METAPHYSICS AS FOUNDATION

METAPHYSICS AS FOUNDATION

Essays in Honor of Ivor Leclerc

Edited by
Paul A. Bogaard and Gordon Treash

State University of New York Press

Published by
State University of New York Press, Albany

© 1993 State University of New York

All rights reserved

Printed in the United States of America

No part of this book may be used or reproduced
in any manner whatsoever without written permission
except in the case of brief quotations embodied in
critical articles and reviews.

For information, address State University of New York
Press, State University Plaza, Albany, NY 12246

Production by Christine M. Lynch
Marketing by Fran Keneston

Library of Congress Cataloging-in-Publication Data

Metaphysics as foundation / essays in honor of Ivor Leclerc / edited
   by Paul A. Bogaard and Gordon Treash.
     p. cm.
   "A bibliography of the published work of Ivor Leclerc" : p.
   Includes bibliographical references and index.
   ISBN 0-7914-1257-1 (alk. paper). — ISBN 0-7914-1258-X (pbk. :
alk. paper)
   1. Metaphysics. 2. Whitehead, Alfred North, 1861–1947.
I. Bogaard, Paul A., 1944–. II. Treash, Gordon. III. Leclerc,
Ivor..
BD111.M564   1993
110—dc20

                               91-43054
                                   CIP

10 9 8 7 6 5 4 3 2 1

Contents

Acknowledgments — vii

Foreword
   Robert C. Neville — ix

Introduction — 1

Section One: Historical Antecedents

1. Kant's Criticism of Panpsychism from the Perspective of the Whiteheadian Metaphysics of Subjectivity [translated from German]
   Reiner Wiehl — 9

2. The Nature of Nature: Kant and Whitehead
   Gordon Treash — 42

3. Leibniz and Modern Science
   Errol E. Harris — 59

4. Metaphysical Lessons of Idealism
   Hugo A. Meynell — 73

Section Two: The Subject as Creative

5. Creativity as General Activity
   Jan Van der Veken and André Cloots — 98

6. Mais Où Sont Les Neiges D'Antan?
   Donald W. Sherburne — 111

7. Perfecting the Ontological Principle
   Lewis S. Ford — 122

8. The Systematic Ambiguity of Some Key Whiteheadian Terms
   George L. Kline — 150

9. To Be Is To Be Substance-In-Relation
   W. Norris Clarke, S. J. — 164

Section Three: The Subject as Foundation

10. Temporality and the Concept of Being
    Albert Shalom — 184

11. The Metaphor of a Foundation for Knowledge
    Edward Pols — 200

12. Collective Guilt
    Jude P. Dougherty — 224

Section Four: Science, Interaction and the Philosophy of Nature

13. Metaphysical Systems and Scientific Theories:
    A Structural Comparison
    Friedrich Rapp — 238

14. The Philosophical Content of Quantum Chemistry
    Paul A. Bogaard — 252

15. The Nature of Chemical Existence
    Joseph E. Earley — 272

16. What is Time?
    Ilya Prigogine — 285

Section Five: Subjectivity and God

17. God, Necessary and Contingent;
    World, Contingent and Necessary; and
    the Fifteen Other Options in Thinking About God
    Charles Hartshorne — 296

18. Persons and God
    Hywel D. Lewis — 312

Contributors — 333

Bibliography — 339

Index of Names — 345

Index of Subjects — 351

Acknowledgments

The editors are most grateful to the contributors to this volume for their generous responses to the invitation to participate in honoring Ivor Leclerc in this way. A special debt of gratitude is also due to the Department of Philosophy, Mount Allison University, for substantial assistance towards this publication from the Marjorie Hastings Fund.

The editors note with sorrow the deaths of Hywel Lewis and Albert Shalom while this volume was in press.

Foreword

Ivor Leclerc is a giant among philosophers in the twentieth century who have contributed to the growth of the grand tradition of metaphysics in the West. For many years a professor of philosophy at Emory University, he trained generations of fine students. Recognizing the importance of professional support for the pursuit of metaphysical philosophy, he has long been an active leader in and contributor to the International Society for Metaphysics and the Metaphysical Society of America; from the latter he received the Founders Medal in 1989 for his own outstanding work in metaphysics. This *Festschrift* in his honor is entirely well-deserved, and I am privileged to be asked to present it.

Despite the prejudice against metaphysics in the twentieth century on the part of so many kinds of modernist philosophies, or perhaps because of the rigors of that prejudice, our century stands out as one of the most creative in the history of that discipline. Perhaps only the ages of Plato and Aristotle, of Avicenna, Averoes, and Aquinas, of Descartes, Spinoza and Leibniz, and of Kant, Hegel, and Schelling are comparable. Each of those was a period lasting from 75 to 150 years and was characterized by a signal genius who evoked a quick sequence of responses of genius. Our metaphysical age began with the mature work of Charles Peirce in the late 1880s, was given brilliant focus by Whitehead, and continues to this day.

Ivor Leclerc saw early on that Alfred North Whitehead had redefined speculative metaphysics for our time. Indeed, part of Whitehead's genius was to prevent metaphysics from being defined *by* our time. His Bloomsbury friends, the other British analytic philosophers, the Vienna Circle positivists, and the Husserlian phenomenologists were all self-conscious about being what we now call modernists, reacting sharply against nineteenth-century bourgeois culture and its philosophies, and setting their own philosophies off as new foundations. Whitehead, by contrast, generously called himself both a Platonist and a pragmatist. He characterized his philosophy as a development of pre-Kantian modes of thought (see the essay here by Harris), and yet clearly was a conversation partner with the speculations of the Kant, Hegel, Schelling era as demonstrated in the essays here by Wiehl, Treash, and Meynell. Whitehead's metaphysics explicitly took its rise as a correction of philosophy in the light of the developments of science, and yet his greatest influence so far has been in the field of philosophical theology, as illustrated here in the essays by Hartshorne and Lewis, and indirectly in those by Ford and Shalom. Within the field of philosophical theology, process theology has found its most fruitful conversation to be with Thomists such as Clarke and Meynell in this volume. Although not represented among the contributors here, another feature of Whitehead's revolutionary metaphysics is that it has provided a language for the Western understanding of East Asian philosophies and religions; Thomas J. J. Altizer has argued that Whitehead's metaphysics provides the explanation for Buddhist experience! And Whitehead was coauthor of *Principia Mathematica*. By no means is Whitehead's metaphysics to be understood as defining itself to be a dialectical reaction against the bogeys of the nineteenth and twentieth centuries. Like the truly great metaphysical systems of the past, it effectively embraces conversation with the whole of its tradition and opens conversation with new partners.

From the beginning Ivor Leclerc saw that philosophy of nature was at the center of Whitehead's system and the revolutionary metaphysics of the twentieth century from Peirce to the present. Leclerc's analyses of Whitehead in *Whitehead's Metaphysics* and *Whitehead's Philosophy*, and his own original work in *The Nature of Physical Existence* and *The Philosophy of Nature* are decisive contributions to understanding and developing our philosphical situation. In contrast to Kant, for whom philosophy of nature was dismissed in favor of either science itself or a special philosophy of philosophy (transcendental definitions of nature), Leclerc has highlighted the continuity of the philosophic discussions of nature from Aristotle through moderns such as Leibniz down to Whitehead and Leclerc's own work. Even Whitehead's contributions to theology consist in new theories of causation for conceiving the role of God and God's relation to the world. The essays here by Rapp, Bogaard, Earley, Prigogine, and Kline contribute to the ongoing discussion of nature in philosophy.

Gordon Treash and Paul Bogaard, the editors of this fine volume, understand the importance of subjectivity in twentieth-century metaphysics, as indicated in their solicitation and grouping of articles. Subjectivity has so often meant consciousness, the immediacy of awareness and feeling as cited by Descartes in his list of mental acts that distinguish mind from body. Consciousness is only a highly derivative notion for Whitehead, however, marking a rare and evanescent phenomenon. Subjectivity, rather, is to be understood in causal terms for Whitehead. Precisely because of this, the "subjectivist principle" (either classical or "reformed") of modernity is nested back in nature, and nature's "bifurcation" is surmounted in the metaphysics stimulated by Peirce and Whitehead. Thus, a Thomist such as Dougherty can treat the subjectivity of personal and corporate responsibility in terms that are both connected with nature and community on the one hand and also with twentieth-century reconstruction of subjectivity on the other. The essays here by Van der Veken and Cloots, by Sherburne and Ford develop the causal underpinnings for that reconstruction of subjectivity.

The idea of "foundation" in contemporary philosophy is ambiguous in the extreme. For the modernists, it is a kind of moral notion, denoting something that must be done in method or categories to escape the errors of the past and to provide an untainted ground for the rest of culture. Postmodernists are excited to deny this moral impulse. For nonmodernist philosophies, however, especially those of twentieth-century metaphysics, "foundation" refers to the most basic and abstract ideas and structures, those that are presupposed or should be presupposed in other parts of culture and that are pervasive. The metaphysical examination of foundations in this latter sense is simply metaphysics. Among the current approaches to foundations in this metaphysical sense are the method of speculative hypothesis pursued by process philosophers, the method of presuppositions pursued by the transcendental Thomists, and dialectical arguments connecting science, experience, and reason, perhaps best typified by Leclerc himself. The essay here by Pols explores all this with wit and imagination.

Although by no means exhaustive of the major options in twentieth-century metaphysics, this volume is a fitting tribute to Ivor Leclerc. It also testifies to the high quality of metaphysical philosophy today.

Robert Cummings Neville
Boston University

Introduction

However much systems of thought which were framed in the classical and in the early modern period may have differed from one another, they held a firm and unshakable conviction in common that it is both possible and necessary to describe the fundamental realities or reality of our world. It is possible to do so because human intelligence is in, or can be placed in, contact with whatever is fundamental, even if acquisition of this insight is an arduous task. Furthermore, it was thought imperative to accomplish the project because only by formulating a clear account of what the ultimate realities are may we understand the origin of all our other knowledge and, in a broader sense, understand the diversity of being that is characteristic of our world. More baldly, there was little, or rather there was no, doubt that resolution of the issues that collectively are described as metaphysical, or which Aristotle associated with first philosophy, was essential as a foundation for all other knowledge, both theoretical and practical. Doubts as to the propriety or possibility of the enterprise were stilled by the necessity of the undertaking and the success of the system proposed.

In marked contrast to classical philosophy, since the beginning of the modern period such foundational work has been accomplished by an exclusive concentration on the knowing subject and the subject's knowledge and cognitive experience. Descartes's *cogito* was the earliest modern effort explicitly directed towards presenting our knowledge of the human soul, the physical world, and God as the result of a searching analysis of the universal exigencies of thought, although it was by no means the only one. Because of this modern focus upon the human subject and human knowledge, the plausibility of metaphysics' playing a foundational role came increasingly to depend upon epistemological investigations. Either implicitly, or in some cases explicitly, modern philosophers assumed that human experience and knowledge are fundamental and irreducible givens so that the foundational role of metaphysics must include an analysis of what human understanding can accomplish. However, because knowledge and experience are fallible and limited, it was only a short step from there to the formulation of trenchant criticisms of any effort to delineate universal and necessary foundations of experience or of the physical world. In the present century many philosophers came to believe such an enterprise was a vain and wrongheaded one. This doctrine—one might say dogma—gained wide acceptance for a time, especially among English-speaking philosophers; but its success was never complete. A large part of the reason why it was not was because—unlike classical and early modern schemes—it was never able to make clear how it is possible to connect the knowing subject's experience to the physical world without invoking a *deus ex machina*.

In the second half of the century Ivor Leclerc has been one of the most consistent and outspoken defenders of the place of metaphysics in the architectonic of human cognition, and therewith he has been one of the most constant and acute critics of the dogmas which have preoccupied contemporary thought. There is a very good reason for this. Leclerc began his investigation with a close study of the writings of A. N. Whitehead, who earlier in the century had come to appreciate the foundational nature of metaphysics as a groundwork for the philosophy of nature, after having attempted unsuccessfully to operate within the framework of the assumption, inherited from early modern thought, which insisted that human experience and human knowledge must be the starting and the endpoint of all rational inquiry. In his mature work Whitehead argued that the chief task of contemporary metaphysics was to go beyond the naive assumptions of modern philosophy and carefully to rethink the notion of subjectivity so as to articulate a clear and adequate formulation of what a subject is, and how to apprehend its relation to the physical world. Human knowledge and human subjects must be understood as important special instances of subjectivity, not as the exclusive focal point of all speculation.

Because they are concerned with these issues, the essays which constitute the present study share several convictions with Leclerc. In the first place they all accept the classical evaluation of metaphysics as being the only coherent foundation possible for the more special disciplines, even if each recognizes that the systematic foundation offered is one which must remain open and is not the articulation of a completed system such as has been proposed in the past. Their agreement on this key methodological issue, however, does not obscure the widely diverse, and in some cases conflicting, positions represented by the papers. Yet such diversity is directed towards the common goal of portraying an aspect of subjectivity through which to intensify, deepen, expand, and reinterpret the conception of the active subject as an ontological category. As such they accent the central aspects of a contemporary metaphysics which will be an adequate foundation for the philosophy of nature as a whole.

SECTION ONE: HISTORICAL ANTECEDENTS

The first four papers of this collection explore significant antecedents within the tradition in order to show how incisive the foundational metaphysics of

Leibniz, Kant and later German idealism have been for clarification of the relation between the subject and the world and to demonstrate their relevance to contemporary debate. Reiner Wiehl and Gordon Treash highlight aspects of Kant's thought which are central to resolution of the issues. Wiehl argues that in raising the issue of how reflective judgment and teleology are connected in the *Critique of Judgment* Kant has anticipated issues to which Whitehead's thought provides significant answers. In the same vein Treash insists that Kant's conception of subjectivity is much richer than Whitehead sometimes recognized, but that it has several systematically significant affinities to Whitehead's positive position. Errol Harris reconstructs Leibniz's thought in order to illustrate that no matter how impressive and startling they may be, the results of empirical science demand the foundational concerns provided by a metaphysical analysis centered upon an ontology of the subject. Finally, Hugo Meynell's examination of idealism, particularly of Schelling's idealism, suggests that proceeding in this direction requires recognition of the transcendent. He contends that Schelling's idealism not only offers a coherent philosophic option, but if supplemented by transcendental Thomism, provides a plausible foundation for the philosophy of nature.

SECTION TWO: THE SUBJECT AS CREATIVE

Whitehead was able to formulate a new metaphysical synthesis by eliciting the notion of creativity into great importance as the root category of his system. More than that, it is the creative activity of subjects—understood from an ontological perspective—which constitutes the central point of Whitehead's thought, and the other novel aspects of his system are related directly to this crucial category. The second section of the book examines some of the implications of Whitehead's having adopted this strategy with special attention to its adequacy as a foundation for our natural knowledge. Jan van der Veken and André Cloots insist that an interpretation of the key Whiteheadian conception of creativity, which is richer than the one usually adopted, is a promising starting point for extending the dialogue between Whitehead and key figures in continental thought, including Spinoza, Hegel, and Heidegger. Donald Sherburne objects sharply to the way in which the past of a creative entity, and indeed the creative subject itself, has been understood by some students of Whitehead's thought. He contends that those whose interpretations he criticizes come much closer to Sartre than to Whitehead. Lewis Ford studies carefully the ontological principle, which is intimately connected to creativity and to the conception of the subject as creative activity, and argues that in the course of his philosophical development Whitehead extended or broadened his use and conception of this principle. George Kline explores the difficulties that Whitehead's syntactical ambiguities have given rise to and shows that many of the problems encountered in Whitehead's philosophical analysis of creative subjects can be resolved by attention to them. Norris Clarke warns against discarding the category of substance altogether, as some interpreters have done. Rather, the category is to be retained, but also understood as involving active and self-communicative agency, so that the relational aspect of being is emphasized.

SECTION THREE: THE SUBJECT AS FOUNDATION

The three papers in this section propose quite different ways in which a more substantial appreciation of the foundational role played by the subject grounds nature and human actions. Albert Shalom examines the close relation that exists between the emergence of the subject, or of subjectivity, and the role of time which he understands as central to physical existence. Again, the activity of subjects is at the heart of Edward Pols's exploration of what may be expected of any foundational metaphysics. Pols argues that although the endeavor to articulate foundations has a useful function, it is no more than a metaphor which must finally be discharged by radical realism—with a strong emphasis on the active and acting subject. While these two papers are concerned with the internal subjectivity of every being or of every actual existent, in the final paper of this section Jude Dougherty directs attention to the relationship between human subjects. He explores in detail some problems of legal and ethical philosophy, which demonstrate clearly the dangerous consequences of attempting to rely upon the notion of responsibility—particularly of groups as reflected, for example, in their collective guilt—without an adequate ontological foundation's having been laid for this form of interaction between subjects.

SECTION FOUR: SCIENCE, INTERACTION
AND THE PHILOSOPHY OF NATURE

The theme of interaction is crucial for the fourth section from another standpoint. If it is true that metaphysical investigation plays the foundational role that this volume contends it can and must do, then concrete manifestations of that role ought to be apparent, particularly in interpretation of the physical world. This section revolves around the insight that it is impossible to achieve such an explication of the physical unless physical entities are construed with essential reference to their mutual interaction. Friedrich Rapp shows that the criticisms which been leveled against metaphysical enterprises conceived as foundational are by no means conclusive, and have proven inadequate within the philosophy of science. A theory of natural science framed within a metaphysical system such as Whitehead's, which is grounded in an ontological interpretation of the subject, is needed to replace the accounts that evolved early in the modern era. Understood in this way, metaphysics plays a role which can be structurally compared to science. Paul Bogaard reviews the difficulties theoretical chemists have recognized in providing a conceptual interpretation of the products of chemical bonding. An explication of the philosophical content of theoretical chemistry makes very doubtful the presumption typically endorsed by philosophers of science that complex molecular systems are reducible to their physical components. That assumption, he insists, ignores the substantive interaction among components, which in turn rests upon an outmoded metaphysical foundation. Joseph Earley relies upon explicit metaphysical foundations to describe the five different senses in which chemical entities may be understood to exist. This description, Earley argues, requires that due consideration be extended to both the nature of compounds and to the interaction of elements within the compound. Finally, Ilya Prigogine examines the nature of time, from a standpoint which, as he explains, derives directly from Leclerc and derivatively from Whitehead. He argues that the irreversibility of time on the phenomenological level, and its direction on a more fundamental one, must be woven into a cosmology in which no object in the universe is regarded as being in equilibrium and in which time-ordering is a statistical description, ultimately dependent upon the interactive correlations of the components involved.

SECTION FIVE: SUBJECTIVITY AND GOD

The final section of the book explores an issue which traditionally has constituted an important aspect of the foundations of knowledge and existence, that is to say the role of God in metaphysical accounts. The last two essays examine the dogma of contemporary philosophy which insists that God, understood in a sense consistent with if not derived from religious practice and natural theology, can play no significant role in our understanding of reality. This dogma means that human subjects are the most complex ones which can be coherently described by rational inquiry. It is a proposition challenged directly by several papers of the collection but is addressed with special intensity by Charles Hartshorne who explores the logic of necessity and contingency as applied to the world in order to argue that metaphysics without God is impossible. That exploration from the perspective of formal logic is balanced by Hywel Lewis, who insists that it is essential to confront the issue of origins in any rational account and that the universe that we encounter must be regarded as grounded in a transcendent reality, which is adequate both to the understanding of human subjectivity and religious experience.

Section One
Historical Antecedents

1

Kant's Criticism of Panpsychism from the Perspective of the Whiteheadian Metaphysics of Subjectivity

Reiner Wiehl

KANT'S CRITIQUE OF PANPSYCHISM AS ONE OF
"SEVERAL SYSTEMS OF THE PURPOSIVENESS OF NATURE"

In §72 of the *Critique of Judgment* Kant distinguished between four different systems of purposiveness in nature and included panpsychism among these four systems. Each of the systems corresponds to a certain kind of metaphysics, and all four understand nature as a whole in teleological terms. Each conceives the science of nature as a whole, that is to say physics, as based on teleological principles of explanation. Among these four systems Kant held the version of panpsychism that he called hylozoism in particularly low esteem. He saw a palpable contradiction in it insofar as the possibility of living matter simultaneously entails the concept of lifelessness because the term 'matter' refers to something that is inert. Living matter, then, is much like the notion of wooden iron; and, as he argues, because of the internal conceptual contradiction it entails, hylozoism cannot be coherently maintained. Kant divided the four different systems of the purposiveness of nature into two classes or ideal types, into an idealism and a realism of natural purposes, and panpsychism is subsumed under the latter class. Idealism is the, "view that all purposiveness of nature is unintentional. Realism is the view that the only instance of it apparent to us (in organized, organic nature) is intentional."[1] Intentionality and the lack of intention thus constitute a complete disjunction of the possible conceptual division of all teleology. Here panpsychism shows itself, as it did previously, to be inadequate for two reasons. It is unsatisfactory in the first place because of the internal contradiction it entails. In the second place it is defective because its extends the domain of intentional purposiveness in nature, from one natural being to any natural entities whatsoever, when this extension is not adequately grounded. Accordingly, and because of the first of these defects, Kant also rejects hylozoism that is limited to certain kinds of natural beings, that is to say to those in which matter is organized in a specific fashion. In view of his proclamation of transcendental idealism, a connoisseur of Kant's transcendental philosophy might well be inclined look for the major deficiency of panpsychism in this realism of purposes. But curiously enough this is not Kant's view at all. For among the four systems of the purposiveness of nature it is the other variety of realism which is distinguished from panpsychism or theism, that Kant always favors. It has the special advantage over all the other forms of explaining nature that, "By virtue of the understanding which it attributes to the creator it best saves the purposiveness of nature from idealism and leads towards an intentional causality for the production of nature."[2] The theoretical advantage of theism over panpsychism is that theism contains no conceptual contradiction, or rather need not contain such a contradiction, and that it can avoid the notion of purposiveness without purpose such as is invoked by idealism. This is a notion which is difficult, if not impossible, to understand. In fact Kant regarded an idealism of natural purposes as hardly worth serious consideration. This was certainly the case for the idealist system that he described as causalism and that he identified with the classical atomism of Democritus and Epicurus. He insisted that this system, "taken literally is so patently absurd" that, "it need not detain us."[3]

Kant regarded the principal absurdity of the causalist system as its contention that, "the relation of matter to the physical grounding of its form, that is to say the laws of motion,"[4] is based on a purely ideal or unintentional purposiveness. This has the effect of calling the notion and the actuality of lawfulness itself into question. By contrast, Kant does not deny that the other system, or idealism, has a certain value. He calls this system fatalism, recalling the expanded understanding of it originating with Spinoza in order to indicate that it, "is universally regarded as being much older."[5] It is not so easy to refute this system because it presupposes a hyperphysical basis of matter and thus points towards a "supersensible" in "which our insight is not so readily adequate."[6] However, Kant regarded this fatalism not only as being refutable but also as being incomprehensible because it invoked the concept of a creator. The difficulty Kant isolates in the conception of such a creator is that, although understanding (*intellectus*) may be attributed to the creator, the connections of purposes that are incontrovertible in nature need not be thought as developing from the nature of this absolute being.

Different criteria for their assessment obviously intersect with one another as Kant assesses the four systems of purposiveness. For one thing, a certain incoherence is apparent from the outset in Kant's conception of the idealism of purposiveness because it involves postulating purposes without intentions. This incoherence is equally a difficulty for the fatalist and the causalist systems despite the advantages claimed for the latter. Initially this incoherence of idealism would seem to speak in favor of the realism of purposiveness. Yet, both the idealist and realistic systems prompt philosophic reflection because the supersensible foundation of the purposiveness of nature they presuppose is difficult to refute. From this perspective panpsychism obviously makes less of an impression because it provides readily available grounds for its own refutation. So, among the four systems, the assumption of theism becomes the only one worth extensive theoretical attention. In fact, in the *Critique of Pure Reason* Kant paid special attention to the refutation of theism, which he described as the system of the purposiveness of nature that is the most difficult to refute and thus whose refutation is the most urgent.[7] It is well known, of course, that Kant rejected all four systems of natural purposiveness as ill-grounded. Their inappropriate extension beyond the domain within which teleology is justified was his reason for doing so. This expansion involved moving from a valid explanation of some natural entities to an invalid explanation of all natural entities. The invalidity of such a progression, of such an expanded use of the teleological mode of explanation, appears from the fact that the distinction between living and nonliving natural entities is confirmed by experience and that only the former, that is only living natural entities, require teleological explanation whereas lifeless natural entities can be explained purely mechanically, and without the addition of teleological causality. Thus, the connection between teleology and reflective judgment, which is countenanced by Kant's theory, means that the use of teleological principles of explanation must be restricted to particular instances in which something living is given. This forbids an extension of teleological explanation to all natural entities.

However, because of its lack of refinement, this suggestive and not entirely misleading exposition of Kant's critique of teleological judgment conceals the problem that needs to be resolved by the connection of teleology to the principle of reflective judgment. The following considerations suffice to clarify the problems. (1) In the first place, the philosophic critique of judgment would be superfluous with respect to possible explanations of nature if empirical observations and experience sufficed to distinguish what is living from what is lifeless, and if it were possible to gain even the principles valid for an explanation of these different natural entities from this distinction. In fact, Kant regarded the derivation of universal and objectively valid principles of explanation from our observation and experience of given natural entities as being quite impossible. This was the reason why he postulated an a priori principle to ground even the case in which teleological principles of explanation are employed. Because of its a priori validity the principle can be grasped prior to, and independently of, any experience.[8] It is no accident that Kant applies the concept of an organized being in the critique of teleological judgment. This concept is not identical to the concept of a living being as is often erroneously assumed.[9] So far as its being and its behavior are concerned, a living being is certainly an organized entity, indeed it is an organized entity *par excellence* from which the essential characteristics of an organized entity can be read off particularly well. But not all organized entities are living entities. No organized entities are given merely as matter. Rather, they are always given as a definite unity of some matter with some definite form. So, because we are human beings, nature is always given to us in such unities of matter and form, whether it is the universal or the particular and individual that is given. For example, it is given to us as the unity of some definite matter with the form of law-like behavior of a definite change of place. The philosophic problem that is raised by the concept of an organized being is the problem of the lawfulness of its unity of matter and form. Inherent in this problem is the question of conceiving the unity of a definite bit of matter under the condition of the lawfulness of that unity. In other words, it is the problem of diverse instances of lawfulness that are related to one another, an original lawfulness that is valid a priori, and the empirical lawfulness of motion.[10] Thus Kant's theory requires that a foundation be provided for the lawfulness of the connection of a given body—as conceived by Newtonian theory—with the universal laws of motion which characterize the behavior of such a body. As organized entities *par excellence*, living beings illustrate this problem especially well. For, even if the behavior of such a living being can be explained as the behavior a material body, the real connection of the parts of this organic living being—that is the motion of the parts with one another and in response to one another in the given whole—cannot be satisfactorily explained by the same laws of motion that do adequately explain the real relations of this living being, as an organic material body, with other material bodies.

As we have seen, Kant's critique of teleological judgment insists that living entities are only specific kinds of organized, natural entities. The distinction between internality and externality, and the mirror image of this distinction that involves the conformity of things to law, are all tied up with the concept of the organized being. An organized being has at its disposal an internal unity inasmuch as it is a unity of form and matter; and simultaneously, as an external unity, such an entity is related to other equally organized beings. This distinction between inner and external unity is valid for all the possible forms of organization it is possible to delineate. The distinction between the states of what is moved corresponds to this distinction between the inner and the outer. This is the distinction between relations involving motion of the parts on the one hand and those that the whole has in relation to other wholes on the other.[11] Thus the distinction between internal and external motion and movability cannot be reduced—at least not without further discussion—to the distinction between relative and absolute motion under universally valid laws of motion. Kant's famous formula, which insists that in an organism, that is in an organized natural entity considered in terms of its internal movability, everything is both goal and simultaneously reciprocally the means, expresses the impossibility of this reduction in teleological form. That formula gains its initial plausibility with reference to living organisms. But, as we have said, in the context of his critique of teleological judgment, living entities for Kant are simply the paradigms of any organized natural things whatever that are characterized by an internal form of purposiveness.

(2) A second argument makes it plain that Kant by no means proceeds simply by limiting the use of teleological principles of explanation to the givenness of living entities that are presented in experience. Teleological explanation is imperative not only in those cases where the behavior of certain given natural entities must be explained, and when that behavior obviously cannot be explained mechanically. The need for this teleological explanation is also manifest when the question about the origin of natural things is raised, and that is the question about the principles and the causes of the being of these things.[12] In the face of this question, the distinction between organized and nonorganized natural things is only secondary. For it is obvious that we cannot explain the origin of matter by recourse to the laws of motion that are valid first of all for organized natural beings. Where we do not attempt to explain their origin, we certainly cannot take refuge in that lawfulness which constitutes the definite form of these organized natural entities. To employ such an explanation would be to proceed circularly. Clearly, it is within the framework of an explanation of the principles of natural events that the need for teleological principles is most apparent. Manifestly, Kant had no particular interest in ordering these different possible questions about the universal knowledge of nature, whose answer seems to lead to teleological principles, systematically and with reference to their categorical differences. For him, prior to such categorical ordering, there is the question of what right we have to apply any sort of teleological principles and the status that must be attributed to a teleological representation when the use of such principles appears to be unavoidable.

(3) If the theoretical foundation Kant provides in his critique of teleological judgment is not primarily intended to limit the use of the teleological principles to a few of the possible instances, primarily to those instances in which living organisms are given by experience, a third argument for this can be cited; and this is certainly the main argument. This foundation is rooted in the conception of human judgment, because judgment is presupposed by any logic of judgment or cognition. The very essence of judgment, or so Kant argues, is that it brings any possible knowledge or cognition under

the forms of judgment and knowledge. These forms are the universal and the particular. Thus, any conception of judgment must distinguish between the particular and the universal in cognition and knowledge on the one hand while simultaneously combining them conceptually on the other. To that extent, the representation of a universal, and accordingly the representation of a certain totality, is always contained in any definite judgment, no matter what sort of judgment it might be. The famous distinction between determining and reflective judgment does not affect anything at all so far as the datum of a universal representation that is tied to every judgment is concerned, for determining judgment subsumes a particular under a given universal, and reflective judgment begins with a given particular and then seeks to find the universal of which this is the particular case.

If judgment, which is one of the human rational faculties, is subjected by a critique of reason to limits that are equally valid for determining and reflective judgment, then this critical limitation can be sought in no higher general kind of representation than the one that judgment entails. Rather, as the axiom of transcendental philosophy has it, this critical limit is to be sought in the universal conditions of the empirical knowledge possible for human beings. However, in their application to a sensible given, these universal cognitive conditions of possible experience lead to knowledge of matter, or to knowledge of what is movable in space, insofar as this is defined by universal laws of motion or by the laws of a universally valid mechanics. If anything remains for a critique of teleological judgment to investigate in the face of such knowledge of the metaphysical foundations of natural science, it is this: How can the unity of this given nature, which is conceived as being not merely the external connection of matter with universal laws of motion, but simultaneously as an inner unity of form and matter whose lawfulness demands teleological principles, be interpreted so as to make this latter comprehensible as the groundwork of that external connection? It is, accordingly, the question about the possibility of nature as a whole, the question about the inner unity of all of nature to which the critique of teleological judgment leads directly in its formulation of its problem. The results of the *Critique of Pure Reason* remain highly significant for this philosophic exposition, and those results insist that theoretical insight into the internal foundations of nature, or empirical knowledge of the internal unity of things in nature, is in principle denied to human beings.[13]

If this is required by a critique of teleological judgment, it also follows from the insight that any possible knowledge of the appearances of nature is always necessarily grounded in the notion of an internal essence and an essential unity, and that it is the task of a philosophical critique of reason to explicate them. Kant attempted to resolve this problem of the inner unity of nature for the appearances that constitute nature, and are the objects of possible empirical knowledge, by interpreting the teleological grounds which determine such an internal unity as principles of a purely reflective judgment content to judge a natural thing as purposive without committing itself to the claim to provide a teleological explanation of natural phenomena. That permitted Kant to avoid positing double causality, both a mechanical and a teleological one, as underpinning universal natural knowledge. Moreover, in this way he could escape the nonsense entailed by having to explain the lawfulness of the internal unity of natural entities from the regularity of the universal laws of motion, which concern matter as given in appearance. Kant's philosophy of nature must pay a high price, one that his critics have often alleged is far too high, in order to avoid these two sources of incoherence.[14] For the critique of teleological judgment leads Kant neither to a metaphysics of life, which permits the multifarious specifications of life to be known in terms of teleological laws, nor to the methodology of inductive knowledge, which allows it to proceed in a stepwise fashion from individual instances of lawfulness in the internal unity of matter and form to more special and general forms of lawfulness and finally to the universal laws of motion themselves. The chief point of this critique of reflective judgment is that it confirms the impossibility of achieving empirical knowledge about the indisputable essence of particular natural things.[15] Thus, in general, the distinction between different sorts of internal unity in nature and the distinction of nature into different kinds of entities plays no role in the argument of the critique of teleological judgment. As such, nature can and must be understood from the standpoint of the inner being of the particular things that constitute it. This is the reason why Kant's critique of panpsychism, that is to say of hylozoism, does not attempt to show that the suggestion of purposiveness in nature is erroneously carried over to the totality of nature. Rather, the critique insists that the system does what all systems purporting to establish the purposiveness of nature do and erroneously regards the principle of purposiveness as a principle of determining judgment when in fact not one single principle of empirical knowledge, and not one single principle for the employment of determining judgment in the metaphysical foundations of natural science, can be deduced from it. Seen this way, Kant's critique of teleological judgment corresponds with absolute precision to the literal formalism of theoretical and practical reason.

To a considerable extent, it is the paradoxical result of the critique of teleological judgment that it demands the use of teleological principles in natural knowledge, while simultaneously it insists these principles are not suited to function as the principles of a priori natural knowledge. Kant's criticism of panpsychism is intensified by this paradoxical result. To show that panpsychism suffers from internal contradiction and incoherence is not its explicit point. Obviously, the notion of living matter, and of nature as such, is somehow thinkable, as for example when it is presented as an animal.[16] What Kant urged against such a notion, from this time on, was that its use as "an hypothesis of purposiveness in nature as such"[17] is scant. This, however, means that any purported employment of it is useless because not one single a priori axiom or principle can be gained from such an hypothesis. Kant's critique of teleological judgment is, then, a conceptual tightrope walk between the two extremes of entirely rejecting the use of teleological principles in the knowledge of nature and of developing the conditions by which they are used as fundamental.

WHITEHEAD'S MODERN METAPHYSICS OF SUBJECTIVITY: REFLECTING CONCRETE PROCESSES INSTEAD OF POSITING ABSTRACT VALUES

Now, against this backdrop, Whitehead's speculative cosmology must be seen as the most significant systematic metaphysics of the twentieth century. Initially this metaphysics appears as a grandiose conceptual portrait of a modern system of panpsychism. Certainly Whitehead's own description of his philosophy as the "philosophy of organism" points in this direction. Its result is to regard the original components of the universe, the most concrete of all concrete actual entities, as organisms. The universe as a whole, consisting of such organisms and of innumerable organic connections of such elementary or atomic organisms, itself appears as a gigantic organism, as living matter and as an animal—to use Kant's terminology—but that is not enough. Whitehead developed a philosophical program for this philosophy of organism which is a program that he attempted to redeem as extensively as possible within the framework of this philosophy. The key to his solution lies in his rejection of what he called "the bifurcation of nature." This is the bifurcation of natural entities that Descartes introduced into modern philosophy, and science distinguishes them as physical and mental things, or as bodies and thoughts. By rejecting the bifurcation of nature Whitehead overcomes this distinction and all of the dichotomies resulting from it. Because he intended to overcome this dichotomy, Whitehead posited a corresponding elementary and irreducible polarity for all of the elementary organisms or atoms of the universe. This is the polarity of the physical and the mental. Accordingly, he spoke of the physical and the mental pole of the original organic atoms. His use of the term 'mental' with respect to the elementary components of the universe was entirely serious and by no means intended metaphorically. Whitehead was perfectly clear that, given the tremendous changes that modern culture—not least of all philosophy—represents, it is futile to take over classical panpsychism and to attempt to render it as the philosophic foundation of the cultural and scientific experience of contemporary man. It is no surprise, then, that a revision of classical panpsychism is explicitly to be found here in Whitehead's speculative metaphysics. Whitehead's revision did not aim at the elimination of the soul or at pure materialism, but rather at an "introduction of the subject" to nature and to natural science.[18]

In this respect, Whitehead's revised panpsychism can be described as a pansubjectivism. Accordingly, the being of the actuality is interpreted as subjectivity, and every concrete actuality is understood as a subject. The revision of panpsychism here does not mean that it is abolished, but rather that it is transformed. But then to a certain degree classical panpsychism also remains in modified form. This panpsychism is not only temporally and historically earlier, but it was later logically and ontologically in comparison to pansubjectivism. It is quite incorrect to regard Whitehead simply as providing an extension of the cultural self-understanding of the moderns, an understanding which subordinates all experience, and not least the experience of science, to human subjectivity. It is not difficult to interpret Whitehead's rejection of the bifurcation of nature as speculative idealism so that all philosophically conceivable contraries and dichotomies are subsumed in the speculative theory of subjectivity. It is certainly true that Whitehead's program is directed against the bifurcation of nature, but it is a program directed against *all* dichotomies so far as they appear in the experience of nature and are carried over into modern science.[19] In this Whitehead proceeds from the historical insight that it has been the introduction of the modern principle of subjectivity which has contributed heavily to the bifurcation of nature and thus to those dichotomies in the natural sciences that must be avoided. Accordingly, pansubjectivism is not only the introduction of the subject into nature and into natural science, but for Whitehead it is as much intended to make the subject a part of nature, and in that way it is a naturalizing of subjectivity.[20] Both must be paid close attention if his contributions to natural science and to philosophy are to be adequately assessed. To understand Whitehead's panpsychism, however, it is necessary in the first place to understand that no matter how far metaphysics may undertake to account for the plenitude and the manifold of human experience, the point of departure for the system is, and remains, that of the scientist for whom the paradigm of scientific activity is in the contemporary period, as it was for Plato, mathematical physics—no matter how mathematical physics may have changed over the course of the centuries and no matter how much human experience and physics' own understanding of itself may have altered. This starting point ultimately renders the revision of panpsychism and its transformation into pansubjectivism intelligible. Whitehead's introduction of the subject into nature and into science may only be read from the perspective of a possible philosophy of biology. The philosophic questions he poses are, for him, the renewal of the philosophic question posed by the ancients and the moderns, but they are posed now under the specifically altered conditions and foundations of science in our century, and this means science in general and mathematical physics in particular. It is the ancient question, asked by Plato and Aristotle, which was renewed in the modern epoch by Leibniz and Kant, of what the most universal principles and the foundations of any scientific knowledge of nature are. It is a question concerning universal principles and causes; and as such it is also the question of metaphysics.

Accordingly, Whitehead's pansubjectivism is the philosophic answer to the fundamental question of metaphysics. It was self-evident to the author of *Process and Reality* that in its eternal "coming-to-be" and "passing-away"— and Whitehead speaks here of "creativity" in the manifold of its developments and the wealth of its forms—nature is always the universe of all universes. It is always one and the same all-inclusive whole throughout all of its changes. Similarly, it is self-evident that in its all-inclusive universality nature must correspond to an idea of science that keeps it moving in the direction of a supreme and all-inclusive universality throughout all the changes to which science is subject. Thus, physics is the name here for a unitary science of universal nature, and it is metaphysics insofar as its principles achieve maximum universal validity. The relation between physics and metaphysics, it follows, is one of a relative difference, a difference between the very most universal principles of scientific knowledge and less universal ones. From Whitehead's perspective it is senseless to speak of a metaphysics of nature. This would be as foolish as trying to describe a more wooden wood or a more iron iron.

The most difficult aspect of involving the subject in nature, or of naturalizing it, is that part of what is entailed by that description of the enterprise is its depiction of metaphysics as standing in close connection with physics. Since Whitehead renewed the fundamental metaphysical question of Plato and Aristotle, and of Leibniz, in an epoch in which electrodynamics has replaced classical physics as the paradigm of science, the question focused on the unity of form and matter and the lawfulness of this unity is repeated, even if it is repeated under different conditions and with essential changes in accent. Whitehead submitted Leibniz's and Kant's attempts at a solution, and therewith the philosophic presuppositions of these attempted resolutions, to a criticism that originated in his own pansubjectivism. In his criticism of Leibnizean metaphysics the outlines of the same criticism that has been directed against this sort of metaphysics of subjectivity since the days of Kant and Hegel can be discerned. This criticism is directed against any analysis that has as a consequence the absolute separation and lack of relation between what are regarded as the two original domains, that is to say the domains of being and knowledge. It is directed against the dichotomy and complete disjunction of being for itself and appearance, against the separation of physics from metaphysics, and against the absence of any relation between the two sorts of knowledge produced by this separation. Furthermore, it is directed against the lack of relation between pure a priori knowledge and empirical knowledge. Finally, it is directed against the separation of metaphysical teleology from physical mechanics.

This classical criticism insists that any critical analysis is senseless if it results in such a lack of relation because the distinctions which the analysis uncovers were designed to explicate existing correspondences better. If philosophic analysis concludes that there is no relation between physics and metaphysics, the danger of skepticism with respect to metaphysics is immanent because it is more difficult to assess experience skeptically than it is to assess it as knowledge which transcends experience. Whitehead's criticism of rational or pre-Kantian metaphysics, and especially Leibnizean metaphysics, falls substantially within the boundaries of this classical criticism. What is unique in this criticism is that it also includes a criticism of the Kantian critique. Whitehead understood Kant's criticism of reason as a contribution to the modern metaphysics of subjectivity, and he regarded it as marking neither epochal nor epoch-making progress in relation to its predecessors. To that degree he read Kant's critique of reason with different eyes than Hegel had, although he agreed at many points with Hegel's criticism of that metaphysical conception of subjectivity. However, he certainly did not by any means follow Hegel's path from a metaphysics of subjectivity to a metaphysics of spirit. Rather, in his own criticism of Kant's critique of reason, he remained on precisely the same level of philosophical reflection as Kant. The common ground was nature and natural knowledge. Nevertheless, the line of sight changes. As he emphasized, Whitehead wanted a critique of pure feeling, not a critique of pure reason. This makes it a critique of the lower, instead of the higher, cognitive faculties and provides an exposition of the original modes of relation rather than of the derivative ones. It will indeed be a critique of reason; not however of pure reason but, if I may put it this way, of impure reason. This undertaking proceeds from the fact that even feelings and sensations, even the most primitive modes of relation, point towards a certain rationality insofar as they are tied to a universal principle of order.[21]

The feelings which constitute the object of Whitehead's critique of reason are the original activities of a subject upon which the distinctions between theoretical and practical reason and a third cognitive function have not previously been imposed. Whitehead has recommended a new way of reading the Kantian critique of reason, a way which is highly fruitful for a metaphysics of subjectivity and in which his own metaphysical conception of subjectivity is expressed. The reading Whitehead recommends is to combine the "Transcendental Analytic" of the *Critique of Pure Reason* directly with the *Critique of Judgment* and especially with part 2, the "Critique of Teleological Judgment."[22] If this suggested reading, which was sketched in the first section of my observations, is adopted, it will be necessary to proceed under the direction of the following question raised from Whitehead's standpoint: How are the manifold forms of the sensible given united to this given itself in sense perception under the condition of universal teleological principles of natural knowledge? How does every genuine unity of organized beings come to fruition under the presupposition of such a synthesis of form and content of the internally given? What sort of forms are involved, and how do teleological principles function, in the constitution of organized beings?

Even if it is true that Whitehead criticizes Kant's critique of reason in general, and objects in particular to what results from the reading of Kant that he recommends, it is also true that all of this obtains on the basis of a common assumption, that is to say their common assumption of the unity of nature. This common element may be helpful in revealing the recurrence of the most profound difficulty of Leibnizean metaphysics in Kant's exposition of reason. The most serious of all the consequences that the lack of relation entailed by the Leibnizean metaphysics involves is the lack of relation between subjectivity and causality. This is, of course, directly related to the lack of relation between teleology and mechanics. Whitehead attached no special importance to the key concept of Kant's critique, the notion of the transcendental. Indeed, he hardly acknowledged the critical distinction between transcendental ideality and empirical reality that Kant had originated in order to replace the classical distinction between physical and metaphysical reality. In Whitehead's view there was no significant merit in making the subject the ground of causality transcendentally while at the same time, and empirically, causality is rendered as a basis of the subject's knowledge. This merely retains the old scheme denying any relation between the principle of subjectivity and the principle of causality that had been inherited from Leibniz, and therewith the old denial of relation between teleological and mechanical principles of natural knowledge is also retained.

We are accustomed to drawing an epochal line of demarcation between classical panpsychism and modern pansubjectivism when we establish the dividing line in history between the classical and the modern periods—thanks to the historical significance of Cartesianism and Kantianism. But again, this was certainly not Whitehead's view. For him, the purported epochal distinction had a merely relative and a subordinate significance, and he regarded contemporary subjectivist metaphysics merely as a version of classical panpsychism. It suffered from one and the same theoretical inadequacy as its predecessor did, or from a related one. Whitehead attempted to bring the inadequacy of classical and modern panpsychism down to its lowest common denominator. He found this in the inadequacy of what he described as an ontological principle which is present in its most original and primitive form in any metaphysics as a theory of reality. This is to say, he found all traditional metaphysics to be dominated by the grammatical scheme of the distinction between subjects and predicates. He insisted that metaphysics elevated this particular and contingent linguistic scheme to the status of a universal ontological principle. Accordingly, Whitehead regarded both classical and modern panpsychism, and indeed the entire traditional metaphysics of subjectivity, as resting on an inadequate ontology of things and of substances. In this ontology the being of what exists, that is to say the original and primitive mode of being of any existent, is the being of substances and things. This ontology conceives things as "subjects" corresponding to the grammatical concept of subjects. They are subjects with definite properties by which they are defined as this or that subject and as being so and so. They express these properties as subjects express predicates. A substance is thought to be a sort of "super thing," different from other things by virtue either of the quality or the quantity of its independence.[23]

The idea that not only substances and things as such, but substances and things to which we ascribe a certain intentionality and therewith also subjectivity, are abstract factors provides the key to understanding Whitehead's transformation of classical and modern panpsychism. In this connection it is also appropriate to speak of Whitehead's criticism of the dogma of the immediate given. Objective data, or in Whitehead's terminology objectified nexūs, are always and unavoidably abstractions. There is always a concrete causal event which is their basis and in which they are embedded. On this basis any one of them becomes an objective datum determined in this and that way for a definite concrete subject. But not even this subject, to which a nexus is given as an objective datum, is an *immediate given*, because this subject is what it is and what it has become only within the framework of a comprehensive context of effects. Just as its objective datum was first a manifold of initial data that developed into a definite objective datum in concrescence, the subject was first an initial subject that developed consistently with its potentiality. The unavoidable illusion of an immediate given is directly tied to the notion of the immediate givenness of an objective nexus as such when what has become, its concrescence and its being as a concrescent, are distinguished in an event or in a process. Where these abstractions and the conditions that prompt them are ignored, Whitehead insists, the result is phenomenalism followed quickly by skepticism.

From this perspective, Kant's transcendental philosophy is also to be included under the rubric of phenomenalism, despite its powerful exertions to avoid Humean skepticism.[24] In the light of Kant's famous proclamation of a "Copernican turn" in philosophy, one is inclined to speak of Whitehead's second Copernican turn. For in the first place the critique of reason as a superior cognitive faculty is completed by a critique of reason inherent in the lower ones; in this way the basis is ultimately provided for the earlier criticism of reason. Secondly, in addition to the Copernican turn prescribed by Kant, the Whiteheadian turn involves his trenchant criticism of the dogma of the immediate given, both in itself and in its various metaphysical applications.[25] The basic presupposition of what Whitehead calls "simple location" is one important application of this dogma, that is the immediate spatial-temporal definition of the physical given within the structure of the universe. The assumption of the immediate givenness of subjects and objects, or of souls and bodies, is another instance of the same presupposition in metaphysics. It is crucial that Whitehead's point not be misunderstood here. His criticism of the immediate spatial and temporal definition of all physical reality within the structure of the universe is not tantamount to the rejection of all possible spatial and temporal definition. Nor does the criticism of the immediate givenness of subjects and objects represent an absolute rejection of the distinction between subjects and objects in philosophical thought. Indeed, to a certain extent Whitehead's metaphysics intensifies rather than weakens the distinction between subjectivity and objectivity. But this ontognostic difference gains a new functional and methodological significance because of Whitehead's criticism of the dogma of the immediate given. In Whitehead's new subjectivist metaphysics the concepts of subject and object not only belong together, as they always have done, but in reality they are inextricably tied to one another within a concrete framework of events and causal relations. Within such an event, subjectivity and objectivity mutually involve one another. There is no well-defined and univocal frontier between the one and the other in such a concrete causal nexus. In the case of any one of these instances of connection the boundary lines between subjectivity and objectivity run parallel to one another in one way and in another way they cross one another. Whitehead's criticism of the dogma of the immediate given rests on the following axiom: Any thing which is given immediately has become that given. As a definite datum, it is what it is because of its concrescence or its coming-to-be and in respect to its unique concrescence. The internalization of this coming-into-being and concrescence of the given is the principle behind Whitehead's criticism of what is immediately given as abstract. Hence, in their functions as determined or as determining, subjectivity and objectivity are abstract moments that must be defined from case to case by means of the internalization of this concrescence.

This perspective embodying the criticism of the dogma of the immediate given is what makes Whitehead's transformation of classical and modern panpsychism so significant. If it is pointless to speak of the immediate givenness of a being in abstraction from its development and its concrescence, it is also senseless to say that any given thing has an immediately given soul, and is for that reason a living being, or even that every being is a subject in its immediate givenness. So, just as we spoke of the functionalization of the fundamental ontognostic concepts of subject and object, a functionalization of panpsychism can be described now. But that means it is untrue that all beings have souls or are alive and as such are mortal and so subject to development and decay. Rather, in order that a definite, concrete datum be recognized as an objective given in its definiteness, and so that it can be defined as cognition, the internalization of original and initiating data is first essential. This internalization can be explicated in the form of the history of the abstractions that condition the concrescence or coming-to-be. However, more is required for the definiteness of something immediately given. This more is the anticipation by an actuality in concrescence of its own development and the internalization by the other givens of its having been given. Thus an entire and complete history pertains to the complete definiteness of a given; this is the history of the past, the present, and the future of this given. In the long run, this history is a complex one: it is the history of the relevant datum itself, which is a history that is unique and particular to it. Simultaneously it is this history from another perspective which is not the standpoint of the datum in question. For the complete definiteness of an objective datum always requires at least two histories, an inner and an outer one.

Whitehead's criticism of the dogma of the immediate given thus points towards a theorem which insists that the internal is always complemented by the outer and privacy by publicity.[26] It is a particularly important element of this criticism that it is not by any means only the subjects which are related to particular data that have their own unique histories. The same thing must be true for the data as well. Even an objective datum has its history in which manifold subjects are involved along with their objectifications. In order that a historical subject be related to data at all, that subject must form a unified, coherent whole of events and effects. Here, Whitehead's criticism of the dogma of the immediate given leads to an inversion in what is meant by the axiom of traditional panpsychism. The deeper significance of Whitehead's second Copernican turn lies in this inversion. The ambiguity of the assertion that everything given is defined as a living being in its immediate givenness obscures the essential difference between traditional and revised panpsychism. For in that assertion the accent can fall either on what is living or on its definition. Accordingly, the proposition can mean that everything given immediately is a living entity insofar as it is completely determined and stands under the conditions of this complete determination. However, it can also mean that everything given immediately is completely determined only insofar as it is a living entity and stands under the conditions imposed by this form of life. In the second case life is seen as a category of the possibility of complete determination, and this in turn is regarded as a condition of the possibility of the complete determination of the given. In this latter case, life is regarded as a category, which category is taken as being a condition of the possibility of the definiteness of whatever is given. Numerous correlative categories pertain to this category of life: for example, concrescence, endurance, decay, and also recollection, internalization, anticipation, and making things present or presentation.

Whitehead's transformation of classical and modern panpsychism results in a decision in favor of the second sense of the ambiguous proposition. Now, it might well be suggested that this interpretation is fundamentally the correct sense of Kant's critique of reason, particularly when the third *Critique*, and especially the critique of teleological judgment, is regarded as being the proper and true foundation of all of Kant's thought.[27] The question of whether in his sketch of a new metaphysics of subjectivity Whitehead did not finally understand Kant better than Kant had understood himself may remain open here. Whitehead's critical stance vis-à-vis Kant, namely that Kant had not totally freed himself from the constraints of traditional substance and thing metaphysics and thus that ultimately he could not escape from the dogma of the immediate given despite having taken significant steps in the direction of this liberation, has several aspects to it. Thus, the precipitate of the dogma of the immediate given is found in Kant's critique of reason, most significantly in the form of the immediate acceptance of all those dogmatic, fundamental distinctions, that provided the methodological instruments for this critique of reason and which, accordingly, were never themselves put seriously into question. The most important of these fundamental distinctions are those between a higher and a lower cognitive faculty, and between sensibility and understanding, that is between the immediate givenness of a sensible appearance and the immediate givenness of a thought entity in itself. An additional and highly important distinction is the one between determination and reflection as a distinguishing function of judgment in which the former subsumes an immediately given appearance under an immediately given concept whereas the latter is designed to search out the concept for any given sensible appearance. The absolutely fundamental distinction between mechanical causality and teleology also belongs among these distinctions.

Now, in Kant's critique of reason, all of these immediate givens provide the foundation for the immediate givenness of the distinction between the a priori and the a posteriori in knowledge. Whitehead's transformation of classical and modern panpsychism is directly tied to his rejection of the dogma of the given. What appears as an immediate given is in truth the coming-to-be and the concrescence of an objective event from initial givens. His critical recension of the Kantian critique of reason, and of the immediate givens that Kant subordinates to it, is to be seen from this perspective. Sensitive and conceivable givens are always and necessarily coming-to-be, and hence they have become. The same thing is true of determinations and reflections, or for causal and teleological connections. Whereas Kant was concerned to construe the connection between what has been differentiated methodologically by employing a philosophic theory, Whitehead proceeds by insisting that the differences just mentioned have a functional significance and that this significance is always conditioned by other previously occurring events. Under previously given conditions the physical-sensible and the conceptual factors are connected to one another within the context of a concrete nexus of events. Thus, in one respect, it is always the physical-sensible, and in an other respect it is the conceptual factor, that is primary. Where conceptual factors predominate in a nexus of events, we always find both functions, those of determination and of reflection. The physically given is determined under given circumstances by conceptual givens, and simultaneously a conceptual given is always sought for any physical or sensible given. In one sense its definition is primary; but in another reflection is. Each nexus of events is a causal nexus, a causal event of what is physically given. As determinate, such an event has definite direction. As a defined and concrete event, it is directed towards a definite goal. Each particular individual causal event has its own unique goal. Its immanent purpose of fulfilling this goal invests causality with a definite activity or energy. The activity and energy is exhausted in achieving this purpose, and the causal history of the event reaches its conclusion in attaining its end. This particular history is completed by the actualization of the immanent purpose. There are innumerably many such histories. In each particular, individual causal event development and decay always proceed together. Only when a causal history is completed by the attainment of its purpose is something definite or determinate developed. Simultaneously, however, something has ended and decayed, a concrete coming-to-be, or a development in which energy and activity were invested.

KANT'S METAPHYSICS OF SUBJECTIVITY AS THE SENSUALIST VERSION OF PANPSYCHISM

Causal Histories and Oscillations

Thus, for Whitehead's contemporary metaphysics of subjectivity the most elementary givens are causal histories. These depend upon other causal histories by which they are occasioned just, as they form causal occasions for other causal histories. As an event directed towards a goal, each such causal history represents a teleological process. In many histories the causal factor predominates. In other histories the teleological one does. Here two conditioned priorities exist side by side as fundamental. In one perspective causality has priority over teleology. For just as there can be no *creatio ex nihilo*, no definite proposition of purposes, that is, no striving, no desiring, no acting, can proceed from nothing. There must necessarily always be causal impetuses for setting definite goals, and for all striving and acting. However, from the other perspective, teleology is prior to causality, for no matter how many causal impetuses coalesce together they would never lead to a definite event, or a definite action, were they not joined in the unity of definite goals proposed. Only under this condition do the many impetuses lead to a definite event. Externality and internality are the two aspects of the two priorities. Viewed from the outside or externally, causality is primary in contradistinction to teleology. From the internal perspective teleology is prior. The point at which causality and teleology pass over into one another cannot be determined with precision, and it is just as little possible to do so for the transition from externality and internality.

Now, in Whitehead's metaphysics of subjectivity the most elementary forms of organization of concrete causal events are oscillation and change of place. Each oscillation, and each change of place, represents a directed and an intentional causal event. A certain dissemination pertains to every oscillation, and the attainment of a place that is always well defined pertains to change of place. For their part, these two elementary motions, oscillation and change of place, are related to one another in a complementary way. An elementary causal event can be described in both ways, that is as an oscillation and as a change of place; such an event must be described as either one or the other under different conditions. Wherever Whitehead describes the concrete, elementary causal process in its characteristic determination of goals as change of place, one cannot avoid impression that for him the second Copernican turn meant a conscious return to the physics of the Greeks, and in particular to Aristotle's physics, rather than a philosophic step beyond Kant's first Copernican turn. That justifies the attempt to regard this return to Aristotle's physics more as a renewal of classical panpsychism than as a specific contemporary reformulation of it. As a consequence, for Whitehead, every causal event is an entelechy insofar as it is a change of place. It is the actualization of a well-defined spatial-temporal datum on the basis of previously given initial data which the distinct potentialities for such an actualization hold out. The causal event of such a definite change of place includes the definite potentiality for such motion as given. In any definite change of place there is a causal process of the place that is natural for and characteristic of it, and in this there is the completion and the fulfilling of the unique event. As such an entelechy, this change of place is not the only form of organization for a definite causal event, but it is the most elementary. Classical panpsychism is relevant to such elementary changes of place because it regarded this, in contradistinction to motion initiated by an other, as the most original sign or characteristic of life.

However, it is quite incorrect to see Whitehead's second Copernican turn as merely a reversion to Aristotelian physics. For, in that way, one misconstrues the complementary relationship Whitehead postulated between oscillation and change of place. The theorem affirming this complementary relation is inextricably tied up with Whitehead's criticism of the two dogmas of the immediate given and of substance and thing ontology. These dogmas, however, are at the center of the Aristotelian physics. For Aristotle things, or the relevant material bodies, are indisputably ultimate and fundamental. Without things' or bodies' being immediately given, there is no motion and no cause of motion. Every motion, and especially every change of place, is the motion of a thing, that is the motion of a physical and material body. Every such body has a nature characteristic of it. This nature is the result of its natural elements, and these elements provide the basis for definition of the natural place to which that natural body moves. Similarily, there are no causes of motion, and there is no power of moving, without the presumption of things or material bodies. The search for such definite causes of motion necessarily always leads to one or more things, to one or more material bodies. Thus, the determinate cause of the motion of a material body is to be sought in the first instance in its own nature and secondarily in other material bodies.

Whitehead's physics and metaphysics complete the liberation of the causal processes and changes of place from their connection to immediately given material bodies, and this liberation is based on his criticism of the dogma of the immediate given.[28] Thus, every causal process and every change of place is a natural event that finds its completion inasmuch as the relevant characteristic place, the "natural place" of the event, has been achieved. Since Whitehead discarded the dogmas of classical and modern metaphysics, and more particularly the dogmas of the immediate given and the dogma of the absolute priority of substances and things over motions and the causes of motion, it was possible for him to develop a new conception of natural motion and of natural place. He retained the Aristotelian conceptions of natural motion and natural place in the context of this new conception, although he retained it in a form that was substantially altered. Every particular and individual causal process is a natural event. This natural event entails a tendency, or an internal impulse, aimed at actualizing a determinate quantum of energy in a definite spatial-temporal region of the extensive continuum. Understood in this way, a natural place is delineated whenever a definite region of the space-time continuum is occupied by a definite quantum of energy. Moreover, this is the place towards which a definite causal process is directed in its striving for enactment or actualization. Simultaneously, however, it is also true that each such particular and unique change of place is inextricably involved in a comprehensive nexus of motion. The actualization of one quantum of energy in a definite region of the world merely represents a transitional phase of the complete event that is the motion. The event, thus, assumes the character of an oscillation.

Accordingly, in Whitehead's metaphysics oscillations or pulsations are the most elementary causal procedures.[29] They constitute a polar event involving both internalization and externalization in which internality and externality are reciprocally related to one another. Thus, Whitehead's universal doctrine of motion is not primarily oriented, as Aristotle's had been, by the paradigmatic motions of natural elements and by the self-motion in space that is characteristic of animals. Rather, in the first instance, it is heavily influenced by the contemporary scientific paradigm provided by electrodynamics. Whitehead's contemporary metaphysics is essentially defined by the fact that it regards the classical paradigm of Newtonian physics as having been replaced by this new paradigm. If it makes any sense at all to speak of panpsychism here that sense must be sought in a metaphysical interpretation of electromagnetic oscillations with the assistance of the category of subjectivity. Certainly the phenomenon of oscillation can be carried over from electrodynamics to other natural processes, in particular the processes of animal life. One thinks here of Goethe's reflections on the diastole and systole. However, something else is involved at the outset: it must first be realized that Whitehead's transformation of panpsychism not only liberates causal processes from the burden of thing-laden substrata that subordinate the causal process to the old substance ontology. In addition, the essential priorities of classical physics and ontology are turned upside down in the transformation. Whereas previously things were the ultimate entities and were prior to motions and causes, now motion is ultimate and things are secondary and derivative. Further, whereas material bodies had been assumed to be prior to any change of place and to moving forces, now the dynamic of causal localization is prior and the givenness of material bodies is secondary and derivative.[30] This inversion of traditional metaphysical priorities is one of the leading premises that permits Whitehead to interpret lifeless material bodies and animal bodies as forms of organization of given groups of actual entities, or as forms of the concrete unity of goal-directed causal processes and the motion between places. For this mode of analysis, the difference between a mechanical and an organic system, or the difference between something living and something that is lifeless, is simply a difference in the various degrees of complexity of different forms of organization and of their causal conditions.[31] From this perspective, the most pressing task of metaphysics is to delineate a categorial scheme and to develop it into the ideal typology of different, and more or less complex, forms of organization. This ideal typology of forms of organization permits a conceptual interpretation of the givenness of human experience. In orienting himself by the scientific paradigm of electrodynamics, Whitehead leaves the domain in which any possible panpsychism, either classical or modern, is valid. In making the difference between mechanism and organism, and between the living and the lifeless, relative he gains a methodologically secure standpoint beyond panpsychism and its rejection.

Thus, Whitehead's modern subjectivist metaphysics has little in common with the panpsychism Kant discussed. That doctrine conceived nature as a living being and as an animal. Indeed, for Whitehead, as a whole and in each of its parts, nature is just what Kant calls into question in the critique of teleological judgment, that is a system of purposiveness. For Whitehead every actual entity, every particular causal process, is such a system of purposiveness—as every form of organization of groups of causal processes is. These systems may be distinguished on the basis of their forms of organization. Animality is only one abstract form of organization among others. At least two considerations speak against the assumption that, as a whole, nature embodies this form of organization. In the first place, it is contradicted by the argument that one of the innumerable forms of organization which nature has produced is posited as absolute, and as absolute is applied to all nature. Further, scientific experience contradicts the interpretation of nature as a whole as an animal. Experience comes closer to confirming that, for the most part, the organizational form of oscillation dominates in nature. In addition, in the endless expanse of the cosmos, the form of mechanical bodies is realized seldom enough, and it is realized even less frequently in the form of a more or less developed organism.

The intention here, however, is not to show that Whitehead's subjectivist metaphysics has little to do with the concept of panpsychism as Kant developed it. What is much more important is the significance that metaphysics achieves inasmuch as it facilitates a criticism of Kant's critical representation of the system of purposiveness, and in this way it facilitates a criticism of his subjectivist metaphysics. It is clear that in Whitehead's eyes the classical dogmas of the immediate given, and the primacy of substances and things over motions and their causes, remain in force in all of the four systems of the purposiveness that Kant criticized. Occasionalism lives on the assumption of the immediate givenness of simple material bodies and physical motions that correspond to the form of these bodies. Fatalism lives on the assumption of a supreme and absolutely comprehensive natural being which possesses the form of substance and determines all the relations of finite things on the basis of this form by means of its attributes and their modifications. Again, for pantheism the immediate given is nothing less than nature as a whole that is understood by means of the universal form of a natural animal. Finally, theism takes the immediate given as an absolute subject, that is as a thing or a substance endowed with the supreme form conceivable, the form of reason; and it acts for rational ends on the basis of this form. As we have argued, from Whitehead's perspective it is not only the case that Kant's way of presenting the various systems that incorporate the purposiveness of nature is dictated by the dogma of the immediate given. In addition, his own criticism of that system, indeed even his own new metaphysics of nature, is under the sway of that dogma. For Kant, substances and material bodies are no longer thought to be the first things immediately given.[32] Rather, to explain the possibility of natural knowledge for human beings, transcendental philosophy insists that something given immediately by the human senses must be assumed, and because of its lawfulness human understanding derives the concept of a material body as the object of possible experience from what is given by the senses.[33]

The History or the Construction of Knowledge

Now, the further development of this dogma of the immediate given in the form of the assumption of the immediate givenness of sense especially characterizes the relation between determination and reflection in Kant's critical transcendental philosophy. Moreover, it also particularly defines the relation between mechanical and teleological causality. For determining judgment presupposes the sensible given in order to subsume this given, by means of the universal laws of the understanding, under the concept of a material body to which the most universal causal laws correspond. Similarly, for its part, reflective judgment presupposes these sensible givens so as to find the most concrete and specific lawfulness for them. Most importantly, in Kant's critical and transcendental philosophy, the new concept of subjectivity remains tied to the old dogma of substance ontology. In the final analysis, subjects are nothing more for Kant than "things with a subject." They are things or substances that are distinguished from other things, "things without a subject," in virtue of their specific capacities and characteristics. Kant's new subjectivist metaphysics diverges—if it may be put this way—from the tradition not by proposing an unmistakable separation between the concept of a thing and the concept of a subject, but rather by a sharp methodological distinction between two interpretations of the subject which are to be separated from one another. What is at stake here is the distinction between a transcendentally ideal and an empirically real subject. Thus, the transcendentally ideal subject is thought as a thing which is outfitted with a cognitive capacity competent to achieve an a priori cognition. By contrast, the empirically real subject is a representing thing in whose representations sensibility and understanding have combined to produce perception and other specifically empirical cognitions. Thus, Kant was primarily concerned to demonstrate that, as a faculty of cognition, a priori transcendental subjectivity forms the basis for the knowing and the thinking of the empirical subject and its empirical cognition, or knowledge based in experience. By means of its cognitive principles, this a priori subject prepares the conditions for the possibility of an empirical subject and for its empirical or experiential knowledge. Thus, empirical subjects, along with their empirical knowledge, were regarded as being the specific objects of a possible experience. The questionable unity of the two sorts of subjectivity and the analysis of the capacity of knowledge of these two forms of subjectivity provide the methodological direction for an answer to the fundamental philosophic question about the essence of human being. For this reason, the so-called higher cognitive faculty, the thematic cognitive faculty, was the one in which understanding and reason in principle exercised dominion over sensibility and through whose possession human beings were distinguished from other rational and irrational beings. If the second Copernican turn in Whitehead is at stake here we are set the task of comparing it at this juncture with the first one proclaimed by Kant.

Kant described the Copernican turn as proposing a theoretical alternative for laying the foundation of metaphysical knowledge which involved him in deciding in favor of one of two possibilities. As he put it, either knowledge must be constituted by the object or else the object must be constituted by cognition, and it is only in the second case, or when it is certain that the object is formed by cognition, that the possibility of metaphysical knowledge is guaranteed. By its very definition, this is pure knowledge, or a priori cognition. If Whitehead's second Copernican turn is contrasted with Kant's first one here, it is easy enough to fall into the error of misunderstanding it as the suggestion that this way the first one is rescinded in favor of the philosophic position Kant had rejected. The consequence of that would be that cognition or knowledge would have to be thought as constituted by its objects. In Whitehead's contemporary subjectivist metaphysics the idea of pure knowledge a priori forms at the most a limiting concept but is never thought to hold the key to all metaphysical knowledge. This is why it is also appropriate to characterize Whitehead's metaphysics as a metaphysics of experience. That, however, also provides the reason why it is impossible to see it simply as a reversion to the metaphysics that Kant had termed dogmatic in contradistinction to his own critical system. Whitehead insists that the theoretical alternative proposed by Kant ultimately is not valid in its exclusions. Rather, it stands among a series of problematical premises, the most questionable one of which is again the dogma of the immediate givenness of things. That alternative proposes that an object is a thing *without* reason and cognition is a thing *with* reason. Accordingly, if rational human knowledge or metaphysical knowledge is to be possible, then things without reason must be constituted by things with reason. Whitehead escapes from that theoretical alternative by a simple conceptual stroke. The object of knowledge must itself have the character of knowledge if any sort of knowledge, and therewith metaphysical knowledge, is to be possible. Thus, in Whitehead's subjectivist metaphysics, the new fundamental relation of the knowledge of cognition is to be found in place of the former fundamental relation of object and knowledge.[34]

For Kant, cognition constituted an absolute whole which could be made into the object of an extraordinary philosophic analysis, or the object of the transcendental analytic. Again, this analytic took the elements of knowledge as immediate givens that in their immediate givenness represented no knowledge or cognition at all. This was the way that the method of the transcendental logic intended to show how knowledge arises from givens that are not cognition and not knowledge. It intended to do so by conceiving these givens as elements of cognition combined under universal conditions of their categorical synthesis in the unity of a transcendental subject. Whitehead regarded such a methodological construction of a concrete entity from abstract elements as absurd—and in the present case the entity to be constructed would be concrete cognition—because, as he argued, knowledge or cognition is always presupposed, and the concrete can never be derived or constructed from an abstraction. Only something abstract can come from something else abstract. By contrast, the concrete must be taken and understood in its given connection with other concreta that are always given with it.[35]

If Whitehead's new metaphysics of subjectivity proceeds from the difference between one concrete cognition and another concrete cognition, rather than from the difference between the object and the knowledge or cognition of the object, all cognition presupposes other concrete cognitions in its relevant concrete givenness. It is related to previously given cognitions. It is initiated, even if it is not defined, by it. As was true for Kant, every individual, concrete cognition is a synthesis and a synthetic cognition, but the elements from which it develops and in which it consists are for their part always cognitions. Every particular cognition is, accordingly, a synthesis of previously existing cognitions. The relevant synthesis is itself a selection and a preparation or a working up of these given cognitions. Seen in this way Whitehead's metaphysics of subjectivity is a metaphysics of cognition. It becomes apparent here just how great the distance is that separates classical from modern panpsychism. This metaphysics of cognition is nothing but a metaphysics of process and of causal events. Every causal process is a cognitive process. Such a cognitive process is related to other given cognitions that causally initiate it and whose causal instigation and effect are themselves apparent in the process under scrutiny. As such, every particular cognitive process has its own unique, discrete self. It is a unique being in and for itself. The actuality and being in itself of such a process means that it is just this process and is not to be confused with any other cognitive process. Since every cognitive process is such a being in itself, the possibility of its development from its own self cognition is given in it. To speak of the fundamental ontological relation of "the knowledge of cognition" thus points towards reflection in this cognitive relation. A given cognition reflects the other cognitions which are given to it and which constitute its causal impetus. It proceeds reflectively by way of these given cognitions because it is impossible for it to be the same cognition as those given to it. The fact that every individual cognition goes beyond the cognitions that have been given previously is not to be equated simply with the superiority of the novel cognition over the older ones given previously, and it is certainly not to be confused with transcendental reflection which imposes an ontological difference between transcendental and empirical knowledge. The relation of reflecting the givens that is apparent in particular and concrete cognitions initially requires only another being, a new particular and a new definite being that cannot be confused with any other being. Further development may be the development of something superior, but this is not necessarily the case by any means. It may just as well be a regression. In order to speak coherently of the diverse connections and comparisons as progressions or regressions, as the development of higher forms or the retreat to lower ones, valid norms for the relevant judgment must be provided and the validity of these for the comparative cognition in question must somehow be shown. Without a doubt, different norms are possible for the judgment and evaluation inherent in the definite view achieved by any concrete comparison. Similarly, each and every individual concrete process of cognition has previously had its external comparison and assessment in which it was assigned its unique significance and particular value. This is why it is highly unlikely that we will be able to start with a higher cognitive faculty, or with reason, as an immediate given. In order for potentially superior cognition to be given, it must be presupposed that simpler and more elementary cognitions lie at hand as those givens from which the more complex givens can, under certain circumstances, be explained.

From the standpoint of Whitehead's new metaphysics of subjectivity, it is apparent that Kant is the most dogmatic precisely where he ought to be the most critical, that is to say in the assumption of the immediate givenness of reason. Whitehead's transformation of classical and modern panpsychism goes hand in hand with a far-reaching revision of the traditional conception of reason. Reason is no longer thought as essentially given in connection with a higher capacity of cognition, and certainly it is not given with the presupposition of the existence of a highly developed entity that possesses reason. Rather, reason is manifest in each individual cognitive event and in every causal process of cognition insofar as this has its unique significance for itself and for other cognitions. Thus, reason is always already present in the most simple sensations and feelings, and it is inherent in the most elementary sensation. Whitehead called his philosophic undertaking a "Critique of Pure Feeling" in explicit contrast to Kant's "Critique of Pure Reason."[36] It follows that Whitehead's point of departure in the metaphysics of subjectivity is the basic relation of knowing cognition in its simplest and most elementary form, as the feeling of feeling, or as the sensation of sensation. From this basic relation, Kant's decision requiring that the object be moulded by cognition becomes highly dubious.[37] Whitehead's second Copernican turn replaces this dogmatic dictum of a critique, which only purports to be one, with an entirely different view. Consistent with this, both of these propositions must be valid: "The object is formed by cognition," and "Cognition must be formed by its object." The propositions will gain their validity in respect to individual cognitions and in respect to their relation to the other cognitions that initiate them causally and ultimately constitute their objects, but that is not the end of the story. If it is true that every individual concrete cognition is a unique and discrete event, a unique causal process, then a further corrective completion is required for the transcendental and critical dictum that decrees objects are constituted by cognition. Not only must cognitions be formed by objects, but no cognition "can, will, or may"[38] be completely formed by the cognitions that causally initiate it and from which it forms its objects. Equally, no object, and no cognition that can be made into an object, is constituted by just the one cognition for which it is an object. It must also be aligned with other possible cognitions for which it is, or may be, an object. Consistent with this, Whitehead spoke of the external freedom and the internal determination of actual entities. That means every individual causal process of every concrete cognitive process is externally free and causally determined in precisely this sense. Kant's transcendental analysis cannot deal with this factor on the basis of his dogma of the immediate given. Since by definition the elements of the transcendental analytic are not cognitions, the construction of cognition from objects of possible experience must be thought as merely a logical construction and the cognitive process must then be conceived as merely ideal.

Whitehead's revision of the traditional concept of reason is not exhausted by his uncoupling reason from a higher human cognitive faculty and by anchoring it in the elementary connections of the feeling cognition of some thing or of some object. Reason is preeminent in any relation of tension and in the complementary relation that exists between external freedom and internal determination. It is not only manifest in the external causal dependence on other cognitive processes that have proceeded it, it is also manifest in the unique lawfulness, and in the discrete particularity, of every singular event. As free, or as determined, this reason can also be understood as the irreducibility of concrete cognitions. No particular cognitive event, no particular cognitive process, can be reduced to abstract elements. Similarly, it is equally impossible to reduce it to other cognitive processes or to cognitive processes of another sort. No such reduction can avoid paying the price of sacrificing the relevant particularity of the process in question. That necessarily will be a reduction of this concrete and unique lawful particularity to an external, universal lawfulness. Whitehead's second Copernican turn is in principle a revision of the concept of reason and of the rational subject present in Kant's transcendental philosophy. This revision is not content to show the continued influence of the dogma of the immediate givenness of substances and things in Kant's concepts of reason and the subject. The revision we have described of the notion of reason rests immediately upon the transcendental concept of the subject. For Kant, its universality is the more important aspect of transcendental subjectivity. Unlike empirical subjectivity, with its comparative universality and in the comparative universality of empirical cognition, transcendental subjectivity is absolutely universal. That means that this subjectivity forms the logical focus of all the universal predicates which we must ascribe to an object if this object is to be conceived as an object of possible empirical knowledge. In this way, the dogma of the immediate givenness of subjectivity comes to prominence in a particularly crass fashion in Kant's conception of the universality of the transcendental subject.

Translation: G. Treash

NOTES

1. *Critique of Judgment* § 72.

2. *Critique of Judgment*, §73.

3. *Critique of Judgment*, §72.

4. *Critique of Judgment*, §72.

5. *Critique of Judgment*, §72.

6. *Critique of Judgment*, §72.

7. Eric Adickes insists that: "The conception of creation which is required by his theistic conception of God is in the background of Kant's thought in the *Opus Postumum* just as much as it was in 1775, although to be sure here it is present in an indistinct fashion and obviously in a form that is not in direct contradiction with the idealistic theory of space and time." Cf. *Kants Opus Postumum dargestellt und beurteilt von E. Adickes* [*Kant's Opus Postumum Edited and Assessed by Eric Adickes*], (Berlin: Reuther and Reichard, 1920), 376. Adickes's presentation of the material remains most useful because of its clarity and open-mindedness even if one can not agree that: "The later work is here, as is often the case, not always the best" and

that: "The mature man of the decade of the three *Critiques* towers above the superannuated dotard of the last manuscript." Adickes, 394. The neo-Kantian Adickes could not reconcile himself to the changes that the late Kant represents over the classical understanding of transcendental philosophy, even when he clearly recognized this change. He had always to brand these changes as Kant's slipping back into dogmatism. Thus, Adickes points to the fact that in the *Opus Postumum*, "The principle of the possibility of experience is from now on applied in a completely new fashion." Adickes, 389.

8. *Critique of Judgment*, Introduction.

9. § 65 of the *Critique of Judgment* bears the descriptive superscript "As Natural Purposes Things are Organized Entities." Cassirer's reading is singularly representative of the interpretation of Kant's *Critique* as basing teleological judgments on a philosophical foundation of biology. Cassirer insists that although the *Critique of Judgment*, "Certainly does not abandon the connection of biology with mathematical physics, yet it does not maintain the methodological 'autonomy', the methodological self-legislation, of the latter any less strongly." *Das Erkenntnisproblem in der Philosophie und Wissenschaft der neueren Zeit* [*The Problem of Knowledge in Contemporary Philosophy and Science*], vol. IV, (Darmstadt: Wissenschaftliche Buchgesellschaft, 1973, reprint of the second edition), 127–131.

10. Part of the essential content of the *Opus Postumum* is constituted by the draft of, "a work that will erect the bridge that has hitherto been lacking between the metaphysical foundations of natural science and physics, and to do this by extending the circle of the transcendental (a priori) considerations so that it includes the concept of matter." Adickes, 155. In this connection Adickes points to Kant's distinction between a metaphysics of corporeal nature (a metaphysical doctrine of body) and the universal or general metaphysics of nature (a metaphysics of nature in general). The latter, "treats the laws that make the concept of nature in general possible, without reference to any one determinate object of experience, and thus as undetermined in respect to the nature of this or that thing in the sensible world." The metaphysics of corporeal nature is different from this inasmuch as, "It has as its foundation an empirical concept, namely that of matter...and it computes the extent of the a priori knowledge that reason is capable of with reference to this object." Adickes, 156–157.

11. Kant still speaks in the *Opus Postumum* as he did in the *Critique of Judgment* (§65) of an organized body as one, "in which the idea of a whole proceeds from the possibility of its parts in respect of its unified motive

forces," and of a material principle in respect to such a body. Cf. Adickes, 225. In this connection Adickes mentions Kant's application of the expression *anima mundi* with reference to Schelling's work of 1798 on the world soul.

12. Cf. *Critique of Judgment* §67: "To judge a thing as a natural purpose because of its inner form is something completely different from assuming that the existence of this thing is a goal of nature. For the latter assertion we require not merely the concept of a possible goal, but rather knowledge of the final purpose of nature which requires a relation of the natural entity to something supersensible. This exceeds by far all our teleological knowledge of nature, for the goal of nature itself must be sought beyond nature." The difference between inner and outer purposiveness that is treated thematically in §§65 and 66 brings into play the distinction between the idealism and the realism of nature's purposes that is spoken of at §72.

13. Kant's well-known distinction between nature in the formal and material sense is significant here. "When the word nature is taken in its merely formal sense to mean the ultimate internal principle of everything that pertains to the existence of a thing there can be as many natural sciences as there are specifically different things, and each of these must contain the internal source of the determinations relevant to its existence." *Metaphysische Anfangsgründe der Naturwissenschaften* [*Metaphysical Foundations of Natural Science*], Preface A, iii.

14. Hegel's assessment of the Kantian teleology is the most thorough. On the one hand, Hegel recognizes that: "One of Kant's great contributions to philosophy consists in the distinction that he drew between relative or external purposiveness on the one hand and internal purposiveness on the other. In this latter he had unlocked the concept of life for the Idea, and in this way he elevated philosophy over the definition of reflection and the relative world of metaphysics and over what the critique of reason is able to accomplish in a negative way, or only obliquely and incompletely." On the other hand Hegel saw with absolute clarity that Kant always allowed this discovery of the Idea of life in the form of internal purposiveness to escape him inasmuch as he tied it to reflective judgment with the result that: "...It is, rather, subjective cognition which, upon occasional provocation, applies one maxim or another depending on the object it regards as appropriate. But for the rest it does not inquire about the truth of these determinations themselves, be they either determinations of objects or of cognition." *Wissenschaft der Logik* [*Science of Logic*], part II, ed. G. Lasson, (Leipzig: Felix Meiner,1934), 387.

15. In our century it was A. N. Whitehead who formulated the sharpest

criticism of Kant's phenomenalism. He regarded this phenomenalism as an inevitable consequence of the misconstrued connection of subjectivity and sensationalism. Cf. *Process and Reality: An Essay in Cosmology*, eds. D. Griffin and D. Sherburne, (New York: Free Press, 1978). Cited hereafter as PR.

16. So in the *Opus Postumum* and in connection with his sketch of a fundamental system of motive forces in which the essential nature of the concept of ultimate causes (organically constructive forces) are confirmed in the a priori and exhaustive division of moving force, Kant can claim that, "the concept of a system of moving forces of matter is at least conceivable and can be allotted the status of a possibility without requiring, or smuggling it in, as a reality." I follow Adickes, 217 here.

17. *Critique of Judgment* §73.

18. I am applying here the well-known formulation of Viktor von Weizsäcker's from his *Der Gestaltkreis: Theorie der Einheit von Wahrnehmen und Bewegen* [*The Formal Circle: The Unity of Perception and Motion*], 4th ed., (Stuttgart: Georg Thieme Verlag, 1968) 168ff.

19. Cf. the article by R. Wiehl "Whitehead's Cosmology of Feeling: Between Ontology and Anthropology," in *Whitehead's Metaphysics of Creativity*, ed. F. Rapp and R. Wiehl, (Albany, State University of New York Press, 1990). On Whitehead's metaphysics as a metaphysics of experience see the articles by F. Rapp and H. Poser in the same volume.

20. Michael Hampe provides strong arguments in favor of naturalism in Whitehead's metaphysics in his: *Die Wahrnehmungen der Organismen: Über die Voraussetzungen einer naturalistischen Theorie der Erfahrung in der Metaphysik A. N. Whiteheads* [*Perception of Organisms: A Naturalistic Theory of Experience in Whitehead's Metaphysics*], (to be published shortly).

21. It was in this sense that Whitehead described the philosophy of organism as a "critique of pure feeling" to take the place of Kant's *Critique of Pure Reason* but which, simultaneously, is to provide the foundation for all three of Kant's *Critiques*. PR ll3[173]. A thorough-going revision of the traditional conception of reason would, of course, be required by this new metaphysical foundation for a philosophy of pure feeling.

22. Thus, in Kant's "Transcendental Aesthetic" Whitehead saw a distorted fragment of what rightly and properly must form the chief object of the critique of reason. PR 113[172–173].

23. Whitehead speaks of the subjectivist principle in terms of the conflation of traditional thing and substance ontology with the modern philosophy of subjectivity in the sense of a philosophy of experience. "The subjectivist principle is that the datum in the act of experience can be adequately analyzed purely in terms of universals." PR 157[239].

24. In fact, Whitehead constantly emphasized that there is only a short distance between the phenomenalism of Kant's transcendental philosophy and Hume's skepticism. Similarly, he criticized phenomenalism and skepticism by reference to the fact that they combine the subjectivist with the sensationalist principle in an analogous fashion. PR 49[78] and 157[238].

25. To speak of a second Copernican turn in Whitehead in contradistinction to the first one in Kant does not involve a return to the concept of substance and stepping away from the concept of the subject. If Whitehead charges Kant with a confusion of the primary and the derivative it is always in the context of insisting that he has taken what is clear, distinct and definite as primary and correspondingly whatever is obscure and indefinite as secondary. This criticism of Whitehead's corresponds to what I will term the primacy of the principle of origin over the principle of validity. Cf. PR 88[135]. Here Whitehead describes his relation to Kant as one of inversion with the result that, unlike Kant, he will not regard the world as arising out of the subject, but rather the subject as emerging from the world.

26. For Whitehead the distinction Kant draws between purposiveness by means of the reflective concepts of internality and externality becomes the positive metaphysical distinction that underlies all concrete reality under the rubrics of privacy and publicity. Cf. especially PR 289ff[443ff]. All concrete reality behaves in a complementary fashion so far as internality and externality are concerned. Thus, whatever has the character of a singular and particular being, what actually has being, is a nexus of such singular entities when it is considered publicly.

27. The extraordinary importance Kant attached to the concept of the organism in his later thought is clear from posing the question of whether this concept belongs more properly to the science he conceived of as being concerned with the transition to physics or to physics itself. Simultaneously, Kant seems to have come rather close to the notion that it is a pure concept of reason. Cf. Adickes, 226–227.

28. Whitehead understands material bodies as corpuscular societies and he defines these as groups of actual entities that can be analyzed as a mani-

fold of societies each with a personally ordered structure. The conception of personality that he applies in this connection is certainly extremely formal and cannot be rendered consistently with our notions of human personality without further discussion. PR 34–35[50–52].

29. For Whitehead the description of this form of motion arises from the paradigm of electrodynamics which directs cosmological speculation in the present epoch of the world. It is not difficult to see, however, that the concepts of oscillation, and of rhythm, have an extensive metaphysical significance that extends well beyond the paradigm of electrodynamics. From this perspective it is of considerable interest to see that in the *Opus Postumum* Kant comes to an analogous interpretation of the forms of motion in his speculations about the ether. Cf. Adickes, 363–375.

30. Since, as a result of this, material bodies are complex societies of primitive actual entities for Whitehead it follows that the change of place of these bodies is not the most elementary form of motion. In addition, this conception of the change of place presupposes that places are real givens in the spatial-temporal continuum. To that extent it requires a cause for the realization of these places. Whitehead found this in the form of the elementary process whose product is just the actualization of a relevant, determinate place. As was the case for Kant, the problem of the change of place by a material body remains an open question. Cf. Adickes, 363 ff.

31. Whitehead's categorial system contains a principle of construction which permits the construction of ever more complex units of organization from the simple givens of experience. This principle of construction makes it possible to bridge the gulf between being in and for its self and appearance which Whitehead criticized as the chief theoretical deficiency apparent in such heterogeneous metaphysical endeavors as those of Leibniz, Kant, and Bradley. Cf. PR 190[289].

32. Significantly, instead of that it is the matter of motion and of forces.

33. Kant's attempt to interpret the ether, that is to say the matter of warmth, as an object of sense that is simultaneously not an object of possible experience is interesting in this connection. Cf. Adickes, 384.

34. For this reason, Whitehead defends the thesis that the difference between the correspondence theory of truth and the coherence theory is not an absolute one but rather a difference only in their perspectival significance. PR 190[289].

35. Whitehead speaks in this connection of the widespread misunderstanding concerning the explanatory function of philosophy. In principle, philosophy is only possible as an explanation of the abstract, not as an explanation of how the concrete emerges from the abstract. PR 20[30].

36. Cf. Note 21 above.

37. Cf. Note 34 above.

38. This is to play on the pentagram of pathosophy of Viktor von Weizsäcker in the form of the pathetic categories of may, must, will, ought, and can. Cf. *Pathosophie* [*Pathosophy*), (Göttingen: Vandenhoeck & Ruprecht, 1956), 60ff.

2

The Nature of Nature: Kant and Whitehead

Gordon Treash

If Whitehead's philosophy of organism marks the beginning of either a revival of concern for the philosophy of nature or a substantiative contemporary metaphysics, then it is quite true that from its outset this movement has been intimately concerned with the problem of how nature is conceived. Neither is it an exaggeration to suggest that by the time he wrote *Process and Reality* a large part of Whitehead's undertaking was defined by his reliance on a sharp distinction between how the philosophy of organism understands nature and what he repeatedly insists is the conception of nature that dominates in modern thought. This modern conception is that nature, its objects and its laws, are "constructs" or, in even more contemporary terminology, "models" framed by individuals or by the members of a school, but not representations of a system or world that is independent of subjects. Whitehead was convinced that such a conception of nature is perverse and must be avoided, as almost the first page of *Process and Reality* makes plain. In the book's preface he lists nine "prevalent habits of thought" that will be repudiated in the course of the ensuing discussion. The seventh of these, and the only one associated with a single thinker is, "The Kantian doctrine of the objective world as a theoretical construct from purely subjective experience."[1] The contrast between the Kantian conception of nature and the one proposed by Whitehead's thought is sharpened in the chapter on "The Order of Nature" when he explains that: "For Kant, the world emerges from the subject; for the philosophy of organism, the subject emerges from the world..."[2]

Whitehead's strategy is to argue that two conceptions of nature are possible, the one proposed by the philosophy of organism and the modern or Kantian doctrine, and that only one of the two can be true. Nature cannot simultaneously be what emerges from the subject or a "theoretical construct from purely subjective experience" and whatever it is from which the subject emerges. So, if the philosophy of organism is true in its major assertions, the

The Nature of Nature: Kant and Whitehead

alternative doctrine must be false. Similarly, should the Kantian conception of nature be accepted, nothing of the illumination provided by the philosophy of organism can be sustained.

The accuracy of Whitehead's historical allusions, especially to Locke and Hume, have been subjected to close examination, but for the most part students have been content to accept his evaluation of Kant at face value. In the first section of the present discussion I will argue that it is incorrect to suggest that there is an irreconcilable contradiction between Kant's doctrine and Whitehead's own position. Rather, in terms reminiscent of the solution of the first and second antinomies, neither the assertion that, "The objective world or nature is primary in both the epistemological and the ontological sense and the subject is secondary to this objective world" nor its contrary, "The objective world or nature is not ontologically or epistemologically primary, but depends upon the subject" can be thought true without certain vital qualifications.

That Whitehead was not a very careful Kantian would be worth no more than a critical footnote. However, to pose the question in these terms has the advantage that it highlights the ambiguity of what a subject is, and that ambiguity is fundamental to the discussion. There can be little question that Whitehead's perspective is through and through ontological. He undertakes to describe the subjects from which all existences are constituted, and the subject is inevitably that unit of experience which he terms the *actual entity* or the *superject*. Kant, by contrast, begins with the cognitive subject. He is concerned to delineate the principles by which not only human cognition, but any thought significantly like human intelligence, proceeds. At first that description seems to suggest that Whitehead was entirely correct to object to any version of the Kantian program because it begins from a perspective diametrically opposed to his own. However, as will be shown, the difference is not an ultimate one, and in fact there are highly important ways in which the two positions reenforce one another. This is apparent when the epistemological implications of the critical program are developed as they are by the first two sections of the paper, and when these reflections are extrapolated to the world conceived by the natural sciences as Kant does extrapolate them in a work which has attracted far too little attention, the *Metaphysical Foundations of Natural Science*. Discussion of this is undertaken in sections three and four, and in this portion of the discussion the importance for Kant of the ontological rendering of subjectivity becomes apparent.

SUBJECTS, OBJECTS AND NATURAL KNOWLEDGE

Textual justification exists for describing the modern conception of nature, according to which it is only a system of concepts or a "model," as Kantian.

In the first edition version of the transcendental deduction, for example, Kant described nature as "...a conceptual whole (*Inbegriff*) that is nothing in itself, but rather a collection of the mind's representations..."[3] It follows of course that, "The order and regularity of appearances that we term *nature* we ourselves introduce, and we would not be able to find them there at all had we, or rather the nature of our minds, not originally put them there."[4]

However, it is not necessarily the case that such characterizations of nature lead univocally to the position Whitehead describes as Kantian, and there is good reason for doubting that they do so. Should the *Inbegriff* terminology be pressed to the point of regarding the world of objects which collectively we term *nature* as merely a theoretical construct from "purely subjective experience," the result is not transcendental but rather Berkeleian subjective idealism;[5] and Kant was not confused this way. He knew perfectly well that no experience is subjective without qualification, even though all experience is the experience of the subject that enjoys it and certainly is "subjective" in that sense. That is a truism from which nothing of the slightest importance follows. What Whitehead begins *Process and Reality* with is the far stronger assertion that nature can be understood as entirely derivative from, and dependent upon, the intellectual life of any particular cognitive subject, and there is no textual justification for reading Kant that way, even if the laws of nature are introduced by the nature of our minds and nature is a conceptual whole, an *Inbegriff*.

The first *Critique* insists strongly upon the dramatically opposed rendering of experience. It, Kant insists, "rests on the synthetic unity of appearances, that is on a synthesis of *an object* of appearances in general according to concepts, without which it would never be knowledge but a rhapsody of perceptions..."[6] If this is granted then the object is manifestly not adequately described as something entertained by an individual subject, unique to that subject and incapable of repetition, so that in more blunt terms it is not a part of the objective world. The *Critique* undertakes to understand the complex nature of experience, and the analysis involves not only the experiencing subject (or the transcendental unity of apperception) but the elements which are given to the subject and the means by which these elements are brought into a coherent unity. Without the categories or rules for its coherent organization, whatever is given to the subject would amount only to what Kant calls a chaotic rhapsody of perceptions and be without cognitive content. But it is equally true that in the absence of anything given there is no knowledge of objects and no objective cognition. "If a cognition is to have objective reality, that is pertain to an object, and have meaning and sense in respect to this object, then the object must be able to be given in some way or the other. Without that concepts are empty and although something has been thought in this way nothing is known through such thought. There is, rather, only a game played with representations."[7] None of this is more than a slight expansion of Kant's insistence on the first page of the Transcendental Logic that, "Thoughts without content are empty. Intuitions without concepts are blind."[8] It does, however, provide strong evidence that the description of Kant's position as one that regards the objective world or nature as the product of each knowing subject's cognition, is seriously incomplete, and that Kant knew that the relations that exist between subjects and objects such as to make each possible is far more complex than such subjective or Berkeleian idealism permits.

It is essential to the first *Critique* and *Prolegomena* that we can adequately characterize our cognition or knowledge only insofar as the given and the conceptual are each realized as being primitive and as irreducible components of any thought about the world. Neither those thinkers who had attempted to reduce human knowledge to sensation, as Locke and his followers did, nor those who with Descartes undertook to derive all our knowledge of the world from thought alone, were able to offer more than half of the truth. In these half-formulations the hope of framing a coherent account of either the world or our knowledge of it is lost. For, without the conceptual element nothing is organized and accordingly there is no order and no nature. The order of nature is the order achieved by this conceptualization. However, a sensible given is equally essential, and without it there is nothing to be thought or cognized.

It is an important indication of what Kant intends that the rules essential to thought about objects are explicitly called categories, and "are named after Aristotle's *categories*, since our intention is identical to his, although it is certainly quite far removed from his in its execution."[9] Moreover, the absolute necessity of these, and only these, categories is a direct consequence of their close connection to the principles of general logic.[10] The categories are the principles by which all rational beings endowed with an intelligence anything at all like our own are able to apprehend the world. They are what makes it necessary for any rational being to think or to cognize the sequence in which one ball on a billiard table strikes another so that the second one moves in a thoroughly predictable fashion as an event. This elementary experience and judgment exemplifies the synthesis of what is given with what the understanding contributes in all cognition of the world. The subject judges and enjoys the experience of causality, but that subject stands under a double constraint. It is constrained by what is given to it, and, further, it is constrained by the rules for cognizing, or thinking about, what is given.

Similarly, some things which we think with perfect clarity cannot be part of any world of objects, and it has been a great error of philosophers to imagine that they can. Our selves or souls, as immortal beings, and God are two such thoughts which we cannot avoid entertaining even though neither refers to an object. It follows that such thoughts cannot possibly entail the synthesizing activity which, as Kant insists, is ingredient in our cognition of the world. Yet even although such thoughts have no sensible objects, and in that sense are not objective, they are not merely the products of unrestrained or free conceptualization. Kant repeats twice, and in nearly identical words, that such thoughts are "ideas" and subject to something quite similar to the transcendental deduction that establishes the necessity of the categories. "No genuine *objective deduction* such as we could accomplish for the categories is possible for these transcendental ideas. For in fact they have no relation to any sort of an object which could be given as congruent to them just because they are ideas. But we can undertake a subjective derivation from the nature of our reason, and in fact that is accomplished in the present section [The Transcendental Dialectic]."[11]

Thus, there are two reasons why it is wrong to ascribe a Berkeleian or a subjective idealism to Kant. It is incorrect, in the first place, because Kant insisted so strongly upon the element of what is given. Where nothing is given, nothing is ever known or cognized. There is merely empty categorization, which can reveal nothing of nature or of the objective world. In the second place, Kant is no Berkeleian or subjective idealist, constructing worlds by reference only to predilection, because he insisted so strongly that what the mind does with what it is given is rule-directed, indeed rule-dominated. These rules are so powerful that even thought which is not tied to objects is not free from their sway.

Nature, it follows, is grounded exclusively in neither the subject nor the object; so the contrast with which Whitehead begins between nature as subjectively grounded and the subject as derived from nature is just that, a contrast, and not a formal contradiction. It cannot be argued then that Kant must be in error whenever Whitehead is correct, or conversely that the transcendental philosophy must perforce exclude any positive connections to the insights embodied in Whitehead's thought. For the present discussion this means that despite the textual reservations it is plausible to treat him with Kant in exploring the status of nature, and that the two are not merely diametrically opposed systems related only by their opposition.

NATURE IN RELATION

A further consequence of the previous section is that neither the epistemological issue of how subjects come to know nature nor the ontological one, focused upon how nature is to be conceived, can be adequately addressed in itself. *Process and Reality* itself provides striking justification of this, for Whitehead's treatment of Kant is not exhausted by the description that was crucial to the previous section. At the end of part II of the book he refers to a passage from Norman Kemp Smith's *Commentary* on the *Critique of Pure Reason*. Kemp Smith had described the objective as what, "...lays a compulsion upon our minds, constraining us to think about it in a certain way. By an object is meant something which will not allow us to think at haphazard."[12] Whitehead freely accepts this adding that, "There is of course the vital difference, among others, that where Kemp Smith, expounding Kant, writes 'thinking', the philosophy of organism substitutes 'experiencing'."[13]

Whitehead finds in Kant, or in Kemp Smith's Kant, the assertion that objects of nature stand in a constitutive and synthetic relation with the cognizing subject. This is considerably stronger than the modest assertion that objects are things which the mind apprehends. In this stronger formulation they are objects *because* they stand in relation to the cognizing subject, and only whatever does stand in such a relation is an object. No object of nature can be adequately understood as simply inert or merely as extension. As an object in nature it is necessarily in relation. The billiard balls, then, are not merely spheres of so much extensive magnitude. They are objects, and claim objective reality, because and only so far as they constitute objects for the subjects that encounter them, and in this case encounter them as events or as the constituents of an event. This means that they are objects just because, for any rational subject, the motion of the one is the cause and that of the other is the effect in the event. Their objectivity is the result of this relation to any possible cognizing subject. Of course, similar requirements exist for objects characterized by the first and third analogies of substance and reciprocity as well. Neither substances nor things in reciprocal relation are objects except inasmuch as they are objects for human intelligence or for an intelligence that is similar in significant ways to human intelligence.

This result stands in sharp contrast to the naive materialism that was prevalent through the modern epoch and which insisted that the fundamental attribute of any natural object is its extension, or its mass, so that per se it is inert. Materialism of this sort had figured in Newton's conception of nature and, consistent with the success of his physics, had dominated thought about nature in the modern era. Critical philosophy begins by demonstrating that such materialism is impossible from an epistemological perspective, but this perspective opens out for Kant as it did for Whitehead. At the very least, it insists none of these objects may be cogently thought as being merely inert units of extension. If so, Kant's thought presages Whitehead's rejection of what he terms *vacuous actuality*. As he had explained early in *Process and Reality*, "The term 'vacuous actuality'...means the notion of a *res vera* devoid of subjective immediacy."[14] If actual objects are the things which do in fact compel any subject to experience in this fashion rather than in any other, manifestly they cannot be "devoid of subjective immediacy." What they are is partially determined by what the experiencing subject makes of them, and indeed they are objective only because of their relation to the subjects who enjoy the experience provided in such relation to objects.

This denial of vacuous actuality is closely tied to another seriously misleading predilection of modern thought that Whitehead termed the *sensationalist principle* or the presupposition that, "...the primary activity in the act of experience is the bare subjective entertainment of the datum..."[15] This element of Whitehead's thought is also sustained by critical philosophy. Kant often uses the terms 'receptivity' and 'spontaneity' to distinguish between the ability to receive impressions and the activity of cognizing those impressions.[16] Neither of these two elements, neither receptivity nor spontaneity, is adequate alone to produce cognition because the act of experience is not merely the reception of what exists independently of any act of subjectivity. Objects, as Whitehead says explicitly invoking Kant, are the result of the relation that must obtain between the two factors. Natural objects, it follows, must be understood then as products and not simply as primitive givens to which all experience and all thought are subject.

That result is achieved by concentrating on the elements which must be recognized in order to complete the account of how human beings understand nature. As has been true of significant statements about human knowledge and understanding since Plato's, it is pregnant with ontological implications and in particular it has an immediate application to the objects that are conceived as constituting nature. It shows how inadequate any conception of nature as consisting of nothing more than bits of extension, or bits of matter, is. Once that epistemological consequence is taken seriously, it has the further consequence that nature requires to be recognized as involving essential forces or as dynamic, and to that degree as not essentially and only extended mathematically.

OBJECTS AND ACTIVITY

Kant was keenly aware that the heightened importance of the dynamic aspect of nature was a consequence of his critical or the transcendentally idealistic interpretation of natural knowledge. In the first part of his discussion of the antinomy of pure reason, for example, he set the dynamic aspect of nature in sharp contrast with the merely quantitative or mathematical. Two terms can be employed to refer to the totality of objects that occupy the attention of men both in their everyday lives and as natural scientists. These are the expressions 'world' and 'nature'.

> The former signifies the mathematical whole of all appearances, and the totality of their synthesis in large dimensions as well as in small ones, which [synthesis] is in the continuation of both composition

and division. But the very same world is termed nature insofar as it is seen as a dynamic *whole* inasmuch as this whole is not concerned with an aggregation in space or in time, in order to synthesize it as a magnitude, but rather insofar as one is concerned with it as a unity of appearances in existence.[17]

Nature is dynamic and is not merely something extended that can be measured mathematically, and Kant is completely consistent with that description when, at the end of his note on the third antinomy of reason (concerning human freedom), he describes nature as the "coherence of appearances necessarily determining one another according to universal laws...."[18]

This description of nature as dynamic—in contradistinction to the world as mathematical—is striking evidence of how strong a connection there is between Kant's critical philosophy and the work he had completed earlier, and especially before the *Inaugural Dissertation* of 1770 on the *Form and Principles of the Sensible and Intelligible World*. This is not difficult to explain historically. At the middle of the century German philosophy was preeminently Wolffian, and Wolff had, or claimed to have, direct connections with Leibniz. It is easy enough for philosophers late in the twentieth century to caricature Wolff. He was graceful neither as an author nor as a colleague, and the esteem in which he expected to be held bordered on the idolatrous.[19] Nonetheless it was he who almost single-handedly brought a positive professionalism to German thought, and it was he who first taught Germans that it was quite possible to philosophize in German. More specifically, it was because of his influence that subsequent generations of German philosophers were exposed to a version of Leibniz's dynamic conception of nature, rather than imbibing undiluted Newtonian materialism. Kant lectured for more than twenty years from the textbooks prepared by an active Wolffian, Alexander Gottlieb Baumgarten, and Baumgarten had developed a conception of nature that is Leibnizean to the extent that it proposes that active monads, which by their very nature exert force, rather than indivisible bits of solid matter, are the foundation and ground of nature.

By the time he came to write his first book in 1746, Kant was familiar enough with the Leibnizean tradition to undertake a correction in the way that school had of computing the living force which was so significant to Leibniz. The correction is interlaced with criticism of Leibniz, but remains firmly within the Leibnizean ambit. The received procedure of computing living force is defective, the young Kant had insisted, and requires to be replaced with a more accurate one. Such a revision is neither sensible or even possible, however, if the leading tenets of Leibnizean thought are not accepted. Of course, the most important of these tenets was the conception of nature as dynamic and active because it consists of dynamic units or substances: without that assumption there are no living forces to be computed. Kant does not use the term 'monad' in his first book, but the conception is very close to the surface indeed. Except for Aristotle, he argues at the outset, all philosophers before Leibniz had attempted to explain motion as imposed upon entities from an external source. External imposition of motion is inadequate because it requires that the source of motion be thought as a motive force. But, he argues, such motive forces explain nothing at all. They simply repeat that motion has obtained, and this vacuity insures that any attempt to ground an explanation of the world on them is doomed. In fact, motion must be explained as a consequence of the substances' fundamental forces, which is what permits them not only to move but to fill space. This force is intrinsic to each substance and is what explains both the motion apparent in the physical world and the extension of bodies. So, far from being reduced to mere extension, a natural entity is active in such a way as to result in extension. The important aspect of Kant's first book here is that in manifest affinity to Leibniz he argues that instead of explaining motion as a consequence of extension, extension is to be explained in terms of the primitive forces characteristic of each substance and that these forces also initiate motion. An intriguing aspect of this early essay is constituted by its suggestion that these fundamental forces may well act in ways requiring descriptions in terms other than those provided by three-dimensional or Euclidean geometry.[20] That hint is not developed further, but it is significant because it is an immediate consequence of the essay's strong insistence that extension, and even more immediately geometry as the science of extension, both are dependent upon how the fundamental beings or substances act upon one another and are not fundamental properties of physical beings in and of themselves.

Ten years after his first work Kant published an essay in Latin, which he hoped would lead directly to his appointment to the chair of logic and metaphysics that had fallen empty upon the death of Martin Knutzen. The full title of the work itself is significant: *The Use In Natural Philosophy of Metaphysics Combined with Geometry, Part One, Physical Monadology*.[21] In this disputation Kant undertook to combine geometry with metaphysics and, as the title promises, to achieve a result that will be useful to natural philosophy, *philosophia naturalis*. The essay develops themes that had appeared in the first book on the living forces, and here Kant uses the term 'monad' in a positive and constructive fashion for the first time. It is unnecessary to follow the entire argument of the dissertation in order to establish the book's significance for the philosophy of nature. This significance lies in its contention that rather than impenetrable and indivisible units of mass it is units of force which are the foundation of all physical being. These units of force are what he now designates as the 'physical monads'. Like the units of mass which the Newtonians had postulated, the physical monads are indivisible.

Unlike the atoms, however, the monads are characterized by their activity. Because they are the elementary parts of any physical body the monads' activities—which consist in attraction and repulsion—are the reason for the physical body's being the way it is. Their ability to provide the explanations of physical bodies is what makes the monads physical ones.

This marks a significant divergence from Leibniz who had posited the parallel but separate realms of monadic activity and physical being so that bodies are properly explained in purely physical terms. "...Bodies act as if there were no souls (to assume an impossibility), and souls act as if there were no bodies, and both act as if each influenced the other."[22] Kant's monadology, by contrast, argues that the monads explain and are the reasons why physical bodies are what they in fact are. Physical bodies are determined by their constituent monads, and he argues at some length that the degree to which they fill space and how they fill space, which is manifestly one of the leading characteristics of body, can be shown to follow from monadic activity alone.

With this Kant obviates the need for the preestablished harmony that Leibniz had been required to postulate between the physical world of bodies and the internal world and life of the monads. Physical bodies are not merely phenomena—even well-founded ones as Leibniz had insisted that they are in the correspondence with de Volder. They are the derivatives from, and the results of how, the monadic substances act. Significant as this difference is, it does not obscure the close agreement of Kant's early philosophy of nature with Leibniz insofar as each understood nature as dynamic and posited active units as the basic elements from which nature, and the objects of nature, are constituted.

A CRITICAL DYNAMISM?

If the preceding description of Kant's early monadology is accurate, it is however, still only an account of an earlier phase of his philosophic development which, it might be suggested, is rendered obsolete by what he accomplished in the critical period. That critical system, as Kant never tires of explaining, restricts the objects of knowledge to the objects of possible experience, and although it is necessary that certain things be cognized as substances or as events with their appropriate causes, only substances or events that may possibly be encountered in experience—either the experiences of ordinary life or the experiences contrived by empirical laboratory scientists—can be characterized by such necessary rules. Neither Leibnizean monads, nor the monads of Kant's early essay can plausibly be proposed as objects of possible experience; they must be thought as no more than the vestiges of a dogmatic metaphysics and as such can play no part in a critical philosophy of nature.

That is a serious historical objection to the attempt to argue that for Kant, as for Whitehead, there is a compulsion to think about nature as dynamic or that nature is a "dynamic whole."[23] On the positivist reading of the first *Critique*, which provides the basis for that objection, any dynamic elements are restricted to the mode of experiencing natural objects. Even though they may be experienced as dynamic, and as involving mutually influencing moments, this description authorizes no conclusion as to how nature is in and for itself, or what the foundation of these experiences is. If that is all that can be established, there may be some similarity between Kant's dismissal of merely extended and vacuous actuality and Whitehead's thought. But since Kant denies all knowledge of the actualities by which nature is constituted the analogy is rendered highly superficial.

The most important refutation of that historical objection is provided by Kant. In an essay first published in 1786, and accordingly one that is indisputably critical, entitled *Metaphysical Foundations of Natural Science (Metaphysiche Anfangsgründe der Naturwissenschaften)*, he admits that the monadology, "...does not at all belong to the explication of natural appearances but is a Platonic concept of the world completed by Leibniz. This concept is correct in itself insofar as the world is regarded not as an object of the senses but as thing in itself, i.e., merely an object of the understanding which nevertheless *lies at the basis of the appearances of the senses.*"[24]

It is vital to insist that the description of the monadology as "Platonic" does not perforce assign it to the dustbin of idle and useless speculation. Although his knowledge of the texts was not extensive (and was mediated by J. J. Brucker) Kant held Plato in extremely high regard, as the section of the first *Critique* entitled "On Ideas in General" makes abundantly plain.[25] Ideas are the media of thought, in contradistinction to categories which are the media of understanding and experience, and thought is an inescapable aspect of our intellectual functioning. If that is so, the passage from the *Metaphysical Foundations* is strong evidence that Kant had not only recognized that the monadology must be admitted as correct within its proper sphere but, more significantly, had insisted that this monadology is the foundation of appearances. Whatever appears is in some way connected with and depends on the monads even although neither the nature of this connection nor the monads is an object of cognition or knowledge.

That renders it inadequate to dismiss the monadology as a matter of Kant's "private metaphysics,"[26] insofar as such a description suggests that Kant accepted a body of opinions which were immune from attack because they were not categorical cognitions, and thus made no categorical claim about the world. Applied to the dynamic interpretation of nature that would mean Kant continued a somewhat irrational attachment to the monadology and to the dynamic understanding of nature which was only a private and

The Nature of Nature: Kant and Whitehead

personal predilection that played no part in his serious philosophy. In such a case the most that could be claimed would be that it did not contradict any of the leading principles of the critical philosophy.

If, on the other hand, the ideas of dynamic nature based upon fundamental forces, which forces are themselves not categorized, are admitted to be essential in significant ways, another difficulty emerges. For, although as the first *Critique* develops the theme, it is possible to derive ideas from the nature of our reason,[27] a monadology or a dynamic foundation of the world is not included among the ideas treated in that way. At the least a further constraint on the reason to think the physical world as grounded in the monadology is required. Although it is never explicitly proposed as a conclusion of the work, such a constraint is the indirect result of the *Metaphysical Foundations*. This was a book designed to provide the basic material for physics without itself actually engaging in the discipline itself. More precisely, as a *metaphysical* foundation for physics it was intended to uncover those "universal laws of thought,"[28] which are not derived from experience but are pure or a priori and as such requisite for all physical science. What is particularly significant about the work from this perspective is its unequivocal dynamic interpretation of matter. "...All that is real in the objects of our external senses and is not merely a determination of space (place, extension, and figure) must be regarded as moving force. By this principle, therefore, the so-called solid, or absolute impenetrability, is banished from natural science as an empty concept, and in its stead repulsive force is posited."[29] More succinctly, "The concept of matter is reduced to nothing but moving forces..."[30] Finally Kant concludes with the bald assertion that, "...A merely mathematical physics pays for the advantage [of working with extension and empty space alone] doubly on the other side, in that it first of all must lay at its foundation an empty concept (that of absolute impenetrability), and secondly must give up all the proper forces of matter."[31]

The objects of nature, or of natural science, are first conceived or cognized under the concepts or categories requisite to all coherent thought about objects. They are a subgroup of those objects because each is material or involves matter. It is fully consistent with this and, as Kant argues, precisely what is to be expected, that the more intense examination of the notion of matter makes it plain that the material, or matter, is not solid impenetrability alone. Rather, it must be conceived as the result of repulsive and attractive force. Force, not extension is the notion fundamental to matter, even if that foundation cannot itself be apprehended, or in Kant's terminology, its possibility understood.

That result corresponds to what Kant had said of the Leibnizean monadology in the first *Critique*'s discussion of the second antinomy (concerned with problems of the simple). Such a doctrine, he recognized, would be correct if the objects constituting human experience were things in themselves instead of mere appearances.[32] This concession is considerably expanded by the *Metaphysical Foundations of Natural Science*. For, in the five years since publication of the first *Critique,* Kant had come to realize that in nature appearances are always the appearances of the fundamental forces that constitute matter. These fundamental forces are not cognizable objects of experience or appearances because they are—and must be thought as being—the basis of any, and of all, appearances in nature. Or equivalently, appearances of matter must be thought as grounded in the operation of forces.

This makes it appropriate to examine the reasons that justify a rejection of materialism. In the course of the discussion Kant cites substantially the same ones that led Leibniz to reject Newtonian materialism. In the first place, materialism requires postulation of empty space between the various bits of ultimate matter. It is apparent to Kant, and largely as a result of the critical insights, that the notion of an absolutely empty space is a conceptual monster. Indeed, it was the first perverse metaphysical proposition to be dismissed by the critical philosophy.[33] Materialism is further unacceptable inasmuch as it posits absolutely indivisible and impenetrable units of matter. Like the notion of empty space, these absolute units can signify nothing given in, or essential to, experience, and accordingly the phrases that employ them rest upon patently empty notions. Finally, atomism is incoherent, Kant argues in the *Metaphysical Foundations*, because it must surrender "all the proper forces of matter."

The point Kant insists upon in the *Metaphysical Foundations of Natural Science* is not merely that the mind has, or may have, a propensity to think about nature dynamically and that this propensity is an individual or "subjective" and private inclination, grounded entirely in the peculiarities of the subject. The argument is, rather, the very much stronger one which insists that nature *must* be conceived dynamically by us as human cognitive agents. The reason it must be is because nature, as we encounter it, is such as to make urgent an explanation of motion, and yet that explanation is impossible for materialism. Thus, although there is no categorical cognition of the forces which stand as the basis of nature, because nature appears to us as dynamic those appearances can only be thought appearances of basic forces.

If so, Kant has argued that the dynamic understanding of nature which characterized his earlier or "pre-critical" philosophy of nature, when it is adapted by the *Metaphysical Foundations* to meet the requirements imposed by critical philosophy, provides the only coherent explanation of nature. In its critical recension it is not possible to demonstrate the existence of these forces in the way that things are demonstrated within the system which rests upon them. This, however, is only an index of how basic and how significant they are. The impossibility of explaining them further, or of schematizing them, is the other side of their function as the presuppositions upon which the conception of nature rests. For Kant, nature and the conception of nature are not radically diverse, and the exploration of this result reveals what it is that makes nature possible. The *Metaphysical Foundations,* expands the inventory of these elements from the schematized categories so that it includes unschematizable force. Thus, if it is to be cognized, known, nature must be thought as dynamic even though the force entailed is not an object of the categorical understanding.[34]

CONCLUSION

There are, then, highly important, and largely ignored, affinities between Kant's thought and Whitehead's philosophy of organism. The conception of the relation between subjects and objects is similar, and so is the rejection of any conception of nature according to which its objects are adequately understood as units of extension. Yet despite the significant similarities, Kant's thought does not proceed to anything like the radical assertions of the philosophy of organism. It cannot do so because both early and late Kant was certain that any entity, monad or substance is complete in and for itself and related essentially only to God who is its creator. This renders it difficult, or impossible, for him to complete the description of nature as dynamic that figures so centrally in the critical description just sketched. For, conceived this way, that is to say as fundamentally independent and as related only accidentally, there is no reason to attribute activity to all actualities. On Kant's theory only those entities involved in relation with other beings need be active, and only some of the possible entities are in relation. This leads to a second difficulty. If even some actualities are active and dynamic, either that activity requires focus and direction or else the world is irrational at base. Just as Kant was incapable of understanding actuality as radically related, he was also incapable of fully explicating purpose and its appearance in nature. The third *Critique* is sharp evidence of how central purpose was to Kant's thought. However, it also makes plain that he did not, and almost certainly could not, progress beyond the purpose attributed by human subjects to some of the phenomena they encounter, to an explanation of the ground of this purpose. That is to allow the root notion to remain inexplicable.

NOTES

1. *Process and Reality*: *An Essay in Cosmology*, eds. D. Griffin and D. Sherburne, (New York: Free Press, 1978), xiii; cited hereafter as PR.

2. PR 88.

3. *Critique of Pure Reason* A114. The second edition employs similar

terminology at B163. Citations from the *Critique of Pure Reason* will refer to either the first or the second edition, or where relevant both. Translations are my own.

4. *Critique* A125.

5. When he returns to discussion of the point in part 2 of *Process and Reality* Whitehead speaks of "subjective experience" without the further modifier.

6. *Critique* A156/B195, emphasis added.

7. *Critique* A155/B194.

8. *Critique* A51/B75.

9. *Critique* A80/B105.

10. *Critique* A79/B104–105.

11. *Critique* A336/B393. Emphasis added. A similar passage occurs near the end of the Dialectic, *Critique* A670/B698.

12. PR 215, fn.

13. PR 215.

14. PR 29.

15. PR 157.

16. *Critique* A50/B74 for example.

17. *Critique* A419/B447.

18. *Critique* A452/B480.

19. Cf. Lewis White Beck's *Early German Philosophy* (Cambridge, Mass.: Harvard University Press, 1969), for a fuller although not very sympathetic, account of Wolff's *Leben und Lehre*.

20. §§9–10, *Kants Gesammelte Schriften* (KGS) I, 23–25.

21. Translated with an introduction by Lewis White Beck, *Kant's Latin Writings*, (New York: Peter Lang, 1986).

22. *Monadology* §81.

23. *Critique* A419/B447.

24. KGS IV, 507. The book has been translated by James Ellington, *Kant's Philosophy of Material Nature* (Indianapolis: Hackett, 1985), 55. Translation altered slightly and emphasis added.

25. *Critique* A312–A320/B368–377.

26. As is suggested by Lewis White Beck, *Kant's Latin Writings*, 10, 111.

27. *Critique* A297/B354, A329/B386, A336/B393, A669–670/B697–698.

28. KGS IV, 473, Ellington 11.

29. KGS IV, 523, Ellington 77.

30. KGS IV, 524, Ellington 78.

31. KGS IV, 525, Ellington 78.

32. *Critique* A442/B470. This is, of course, a major reservation, but nevertheless it is strong evidence of how completely aware Kant was of Leibniz's metaphysics and how much sympathy he had for its systematic motivations. The "Amphiboly" with which the "Analytic" ends suggests much the same thing. During the five years that followed the first publication of the *Critique of Pure Reason* Kant transformed that sympathy into the conception of the *Metaphysical Foundations*.

33. It is first discursively because it occurs in the first major section of the *Critique of Pure Reason*, the "Aesthetic." Chronologically it was the first inasmuch as it was rendered impossible by the interpretation of space offered by the *Dissertation* of 1770.

34. George R. Lucas, Jr., devotes the fifth chapter of his recent book, *The Rehabilitation of Whitehead* (Albany: State University of New York Press, 1989), to an examination of the relationship between Whitehead and Kant. The chapter betrays surprising infelicities with regard to Kant's text. For

example Lucas insists that "Only *der Schein,* however, has the connotation of 'appearance' in the sense of 'pretence' or 'illusion', as Bradley seems to mean by the term 'appearance'. And Kant never uses this term" (82). In fact, Kant uses *der Schein, scheinbar,* and the verb *scheinen* more than 130 times in the first *Critique*. Cf. *Sachindex zu Kants Kritik der reinen Vernunft (Subject Index for Kant's Critique of Pure Reason)* edited by Gottfried Martin (Berlin: de Gruyter, 1967) 241. However, despite such inaccuracies, Lucas's discussion is a useful contribution to the Kant-Whitehead discussion inasmuch as he argues that Whitehead was incorrect to ascribe what he calls Bradley's idealism to Kant and because he insists that he can "…rescue Kant's reputation as a systematic thinker possessed of a wider interest than merely conducting an anti-metaphysical epistemological polemic and to place this at the service of contemporary pluralistic and post-Critical systematic metaphysics in the aftermath of Whitehead" (87). Lucas concludes this chapter of his book by speculating that Whitehead might well have found Kant's treatment of moral and aesthetic experience in the third *Critique* "most welcome indeed" (92). That is a promising beginning, but although Lucas is aware of the limitations of positivist interpretations of Kant, he does not exploit fully the implications for metaphysics of some of the themes sounded here, and accordingly Kant's concern for the beautiful and good—and the purposive—will appear as though they were superadded to the epistemology of the first *Critique* rather than as being continuous with the primary concerns of that book, which concerns are by no means entirely epistemological.

3
Leibniz and Modern Science

Errol E. Harris

I

AMBIGUITY OF THE PHRASE 'MODERN SCIENCE'

The phrase *modern science* is ambiguous because sometimes it is used to refer to the science which has developed since the publication of Copernicus' *De Revolutionibus Orbium Coelestium* in the late fifteenth century, and at other times to refer only to contemporary science—the physics of relativity and quanta and the biology of evolution and Mendelian genetics.

Many people regard the development of modern science from Copernicus to the present day as continuous and in a straight line, being simply an enormous accumulation of successively discovered facts. This conception of the development of science is seriously erroneous; for although there has been continuity, it has not been in a straight line, nor has it been simply cumulative.

A better image would be to describe it as a spiral movement, in which a new conception of the world was developed, as if by a trend which came full circle with the work of Newton, and then continued to develop throughout the eighteenth and nineteenth centuries in a new and wider circle culminating in the work of Einstein, Planck, Eddington, and Heisenberg. This is, of course, a gross oversimplification, but it serves to show that modern science includes two distinct, though connected and continuous developments, involving two different world-views and different philosophical concepts.

SCIENCE AND PHILOSOPHY

The philosophy of the seventeenth century was an outgrowth and a consequence of the new world concept developed by the new science. Or, more correctly, it was the expression of this *Weltanschauung* and the logical unfolding of its implications for knowledge and human conduct. The same is true of contemporary philosophy, though the connection is more complicated. But by an odd historical anomaly, certain contemporary movements in philosophy have been a throwback to seventeenth-century thought, while Leibniz in the seventeenth century reacted against some of the tendencies of his day so as to anticipate twentieth-century ideas.

EFFECT OF THE COPERNICAN REVOLUTION

The effect of the Copernican revolution is frequently misrepresented. It is generally alleged that by removing the earth from the center of the universe, Copernicus put man in his right perspective, downgraded him making it no longer plausible to regard man and his domain as the hub of the universe, that for the sake of which all else existed. In actual fact the long-term effect of Copernicus' innovation was the precise opposite of what is usually alleged.

In the first place, it does not in the least follow that because something happens to be in the center of a system it is the most important thing in that system. For Aristotle and his followers, man was never regarded as the most important creature in the universe, nor the earth the most important part. The outer heaven, at the circumference, was regarded as supreme, and it was God, not man, for the sake of whom all else existed. Boethius, in the sixth century A.D., wrote:

> Thou hast learnt from astronomical proofs that the whole earth compared with the universe is no greater than a point, that is, compared with the sphere of the heavens, it may be thought of as having no size at all. Then, of this tiny corner, it is only one quarter that, according to Ptolemy, is habitable by living things. Take away from this quarter the seas, marshes and other desert places, and the space left for man hardly even deserves the name of infinitesimal.[1]

Secondly, Copernicus, by removing the earth from the center, made it one of the heavenly bodies, and so, according to the Aristotelian scheme, greatly enhanced its dignity and status. But the long-term effect of this translation was altogether to break down the distinction made by Aristotle between the celestial and the sublunary spheres; and when Newton, building on foundations laid by Galileo and Kepler, demonstrated that the laws governing the revolution of the heavenly bodies were the same as those regulating terrestrial motion, the whole universe came to be regarded as a vast machine, created by God and set in motion by Him according to universal mechanical laws, once and for all, so that without His further intervention, it would continue, like a well-regulated clock, to work and move eternally. In this purely mechanical work all explanation of events was by efficient causation. As Laplace said a century after Newton, a sufficient intelligence, knowing the position and velocity of every particle in the universe at any one time, could calculate the position and velocity of every particle in the universe at any other time, earlier or later, and so would know the complete state of the world at all times. Final causation, teleological explanation, purpose, had no place in this scheme of things.

Accordingly, the crucial philosophical questions arising out of this conception of the world, to which the philosophers of the seventeenth and eighteenth centuries had to address themselves, and which are still with us, were how to conceive the relation to the world machine of the human mind, its knowledge, its purposes, and its responsibility. The machine included everything material, all animal bodies (which Descartes regarded as mere automata) as well as human, as Hobbes wrote: "For what is the *Heart*, but a *Spring*; and the *Nerves*, but so many *Strings*; and the Joynts, but so many *Wheeles*, giving motion to the whole Body..."[2] But human beings are directly aware of their own conscious being; so, as the only self-conscious and intelligent creatures in the phenomenal world, they are promoted by the Copernican revolution to the most important and dignified position in that world, everything else being merely matter in motion obeying mechanical laws.

What I have outlined so far constitutes the first cycle of development of modern science. The Newtonian ideas were worked out in detail and widely applied in the eighteenth century, achieving spectacular success, but early in the nineteenth century the second cycle began with the discovery by Faraday of electromagnetic induction and the introduction into physics of the conception of fields by Clerk Maxwell. At the same time, the rise of the sciences of life, culminating in the theory of evolution, contributed to the gradual emergence of a new conception of nature, which is hardly established even today.

THE CONTEMPORARY WORLD-VIEW

On the side of physics, the new developments led eventually to the conflicts and problems connected with electromagnetic fields and the ether which were finally solved only by the theory of relativity. Another phase of the same development led to Planck's discovery of the quantum of action and its paradoxical consequences for the conceptions of matter and energy. The result of these new theories was the complete collapse of the mechanistic conception of nature. All the ideas contributing to it had to be modified.

Space and time could no longer be regarded as absolute entities containing the things and events of the world. Relativity made it no longer possible to locate objects simply, either in space or in time. The position and velocity of a particle is relative to the frame of reference used, and no absolute or privileged frame can be found. Measurements of space, time, and movement, therefore, all become dependent upon the conditions of observation. They describe nothing absolute or self-existent but only the relations which obtain between physical events and the observer.

At the same time, the quantum theory made the notions of wave motion and particle projection problematical. As a result of the theory of relativity, the wave concept, which had long been the basis of electromagnetic theory had already suffered by the abolition of the medium of undulation—the ether. Now waves were seen to behave at times like particles, and particles at times like waves, yet without a medium to support them. Further, Heisenberg declared the impossibility in principle of knowing the precise position of any particle unless the knowledge of its precise velocity is relinquished, or the precise velocity unless we forego all knowledge of its position. Consequently, the whole foundation of Laplace's conception of nature crumbled away.

On the side of biology, the phenomena of life defied complete and satisfactory explanation purely in terms of mechanism, and the idea of evolution, as a process of development in which organisms increase in complexity and efficiency of self-maintenance runs directly counter to the fundamental principle of mechanism—the constant running down of the machine, the necessary increase of entropy. Further, the notion of organism and its maturation stresses the domination of the whole and its principle of organization over the part, and of the mature system in which a process culminates over the phases through which it develops. A similar priority of system to element is also evident in the new physics, reemphasizing the importance of teleological explanation in a new and more sophisticated form.

PHILOSOPHICAL PARALLELS AND ANOMALIES

These developments were reflected in the philosophy of the corresponding periods. In the seventeenth century, Hobbes and Gassendi expounded a philosophy of materialism and mechanism and, for Descartes, the entire spatio-temporal world, including the human body, was to be explained in mechanistic terms. The problem of knowledge was met by Descartes by making a sharp separation between mind and body and relying on the beneficence of God for the truth of our perception of the external world. Locke tried to solve the problem by a theory of causal relations between external objects and the mind, which (as only effects and not causes occurred in the mind) made the truth of our perceptions untestable and unknowable. This was the problem set by the mechanistic conception of nature, and the subsequent development of empiricist philosophy in the eighteenth century revealed its inherent difficulties.

The late nineteenth century and the early twentieth produced the philosophy of evolution and process, which brought a new approach to this and other philosophical problems. Where the mechanistic conception of the world forced upon philosophers the choice between explaining mind in terms of matter (materialism), or all matter and mechanism in terms of mind (idealism), the new approach attempted to build a bridge between the two by means of some sort of evolutionary process. The philosophy of Whitehead is perhaps the most typical product of reflection upon the contemporary scientific world view, and comparison between his thought and that of Leibniz will help to illustrate the thesis I am about to develop: that each period produced an anomaly. In our own day there has been a phase of regression to the empiricism and materialism of the eighteenth century in philosophy; and in the seventeenth century Leibniz anticipated many of the features of modern scientific and philosophical thinking.

II

THE SPACE-TIME CONTINUUM

For Newtonian physics the world ultimately consisted of separate particles activated towards or away from one another by forces depending only on their position and motion in space. Space was a vast inert receptacle in which these motions occurred, and time was similarly a kind of one dimensional extension in which successive events (i.e. motions of particles) took place. Both might be conceived as empty, and the particles were conceived as related only externally, both spatio-temporally and physically. It was thus a pluralistic, particulate world.

While it seems a simple matter to imagine a world of this sort, it is very difficult to think consistently about it. First how can particles be in space and not be *of* it. If they are (as they were held to be) material, they must have size and so must be themselves spatial (as it were, parts of space)? If so, would they not be, like space itself, infinitely divisible? But then how can an aggregate of infinitesimals constitute a finite quantity? If particles are not divisible—if they are atoms—and are nevertheless extended in space, how are their (spatial) parts distinguished and related? Again, if there are forces acting between them, what is their source and how do they act at a distance? If they do not, what is the medium through which they act? Moreover, if bodies act on one another, in what sense are they mutually independent?

Leibniz was acutely aware of the paradoxes which arose out of the Newtonian mechanistic world-view, and it is in his efforts to solve them that he anticipates twentieth-century ideas. These same conceptual difficulties were what eventually led to the Einsteinian revolution; so this philosophical prescience was no mere accident.

The conclusion to which Leibniz came in his reflection, upon what he describes as "the two famous labyrinths in which our reason often goes astray" (i.e. continuity in extension, and the freedom of the will), was that bodies in space and time are only the way we perceive a scheme or pattern of relations between entities which are themselves not material or spatial at all. Space and time, he thought, are not receptacles but schemata of relations of a purely mathematical kind, the terms of which are not bodies with material parts, but are purely metaphysical or spiritual beings which he calls monads. Physical bodies are just appearances resulting from confused perception of these relations, but as the monads and the relations between them are real, the appearances are reliable or well-founded (*phenomena bene fundata*).

This view is very close to what twentieth-century physics teaches; and twentieth-century physics arose out of the breakdown of the classical notions of the relation between material particles and the medium through which electromagnetic forces were transmitted. Newton himself was concerned about action at a distance, and some of the forces acting between particles were much later found to be electrical and magnetic. It was the medium of electromagnetic waves that gave the late nineteenth-century physicists all the trouble that eventually led, by their failure to detect its presence, to the emergence of relativity theory.

This brought about a complete revolution in the conception of space, and time, and its relation to matter and motion. First, the special theory of relativity united space and time into one continuous four-dimensional manifold in which measurements depended upon the coordinate system conventionally imposed upon it. None of these measurements were therefore absolute, although they did reveal some *invariant* quantities. Next it undermined the distinction between matter and energy. Energy and its effects are presented in terms of a field, and the general theory of relativity represents the field as a modification or 'distortion' of space-time—a feature of its geometrical properties. Consequently space-time comes to be thought of as 'the metrical field' and is continuous with matter (which Eddington liked to call a crease or pleat in space-time). The whole physical universe, in consequence, becomes a single continuum in which the parts are all essentially related to one another. Matter is no longer separable from space and time nor particle from the forces acting on it or which it exerts. The relativistic world is all one great metrical field with varying geometrical properties.

A metrical field, however, is a scheme or framework of relations, just what Leibniz said was the nature of space and time. Moreover, the terms of the relations for modern physics are no longer solid impenetrable atoms. These have not merely been resolved into subordinate elementary particles but have proved to be Gestalten or *patterns of energy*, so that what are related in space-time are not material bodies but rather *events*, entities (whatever they may be) that seem purely dynamic and are describable only in mathematical formulae.

THE DYNAMICAL CONCEPTION OF SUBSTANCE

Once more, there is a significant parallel in Leibniz' conception of the world. He dissented from the views of the Cartesians, that material substance was mere extension. The facts of motion and change, he thought, could not be understood purely in forms of space and time. The reality, whatever it was, must be dynamic to account for change. He thus asserted that the monads possessed what he called *vis motrix*, motive force, or appetition. The first term emphasizes their dynamic character, the second implies that the urge is teleological.

Modern physics has discovered that matter is not just inert, or rather that its inertia is dynamic. Einstein propounded the equation:

$$E=mc^2$$

which establishes an equivalence between mass and energy. Elementary particles have proven to be particles of energy, in a very real sense. An electron and a positron can be united and converted into radiant energy and can also be produced out of radiant energy. There is no longer any hard line of distinction between photons, which are particles of radiant energy, and other sorts of particles, such as mesons, hyperons, bosons, and the like. Physical entities, in short, might well, in accordance with contemporary scientific ideas, be the manifestation of a reality imbued with *vis motrix*.

Whitehead held this basic reality to be a process of activity—he called it creativity—in which 'prehensions', or a sort of primitive form of perceptions, were integrated at nodal points into events or 'actual entities'. A prehension was the expression of a relation between the actual entity and others. So, again, we have a network of relations between entities which are not material but are the subjects of a sort of perception—i.e., incipient minds.

This is almost exactly the sort of view that Leibniz propounded. For him, the elements of the universe were monads each of which was a soul constituted of 'perceptions', some rudimentary and unconscious, some conscious but 'confused', and some clear and distinct. What Leibniz called unconscious perceptions are very like what Whitehead called prehensions. Moreover, every actual entity in Whitehead's theory prehends every other, so each is a microcosm from its own point of view of the entire universe. Exactly the same is true of the Leibnizian monad.

THE UNITY OF THE WORLD

What, in modern scientific theory, these views reflect, is the essential interrelatedness of things and events in the world. In relativity theory, all measurements of length, duration, and motion are essentially interrelated. They depend upon the coordinate system used and the velocity with which it is moving relative to the objects measured. Every co-ordinate system moves relatively to every other, so that all measurements whatsoever are essentially interrelated. Moreover, because of these facts the spatio-temporal manifold has to be thought of as a single four-dimensional continuum in which space and time are inseparable.

Largely as a consequence of this, every physical quantity and every physical event has consequences and relationships throughout the universe. This implication is already present in the idea of the field which has no absolute spatial limits, even though its intensity may decrease rapidly beyond a certain point. Strictly speaking, every field of force extends throughout the whole of space.

Further, the structure of space is dependent upon the mean distribution of matter and the gravitational relations of material bodies are consequences (according to Einstein) of the geometrical properties of space. Cosmologists like Einstein and de Sitter were able to express the general character of these geometrical properties in a single mathematical formula from which not only the relative motions of gravitating bodies could be derived but equally the fact that very distant accumulations of matter (like the extragalactic nebulae) were receding from one another with velocities proportional to their distance. Thus, from a single formula, the nearest and most distant phenomena could both be derived.

Sciama stresses the unity of the universe by elaborating Mach's theory that inertial centrifugal and Coriolis forces[3] are really the effect upon accelerating bodies of the fixed stars—of all the other bodies in the universe—and Eddington somewhere remarks that to perform a physical experiment under perfect conditions one would have to remove the fixed stars because they exert at least some modifying influence on physical effects in the laboratory.

More recently, this emphasis on the unity of the physical world has been even more strongly reinforced by developments in particle physics, which have revived the conception of the unified field (originally conceived by Einstein, Schrödinger and Weyl). Contemporary S-matrix and grand unified theories, and the yet newer superstring theory, project a single field of energy diversified in accordance with one complex mathematical formula, from which all the primary physical laws and forces can be derived.

This unity and interrelatedness of the world was something Leibniz constantly insisted upon. He held that every monad in its perceptions mirrored the whole universe so that any change in any monad affects every other thing in the world. "The universe is a whole," he writes to Count Ernst von Hessen-Rheinfels, "which God sees through and through with a single glance" and, again, in response to a letter from Arnaud: "...in reality because of the interconnection of things, the universe with all its parts, would be wholly different and would have been wholly different from the very commencement of it if the least thing in it happened otherwise than it has." "The slightest movement," he says in the same context, "is communicated as far as matter extends."[4] This unity of the world is essential to the whole of Leibniz' thought.

PRIMACY OF WHOLES

As each monad 'perceives' or represents in and to itself every other, and is an epitome of the entire universe, the interrelatedness of things is hardly to be wondered at, and because the universe is a single and complete system each monad is likewise a single and self-contained whole.

Leibniz says that each is a "simple" substance. From what has already been said it is clear that this simplicity cannot be due to the absence of internal differentiation for the variety of the whole universe is mirrored in every monad. What sort of simplicity is it? Leibniz tells us merely that the monad is not a compound of separable parts and is in that sense simple. But if something is internally variegated, yet not compounded of separable parts its simplicity is nothing other than its organic unity. It is a single indivisible whole, and its indivisibility is due to the fact that all the internal differences, and their mutual relations, are determined by and dependent upon the essential nature of the whole—what Leibniz refers to as its substantial form. To put this in more modern language, the principle of order or organization, which constitutes the whole, is prior to, and determines the nature and relations of the internal differentiations which it orders and integrates.

For Leibniz this systematic interrelation between the perceptions of the monad is a reflection of—is really the same as—the systematic interrelation between monads in the world. The perceptions in each monad are not all clear and distinct, however, and it has an urge to clarify them. The changes which it undergoes are the consequence of this urge, which he calls appetition. To this I shall presently return; what I want to stress here is the primacy for Leibniz of the whole.

At the present time we find an increasing tendency in all (or most) sciences to stress the same kind of priority of system over its constituents. In atomic physics the energy system and the way it is organized determines the disposition and behavior of the particles within it. The exclusion principle in quantum mechanics, which states that no two similar particles can have the same state of motion, imposes upon the electronic shells of the atom a structure which determines the character and properties of the whole, and at the same time the number and disposition of the electrons. Again it is the energy state of the atom as a whole that determines the orbits in which its electrons will be found.

In crystals, to take another example, the molecules are geometrically structured and their pattern is determined by the disposition of the atoms in the molecule, and that again by the systems of electronic shells in the atoms.

The crystal functions as a whole, and its physicochemical properties depend on the principles of order which determine its structure.

Finally, almost all biological phenomena are subject to regulation by the structural system of the organism, which is both highly complex and self-maintaining, in such a way that the structure of the parts, their behavior and development are adjusted to one another so as to maintain the same overall systematic balance of organic functions.

These are but a few examples of complex wholes with parts which we should ordinarily describe as separable. But in principle, or in the light of their organic interrelation, they are not really separable if the whole is to be maintained and the internal order not to be destroyed. They have, therefore, a character akin to the so-called simplicity of Leibnizian monads, and the principle of organization that dominates each of them corresponds to Leibniz' substantial form.

Moreover as Leibniz alleged that there was an urge in the monad towards greater clarification (i.e. precise elaboration) of its inner diversity, so modern science discovers a constant tendency in nature towards greater complexity and more intimate integration of wholes. This shows itself in a scale of natural forms, though the actual form of energy involved and the so-called mechanism of development is not yet fully understood. We go from the wave-packet (or elementary particle) to the atom, from atom to molecule, from molecule to crystal, and from crystal to living organism. The development of the organism is much more obviously an urge to greater integration, and emerges in the higher organisms in conscious behaviour and ultimately in the various forms of intellectual activity, where appetition proper and conscious purpose are manifest.

My use of the phrase "urge to greater integration" is inspired by Whitehead, who speaks of the actual entity having a subjective aim at further integration, again a similarity to Leibniz which is in this case derived from reflection upon the conclusions of contemporary science.

ORGANISM

It is not, therefore, surprising to find both Whitehead and Leibniz insisting upon the notion of organism as the appropriate and dominant concept for understanding the world. Leibniz maintains that all things are organisms and that their parts are organisms and theirs again. A partial analogy though not altogether apt is the doggerel:

> Great fleas have little fleas
> Upon their backs to bite 'em,
> And little fleas have lesser fleas,
> And so ad infinitum.

Less flippantly, Leibniz' contention was that every substance is an organic whole and that material phenomena reflect this fact in that each is, or is a factor in, an organic whole the parts of which are equally organic wholes.

Modern science bears this out. Certainly the living organism is an example *par excellence* of wholeness, and it is made up of cells each of which is an organism in itself. But we need not stop there. The matter of living things is very largely composed of proteins, and the protein molecule is not only highly complex but displays holistic characteristics like an organism and may even be self-reproductive. Complex protein structures like viruses have the form of a crystal, in which as we have seen the principle of order and wholeness predominates. Below this again are the physical wholes of which I have already spoken.

There is full justification therefore for Leibniz' contention and for Whitehead's claim that actual entities are activated by an urge to integration. It is significant that Whitehead calls his own system the philosophy of organism. The whole point of the modern doctrine is the evolution of the complex organisms from antecedent states of less complex organisms. The doctrine thus cries aloud for a conception of organism as fundamental for nature.

EVOLUTION

This brings us to another contemporary scientific concept, evolution, of which Leibniz' theory was, in a remarkable way, prophetic. As I have mentioned he maintained that the monads, the real constituents of the world, were appetitive and each experiences an urge towards clearer self-elaboration and self-knowledge. The status of a monad in the scheme of things depends on the degree of the clearness and distinctness of its perceptions. This is the same thing, for Leibniz, as its activity, for a monad is active so far as it perceives clearly and distinctly and passive so far as it perceives confusedly. Monads, therefore, are ranged in an order according to their degree of passivity and activity from the most confused and relatively inert to the most intensely active which perceive with a high degree of clarity. The one monad whose ideas are all clear and who is pure activity is God. Thus, the monads form a series or order of reals which, as a whole, constitutes the universe, and it is a scale of increasing adequacy or perfection—an evolutionary scale. Not only is the world constituted by such a scale, its parts and elements are not static but are constantly striving to climb up the ladder, so to speak. Each monad's appetition is towards greater clearness and fuller activity; so there is prevalent movement upwards. The constituents of the world are all engaged in a constant process of evolution.

For Whitehead this process is what he calls creativity. It is constant and perpetual and its tendency is a progressive realization of the potentialities inherent in the primordial nature of God.

There is no need to remind modern readers of the prevalence of the idea of evolution in contemporary science. It is too familiar. Scientists today expatiate upon the evolution of the universe, the evolution of the earth, the evolution of living organisms, the evolution of mind, of art, of education, of the motor car, of aircraft, of what not. Our approach to almost every subject is in evolutionary terms. So pervasive is this concept that I need not argue for its widespread influence, but it raises an interesting and difficult question of logic and scientific method which is often rejected even by those who most indulge in the use of idea of evolution itself.

TELEOLOGY

What evolves progresses. If it does not we have on our hands a process of change but not of evolution. Not only must there be progress of some sort, but the outcome must in some sense have been implicit in that from which it evolved, as the tree is implicit in the seed or the man in the child. Evolution, therefore, requires the notions of potentiality and actualization.

Properly to understand what is potential in something, we have to know what it is becoming—that is, we can understand it best only in the light of what is being produced, and this becomes apparent only at the end of the process. Full understanding or explanation, therefore, must be in terms of the end; that is, teleological.

Teleological explanation, however, is very unpopular among modern scientists and philosophers and has been in disfavor ever since Francis Bacon made fun of it long before Leibniz wrote. Nevertheless, Leibniz reasserted the importance of what he (following Aristotle) called final causes, maintaining that ultimate explanation could only be in such terms, because it was the final cause that determined the efficient causes.

The modern unpopularity of teleological explanation, however, is, due to a misconception and the scientists who despise it are, for the most part, unwittingly using it all the time, in a way we have already noticed. The misconception is the belief that, because the potentiality is realized only at the end of the process and it is to this that we are referred for explanation, it is being maintained that future events are the real causes and determinants of present events, which appears to be (and in terms of efficient causation is) nonsense. Because the future remains unknown, the teleologist contents himself with empty statements, like: "the reason why bodies gravitate is that they have a gravitational tendency."

However, this is not really the nature of teleological explanation, and perhaps the name is ill-chosen. It can best be explained by using human activity as an analogy. The 'end' at which a person aims is what he or she plans or designs to do. If you want to understand what he or she is about, you must discover his or her intentions. These, of course, refer to the future, but knowledge of them does not require knowledge of actual future events. To understand what a general is doing who is about to fight a battle we must discover his plans. Now a plan is a system of interrelated actions and their expected effects. It is a structure or whole—a design. Accordingly explanation of this kind is not in terms of the future but in terms of the design or whole.

Now this form of explanation is precisely what Leibniz recommended and is exactly what modern science in all its branches demands. Whether they realize it or not it is what all modern scientists are constantly seeking. The physicist explains motion, gravitational or other, in terms of the structure of the space-time configuration in which it occurs; he explains electrical phenomena in terms of field, nuclear phenomena in terms of the energy system. The crystallographer explains the chemical and physical properties of the crystal in terms of its lattice structure (or leptocosm). The biochemist traces the chemical functions of an enzyme to the form of its molecular pattern. The biologist explains organic activity in terms of the needs of the organism to maintain its integrity, and the course of evolution in terms of, what is really the same thing, the "survival value" of characters. In the realm of psychology the holistic or teleological form of explanation is still more appropriate and persists despite the efforts of behaviorists to avoid it—but I shall not multiply examples. If holism asserts itself in physics, chemistry, and biology, it would indeed be strange if it were not admitted in psychology which was, at least at one time, defined as the science of purposive behavior.

In short, modern science has rediscovered in a new and more satisfactory form, the importance, on which Leibniz insisted, of final causes.

The point is that teleological explanation is not in principle, and so not in all cases, an appeal to deliberately intended objectives, nor to the causal effects of future events, but is the explanation of the part in terms of the structure of the whole to which it belongs, and of the process by which the immature becomes mature in terms of the systematic whole that is being generated. The type of causation involved is thus final, which does not exclude efficient causation. It is simply the guidance of efficient causes to the construction of a system, the principle of whose organization prevails throughout the process. This kind of causality is what Leibniz recognized and what Whitehead sought to describe, and it is, as we have seen, prevalent in the procedures and theorizing of the contemporary sciences.

CONCLUSION

How is it that a philosopher writing in the latter part of the seventeenth century could, in so extraordinary a way, have anticipated the thought of scientists two and a half centuries later? I can only suggest that these ideas were already latent in the mechanism of his own day, and his incisive criticism of the philosophical difficulties inherent in mechanism revealed them to him. Perhaps what we have here is another example in the realm of ideas of new concepts developing out of earlier doctrines in which they were already potentially present; another example of teleology—a possibility which should warn us not to treat any man's philosophy as worthless and outdated just because it was written a long time ago.

NOTES

1. *The Consolation of Philosophy*, book 2, prosa 7.

2. *Leviathan*, Introduction.

3. Forces which, when the earth is taken to be at rest, must be postulated to account for the deflection of projectiles resulting from its actual rotation.

4. Correspondence between Leibniz and Arnauld, May 1686.

4
Metaphysical Lessons of Idealism

Hugo A. Meynell

Metaphysics has not, in general, been at all fashionable among the philosophers of the twentieth century. However, they have not clearly shown that it is dispensable, and it may well be claimed that most of those who have opposed metaphysics have shown clear evidence of being dominated by uncriticized metaphysical assumptions.[1] Ivor Leclerc, in consistently advocating and vigorously practising metaphysics over many years, has shown an admirable disregard of fashion.[2] It is a great privilege to contribute to a volume in honor of him and of his work.

In opposing metaphysics, many people have had at the forefront of their minds the idealism generally supposed to have reached its culmination in the philosophical system of Hegel. While not myself supporting any version of idealism, I believe that it ought to be taken very seriously by philosophers. The principal lesson that has to be learned from it is that reality is essentially intelligible, able to be known for what it is by the exercise of intelligence and reason. The principal defect of idealism is its failure to account for that element of matter-of-fact which is just as ineluctably characteristic of reality. I hold that the only brand of contemporary philosophy to do justice to both aspects of reality is transcendental Thomism, and I shall attempt briefly to argue this.

In attempting to show what there is to be gained from a study of idealism, I shall concentrate attention on the philosophy of Schelling. In comparison with Hegel or even with Fichte, Schelling has been neglected by writers in English; but I am convinced that no one shows better than he does both the merits and the limitations attributable to this kind of philosophy.

I

C. S. Peirce, generally considered to be the greatest of all American philosophers, confessed to being "a Schellingian of some stripe." Schelling himself was a Schellingian of different stripes at different times in his career. It is convenient to distinguish four phases of his work: (1) discipleship of Fichte; (2) the philosophy of nature; (3) the philosophy of identity; (4) the antithesis of "negative" and "positive" philosophy.[3]

What gave rise to German idealism in the first place was a following-through of the principles of Kant's critical philosophy, together with rejection of Kant's conception of the "thing-in-itself." Things in their sensible aspect were relative to sense experience, and things in their intelligible or "rational" aspect were due to the active powers of mind, as Kant had shown; where he erred was in postulating unknowable "things-in-themselves" which somehow "caused" or gave rise to sensible phenomena. This was inconsistent with his own insight that causality was a category imposed by the mind upon experience, rather than derived from an independently existing reality.[4] The way out taken by Fichte and his followers was recourse to a spiritual reality, somehow identical with or at least expressing itself through the human subject, which gave rise to the whole of nature and of the human thought which seemed to reflect it.[5]

Fichte had seen nature merely as an object subordinate to humanity, postulated by spirit as an arena for the expression and fulfilment of moral principles. As against Fichte, Schelling stressed from the first (1795) the distinction between the empirical human subject and the Absolute.[6] The Absolute is to be characterized not as any kind of thing, but as infinite freedom; it is from this infinite freedom, and not from the empirical human subject, that the system of the sciences is to be derived.[7] Schelling argues that consciousness and objects condition one another; one cannot have either alone. In approaching the problem of the relation of conscious subject to object, he compares and contrasts the views of Fichte and Spinoza. As Copleston expresses it, "Spinoza reduces the finite self to the absolute Object: Fichte reduces it to the absolute Subject or, more precisely (since the absolute ego is not properly a subject), to infinite activity or striving."[8] Schelling remarks that it is difficult for anyone to endure "the idea of working at his own annihilation, of annulling" in himself "all free causality and of being the modification of an object in the infinity of which he sooner later finds his moral destruction."[9]

As Schelling saw it at this time, reflection had brought about a split between subject and object, ideal and real; human beings by means of reflection had distinguished between external things and their subjective representations of them, and furthermore had become objects for themselves. The split cannot be healed by a mere return to the original situation of reflective immediacy. Spinoza and Leibniz both obscurely glimpsed the truth that the real and the ideal are one in the last analysis; though Spinoza failed to explain the relation of his two fundamental attributes of substance (thought and extension), while Leibniz merely affirmed rather than accounted for the preestablished harmony which he claimed to exist between them. It is the ultimate identity of real and ideal, of objective and subjective, which is the business of the philosopher to display; with nature as "visible Spirit" and Spirit as "invisible nature."[10] Philosophy must show forth nature as a unified system which aims towards consciousness of itself through human thought. In the representation of itself through conscious human subjects, sleeping spirit awakens, and nature comes to knowledge of itself. "The Absolute is the 'pure identity'[11] of subjectivity and objectivity. And this identity is revealed in the mutual interpenetration of Nature and Nature's knowledge of itself in and through man."[12] The temporal order is a manifestation of the Absolute, and is related to it as consequent to antecedent.[13]

In his *Ideas Towards a Philosophy of Nature* (1797) Schelling declared that, in physics as understood at that time, there was confused a mere empiricism with science properly speaking.[14] A really philosophical physics would not take for granted natural forces, such as gravitation, as mere givens but would derive them from first principles. A fully adequate account of nature, furthermore, would account for the lower in terms of its orientation to the higher; the materialist, on the contrary, seeks to reduce the higher to the lower, and consequently fails to see nature as unconsciously aiming at the production of organisms through mechanical laws. While the activity which is at the foundation of nature is unlimited and infinite, and of the nature of force or will,[15] it must be checked if we are to have an objective and finite nature; the overall structure of matter may be shown to derive from this. If we think of repulsion as corresponding to the unlimited activity, and attraction to the checking force, matter may be thought of as a synthesis of the two. The drive of unlimited activity asserts itself again, to meet with a further check, which results in universal mechanism. Yet another repetition of the same process issues in the coming into being of the realm of biological organisms. Schelling remarks that a theory of emergent evolution fits in well with this scheme, but does not dwell on the matter;[16] what he is concerned with is the theoretical construction of nature and not its genetic history.[17]

The *System of Transcendental Idealism* (1800) starts from the subject rather than the object, the opposite end to that from which the philosophy of nature begins. Subject and object are one in knowledge; and in order to explain how this can be so, we need not only to start from objects, and show how unconscious nature comes to be represented. We must also show how objects come to exist for subjects. The mutually complementary character of the resulting systems of thought will display the Absolute as identity of ideal and real, of subjective and objective. "The ego is nothing else than a producing which becomes its own object" through what Schelling calls "intellectual intuition."[18] The overall structure of Schelling's transcendental idealism is close to that of Fichte. The ego is unlimited activity, and to become its own object it must limit itself, which it does by setting up the non-ego against itself. Ultimately, the subject reflectively differentiates itself from objects, and recognizes itself as intelligence. While the philosophy of nature treats of unconscious spirit, that of transcendental idealism deals with conscious spirit, including its self-objectification in moral action and the creation of a political order. It may be asked whether there is a concrete way in which the identity of conscious and unconscious, ideal and real, is presented to the subject itself; the answer is that there is, in the arts. The essence and significance of art and poetry is that they bring to consciousness the unconscious art and poetry of the spirit which exist in nonhuman nature. For this reason the philosophy of art may be called "the keystone of the whole arch" of philosophy.[19]

In the *Exposition of My System of Philosophy* (1801), Schelling proceeds to set out the philosophy of identity.[20] "I give the name Reason (*Vernunft*) to the absolute Reason or to Reason in so far as it is conceived as the total indifference of the subjective and objective."[21] The business of philosophy is to apprehend the relation between things and this Absolute, between finite and infinite, but there are difficulties in describing this relation. The Absolute, being infinite, must contain all reality within itself; so it cannot *cause* the universe of finite things, but must rather *include* them. "The absolute identity is not the cause of the universe, but the universe itself. For everything which exists is the absolute identity itself and the universe is everything which is."[22] However, it must also be insisted that all distinctions lie outside the Absolute;[23] so what is finite must after all be external to the Absolute. Schelling is consequently compelled to say, that it is only from the point of view of empirical consciousness that there are finite things at all, or that there is a distinction between subject and object. He does not explain how the existence of empirical consciousness with its point of view is itself to be accounted for.[24] At all events, Schelling feels that the theory of identity enables him to overcome all the disputes between realism and idealism; the former of which assumes that one has to subordinate the subject to the object, while the latter makes the opposite assumption. Once we realize that they are one in the Absolute, the controversy loses point. So one may call the system of identity real-idealism.[25]

Given the anomalies and paradoxes manifestly latent in this position, Schelling could hardly have remained contented with it.[26] In *Philosophy and Religion* (1804), he proposes that the Absolute manifests itself in eternal ideas, all of them comprehended in one idea,[27] in which nature in all its aspects is eternally present. How do finite things actually come into existence? Following Jacob Boehme, who was a powerful influence on him from about this time,[28] Schelling introduced the idea of a cosmic "fall" as an answer to this problem. This fall is to be conceived as abrupt rather than a continuous transition;[29] it is eternal rather than taking place in time.[30] It cannot be explained;[31] thus the world of finite things cannot even in principle be deduced from the Absolute. But we can say that the ground of its possibility is freedom.[32] The fall amounts to a centrifugal splitting from the Absolute or God; however, this is counteracted by a centripetal movement of return. No particular sensible thing, as has been said, derives from God as its immediate cause. Similarly, things do not return immediately to God but do so through the capacity of human reason to transform the objective into the subjective (by thinking about it and explaining it), and to refer things to their divine origin and exemplar. From one new point, the finite self represents "the point of furthest alienation from God,"[33] in its self-possession and self-assertion. However, being one in essence with the infinite, finite reason can rise above its selfish point of view and return to the true center from which it has been alienated.[34] Schelling at this point still wants to stress, against Fichte's moralism, the capacity of nature to mediate the divine.[35]

In the preface to his *Philosophical Inquiries into the Nature of Human Freedom* (1809),[36] Schelling takes up the charge that his philosophy is pantheistic and leaves no room for free action in human beings. He insists that he teaches neither that finite things do not really exist, nor that the visible world is identical with God. Insofar as pantheism implies merely that all things are immanent in God, Schelling admits that he is quite happy to be called a pantheist; as he points out, St. Paul himself teaches that we live and move and have our being in God.[37] He still wants to claim that there is a sense in which God and the world are identical; "the profound logic of the ancients distinguished subject and predicate as antecedent and consequent...and thereby expressed the real meaning of the principle of identity."[38] At this rate to assert the identity of God with the world is just to say that the world stands to God as consequent to antecedent. The essence of human freedom is the power to choose between good and evil.[39] However, Schelling is too devoted to explanation in terms of antecedent and consequent to be quite content with the notion that real alternatives are open to human agents from moment to moment as they live their lives. He, thus, asserts that a human being's choices are determined by his or her essence or character, which is founded upon a primordial choice on the individual's part that does not take place in time.[40] The upshot of all this is that human actions are at once free and in principle predictable; freedom and necessitation "are mutually immanent, as one reality which appears as one or the other only when looked at from different sides...."[41]

Even in God, granted divine freedom, one has to postulate an impersonal ground of existence, which may be interpreted as will without understanding.[42] To be really personal, God must be self-creative out of this ground, which he is as reason and love.[43] However, one must not think of these two aspects of God, the impersonal and the personal, as in temporal succession; they are simultaneous.[44] The unity of aspects which is indissoluble in God is dissoluble in human beings; hence their capacity for good or evil.[45] What is eternally accomplished in God, the triumph of reason over the lower will, is brought about in human beings over the course of history.[46]

In the latest phase of his thought, Schelling is preoccupied with the difference between the negative philosophy of mere concepts and essences, which he sees exemplified in the work of Hegel; and the positive philosophy which takes real existence into account.[47] From a mere "what" no "that" can be derived; positive philosophy begins from God "as a pure That."[48] Schelling does not maintain by any means that there should be war *à outrance* between negative and positive philosophy, though he sees much of the history of philosophy in terms of conflict between them; he rather finds desirable a unity between the two.[49] How is one to make the transition from negative to positive philosophy? The transition cannot be made by thought alone because thought provides nothing but essences and deductions from them. So recourse must be had to the will, "which demands with an inner necessity that God should not be a mere idea."[50] The human subject is conscious of her fallen state, and knows that this can be overcome only by the gracious action of God; so she demands the existence of God not just as a transmundane ideal but as a real person.[51] So we move to actual religion, in which we are brought into the presence of such a God; the upshot of negative philosophy is only possible religion.[52]

The foregoing does not amount to a natural theology, a basis for belief in God in reason alone, in the traditional sense.[53] One may circumvent the need for this, on Schelling's account, by attending to the history of the development of human religious consciousness, in which are to be found both humanity's search for God and God's response to this search. This is why Schelling in his latest work is concerned above all with mythology and revelation; here are to be found the successive stages of divine revelation to and redemption of humankind. The eternal becoming of God in himself is displayed temporally in the history of religion. It was necessary for myth to come before revelation;[54] it corresponds to the dark lower principle in God.[55] While myth is a necessary process, the revelation in Christ is an act whereby God "freely gives or has given of himself to mankind."[56] One may properly regard revelation as the truth to which mythology points; this is why so many anticipations of Christian truth can be found in paganism.[57]

II

When he heard Schelling's final lectures in Berlin, Kierkegaard expressed disappointment that Schelling did not rethink his whole position in light of the distinction between negative and positive philosophy, rather than treating his hearers to discourses on myth and revelation.[58] I share that disappointment, and would like to speculate on what the results of such a rethinking might have been. It appears to be implicit in the whole enterprise of science that the world is subject to explanation by human thought; yet there seems to be no good reason why such explanation should not be loosened from the necessitarian, antecedent-and-consequent pattern which so obsessed the idealists. In the case of human action, to explain why I went to lunch at a certain time is not to explain why I could not but have gone to lunch at that time. To say, "In that case the explanation would be incomplete," is merely to invite the retort, "On what basis does one have to assume that explanations of that kind and degree of completeness are available in human or in natural affairs?" It is well known that contemporary science, as opposed to classical science, provides no sanction for the expectation of such completeness of explanation. In explaining the evolution of the opossum, the zoologist does not aspire to state why this kind of animal had to come into existence exactly when and where it did; she rather tries to show how, given the nature of its immediate ancestors and the environment, an animal with that particular set of characteristics was liable to come into existence and to survive. In the present state of physics, it is unknowable exactly when any particular atom of a radioactive element will emit an alpha or a beta particle; all that can be confidently declared is that half of the atoms of any sufficiently large sample of the substance will thus have decayed in anything from a few microseconds to many millions of years. The moral is that explanation can have a completeness which is adequate for the purposes of science without being deterministic and, thus, without raising problems for the freedom of the will. This is the short answer, I believe, to the problem which exercized Schelling for so much of his career, of how a systematic understanding of things can be reconciled with human freedom.

What corresponds to Schelling's negative philosophy is the scientific a priori that reality will turn out in the long run to be intelligible, to be patient of explanation by conscious subjects; corresponding to his positive philosophy, the principle that which kind of intelligibility is actually realized in the world can be known only by empirical investigation. The puzzle about the relation between the subjective and the objective, which so preoccupied Schelling, is to be resolved by the theorem that the objective world is nothing other than what is to be known by conscious subjects who conscientiously attend to the data of the senses, invent possible explanations for them, and judge to be so the explanation best corroborated by the data. Such judgments may be of fact or value; a beneficent free being will decide to act on the basis of judgments of fact and value which he has authentically made. While the determinism of classical science set intractable problems for Spinoza, Hume,

Kant, and many others, including Schelling himself, about this matter, there is no good reason why contemporary science should do so for us. As the idealists all rightly insisted, such an intelligible world, if not dependent on the (conscious) human subject, gives every sign of being dependent on something either associated with or analogous to that subject. The intelligibility of the universe (as affirmed by the negative philosophy), and its irreducible element of fact (as alluded to by the positive), are both perfectly explained as due to an intelligent being, which conceives and wills a universe with the particular intelligibility which ours is progressively found to have, rather as we human beings conceive and will our own actions and products.

It is cardinal to the central European metaphysical tradition which stems from Plato that reality is intelligible, that it is essentially *for* mind.[59] In the course of summarizing Schelling's philosophy of nature, Fr. Copleston writes: "Schelling is convinced that all scientific inquiry presupposes the intelligibility of nature. Every experiment, he insists, involves putting a question to nature which nature is forced to answer. And this procedure presupposes the belief that nature conforms to the demands of reason, that it is intelligible and in this sense ideal."[60] On this matter Schelling seems to me to be absolutely right.[61] In impatiently brushing aside this insight and the consequences which flow from it, the many schools of thought which have followed Kierkegaard, Marx, and Moore in repudiating idealism with more or less contempt, have led us inevitably to our present notoriously chaotic and fragmented view of the world.

I have suggested already that it is helpful to see Schelling as groping towards a fundamentally transcendental Thomist position. It surely cannot reasonably be claimed that what was perhaps Schelling's fundamental project, of reconciling objectivity with subjectivity, of showing how objects which exist prior to and independent of human minds can come all the same to be really known by such minds, has been satisfactorily resolved by most later schools of philosophy. The problem is often impatiently dismissed, but that is another matter. Exponents of the reductionistic objectivism characteristic of what is called scientism, and the champions of unbridled subjectivism, seem to face one another, now even more than in Schelling's time, over an unbridgeable ideological crevasse. One of Schelling's very earliest works is concerned with the problem of reconciling the claims of subjectivity, represented by Fichte, with those of objectivity, represented by Spinoza's rigidly deductive and necessitarian system of nature.[62] For transcendental Thomism, at least as set out in the work of Bernard Lonergan,[63] "genuine objectivity is [nothing other than] the fruit of authentic subjectivity,"[64] and the world or reality is simply what is to be known by conscious subjects.

There are three elements in knowing: experience, understanding, and judgment. Understanding is the creative business in knowing, where one envisages a range of possibilities to explain phenomena within one's experience, one affirms one of these possibilities as more or less probably the case, as verified by the relevant experience more than its alternatives.[65] The permanent achievement of idealism, I believe, is to show that the world or reality can be nothing other than what is to be known through such creative acts of understanding, and that this has to be taken into account by any overall theory of the nature and structure of things. The subjective idealist infers that the world is actually created by such acts of understanding on the part of human subjects. This does not only fly in the face of common sense—which, for better or for worse, will hardly let pass the view that we ourselves create the thoughts of other persons, the historical past, and the very stars in their courses, in the act of thinking about them—but it also neglects the fact that some envisaged possibilities, grasped by creative understanding, are verified as more liable to be true than others—the existence of oxygen rather than phlogiston, the truth of the theory of biological evolution rather than that of special creation, and so on. So, it seems that subjective idealism is to be rejected.

However, none of the three great German idealists was a subjective idealist in this sense; even Fichte, who seems most closely to approximate to the position in his earlier writings, claimed later that he never was such. It is not, for these idealists, the conscious empirical human subject that gives rise to the world, but something closely related or analogous to this, which is variously conceived, as we have seen, at the different stages of Schelling's philosophy. According to transcendental Thomists, the world and all the things within it have not only a *what* (essence) to be grasped by creative acts of understanding, but a *that* (existence) to be affirmed in judgments. Many worlds or no world were possible; the one that actually exists is to be known by the threefold process (having experiences; conceiving possibilities which may explain these experiences; and affirming to exist, to be real, those possibilities best supported by the experiences) previously summarized. The existence and nature of such a world are best to be explained, according to transcendental Thomists, by a being who conceives all possibilities, and wills those to exist which actually obtain;[66] and that, as Aquinas would say, "all call God."[67]

"To me," writes Sir Karl Popper, "idealism appears absurd, for it... implies something like this: that it is my mind which creates this beautiful world. But I know I am not its Creator."[68] "Something like this" is indeed the case, though we do not create the world, we do, as the phenomenologists put it, in a sense "constitute" it. As was in effect forcefully argued by Kant, to know the world involves creative mental acts; we get nowhere in coming to know the world if we simply allow the data of experience to impinge upon us. Popper's own theory of knowledge, with its stress on the role of active conjecture, is itself a powerful illustration of the point. But that we cannot come to know it except by means of creative mental acts does not of itself demonstrate the subjective idealist's conclusion that it is actually created by acts of our minds; though it is a strong hint at least, as idealists of other kinds and rational theists[69] would maintain, that it is due to some entity or entities[70] analogous to our minds.

Fichte and Schelling were in correspondence with one another on philosophical questions around 1800. As Fichte saw it, Schelling did not take sufficient account in his thinking of what Fichte saw as the only sure basis for philosophy, the certainty that the conscious subject has of herself; whereas Schelling retorted that Fichte had not reached the proper ground for philosophy in the Absolute, which comprehends both spirit and nature, the subjective and the objective.[71] The transcendental Thomist would agree with Fichte that the human subject is indeed the basis for cognition; it is self-destructive to understand and judge that one is not a being capable of understanding or judging, and the world is nothing other than what I tend to come to know about so far as I exert understanding and judgment to the uttermost. She would agree with Schelling so far as to insist that what is basic to cognition is not basic to reality because each of us has excellent reasons for supposing that the world of material things and persons existed prior to and independently of our knowledge of it. But if what I have already argued is on the right lines, there are good reasons for supposing that what is basic to reality is analogous in important respects to what is basic to cognition.

Once it is clear that what is first in the order of cognition or knowledge is not first in the order of reality, but only in some important respects analogous to what is so, the basis is removed for any tendency, as in all three great German idealists, to merge the empirical human subject with the Absolute or the divine subject. Nor is there any risk of the "moral destruction" of the former, through engulfment either by material causality or by absolute spirit. The human subject can know things in part, and can choose between options really open to her in accordance with her knowledge. Though she clearly cannot know everything, she can get a second-order grasp of reality as a whole (as whatever is to be known), and so in a manner transcend her finitude and temporality. It is not exactly that the "real and ideal are one," as the philosophy of identity would have it; rather, the real is in the last analysis nothing other than what is to be known in terms of the ideal, judgments arrived at by the threefold process sketched above.

To what extent is it true, as Schelling says, that human beings have by reflection created a split between subject and object, and between external things and their representations of them; or that they have made objects of themselves? And so far as such dichotomies are to be overcome, how should we set about overcoming them? I think it is very important here to distinguish sharply between two radically different senses of the terms 'object' and 'objective'.[72] In one of these senses, to consider a human subject, oneself or another, "objectivly," is to treat her as though she had none of the special capacities of subjects to think, to feel, to understand, to make choices, and so on. This, notoriously, is the way in which behaviorists and reductive materialists wish to talk of human subjects. In the other sense, to consider anything objectively is to try to think of it as it really is, rather than in accordance with one's own feelings or preconceptions or prejudices. In that sense, to treat human subjects as though they were *not* human subjects is the very reverse of treating them objectively. Let us distinguish these two senses as "objective$_1$," and "objective$_2$." To make oneself or another into an object$_1$, except perhaps for a very circumscribed and limited purpose like curing a disease (where it may indeed be appropriate to treat a human being as a mere chemical machine or assemblage of organs), is at once morally monstrous and theoretically mistaken. But nothing is more desirable than to aspire to make objects$_2$ of ourselves and others, to aspire to know them as they really are. To do this effectively is nothing other than to apply to them the threefold process described above. Our tendency to treat things and persons exclusively as objects$_1$ is increased by our need to get control over our environment. This is desirable so far as it goes, but when taken too far leads to a terrible spiritual barrenness and "disenchantment" with nature. To treat reality in terms of objectivity$_2$ is to be delivered from such disenchantment; as Schelling well understood, nature from this point of view is full of spiritual nourishment for human beings, and perhaps even a medium of divine communication to them.

As for the split between subject and object$_2$, I may certainly come to judge for good reason that I am a human subject, capable of thought, feeling, and will; that I inhabit a world which includes other such subjects distinct from myself; and that this world consists largely of things which are not subjects, but which are in principle intelligible to me. For such reflection, there is no need whatever to turn myself into an object$_1$, and no danger of my doing so, once I have grasped the distinction between the two sorts of objectivity. When it comes to things and our representations of them, we may distinguish things as objects of naive perception, and things as known in terms of a mature science. At the ideal term of science (where the threefold process has been carried through indefinitely), things are known as they really are, and our perceptions of things are explained in terms of their interaction with our sense organs. To conceive of things in such a way is very different from envisaging them in terms of naive realism, where the distinction of things from oneself and one's thought is simply taken for granted.[73]

A very brief comment seems in order on the central place in metaphysics attributed to art in the *System of Transcendental Idealism*. To summarize what I have tried to argue elsewhere,[74] art satisfies us by exercizing and clarifying activities of mind which are usually unconscious or at best half-conscious, and which are involved in getting to know, and so in a manner "constituting," the reality which exists independently of ourselves. Thus, in the arts we may be said as it were to cocreate nature; and this would seem to give us some kind of insight into the work of the spiritual principle, if there is one, which gives rise to nature. I believe that Schelling's philosophy of art approximates quite closely to these positions.

Hegel declared, in a famous phrase, that the real is the rational, and the rational, the real. This statement may be felt to express the quintessence of idealism, and it seems quite a good idea, in trying to assess idealism as a whole, to try to make up one's mind about the right and the wrong of it. As critics of Hegel from the later Schelling to Lonergan[75] have pointed out, it seems not to do justice to the element of contingency, of matter of fact, in the universe. Even if all phenomena could be derived, as a matter of iron necessity, from a few basic laws and initial conditions in the universe, these laws and initial conditions themselves could hardly be anything else than contingent matters of fact. Yet, it remains an imperative demand that every phenomenon should be explained, and science is an impressive witness to the proposition that this demand corresponds to the truth about things. The transcendental Thomist takes her first step towards resolution of this dilemma by distinguishing two elements within reason: the understanding that envisages possibilities and concocts hypotheses, and the reason (in a narrower sense) which affirms on good grounds that some of these hypotheses are probably or certainly true. The real is intelligible, susceptible to understanding; it is the business of reason to determine which of the intelligible possibilities in fact are so. However, it is wrong to say that the intelligible is the real, since there are an infinite number of possible (and so intelligible) worlds which might have been instantiated, but are "unreal" because they happen not to have been. The intelligibility of the universe, according to the transcendental Thomist, is to be explained as due to the intelligence of that being which ultimately accounts for it, its element of contingent fact to that being's will. At this rate all the complicated manoeuvres of Schelling's philosophy, in the years immediately after 1800, to explain how a contingent world could possibly have arisen, turn out to have been unnecessary.

The aim of Schelling in his philosophy of nature, to deduce from first principles all the basic characteristics of reality as discovered by the sciences, was certainly doomed to failure. However, it should not be inferred that nothing like a philosophy of nature is possible at all. Considerations advanced by the idealists tend to show that an unintelligible reality, an actuality which does not realize a possibility to be grasped by any conceivable intelligence, is in the last analysis incoherent. An intelligible world is only fully to be explained as due to an intelligent will. Such a will may freely decree initial conditions and laws, such that certain types of beings are liable to evolve and survive, which in turn constitute a foundation for the coming into existence of other types of being, and so on. Such is the general schema of what has been called emergent probability, to which it has been clear for over a century that our universe conforms. The upshot of such reflections, very general as they are, is by no means empty or trivial; it is theistic, and such that subjective idealism together with all forms of materialism are ruled out.

However, it may still be claimed that radical free will in God or human beings, in the sense of a real capacity to choose between alternative courses of action when all factors are taken into account, is inconceivable. The underlying assumptions seem to be as follows: that free will is inconsistent with necessitation; that whatever is not necessitated is arbitrary; and that an action which is arbitrary is not properly to be attributed to free will. Many philosophers, including Schelling himself, have contested the first assumption; I myself believe that they would have done better to contest the second. It certainly seems proper to concede the third. If I suddenly stand on my head and sing the "Marseillaise" for no reason, you are more likely to attribute this to some kind of fit caused by electrical or chemical stimulation of my brain than to my freedom of will. A typical free action, on the contrary, can be seen to be performed for reasons; and given that the agent has the reasons, and performs the action in accordance with them, it is easy to infer that she is determined to do so.[76] I think that this inference is a specious one. Consider an example of the kind that specially preoccupied Schelling in his later writings, where I am poised between good and evil; say, where I can amuse myself by addressing a humiliating and spiteful remark to someone, or forego the amusement by saying something charitable and restrained. Whichever course of action I take, it will not be arbitrary; both the worse and the better will be susceptible of explanation. In the one case I will have yielded to the bad impulse; in the other I will have resisted it. "But if you yield," it will be objected, "this can only be because the impulse was stronger than the tendency to resist it." However, this way of talking presupposes determinism, and so cannot properly be used to establish it. There is nothing incoherent about the libertarian view of this matter, that either issue is really possible until I take my decision.

"But even if determinism were acknowledged to be true," it may be said, "this would make no difference to the common-sense notion of freedom, or to the uses of our moral language which presuppose it. If the kind of freedom which is opposed to determinism turns out to be illusory, we are still left with the kind which is opposed to constraint." Even in a deterministic universe, there is a difference between a person who leaves a room because she sees good reason to leave it, and one who does so under physical or psychological compulsion. If it were universally acknowledged that determinism is true, moral language might still have a use in shaping conduct, of reinforcing the sorts of dispositions of which we approve, and decreasing the probability of the kinds of behavior that we deplore. I would concede that moral language might retain some function among consistent persons who believed the universe to be deterministic, but I insist that it would lack presuppositions that are now rather central to it. For example, we are apt to assign blame for some actions committed by ourselves and others in the past, but such blame presupposes that we or they really could have done otherwise, even when the whole situation in which we or they acted is taken into account. Kant's maxim that "ought" implies "can" is deeply built into the assumptions underlying our moral language as it now is; and this entails that "ought to have done otherwise" implies "really could have done otherwise." However, that only pushes the difficulty one stage further back. I can scarcely say "she ought to have done otherwise, in that she ought to have reflected further"; while at the same time admitting that, given that she *did not* reflect further, taking all the circumstances into account, she *could not* have reflected further.[77]

I conclude that it is after all a necessary presupposition of our moral language as it is now, as well as a *prima facie* implication of our common-sense experience of choice, that we *can* sometimes act otherwise than we do, even when all circumstances are taken into account. Let us call this capacity radical freedom. That an agent is radically free is incompatible with the total predictability, even in principle, of her actions; for all that such compatibility was accepted by Schelling, in common with Hume and his many followers among philosophers at the present time. (Schelling seems to have been at least half aware of the unsatisfactory nature of such compatibleness, driven as he was to postulate a timeless choice by which agents opt for the character which determines the particular choices of their lives. As Copleston reasonably remarks, how this timeless choice by human agents can take place is obscure.[78]) Such radical freedom is, as I have said, quite coherent with contemporary science, for all that it seemed not to be so with science as it existed from the seventeenth to about the end of the nineteenth century. There is a sense in which science as such presupposes that everything is to be explained, but such explanation, as was illustrated above in the cases of evolutionary biology and nuclear physics, leaves open a margin of indeterminacy for particular events. Now Schelling, as Heidegger and Alan White have pointed out, was preoccupied throughout his career with the question of how system could be reconciled with freedom.[79] I believe that the answer is to be found in the basically transcendental Thomist position which I have sketched.[80]

Radical freedom may be attributed either to human beings, in the manner that I have just summarized, or to God. According to the view of classical theism which is exemplified in Thomism, whether traditional or transcendental, God could have created a universe quite other than this, or refrained from creating at all. Perhaps it is in Schelling's doctrine of God that the trend of his thought towards a basically transcendental Thomist outlook is most clearly seen. There is a remarkable variety in Schelling's attempts to characterize the Absolute in the earlier stages of his work. Plainly, to view the Absolute as "force" is not quite the same as to view it as "will," or for that matter as "reason." So far as the Absolute is supposed to be unconscious, it does not seem to explain what needs to be explained, the amenability of things to rational explanation. If nature is *orientated* towards rationality and consciousness, as Schelling maintained throughout his career, what less than a rational and thus conscious ground is fully to explain this orientation? Schelling's move from idealism to theism, therefore, seems fully justified. However, there is no room within the Thomist scheme for the later Schelling's conception of prior and subsequent moments in the divine life, any more than for the very similar distinction made by modern "process" theologians between the "primordial" and "consequent" natures of God. For the Thomist, God is eternal and so changeless, in no sense undergoing progress or development; eternally willing that a universe should exist, and time and change along with it. In the Thomist technical terminology, God is eternal "act"; in time, finite beings progress from "potency" to "act," acorns becoming oak trees, kittens cats, and human children mature women and men. Evil is a matter of a finite thing's failure to be what it should be, physical evil being impairment of a part or a function of something, moral evil of misdirection of the will; there is no question of a power existing somehow prior to divine consciousness, precariously surmounted by the latter in the act of creation, and later giving rise to the possibility of evil in the creature. Schelling's contention, that development of a kind is required in God if God is to be conscious or personal at all, the transcendental Thomist would deny outright. What is utterly and unsurpassably supreme in the category of personality is unrestricted understanding and all-powerful will; it is by virtue of their finitude that human persons are subject to change, and so to progress or regression.[81]

Since the doctrine of successive moments in God, even moments which, as in the later Schelling's view, are not exactly to be conceived as in time has no place in the Thomist theology. Therefore, Schelling's account of the relation between myth and revelation, as reflecting these moments, can have no place there either. But Schelling's idea that myth somehow anticipates and corresponds to revelation, and that the study of each is liable to enhance our understanding of the other, may well find support within a transcendental Thomist perspective. As is apparent especially in the work of Carl Jung and his followers, myth expresses age-old intuitions about the human condition in the world, and about the basic crises apt to befall human beings in themselves and in relation to one another; if there is a divine reality, myth is likely to contain intimations of it. In the life of Jesus, it may well be maintained that "myth became fact"; the narrative of the Gospels has after all the structure and basic content of the career of the cult hero, as found, in more or less fragmentary or complete forms, among human groups widely removed from one another in place, time, and culture. Would it not be very fitting if, in order to inspire our devotion, and to hearten us in overcoming the ravages of evil in ourselves and others, God had come among us in the form of a human history which had the structure of myth, thus providing a key which uniquely fitted the lock constituted by the human psyche?[82]

When Schelling delivered his final Berlin lectures in 1841–42, it seemed to his hearers, or at least to those of them who were to become most influential, that his critique of Hegel's philosophy was wholly convincing but that what he put in its place was totally inadequate. The result of this was to confirm the tendency of intellectuals from that time onwards to feel that the whole business of metaphysics had been put into disrepute. To this extent Schelling was a true prophet when he suggested that people, in rejecting Hegel's teaching, might even conclude that "there shall be no more philosophy at all."[83] On the other hand, Schelling had opened up a vein of inquiry into the human subject and her capacity for decision and moral choice that had been comparatively neglected by his predecessors, and was to lead in time to existentialism. Was Schelling perhaps right after all in thinking that speculative metaphysics is a possible and important enterprise? And, if he was, what if anything is to be learned from his own efforts in that direction?

It seems to me that metaphysics is indeed possible and that it has seldom if ever been more timely than at present, with our chaos of dangerously conflicting views about the nature and destiny of human beings and their place in the world at large. What is mainly to be learned from Schelling, I suggest, may be summed up in the following four points: (1) the question of the relation between thought and the physical world, and the related question of the nature and reality of human freedom, are among the central topics of philosophy; (2) the susceptibility of nonhuman reality to investigation by human reason is a vital clue to the nature of that reality, and to the nature and existence of any Absolute which may be at the basis of the world; (3) the element of contingency, both in nature at large and in human free action, should be accounted for rather than explained away by a satisfactory general philosophy; (4) the requirement that everything is to be rationally explained remains all the same a proper one once certain qualifications have been made. The many enemies of idealism have repudiated its conception of the relation of thought to the material world; their alternative accounts, so far as they have bothered to offer them, have usually evaded rather than confronted the problems pointed out by the idealists. Points 1, 2 and 4 are common to idealists in general; point 3 is the central point of difference between Schelling and Hegel. The anomalies in Schelling's own thought, and particularly in the position taken up in his latest work, derive quite largely from the difficulties in reconciling 3 and 4. I have argued that in the course of finding the way to reconcile them, one also comes across reasons for abandoning the idealist's Absolute for the theist's God, an unconscious or quasi-conscious Being from which the world necessarily emanated, for an intelligent Agent from which it issues by an act of free will. Schelling largely grasped this point during the later phases of his work,[84] but was prevented from following his insight all the way through by elements left over from his earlier idealism and the restrictive account of explanation which it entailed.[85]

The Absolute postulated by Schelling at a comparatively early stage in his career, an indescribable somewhat which indescribably gave rise to the secondary realities or illusions that constitute the finite world of objects and subjects, or nature and conscious spirit, was sarcastically dismissed by Hegel, in a famous phrase, as "the night in which all cows are black."[86] In fact, the "unrestricted act of understanding,"[87] which lies at the foundation of the world, is rather to be described as the eternal noon in which every cow is incandescent.

NOTES

1. Cf. the sublime remark heard at a recent conference on metaphysics: "Oh no, materialism isn't a metaphysics; it just happens to be true."

2. See especially his books, *Whitehead's Metaphysics* (London: Allen and Unwin, 1958); and *The Nature of Physical Existence* (New York: Humanities Press, 1972). The latter has claims to be the most considerable work of metaphysics to have appeared since the Second World War.

3. Cf. Adam Margoshes, "Schelling," *Encyclopedia of Philosophy*, ed. Paul Edwards, (New York: The Macmillan Company and the Free Press, 1967), vol. 7, 306.

4. Cf. Bertrand Russell's comment: "This inconsistency is not an accidental oversight; it is an essential part of his [Kant's] system." *History of Western Philosophy* (London: Allen and Unwin, 1946), 735. Kant was attempting to respond to David Hume's sceptical account of causality, *Enquiry Concerning Human Understanding*, sections IV, V and VII.

5. As Alan White remarks: "As both Fichte and Schelling take Kant's first *Critique* to reveal, the philosophizing subject reflects on itself as well as on its object and thus attains the transcendental level, beyond the finite realm of the subject-object opposition." *Schelling: An Introduction to the System of Freedom* (New Haven and London: Yale University Press, 1983), 23.

6. Fichte made the distinction clear in his later writings, insisting that, in spite of appearances, he had never meant to identify the absolute with the empirical human subject; cf. F. C. Copleston, *A History of Philosophy*, vol. VII (London: Burns and Oates, 1963), 44. As F. Bolman puts it, "While Fichte envisaged a world which is the scene of man's duty and the condition of his moral freedom, Schelling, seeking greater objectivity, led the way to Hegelian absolute idealism." For Schelling and Hegel, whatever the differences between them, "the real was the process of reason progressing in the world by action and reaction to its consummation in the perfect, unified expression of truth." "Introduction" to Schelling's *The Ages of the World*, ed. Bolman, (New York: Columbia University Press, 1942), 4. But Schelling himself at this early period does see some kind of identity between the Absolute and human subjects, out of which he makes ethical capital in Fichtean fashion. As White expresses it, "Philosophy (according to Schelling) must teach us that we are infinite or absolute as well as finite. When our essential identity is grasped by all, all will come to 'obey the same laws of freedom, as one complete person'." Schelling, *Works*, la:158; White, *Schelling*, 28. References to Schelling's works with an "a" suffix will be to the edition brought out by his son, K. F. A. Schelling (Stuttgart and Augsburg: J. G. Cotta'scher Verlag, 1856–61); others to that of M. Schröter (Munich: C. H. Beck'sche Verlagsbuchhandlung, 1927).

7. *Works*, 1:100.

8. Copleston, *History*, 102. I am heavily indebted to Copleston for this and the next nine paragraphs.

9. *Works*, 1:263. As H. B. Acton comments: "The dogmatic realist [i.e., one who takes her stand on the objective] cannot make the step from the absolute object to any sort of subjectivity, and the idealist cannot make the step from the absolute subject to its finite counterpart." "The Absolute," *Encyclopedia of Philosophy*, Vol. 1, 8. Copleston, *History*, 94, 99, 100, 102, 105.

10. *Works*, 1:706.

11. *Works*, 1:712. Schelling saw the underlying maxim of Spinoza's *Ethics* as: "Strive to become identical with the infinite, to drown in the infinity of the absolute object." *Works*, la:315; White, *Schelling*, 32.

12. Copleston, *History*, 107.

13. Copleston, *History*, 105–107, 109.

14. *Works*, 2:283. Cf. the long extract in E. Behler, ed., *Philosophy of German Idealism* (New York: Continuum, 1987), 168–200.

15. Cf. Margoshes, "Schelling," 306.

16. *Works*, 1:417.

17. Copleston, *History*, 109–112. For a brief account of Schelling's philosophy at about this time, see Bolman's "Introduction," 12–13; and for a comprehensive treatment of Schelling's philosophy of nature, see Joseph L. Esposito, *Schelling's Idealism and Philosophy of Nature* (Lewisburg: Bucknell University Press, 1977). Esposito makes an instructive comparison between this aspect of Schelling's work and contemporary General Systems Theory.

18. *Works*, 2:370.

19. *Works*, 2:349. As Acton expresses Schelling's position on art: ". . . whereas in nature the Absolute is embodied in an unconscious way, in works of art it is consciously embodied so that through his productions the artistic genius reveals the Absolute to mankind." "The Absolute," 7. For this paragraph as a whole, cf. Peter Heath's translation of the *System of Transcendental Idealism* (Charlottesville: University of Virginia Press, 1978).

20. Cf. Bolman, "Introduction," 15.

21. *Works*, 3:10. As Margoshes expresses Schelling's view of the matter at this time: "The absolute identity of nature and intelligence is found in their common neutral source, reason. Reason is one and infinite, embracing things in themselves, and knowledge of things. In reason there is no object, no subject, no space, no time." *Schelling*, 308.

22. *Works*, 3:25.

23. Cf. *Works*, 3:21.

24. Cf. White, *Schelling*, 77. Schelling seems to be reproducing here the problems of the classical Indian *Advaita* philosophy, of which Shankhara is the greatest representative. For an exposition of Shankhara's philosophy, see C. Sharma, *A Critical Survey of Indian Philosophy* (London: Rider, 1960), chapter 15.

25. Copleston, *History*, 123–125.

26. White points out that Schelling's *System of All Philosophy* (1804) deals with the problem of the existence of finitude in three incompatible ways, *Schelling* , 92, 94. Cf. Bolman, "Introduction," 17.

27. *Works*, 4:23–24.

28. For the influence of Boehme on Schelling, see Robert F. Brown, *The Later Philosophy of Schelling* (Cranbury, N. J. and London: Associated University Presses, 1977).

29. *Works*, 4:28.

30. *Works*, 4:31.

31. *Works*, 4:32.

32. *Works*, 4:30.

33. *Works* 4:32.

34. Copleston, *History*, 126, 128–129.

35. Bolman, "Introduction," 24–6. Cf. *Works*, 7a:140–141, 32–34.

36. Cf. Bolman, 22–24; and the profound study by Martin Heidegger, *Schelling's Treatise on the Essence of Human Freedom* (London and Athens, Ohio: Ohio University Press, 1985).

37. *Acts*, 17:27.

38. *Works*, 4:234.

39. *Works*, 4:244.

40. *Works*, 7a:386–387; White, *Schelling*, 125–126.

41. *Works*, 4:277; Copleston, *History*, 130–131, 133.

42. *Works*, 4:251; cf. White, *Schelling*, 118–119.

43. This, together with much in the later Schelling, plainly anticipates contemporary "Process Theology." One could hardly find a better account of

the distinction in this theology between the "primordial" and "consequent" nature of God than the following: "I posit God as first and last, as alpha and as omega, but he is not as alpha what he is as omega." *Works*, 8a:81; cf. White, *Schelling*, 136.

44. *Works*, 4:326.

45. *Works*, 4:256. Cf. White, *Schelling*, 120; and *Works*, 7a:364.

46. Cf. *Works*, 4:296. Copleston, *History*, 130–2, 135. Creation itself for Schelling is a kind of victory of good over evil, cf. *Works*, 7a:401; as White puts it, "the dark ground principle is aroused by the act of creation, but it is at the same time subordinated to light and understanding and, thus, to the good." *Schelling*, 131. Schelling's view on this matter anticipates Karl Barth's curious doctrine of evil as consisting of possibilities which God rejected in creating, but which all the same are active within God's creation; see his *Church Dogmatics* (Edinburgh: T. and T. Clark, 1936–64), 111, 295–367.

47. As Schelling saw it, Hegel failed to justify the transition from his "Logic" to philosophy of nature and philosophy of spirit, the parts of his system which dealt with matters of experience; cf. White, *Schelling*, 155–156. For Schelling on Hegel in general, see White, *Schelling*, 151–157. Cf. E. Bréhier, *Schelling* (Paris: Felix Alean, 1912), chapter 4.

48. *Works*, 5:746.

49. *Works*, 5:746.

50. *Works*, 5:746. "In a sense the forerunner of Schopenhauer and Nietzsche, he (Schelling) conceived voluntarism to be the ultimate critique of all forms of rationalism." Bolman, "Introduction," 4.

51. Cf. *Works*, 5:748.

52. *Works*, 5:750; Copleston, *History*, 136–137.

53. Though a complete natural theology does seem to me implicit in the statement: "If there is or is to be a rational (world), then I must presuppose (absolute) spirit." *Works*, 13a:247; cf. White, *Schelling*, 173.

54. *Works*, 5:437.

55. *Works*, 6:396.

56. For a more detailed account of the relation between myth and revelation in the later Schelling, see White, *Schelling*, 178–186; also Paul Tillich, *The Construction of the History of Religion in Schelling's Positive Philosophy* (Lewisburg: Bucknell University Press, 1974). Schelling's final lectures at Berlin have been published as *Schelling: Philosophie der Offenbarung 1841/42*, ed. and Introduction by Manfred Frank, (Frankfurt am Main: Suhrkamp Verlag, 1977).

57. Copleston, *History*, 138, 140.

58. Copleston, *History*, 138.

59. In this matter it seems to me better to envisage Aristotle as rather proposing a corrective to Plato than being in fundamental opposition to him. I have tried to argue this in a paper, "On Being an Aristotelian," prepared for and accepted by a meeting of the International Society for Metaphysics in December 1988.

60. Copleston, *History*, 107.

61. I have argued this at length in *The Intelligible Universe* (Totowa, New Jersey: Barnes and Noble, 1982).

62. *Philosophical Letters Concerning Dogmatism and Criticism* (1795); *Works*, la:281–342.

63. The principal work in which he does so is *Insight: A Study of Human Understanding* (London: Longmans, Green and Co., 1957). For a simplified account, see H. A. Meynell, *An Introduction to the Philosophy of Bernard Lonergan* (London: Macmillan, 1976).

64. Cf. Lonergan, *Method in Theology* (London: Darton, Longman and Todd, 1972), 265, 292.

65. This account of knowing may be defended on the ground that its denial is self-destructive. Suppose someone does deny it. Does she put forward her denial as the possibility which best explains the relevant evidence? If she does, she is employing in vindication of her knowledge-claim the very mental operations she is maintaining to be irrelevant in the vindication of knowledge-claims. If she does not, it seems pointless to pay any attention to her denial, which is *ipso facto* groundless.

66. Cf. *Insight*, chapters 12, 14, 16, and 19; Meynell, *Introduction*, chapters 3 and 6.

67. Thomas Aquinas, *Summa Theologica* Part I, question 2, article 3.

68. Karl Popper, *Objective Knowledge* (Oxford: Clarendon Press, 1972), 41.

69. I.e., those theists who maintain that belief that there is a God may be shown, by arguments which do not explicitly or covertly assume what they set out to establish, to be better founded than the belief that there is not.

70. It does not seem in place here to consider the possibility of polytheism at length; monotheism may be argued from the fact that the universe seems to be a single intelligible structure. J. M. E. McTaggart is notable among idealists for his view that the Absolute is to be regarded rather as a college than as a single being.

71. "Schelling," *Encyclopedia Britannica*, 1974 edition, vol. 16, 339.

72. Cf. Lonergan, *Insight*, 375–380, 412–416. On the continuing difficulty of relating the objective to the subjective, see J. Kekes, "Link–Concepts and Epistemology," *Ratio* (December 1985): 107–120.

73. G. E. Moore took idealism to task for implying, "(1) that the universe is very different from what it seems, and (2) that it has quite a large number of properties which it does not seem to have." "The Refutation of Idealism," *Philosophical Studies* (London: Routledge and Kegan Paul, 1922), 1. If what I have said is on the right lines, the arguments advanced by idealists at least go to show that the universe is very different from what it seems to be to the naive realist; indeed, one might infer the same conclusion from a brief consideration of contemporary physics. It does not seem to be as a whole spiritual, but I do think that idealism indicates that it shows signs of being as a whole due to something in the nature of spirit.

74. Cf. Hugo Meynell, *The Nature of Aesthetic Value* (London: Macmillan, 1986).

75. See Lonergan, *Insight*, 373: Hegel "views everything as it would be if there were no facts."

76. The classical exposition of this argument is due to David Hume,

Enquiry Concerning Human Understanding, section VIII. For the notion of "emergent probability," see Lonergan, *Insight*, 123–130, 132–134.

77. The dilemma between freedom and universal determination is set out with marvellous brevity and clarity by R. Chisholm in "Responsibility and avoidability," *Determinism and Freedom in the Age of Modern Science*, ed. S. Hook, (New York: Collier Books, 1961), 157–159.

78. Copleston, *History*, 134. Acton blames Schelling for following Kant in taking human choice out of the ordinary world of events, "The Absolute," 9.

79. Cf. *Works*, 10a: 36; White, *Schelling*, 159.

80. Cf. Lonergan, *Insight*, 620–621.

81. For a full exposition of the Thomist view of God, see Lonergan, *Insight*, ch. 19; cf. Thomas Aquinas, *Summa*, Part I, questions 3, 7, 9 and 10. On God and evil, see Lonergan, *Insight*, 666–668, 688–694; Thomas Aquinas, *Summa*, part 1, question 48.

82. Cf. Lonergan, *Insight*, ch. 20; C. G. Jung, *Psychology and Religion* (London: Routledge and Kegan Paul, 1958), 154f; C. S. Lewis, "Myth Became Fact," in *Undeceptions*, ed. W. Hooper, (London: Geoffrey Bles, 1971), 39–43.

83. *Works*, 13a:364; White, *Schelling*, 148.

84. As Schelling says, to recognize that Absolute Spirit can give rise to the world of finite things only by choosing, and by being positively free in doing so rather than merely uncompelled, is necessarily to think of Absolute Spirit as God; *Works*, 13a:269. This is a radical change in relation to his earlier works, in which the freedom of absolute spirit is conceived as equivalent to strict necessity, action in accordance with essence. Cf. White, *Schelling*, 175.

85. According to Copleston, Schelling never entirely renounced the idealist view that God is related to the world as antecedent to consequent. *History*, 175.

86. Schelling had himself compared the Absolute in its primordial nature with night. Cf. *Works*, 2a:66, 4a:278; and 6a:154; White, *Schelling*, 1.

87. Lonergan, *Insight*, 648, 651.

Section Two
The Subject as Creative

5
Creativity as General Activity

Jan Van der Veken and André Cloots

One of the most distinctive features of Whitehead's metaphysics is the distinction between creativity and God, or between the metaphysical and religious ultimates—a distinction essential for any contemporary metaphysics. This distinction is also an integral part of Heidegger's overcoming of traditional metaphysics in his *Seinsdenken*. The questions, however, are how the metaphysical place of creativity should be conceived and how the religious notion of God can be conceptualized in conjunction with it.

In this paper, we wish to stress the possibility of—and even the need for—a "rich" interpretation of Whitehead's notion of creativity on the one hand, and a less "entitative" understanding of his conception of God on the other. We also wish to show that, as a result, the relationship between God and creativity can be reinterpreted. Whitehead's first metaphysical project, as expressed in *Science and the Modern World* (SMW), will here be our illuminating guide.

* * *

If one is engaged with process philosophy in Europe and takes a generally positive approach to it, one has to grant that the very same difficulties will repeatedly present themselves. We shall assess several of these recurring difficulties in order to investigate whether a connection holds between them.

One objection frequently voiced is that Whitehead was a typical practitioner of "onto-theology," as this concept was defined and criticized by Heidegger. Heidegger reproached traditional metaphysics, beginning with Plato's, for its onto-theological character, which means that for Heidegger the quest for Being (*Sein*) has been transformed invariably into a question concerning beings (*Seienden*): substance, first cause, God. Even though Whitehead and Heidegger were mutually ignorant of the other's work, Heidegger's overall critique of Western metaphysics is nonetheless especially significant for Whiteheadians.

It seems—at first reading—that Whitehead concerns himself solely with beings, i.e., *Seienden*, or entities that exist. Although his "actual entities" are conceived dynamically, they are nonetheless always entities, or beings. God, too, is for Whitehead—at least since *Religion in the Making* (RM) and *Process and Reality* (PR)—an actual entity, even if the sole nontemporal one. Does this mean, then, that Whitehead is not at all concerned with Being itself? In Whitehead's system the analogue of what the tradition understands by Being cannot be a determinate actual entity—not even God—but creativity.[1] Creativity is *das Ereignis*, the coming into the fore of beings. Substantial activity is for Whitehead (as Being is for Heidegger) "the Occurrence," that which appears in everything that happens yet which never reveals or exhausts itself in any specific occurrence. Later, however (i.e., after SMW), Whitehead moves toward an understanding of creativity as a purely formal, general characteristic, "without a specific character of its own." If one ascribes to creativity a richer, not merely formal meaning—that is, if one conceives creativity as truly active—then the discussion with Heidegger can be far more fruitful. Then, too, it is not necessary to conceive God as the highest being, or as an actual entity among others. Instead God can be conceived as a dimension of creativity (somewhat like *das Heilige* as conceived by Heidegger) without being creativity itself.

Another objection is raised by the neothomist Norris Clarke, who enters into a dialogue with Whitehead.[2] Here the main topic is also the relation between God and creativity. Clarke is willing to attribute to creativity a certain role, but for him it cannot be the ultimate role, for the "creative advance" of the finite has itself been created by God. Clarke is well aware that Whitehead has a good reason to reject the traditional concept of creation. If God alone has created everything, without any other ground, in an unconditioned and free decision, then He is "the supreme author of the play"[3] and is responsible for the bad as well as the good. So even Clarke must concede that God does not decide everything. Therefore, also from this standpoint, a distinction between general activity and divine agency is important.

Finally, there remains the dialogue with German idealism, which could be very stimulating for a creative interpretation of Whitehead. Through such a dialogue it would become clear that the analogy with philosophies of the Hegelian school is, in fact, not accidental but that, as far as our theme is concerned, a rethinking of the relation between the Absolute and God is necessary: the Absolute, or the ultimate, should not have a mere formal role in relation to the finite.

All these problems seem to have a common background and an inner connection. The real problem seems to be (in non-Whiteheadian language) the relation between the Infinite and the finite, between Being and beings, between Reality and realities. Here, we touch one of the central problems of classical philosophy: "In all philosophic theory there is an ultimate which is actual in virtue of its accidents."[4]

When he approaches this problem for the first time in his metaphysical works (viz. in SMW), Whitehead turns to Spinoza, as his use of the term 'substantial activity' shows. Whereas for Spinoza substance and God coincide, for Whitehead this is not the case. As a result, Whitehead faces the question, which Spinoza does not face, of the relationship between the ultimate metaphysical principle and God.

Whitehead holds that there are good reasons why God (the religious ultimate) and creativity (the philosophical ultimate) *do not* coincide. First, he conceives of freedom as a universal category: if there is *an* instance that decides everything, then there is no place left for the self-determination of actual entities. Second, he refuses to deny, or explain away, the problem of evil. If God, however, were the sole determining instance, then He would be responsible for everything, evil included. In this respect, Whitehead sides with David Hume, who criticized traditional theism and its conception of God as the all-powerful creator, i.e., God as, at one and the same time, the philosophical and the religious ultimate.[5] In so reacting to the traditional creation doctrine, Whitehead moves the specific activity of actual entities into the foreground: they must not only exist in themselves, they must also be the "creator" of themselves; they are *causa sui*.

In order to conceptualize this *causa sui* characteristic of actual entities, Whitehead introduces the notion of creativity, which, together with the notions of the one and the many, is constitutive of "the Category of the Ultimate." Creativity, not God, is the metaphysical ultimate. Then, the basic question is how to conceive this "ultimacy of creativity."

Central to Whitehead's system is the "ontological principle," which makes of his metaphysics an ontological pluralism. Actual entities are all that exist. This principle is also a category of explanation: "no actual entity, then no reason."[6] What, then, is the ontological status of creativity? Creativity is clearly not an entity, not even the highest or all-encompassing one, in which respect it differs radically from Spinoza's substance. Does this mean that creativity is "nothing," because "in separation from actual entities, there is nothing, merely nonentity—'The rest is silence'"[7]? The ontological principle has often been said to be the main reason for interpreting creativity merely as a general characteristic of all actual entities without itself having any metaphysical reality or activity.

It is vitally important, however, to interpret correctly the ontological principle. Whitehead calls it "the principle of efficient and final causation,"[8] which "means that actual entities are the only *reasons*; so that to search for a *reason* is to search for one or more actual entities."[9] In other words, the ontological principle delineates the domain within which reasons can be sought. Nonetheless, the ontological principle—providing reasons in this sense of the term—cannot be the final explanatory word. Actual entities can be invoked to explain specific conditions for concrete actualities, further explanation is required to establish that there is causation at all, that reasons can be invoked, that reality continually reestablishes itself from the causal efficacy of the past. The ontological principle is not its own foundation. It eventually refers to the Category of the Ultimate, which is presupposed in all the more specific categories.[10] In this respect, the principle of creativity transcends the ontological principle and is prior to it as far as metaphysical explanation is concerned. That is, creativity is not a reason on the same level as are the actual entities. Nevertheless, it has explanatory power. It is the ultimate descriptive notion, but at the same time is the ultimate explaining principle. It is the formative element, "whereby the actual world has its character of temporal passage to novelty."[11]

In any philosophy of becoming, one basic issue is how to understand "ongoingness."[12] It is one of Whitehead's main concerns when he introduces the notion of creativity, which refers to the activity of reality whereby new actuality continually comes into existence. Creativity is the ever-urging drive that pushes reality forward. "The creativity of the world is the throbbing emotion of the past hurling itself into a new transcendent fact. It is the flying dart, of which Lucretius speaks, hurled beyond the bounds of the world."[13] In order to understand ongoingness, the notions of "transition" *and* "concrescence" are essential, even though in themselves they are not sufficient. The coming into existence of new actuality cannot be fully, or exhaustively, explained by either the causal efficacy of the past or the self-creativity of the present. Insofar as the coming into existence of new actuality would be understood merely in this way, a gap would remain between the past and the present, between the urge of the past and the taking up of the past into the self-creativity of the new entity. Transition and concrescence are two aspects of one and the same creativity, two sides of the activity pervading all reality, pushing reality toward the future. For the past is efficient causation only because it qualifies transcending creativity, and the present is final causation because it is an instance of the creativity of the universe. Here the notion of creativity is necessary as the unifying, but at the same time, fundamental principle: "the fundamental, inescapable fact is the *creativity* in virtue of which there can be no 'many things' which are not subordinated in a concrete unity."[14] Or, in terms of RM, creativity is the formative element "*whereby* the actual world has its character of temporal passage to novelty."[15]

Nonetheless creativity is not just one formative element among others: it is "that which is left out in the analysis of the static factors of the metaphysical situation."[16] Exactly this is what Whitehead means when he speaks of substantial activity and its attributes.[17] Creativity is the universal activity, characterized by the other formative elements. As universal activity, creativity is not actual except in its "accidents," or "modes." Yet it cannot be reduced to them. Creativity is the activity of reality, or, in other words, reality as activity. As such, creativity *does* something, even though its activity is never independent of the *activities*. Reality is never exhausted by, never limited to, what is; it always has—or, better, *is*—the power of reestablishing itself, given the conditions of the past.[18]

Moreover, there is the *unity* of the ongoing universe: it is a *uni*-verse, not a mere multiplicity. "There is the one all-embracing fact which is the advancing history of the one universe,"[19] which, too, finally can be "explained" only by creativity. There is a uni-verse, and there always will be one (a priori), because of never-ending creativity as the activity of integration, inherent in reality. We must refer to this activity in order to gain a final understanding of "the general interconnectedness of things." Creativity is that which "transforms the manifoldness of the many into the unity of the one."[20]

From all this it becomes clear that Whitehead must ascribe *explanatory power* to creativity, even though creativity as such is not an actual entity, and in the latter's sense is not a reason. It is "no-thing"—but that does not mean that it is merely nothing. Rather, it is general activity, which is the ultimate metaphysical explanation of "the advancing history of the one universe." In what follows we shall attempt to show how creativity as universal activity can be interpreted in a fuller sense and how, thus interpreted, it is able to be limited in such a manner that the religious person is permitted to recognize the principle of limitation as the divine lure towards value, beauty, and harmony.

* * *

In order to elicit what Whitehead wants to say, one must understand what creativity is not: "The creativity is *not* an external agency with its own ulterior purposes."[21] I.e., creativity is not exterior to, or outside of, actual entities. It does not follow from this text, however, that creativity is not an agency, or an active principle. What is more, the text suggests that creativity is an *internal* agency; it is, so to speak, immanent. Whitehead's term is 'substantial activity',[22] "the pure notion of the activity conditioned by the objective immortality of the actual world."[23]

As such, creativity in itself is not nothing. L. J. Eslick calls creativity "existing non-being,"[24] and Walter Stokes, in his well-known dissertation on the function of creativity, offers a similar interpretation: "[Creativity is] totally ordered to the actualization of new occasions. [It] is the ultimate subject to which the process of actualization is ascribed. Though not actual, creativity is as real as actual occasions."[25] "Creativity is not a name for a general fact, it is a reality, though it is non-being."[26] "The efficient cause of the novel actual entity is creativity conditioned by the actual entities of the actual world."[27] Interpreted in this way, creativity has explanatory value; it explains not in a causal but in an ultimate metaphysical way that there is a unified, dynamic universe. "The 'creative advance' is the application of this ultimate principle of creativity to each novel occasion which it originates."[28]

All of these themes converge in the text of AI (one of Whitehead's latest texts on creativity), wherein creativity is described as a featureless "reason." Reacting against the idea that an occasion of experience arises out of a passive situation that is a mere welter of many data, Whitehead retorts:

> The exact contrary is the case. The initial situation includes a factor of activity which is the *reason* for the origin of that occasion of experience. This factor of activity is what I have called 'creativity'.... This basic situation, this actual world, this primary phase, this real potentiality—however you characterise it—as a whole is active with its inherent creativity, but in its details it provides the passive objects which derive their activity from the creativity of the whole.... Thus, viewed in abstraction, objects are passive, but viewed in conjunction they carry the creativity which drives the world.[29]

This late text connects remarkably well with his earliest texts on creativity, found in SMW. In these earliest texts Whitehead speaks of substantial activity and of the concrete realities (later portrayed as actual entities), which are its modes. "In the analogy with Spinoza, his one substance is for me the one underlying activity of realisation individualising itself in an interlocked plurality of modes."[30] This reference to Spinoza makes clear that Whitehead understands an ultimate metaphysical explanation to be more than a mere description, while at the same time to be different from an ultimate reason in the sense of a cause. Such an explanation is a reference to that basic element in reality from which all further explanation starts, leaning as far as possible to "the nature of things."[31]

Current thinking about creativity has been perhaps too strongly influenced by the idea that Whitehead conceived creativity as analogous to the Aristotelian principle of matter: "'Creativity' is another rendering of the Aristotelian 'matter', and of the modern 'neutral stuff'. But it is divested of the notion of passive receptivity, either of 'form', or of external relation; it is the pure notion of the activity conditioned by the objective immortality of the actual world."[32] The second sentence here is nearly as important as the first: creativity only *resembles* the Aristotelian principle of matter, and then only insofar as it has no specific character.

Another model for the interpretation of creativity, suggested by Stokes, is that of a receptacle.[33] Although creativity can be viewed as similar to a receptacle in its unifying function (though in AI the Platonic *hypodochè* is compared to the "extensive continuum"), the analogy should not be pressed too far. In order to fulfill its basic unifying function (the category of the ultimate encompasses not only creativity, but also the one and the many), creativity must be more than either prime matter or a passive receptacle. Accordingly, we propose that creativity be interpreted not primarily as Aristotelian *hylè*, or *materia prima*, but rather as substantial, or all-pervading, activity. It is no accident that substantial activity is the term Whitehead himself first used, viz. in SMW.[34]

Spinoza's substance is unequivocally *causa sui*; further it is necessary, for it simply cannot fail to exist. In the end, for Spinoza, only substance exists. Likewise for Whitehead, because nothing exists (nor can exist) outside of creativity, creativity (as the metaphysical ultimate) is *causa sui* and necessary. That creativity should have another cause besides creativity itself would be absurd, but because the ultimate is thought of in terms of creativity, all actual entities and their mutual relatedness should be interpreted as creative, or *causa sui*. If one interprets creativity more along the lines of Spinozistic substance than along the lines of a nonexisting *hylè*, then creativity better fulfills the function Whitehead allots to it (albeit implicitly).

Thus, our proposal amounts to this: creativity should be conceived first and foremost as substantial or universal activity—in a particular and focused, and not as a merely formal principle. This interpretation can be vindicated by a reading of certain of Whitehead's earlier texts. One should note here that PR is not the whole of Whitehead: it might be, after all, not as final a statement as has been so frequently claimed. There are texts prior and posterior to it that cannot be brought entirely into accordance with the *opus magnum*. Perhaps his earlier perspectives—whether or not fully formulated—are the most intelligible.[35]

From the perspective of SMW, wherein Whitehead describes creativity as substantial activity with "an interlocked plurality of modes," God is not a real entity, or *Seiendes*, but rather the first limitation of being, i.e., the first and foremost characterization of substantial activity. If we conceive creativity as universal activity that is necessarily limited (some particular "how" being necessary), then we need not conceive this limitation of creativity as a distinct actual entity. On the contrary, we should conceive the *limitation of creativity* to be as ultimate a principle as creativity itself because an actual entity could never possess the selfsame philosophically ultimate meaning.

Whether the first limitation of creativity can or should be understood as God is, however, another question. Since 'God' is a religious word, therefore, the question about the divine nature of the first limitation amounts to the following: does the sustaining and driving power at work in the universe reveal the characteristics that the religious person ascribes to God? In other words, is creativity internally directed towards truth, goodness, and harmony—or is it rather directed by fate, an anonymous, indifferent power? This question can be answered, if at all, only on the basis of one's own personal experience. For this reason, the issue of the variant meanings of "the particular how" of the limitation of creativity is a religious, and not a purely philosophical, matter. The issue becomes a philosophical matter, however, because it must be possible, within the universal connections of a philosophical system, to express what the religious person says about the final limitation of the ultimate. In this sense, God is not an exception to the metaphysical principles, and that is why for Whitehead God, too, is an actual entity, albeit an eternal one, but God need not be an actual entity like all the others. In Whitehead's system it is clear that God is an exception: God is an actual entity but not an actual occasion,[36] being eternal and everlasting; He is an actual entity in which the mental and physical poles are related in a different way from how they are related in all other actual entities. If God is an actual entity among others, the question remains whether an actual entity can be immanent to all other actual entities, which is necessary if God is to fulfill his ontological functions.

In a highly original but controversial interpretation, Laurence F. Wilmot[37] emphasizes the theme of the immanence of God in each actual entity. He advances the thesis that Whitehead abandoned the implicit Platonic scheme of PR when he came to write AI and that Whitehead there claimed that one must give special attention to the immanence of God in the World, as this was examined, incidentally, by the Alexandrian theologians of the fourth century.[38] Although Wilmot seems to demonstrate too much of a good thing, one is able to agree with him that Whitehead did abandon the Platonic solution as insufficient to meet the problem of the relationship between God and the world. The Whiteheadian texts mainly establish that one should go further than Plato; and they establish, if a bit less firmly, that one should go further than PR as well.

God's immanence in the world must now be considered. Whitehead's earlier positions on this problem are unsatisfactory, for it is not sufficient to say that God is present (or is prehended) only through the "initial aim."[39] Rather, only as the primordial limitation, or qualification, of creativity and not as an actual entity can God be "in unison of becoming with every other creative act."[40] Were God exclusively consequent to the genesis of particular actual entities, we would be able to talk of "the objectification of the world in God" but not of his being "with all creation,"[41] (or, even more to the point, *in* all creation).

The teleological influence of God on the process of becoming is in any case of such significance that Whitehead speaks of creation[42] in precisely the preceding sense. If God is not truly active *in* each new occasion, then these occasions are just *causa sui*, which negates the notion of God as creator in any meaningful sense. The relationship between creativity and God can be interpreted differently; that is, creativity can be viewed as universal activity, which is efficacious in all events, and God can be viewed as the primordial limitation of this process, which coordinates all events from within. Then it becomes much easier to accept the immanence of God in all events. Such a reading need not be un-Whiteheadian. In fact, it closely follows the arguments of SMW, where Whitehead does not yet think of God as a distinct actual entity and explicitly conceives creativity as substantial activity.

The distinction between creativity and God—and so between the creative advance, or reality, on the one hand and God on the other—is very important, but the distinction between God and the modes, or actual entities, is likewise to be maintained. It is not enough to say that God is not an exception to the metaphysical principles. Creativity *is* the exception—for it is the final, or all-encompassing, metaphysical category—and God is its first qualification. God is an exception to other actualities, both for religion and also for philosophy—even in Whitehead's system. Thus, the question is whether the conceptualization of God as *an* actual entity is the best conceptualization, seen from the standpoints of religion and, even, philosophy. We think it is not—from both standpoints. Certainly in SMW Whitehead conceives God, not as a determinate reality over against other realities but as the religious limitation of reality, a definite manner in which to interpret, or to impart a specific (i.e., religious) meaning to, the "Principle of Concretion." Whitehead seems to go in the same direction when in AI he speaks of God as the "Eros of the Universe."[43] In other words, for Whitehead 'God' is a religious name, given intuitively by believers to the all-encompassing process (reality, substantial activity) as they "see," or interpret, it from the perspective of their particular experiences. 'God' is a specific, religious name—in terms of meaning—given to reality, as it is experienced within a specific community, by the religious person. In this sense, 'God' is a "category of meaning" and not a "category of being."

One is not to expect, of course, that objections against a system of thought can be cleared away by the proposal of a single revision. Such would be too far-reaching a goal. What we have attempted here is only a "research project," which, it is hoped, will incite and contribute creatively to a dialogue with the great philosophers (Spinoza, Hegel, Heidegger), a dialogue that Whitehead and Whiteheadians have begun—and in an important respect have only begun.

NOTES

1. Or, more exactly, creativity as characterized by God.

2. W. Norris Clarke, *The Philosophical Approach to God: A Neo-*

Thomist Perspective (Winston-Salem, N.C.: Wake Forest University Press, 1979).

3. SMW 223.

4. PR 7 [10].

5. "...God in the image of an imperial ruler, God in the image of a personification of moral energy, God in the image of an ultimate philosophical principle. Hume's *Dialogues* criticize unanswerably these modes of explaining the system of the world." PR 342–343 [520].

6. PR 19 [28].

7. PR 43 [68].

8. PR 24 [36–37], Cat. of Explanation xviii.

9. PR 24 [37].

10. The ontological principle is one of the Categories of Explanation. But "the Category of the Ultimate expresses the general principle presupposed in the three more special categories" (PR 21 [31])—viz. in the Categories of Existence, the Categories of Explanation, and the Categorial Obligations—and so in all further explanation.

11. RM 88. However, it is not simply one of the formative elements: the other elements can only be formative "thanks to" creativity. Creativity is, "that which is omitted in any analysis of the static factors in the metaphysical situation." That is also the reason why in SMW Whitehead refers to Spinoza's substance and its attributes: "the analyzed elements of the situation are the attributes of the substantial activity." SMW 238.

12. Or as Whitehead puts it in his earlier work, "the passage of nature" (e.g., CN 73).

13. AI 227.

14. PR 211 [321–322]; emphasis added.

15. RM 90; emphasis added. Cf. RM 92: "The reason for the temporal character of the actual world can now be given by reference to the creativity and the creatures."

16. SMW 238.

17. SMW 238, 255.

18. As such, creativity certainly has affinities with Bergson's *élan vital*, and even with Nietzsche's *Wille zur Macht*, the latter of which is "not Being, not Becoming, but 'Pathos'." *Werke*, ed. K. Schlechta, (Berlin: Ullstein Verlag), vol. 3: 778.

19. AI 192.

20. AI 192.

21. PR 222 [339], emphasis added.

22. SMW 220.

23. PR 31 [46–47].

24. L. J. Eslick, "Existence and Creativity in Whitehead," *Proceedings of the American Catholic Philosophical Association* 35 (1961): 158.

25. W. Stokes, *The Function of creativity in The Metaphysics of Whitehead* (Ph.D. diss., St. Louis University, 1960), 104.

26. W. Stokes, "Recent Interpretations of Whitehead's creativity," *The Modern Schoolman* 39 (1962): 326.

27. W. Stokes, *The Function of Creativity*, 153.

28. PR 21 [32].

29. AI 230–231; emphasis added. I (Cloots) first met Ivor Leclerc at the International Congress of Philosophy in Düsseldorf in 1975. Working on a dissertation on the problem of the Ultimate in Whitehead and Hartshorne, I was always bothered by the fact that creativity was so often almost identified with concrescence, obscuring in that way the place of transition and also the ultimate explanatory function of creativity. Leclerc, in his book on Whitehead's metaphysics, seemed to go a long way in that direction as well. So at our first meeting we discussed this issue. It seems that he has come to realize the importance of this text of AI for the understanding of creativity. See Ivor Leclerc, "Whitehead and the Dichotomy of Rationalism and Empiricism," in

Whitehead's Metaphysics of Creativity, ed. F. Rapp and R. Wiehl, (Albany: State University of New York Press, 1990), esp. 8. At the same conference Van der Veken read a paper that contains the core of our position on creativity. See Jan Van der Veken, "Creativity as Universal Activity," in *Whitehead's Metaphysics of Creativity* (Albany: State University of New York Press, 1990), 178–188.

30. SMW 102.

31. Cf. SMW 135.

32. PR 31 [46].

33. W. Stokes, *The Function of Creativity*, 153.

34. SMW 220.

35. Arthur E. Murphy, "Whitehead's Objective Immortality", *Reason and the Common Good: Selected Essays of Arthur E. Murphy*, ed. W. H. Hay, M. G. Sinder and A. E. Murphy, (Englewood Cliffs, N.Y.: Prentice-Hall, 1963), 163–172, poses the question, Which Whitehead will be "objectively immortal?" Is it the systematic Whitehead of PR or, "the explanatory Whitehead, insisting on the endless resourcefulness and many-sidedness of thought, confronting all intellectual systems (including that of PR) with the importance of their omissions, and providing in his own thinking some fine examples of ways in which this can in fact be done, in which the as yet unsayable can be said, if we have the wit and wisdom to fit our language to the structure of the concrete facts and not merely to the 'rationality' of our system. One or the other of these Whiteheads can follow, but not both" (Murphy, 172). Murphy also criticizes the ontological principle and the drastic conclusions Whitehead draws from it ("The rest is silence"): "But even here his teaching remains equivocal and a choice must be made. Philosophers look for reasons, but what kind of reasons?" (Murphy, 172). Therefore, Murphy prefers the earlier Whitehead to the one of PR. He interprets the consequent nature of God as a kind of ad hoc concept: "But it left me profoundly dissatisfied. I could see it then, and I can see it now, only as an unhappy expression of that hardening of the categories in which ideas that have ceased to function as ideas are set up as the necessary structure of existence to which, in the name of rationality, all our thinking must finally conform" (Murphy, 166). In her contribution to the International Whitehead Symposium in Bad Homburg, Dorothy Emmet also prefers the earlier Whitehead and the Whitehead of SMW, where more justice is done to his basic

insight than is done in PR. Dorothy Emmet, "Creativity and the Passage of Nature," *Whiteheads Metaphysics of Creativity*, 59–69.

36. PR 88 [135], 77 [119], 22 [33].

37. Laurence F. Wilmot, *Whitehead and God: Prolegomena to Theological Reconstruction* (Waterloo, Ontario: Wilfred Laurier University Press, 1979).

38. The key text to which Wilmot refers is AI 213–216: "These Christians have the distinction of being the only thinkers who in a fundamental metaphysical doctrine have improved upon Plato.... What metaphysics requires is a...solution which exhibits the World as requiring its union with God, and God requiring his union with the World.... The problem came before the Christian theologians in highly special forms.... I am not making any judgment about the details of their theology.... My point is that in the place of Plato's solution of secondary images and imitations, they demanded a direct doctrine of immanence."

39. PR 224 [343], 244 [373].

40. PR 345 [523].

41. PR 343 [521].

42. "In this sense, God can be termed the creator of each new temporal actual entity." PR 225 [343].

43. AI 326.

6

Mais Où Sont Les Neiges D'Antan?

Donald W. Sherburne

"But where are the snows of yesteryear?" wondered the fifteenth-century French poet Francois Villon in the haunting refrain which closes each stanza of his best-known poem, the *Ballade of the Ladies of Byegone Times*. His question haunts us still. The question of the status of the past is particularly insistent for those of us oriented toward the process metaphysics of Alfred North Whitehead. In recent years the question of the status of the past has become even more urgent to me personally because two of my friends whom I admire very much as interpreters of process thought—Lewis Ford and George Kline—have advanced an understanding of the process account of the status of the past which I find puzzling and wrongheaded. For some time I have been toying with ways of responding to their claims. Just recently I have been reading in Sartre's *Being and Nothingness* with some students, and, wonder of wonders, I found myself gaining from that unlikely source insights about how I might respond to the Ford/Kline interpretation. I hasten to note that I have no intention of defending a Sartrean position in this paper; to the contrary, some of the insights I will draw upon emerged as I read criticisms of Sartre advanced by Marjorie Grene in her book, *Sartre*. What has struck me, though, as I have pursued these ideas, is the fact that the more one thinks Whitehead and Sartre together, the more interesting the fruits of their juxtapositioning become. Finally, the line from Villon sprang to mind not only because I have been thinking in a Gallic mode, but because, having just recently arrived for a working vacation in Florida in a rare snow and ice storm, I now find myself looking out over a warm sandy beach to the ocean beyond deeply grateful that wherever those snows of yesterweek may be, they most assuredly are not here and now.

Ford and Kline have torn apart being and becoming[1] whereas I believe that, considered from within the process perspective, they are most happily viewed as one. Ford and Kline wish to say that an actual entity enjoys its process of becoming, the becoming runs its course, and then the actual entity acquires the status of being, which persists for a long time in some cases, and not so long in others. In contrast, I hold that an actual entity's becoming *is* its being, and that when the one perishes, so does the other. The whole point of the process point of view, it seems to me, is to insist that *ousia*, that which is, being, is process, becoming, and not an enduring, persisting, substantial substrate. Another way of getting at what I perceive to be the difference between the Ford/Kline position and my own is to consider the title of Whitehead's magnum opus, *Process and Reality*. Is there a redundancy in the title or not? Bradley's famous title, *Appearance and Reality*, clearly does not involve a redundancy—Bradley is most assuredly out to separate appearance, on the one hand, from reality, on the other. Is Whitehead doing the same thing in his title, as persons influenced by the Ford/Kline arguments have suggested? I think not. Rather, Whitehead, who is, for starters, totally opposed to Bradley's distinction between appearance and reality, seems to me to be (probably deliberately) building that opposition into his own title. I understand Whitehead's title to be an emphatic statement of his commitment to the intuition that reality *is* process and that process *is* reality. On this view, it makes no sense to claim that once the becoming of an actual entity is finished, once it achieves its satisfaction, then it enters upon its being and continues to exist in this mode for a shorter or longer time depending on the scope of its impact down through the years or ages, as the case may be.

Now wait a minute, one might well say. Surely, it might seem, on a question such as this Whitehead must have unambiguously tipped his hand, must have clearly articulated his position. So why, it seems natural to ask, would anyone propose to run off to the concepts of someone as un-Whiteheadian as Sartre in order to cast light on what Whitehead meant in the very title of his most famous book? Alas, Whitehead was not asking just the sorts of questions about the past that many of us want to ask now, and when he did write around in the neighborhood of these sorts of questions, his words take on a frustrating ambiguity. There is no more vivid example of this exasperating ambiguity than the wording of Category of Explanation ix: "That *how* an actual entity *becomes* constitutes *what* that actual entity *is*; so that the two descriptions of an actual entity are not independent. Its 'being' is constituted by its 'becoming.' This is the 'principle of process'."[2] That word 'constituted' in the penultimate sentence has been the focus of a good deal of debate. On the face of it, it seems clear to me that this ninth Category of Explanation, presenting the principle of process, makes my case, but the Ford/Kline axis hastens to point out the ambiguity of 'constituted.' It can mean to make up, to form or compose—this is the way I would naturally read the word, giving the conclusion that Whitehead is presenting being and becoming here as identical. My opponents read the word 'constitute' in a different sense, the sense of establishing, setting up, founding. This is a perfectly legitimate dictionary meaning of the word (as is, I hasten to add, the meaning I would prefer to give it). Given this second sense of 'constitute,' the Ford/Kline camp gleefully asserts that what Whitehead is saying in his ninth Category of Explanation is that becoming sets up, shapes, founds that which comes later, namely being. Here we seem to have reached an impasse.

This impasse is very real—it seems to be the case that whatever further evidence either side hauls out of the text to buttress its understanding of the proper way of reading 'constituted,' the other side finds a way of interpreting the new evidence as either supporting, or at least not threatening, its reading.[3] Given this standoff, the tactical move of David Hume, to beat around a bit in the bushes lining neighboring fields in hopes of stirring up new game, doesn't sound like such a bad idea. Sartre's phenomenological analyses may not sound like a very close "neighboring field," but the possibility that there is new game there will hopefully justify the journey.

First, more about the Ford/Kline interpretation of being, for it is here that contact with the ideas of Sartre will first occur. As Ford sees it, the extent of the persistence of the being of an actual entity is a contingent matter. Something continues in its being as long as it continues to be taken into account by actually concrescing actual occasions. As its connectedness to the actual, concrescing present becomes more and more tenuous, the being of that something becomes more and more tenuous—finally, when all connectedness to the present vanishes, so, too, vanishes the being of that something. Cleopatra and Napoleon continue in being, whereas the being of, respectively, their handmaidens and manservants has slid over the horizon, has perished, has vanished into nothingness.

Traditional understandings about the notion of being are engaged here. Since the time of Plato philosophers have recognized the idea that the hallmark of being is to be effective in some way or other. The Ford/Kline orientation clearly plays to that traditional understanding. There is also a legacy from the Greeks, from Parmenides as well as Plato, that being is unchanging. Again, the Ford/Kline position makes contact with that dimension of the tradition, for it is very clear that Whitehead insists that once an actual entity has completed its concrescence, its becoming, its decision making, its process is over, used up, finished, passed by, never to reappear. This same tradition, however, carries with it the conviction that being is more perfect that becoming, that it is the domain of the real as opposed to the domain of appearance, the locus of value, the natural domain of rational activity. These features of the tradition ought to make adherents of the Ford/Kline position a bit uneasy, as these are all features or factors which it is clear Whitehead associates with becoming, process, immediacy, subjectivity. However, arguing out the issues regarding the past in these terms is very difficult, very slippery, very tricky, and probably as inconclusive as the debates surrounding the word 'constituted.' So on to Sartre and *Being and Nothingness*.

I hear very strong echoes of the Ford/Kline position in the following passage from Sartre:

> Today I alone am responsible for the being of the dead Pierre, I in my freedom. Those dead who have not been able to be saved and transported to the boundaries of the concrete past of a survivor are not *past*; they along with their pasts are annihilated.[4]

Note that Sartre is speaking of the "being" of the dead Pierre, just as Ford would speak of the being of Napoleon or Cleopatra. Pierre, Napoleon, and Cleopatra are past beings because they lie within the boundaries of the concrete past of at least one survivor; those handmaidens and manservants, alas, have fallen outside the boundaries of the concrete past of any and all survivors, and hence they have been annihilated. (This appeal to the concept of annihilation puts one in mind of Whitehead's observation that "...in separation from actual entities there is nothing, merely nonentity—'The rest is silence.'"[5])

Now that we have seen that there is a certain similarity between the way that Sartre speaks about the past and the way that the Ford/Kline interpretation leads one to speak about the past, we need to say just a brief word about the conceptuality that leads Sartre to his way of speaking. If it should turn out that the conceptuality that leads to Sartre's way of speaking is wildly at odds with the Whiteheadian conceptuality, then it might be that the point of difference is just that "neighboring field" in which we can scare up some game.

Sartre's discussion of the past centers around his notion of the for-itself. Part II of BN is titled "Being-for-Itself" and the first chapter of part II is titled "Immediate Structures of the For-itself." The second chapter, from which our Pierre quote comes, provides a deepening of our understanding of the for-itself by exploring its relation to the temporal dimensions. *For-itself* is Sartre's term for conscious human being. Consciousness is a "no-thing," a nothingness. As a "decompression" from the infinite density of being-in-itself, being-for-itself is a hole in being, detached, a lack that experiences itself as a freedom. Expressed in temporal terms, for-itself is, to use Heidegger's expression, "out-ahead-of-itself-being." That consciousness, that nothingness, that lack, that freedom experiences itself from within a temporal thickness where its own being lags behind it, never quite catching up with it, which is why Sartre can say that the being of consciousness is not what it is and is what it is not.

This temporal structure radiates out from consciousness, from nothingness. Being-in-itself, infinitely dense material stuff, does not admit of temporal structures. "These observations enable us to refuse a priori to grant a past to the in-self..."[6] Temporality is indissolvably linked to the for-itself; "We have seen that the Past is an ontological law of the For-itself..."[7] This is the context within which Sartre and other phenomenologists employ the concept, "horizon." Past and future spread out as horizons for the for-itself which I am. The dead Pierre still lies within the horizon of my past; when he slides over that horizon Pierre is "annihilated."

I have long been perplexed by a nagging question that arises for me out of this horizon talk: Can one take this horizon talk seriously and still take evolution seriously? I mean, *really* take evolution seriously? What happens to the conviction which is an integral part of the modern world that there was a time, about which we know a great deal, before consciousness arrived on the evolutionary scene? I recall that Teillard de Chardin, in *The Phenomenon of Man*, wrote something to the effect that it was from now on impossible to philosophize seriously without keeping the theory of evolution constantly in mind. I agree with this observation wholeheartedly. I have the very uneasy feeling when I hear the continental talk of "horizons" that evolution has slipped out of the picture. When I ask existentialists or phenomenologists about evolution, I get what seems to me to be an unsatisfactory, evasive response, a response that says, "Evolution, oh sure, but when you consider evolution you are always considering it from within the horizon of your own immediate experience." Well yes, but no! Of course evolution, and all those fossils, and all those DNA mappings are grasped and understood by human beings, but that thinking and those understandings are, for me, filtered through the strong, uncompromising realism of Whitehead's ground-floor metaphysical instincts. For me, evolution is no complex of structures within the horizon of human experience but, rather, a window out on to a wider reality of which human being is a part and to which human being is attached, but which transcends human being as assuredly as France transcends Paris.

This is something like the point made by Marjorie Grene in her very astute study, *Sartre*.[8] Grene's book is most insightfully faithful to the spirit and meaning of Sartre's texts, an achievement quite remarkable for one who nevertheless has serious reservations about the starting assumption of the whole Sartrean project. That starting point is the Cartesian starting point. Concerning Sartre, Grene writes:

> He is the ultimate and most consequent Cartesian, carrying what remains of the Cartesian either-or to its terrifying logical conclusion. We have seen how he does this by weaving together phenomenological *motifs* with dialectical methods, but always on the strict conceptual ground of Cartesian consciousness, Cartesian freedom, and Cartesian time. Thus, it is that the Sartre of *Being and Nothingness* and even, in a way, of the *Critique*, represents for us the 'tragic finale' of a tradition initiated in the seventeenth century—the tradi-

tion that conceived of a pure, and purely rational, center of conscious activity seeking to control a purely passive material world.[9]

When Grene turns to her sharpest criticism of that starting point,[10] she zeroes in on the notion of the prereflective *cogito*: "This prereflective *cogito*, then, is the condition of the Cartesian *cogito*, as of every *cogitatio*. It is [for Sartre] the absolute beginning of philosophy."[11] It is precisely here, at the stage of the analysis of this prereflective, nonthetic, nonpositional consciousness, that, in Grene's view, Sartre has made his fatal error. Grene's analysis is subtle and complex; the heart of her critique is the claim that Sartre is in error when he insists that it is a necessary condition of prereflective consciousness that it be conscious of being conscious of whatever it knows. Sartre insists that:

> The necessary and sufficient condition for a knowing consciousness to be knowledge *of* its object is that it be *conscious of itself* as being that knowledge. This is a necessary condition, for if my consciousness were not consciousness of being consciousness of the table, it would then be consciousness of that table without consciousness of being so. In other words, it would be a consciousness ignorant of itself, an unconscious—which is absurd.[12]

Is an unconscious an absurd notion? Freud certainly did not think so, and Sartre's assumptions in his argument in BN with Freud on this point (90–94) can certainly be challenged. The notion of "consciousness that is not conscious of being conscious of X" does not seem to be quite the same as the notion of "an unconscious consciousness." Grene makes this point as follows:

> Nor is forgetting myself in my concentration on what, *via* the nonthetic, I seek to posit, to be identified with unconsciousness. Quite the contrary: the outward thrust of subsidiary awareness is the very transcendence of self that makes intentionality possible.
> Why does Sartre fail to see this? Why does he argue that a nonself-conscious consciousness would be unconscious? Clearly because for him, in *Being and Nothingness* as already in the *Emotions*, the *cogito* has been taken as the unique and indispensable starting point of all philosophy.... In moving the content of consciousness out into the world, Sartre has nevertheless retained the Cartesian thesis that the first unique moment of thought must be thinking about thinking: consciousness, to be consciousness, must be self-directed and self-contained.[13]

Grene's repudiation of Sartre's fundamental assumption has its roots, not in

Whitehead, but in Michael Polanyi. Following Polanyi, she denies that all cognitive consciousness is thetic; rather, she believes that it is "the case that there is always a nonthetic foundation, a foundation of what Michael Polanyi calls subsidiary awareness, at the root of even the most plainly intuitive, positional (or, in Polanyi's language, focal) awareness of an object."[14] Grene's conclusion is that such:

> Non-thetic consciousness is essential, not only to the being of the for-itself, but to knowledge—that is, to the relation of the for-itself and the in-itself. It is not prereflectively reflexive, but outward directed; it directs the for-itself toward the in-itself. To see this, however, would have meant for Sartre a radical denial of his Cartesian starting point. And then he would not be Sartre.[15]

We have done a considerable amount of beating around in our neighboring field, but at last we are in sight of our prey. What emerges from all this is an appreciation of the stark contrast between the position of Sartre and the alternatives offered by a Polanyi or a Whitehead—Sartre begins with the *cogito*; they begin with relatedness. Grene's nonthetic foundation, Polanyi's subsidiary awareness, and Whitehead's prehensive relationship are all three, alike, ways of abandoning Sartre's Cartesian starting point. Whitehead could be just as well gently mocking the Cartesians and the post-Hegelian British idealists as Kant when he wryly observes that Kant was "led to balance the world upon thought—oblivious to the scanty supply of thinking."[16]

Now back to the Ford/Kline account of the past, back to Cleopatra, Napoleon, the dead Pierre, and those handmaidens and manservants. Given his starting point, Sartre is locked into his account of "the being of the dead Pierre"—"being," to begin with, is "back there" as opposed to the nothingness of the present for-itself, and further, "the being of the dead Pierre" is suspended in its being only by the present nihilating Sartre, who is "responsible for" it. However, abandon that Cartesian starting point, and abandon it in the particular way that Whitehead does, and everything changes. Consciousness no longer supports the past; rather, it blossoms out of a prior ground that supports *it*. As Whitehead writes, "For Kant, the world emerges from the subject; for the philosophy of organism, the subject emerges from the world...."[17] This relationship implies that "consciousness is the crown of experience, only occasionally attained, not its necessary base."[18] From a Whiteheadian perspective that ground in the past from which consciousness arises, which supports and generates consciousness, enjoys its ontological fullness quite apart from, quite independent of, the consciousness to which it gives rise. To suggest that that ground in the past is dependent *in its being* on the persisting presence of its conscious entertainment is simply to fly in the face of those doctrines at the very heart of Whitehead's reorientation of the Cartesian subjectivism. So yes, I am aware of the stories of Cleopatra and Napoleon, and yes, their handmaidens and manservants, however, have been lost in the haze of temporal and historical indistinctness. Can that mean that Cleopatra and Napoleon enjoy an ontological status now lost by the hired help? In the context of Sartre's account, his entire analysis of being and nonbeing demands the answer, "Yes!" In the context of Whitehead's account, to give a different ontological status to the historical "principals" on the one hand, and the historical "extras" on the other, makes no sense at all.

What have I done here? I certainly have not provided anything like a coercive proof of the position I hold. I have argued that the Ford/Kline interpretation has a striking similarity to the position of Sartre concerning this business of the being of past entities; I have then exposed the fundamental philosophical assumptions that lead to the Sartrean position; finally I have shown that Whitehead's fundamental assumptions are diametrically at odds with those assumptions which lead to the Sartrean viewpoint. Thinking of the issue in terms of these relationships opens one up, I hope and believe, to my reading of Whitehead's account of being, becoming, and the past. That reading is as follows. Each generation of actual entities pours the structures of its completed satisfactions into the subsequent generation of emerging, becoming occasions. The wrapping up of its own process of becoming marks the perishing, the death, of each actual entity. "In this process the creativity, universal throughout actuality, is characterized by the datum from the past; and its meets *this dead datum*..."[19] In perishing, each actual entity is also objectively immortal in that it has poured the structure of its completed satisfaction into the generation of actual entities that supersedes it. So Napoleon has indeed perished and gone—dead. Yet he is objectively immortal in that the structure of his life impinged upon what followed it. Those manservants are on a complete ontological par with their master—they also have perished and gone, and yet they are objectively immortal in precisely the sense that Napoleon is, namely, the structures of their lives impinged upon what followed them in precisely the same metaphysical manner as did the structures of the life of Napoleon. The "width" and/or the "depth of persistence" of that influence can vary greatly—and in the case of Napoleon and his manservants they obviously do—but the ontological significance of this width and persistence is, in the case of Whitehead (unlike that of Sartre), absolutely nil. How puzzling, then, it is that any Whiteheadians would want to maintain, as does Ford especially, that Napoleon persists in his being while those inglorious manservants have receded into nonbeing. Sartre can maintain that distinction; for a Whiteheadian it makes no sense!

* * *

A gloriously warm Florida January has swiftly passed as I have alternately sketched out this article and done Florida-type things. Those unusual snows of late December, like Napoleon, have perished, gone—though their effects on the citrus crop linger on. As I depart now for a February, March, April, and May at Carleton College in Minnesota, I know I will encounter many snows in the months ahead. Whichever of the twenty-eight varieties of snow that the Eskimos distinguish they may be,[20] of one thing I am quite confident: *les neiges d'antan* do not lie in wait for me there, or anywhere else, for *they be not*.

NOTES

1. Ford and Kline have edited a collection of essays in which each has a contribution which argues the position in question. The book is titled *Explorations in Whitehead's Philosophy* (New York: Fordham University Press, 1983). Kline's article is entitled "Form, Concrescence, and Concretum," and Ford's views are most clearly presented in the final essay in the book, titled "Afterword," especially pages 318-331.

2. PR 23 [34-35].

3. I will cite just a few of these examples. In his seminal study, *Whitehead's Metaphysics: An Introductory Exposition* (London: G. Allen and Unwin, 1958), 69, Ivor Leclerc quotes the following passage from Whitehead's *Modes of Thought*, 131: "...that 'existence' (in any of its senses) cannot be abstracted from 'process.' The notions of 'process' and 'existence' presuppose each other." This sounds rather convincing to me, and Ford is clearly aware of the passage—he refers, in the essay I have identified in endnote 1, to Leclerc's use of the passage, but promptly denies it any significance. Here is another passage which occurs a few pages from the end of chapter 4 in Whitehead's earlier book, *Science and the Modern World*: "Thus nature is a structure of evolving processes. The reality is the process." Now that statement seems to me to be very close to conclusive evidence for my point of view. Ford knows the passage well, but with his fixation on the genetic analysis of the composition of Whitehead's works, he can shrug off the passage as an early, imprecise statement. One final example: in a short piece titled "Whitehead as I Knew Him," published in Kline's early collection of essays, *Alfred North Whitehead, Essays on His Philosophy* (Englewood Cliffs: Prentice-Hall, 1963), 8, William Ernest Hocking quotes Whitehead as having said, "Reality is becoming; it is passing before one—a remark too obvious to make.... You can't catch a moment by the scruff of the neck—*it's gone*, you know." (Italics in the text.) I happen to think that by "gone" Whitehead really meant gone!

4. J. P. Sartre, *Being and Nothingness* (New York: Washington Square Press, 1966), part II, chap. 2 ("Temporality"), 166, of the standard Hazel Barnes translation. All future quotes from *Being and Nothingness* will be identified by BN and page number.

5. PR 43 [68].

6. BN 167.

7. BN 175.

8. Marjorie Grene, *Sartre* (New York: New Viewpoints, 1973).

9. *Sartre*, 268.

10. Cf. *Sartre*, 119–123, 136

11. *Sartre*, 122.

12. BN 11.

13. *Sartre*, 121.

14. *Sartre*, 120–121.

15. *Sartre*, 136.

16. PR 151 [229].

17. PR 88 [135–136].

18. PR 267 [408].

19. PR 164 [249], italics added.

20. Since arriving in Minnesota I have read an amusing and persuasive piece by Geoffrey K. Pullum in *Natural Language & Linguistic Theory* 7, no. 2 (May 1989) titled "The Great Eskimo Vocabulary Hoax." Pullum holds that the widely disseminated view that there are many words in Eskimo for snow is a myth, a myth for which questionable scholarship on the part of Benjamin Lee Worf, among others, is largely responsible. The conclusive

evidence for Pullum's view point is found in an article by Laura Martin titled "'Eskimo Words for Snow': A Case Study in the Genesis and Decay of an Anthropological Example," *American Anthropologist* 88, no. 2 (June 1986): 418–423. I am a bit disappointed with the imagination of Eskimos, but join with Pullum and Martin in the campaign to dampen down this fascinating falsehood.

7
Perfecting the Ontological Principle

Lewis S. Ford

Perhaps the most influential version of the ontological principle is one proposed by Ivor Leclerc in the second chapter of *Whitehead's Metaphysics: An Introductory Exposition*.[1] By showing the generality of 'entity' and of 'actual entity' to refer quite impartially to many different metaphysical systems, Leclerc demonstrates the power of the ontological principle quite apart from its special meaning for Whitehead, while at the same time showing its centrality to Whitehead's endeavor. We do not wish to challenge its essential truth which we find to be largely correct, but we do wonder whether Leclerc's account is really an interpretation of Whitehead's own formulation, or more a modification thereof. Moreover, if it is a modification, the way may be open to modifying it still further in the interests of obtaining still greater coherence, as I hope to show in the final section.

I

Leclerc introduces the ontological principle by way of the distinction between primary and second being in Aristotle's metaphysics. Primary beings, substances, exist in the fullest sense of the term, while all other entities are secondary, deriving their existence from their dependence on primary beings. Whitehead's primary beings are actual entities, not enduring substances, but otherwise this same principle is adopted: "The general Aristotelian principle is maintained that, apart from the things that are actual, there is nothing—nothing either in fact or in efficacy" (*f1*).[2] This general Aristotelian principle is then identified with the ontological principle, even though it may be only a corollary thereof. Then, under the influence of Aristotle that acting is a generic feature of actuality, Leclerc argues that "Whitehead identified 'being' and 'acting'; an *actual* entity is an *acting* entity" (WM 85f; cf also 70, 100, 107), such that past actualities "are, in the strict sense, no longer 'actual'" (WM 101). This paves the way for Leclerc's distinctive formulation: "by the ontological principle, an 'entity' can exist only

122

either as itself 'actual' (i.e.acting), *or* as implicated in the activity of some actuality" (WM 102).

In section 3, I shall propose as my version of the ontological principle: "all being is derivative from becoming." In the first place this substitutes 'becoming' for 'acting' where Leclerc has the existence of all entities derivative from 'acting.' Leclerc presumably would not accept this substitution, however, for he understands the principle of process to identify becoming with (a part of) being, whereas I follow Jorge Nobo in interpreting the principle that "its 'being' is constituted by its 'becoming'" (PR 23 [34f]) to mean that its being is produced by its becoming (PS 4:275-84). Becoming 'constitutes' being in the sense that concrescence results in being or satisfaction as its outcome, not in the sense that (primary) being is identified with becoming (so WM 69f, 71).

To be sure, if we identify primary being with that upon which all other entities depend, as in Aristotle, then a good case can be made for identifying it with the individual acts of concrescence. I suspect that Aristotle's distinction between primary and secondary being is foreign to Whitehead's conceptuality. First we must determine: which is primary, being or becoming? The tradition has overwhelmingly endorsed the former. The thrust of Whitehead's philosophy is towards the latter: all actual beings (past occasions as objectified) are the result of concrescence, the way beings come to be. Or, bearing in mind the traditional convertibility of being and unity, just as all composite unity results from unification, being results (and is derivative) from becoming.

Yet Whitehead never formulated his philosophy in this way. His own version of the ontological principle cannot be used for this purpose, for two reasons: (a) Whitehead proposed a different meaning of 'actuality' than that employed by Leclerc, and (b) he had other purposes for this principle which he never finally repudiated (at least in PR), which depend on past actualities, and not simply upon present, acting entities.

(a) Traditionally, 'actual' has been given two different meanings: (i) 'acting' (as in Aristotle) and (ii) 'concrete determinateness.' Whitehead may have found a way of unifying these two meanings in the notion of 'decision.' Deciding is a form of activity accomplished in concrescence, where the outcome of this finite activity is concrete determinateness. These can thus be conceived as the two temporal aspects, past and present, of actuality, embraced by the same term, 'decision.' While this may not have been immediately Whitehead's intention,[3] the specification of actuality by 'decision' could have led to this conclusion: "Just as 'potentiality for process' is the meaning of the more general term 'entity' or 'thing'; so 'decision' is the additional meaning imported by the word 'actual' into the phrase 'actual entity.' 'Actuality' is the decision amid 'potentiality'" (PR 43 [68]). Actual entities, both present and past, are equally decisive and hence actual. In other uses, perhaps, they cannot be actual any longer when past, but not according to Whitehead's use of the terms.

On this understanding of 'actuality' we cannot identify 'actuality' with that which primarily exists, if that means what is presently acting or concrescing. For this would not be true of past or objectified actualities.[4]

(b) The ontological principle in Whitehead's hands is not simply the principle that all other entities are dependent for their existence upon presently concrescing actual entities. It is also a principle of explanation concerning the origin and constitution of an actual entity. This comes out more clearly in an earlier formulation which Whitehead presented to his Harvard class in October 1927: "That every condition to which a process of becoming conforms in any particular instance has its *reason* in the character of some actual entity whose objectification is one of the components entering into the particular instance in question (the ontological principle—or principle of extrinsic reference)" *(c1)*.[5]

If this were Whitehead's sole formulation of the ontological principle, there would be no basis for Leclerc's reference to *acting* entities because it only appeals to objectified determinate actualities. However, the ontological principle has many different formulations as the principle developed.

The principle of extrinsic reference (as I shall call this early formulation) is perhaps best understood as Whitehead's version of the principle of sufficient reason. This principle has become indelibly associated with Leibniz's metaphysics, which assumes that all actualities are created in every detail by God, and that God always acts for the best. In such an economy each actuality is what it is in accordance with some reason why it is so and not otherwise. In Whitehead's early philosophy, the reason why the objective constitution of an actuality is so and not otherwise is to be found rather in the actualities of the past actual world. They, and not God, comprise the decisions for it, for it is merely the synthesis of these reasons. "'Decision' cannot be construed as a casual adjunct of an actual entity. It constitutes the very meaning of actuality. An actual entity arises from decisions *for* it, and by its existence provides decisions for other actual entities which supersede it" (PR 43 [68]).

The principle of extrinsic reference differs verbally in several details from the precise formulation of the eighteenth category of explanation, but substantially in just one respect: the latter formulation locates the reasons for things *also* "in the character of the subject which is in process of concrescence" *(i2)*. In other words, it grounds reasons in acting entities as well as in those which no longer act. Without this added proviso Leclerc's interpretation of the ontological principle in terms of acting entities would not have been possible.

Whitehead had called the principle of extrinsic reference an ontological principle because the reasons vested in past actualities, when fused with the creative activity of unification, call concrescent actualities into being. At this point 'decision' is seen only extrinsically. When Whitehead comes to formulate the final ontological principle, it is a principle of extrinsic and intrinsic reference, for the self-decision of the concrescing occasion now becomes a reason for its very being. At this juncture Whitehead's theory becomes existential.

Between the principle of extrinsic reference (*c1*) and the final formulation (*i3*), there are several variations. For example, when Whitehead reconceived God as the nontemporal concrescence of all eternal objects (*f1*), he found a way to ground the unrealized ones in God's experience, a matter which had proved difficult as long as God was conceived as a pure impersonal principle, as God seems to have been conceived up to this time.[6] This shift also made it possible to reconceive 'actuality' as concrescence instead of as 'decision' because the nontemporal actuality was now a concrescence. This prompted a reformulation of the ontological principle in order to express the intrinsic relation between reasons and actualities: "The ontological principle can be expressed as: All real togetherness is togetherness in the formal constitution of an actuality" (PR 32 [48]). This position is also reflected in the formulation of the [revised] subjectivist principle, "that the whole universe consists of elements disclosed in the analysis of the experiences of subjects" which is expressly identified with the ontological principle (PR 166 [252]).

What is not clear from this formulation is whether past actualities also function as reasons. Perhaps Whitehead left the issue deliberately open. In any case, the final formulation of the ontological principle combines this reinterpretation with the extrinsic principle such that both presently concrescing and past actualities serve as reasons.

Whitehead usually refers to "the ontological principle" as if a single principle, such as the general Aristotelian principle, were meant, or as if a single definite formulation were intended. This can be misleading because the principle of extrinsic reference, and not its final formulation, was the way the ontological principle was specified in October 1927. This means that anything written prior to that date and preserved in the final version of *Process and Reality* that referred to "the ontological principle," originally meant that restricted principle. By my calculations this included what I call "the Giffords draft," the nine and half chapters he had drafted that summer for the ten Gifford lectures he was to give in June 1928.[7] This may comprise as much as two hundred pages of *Process and Reality*.

Thus, in order to fully appreciate the role of the ontological principle as it developed in Whitehead's hands, we need to examine its various formulations *seriatem*, arranged as much as possible according to their probable order of composition. Then we shall be in a position to reflect on some possible ways of extending the Whiteheadian trajectory further. After briefly summarizing the findings of the compositional analysis I will speculate about generalizing the principle to apply not only to actualities but to all entities.

II

THE ONTOLOGICAL PRINCIPLE AS FIRST FORMULATED

The first explicit mention of our principle antedates *Process and Reality* and may be found as the fourth of six metaphysical principles presented to his students at Harvard in the fall of 1926:

> *a1*. The ontological principle. The character of creativity is derived from its own creatures and expressed by its own creatures. (EWM 313)

This is clearly *an* ontological principle, although it is not yet recognizable as Whitehead's mature principle. It derives from his earlier monism in *Science and the Modern World*, where events are conceived as modes or spatiotemporal portions of the underlying substantial activity. In *Religion in the Making* actual occasions become the final reality, while the underlying substantial activity is reconceived as creativity, one of the formative elements of these occasions. Creativity in its concrete form is then to be explained in terms of these entities more actual than itself. In itself creativity has no character. "It is only then capable of characterization through its accidental embodiments, and apart from these accidents is devoid of actuality" (PR 7 [10f] *C*).

AS FIRST MENTIONED IN PROCESS AND REALITY

Though "The Categoreal Scheme" (PR I.2)[8] seems to come from several different compositional strata, some quite late, the following passage may well be Whitehead's first mention of the ontological principle:

> *b1*. The ontological principle broadens and extends John Locke's notion of power by transforming it into the notion that the reasons for things are always to be found in the composite nature of definite actual entities—in the nature of God for reasons of the highest absoluteness, and in the nature of definite temporal actual entities for reasons which refer to a particular environment. The ontological principle can be summarized as: no actual entity, then no reason. (PR 18f [27])

So *b1* restates *a1* in a more general form because it refers not merely to "creativity" but to "things"—things whether actual or nonactual.

By "reasons of the highest absoluteness" Whitehead apparently means the way in which God as the principle of limitation determines what is actualizable, while particular reasons are based on contingent experience. By *a*, the character of creativity is expressed by its own creatures, God being the supreme creature (EWM 313); therefore, God expresses himself by the principle of efficient causation, contributing "to the character of processes" superseding itself. God's contribution is general, effecting the metaphysical limitation, while particular occasions contribute particular characteristics. Thus, in the light of this situation, why some particular occasion has the characteristics it does can be attributed to the character of actualities lying in its past.

By concentrating on the reasons why things are, Whitehead transforms what has been a principle concerning ontological grounding in creativity into something approaching Leibniz' principle of sufficient reason as transposed on a more pluralistic basis (thereby allowing for interaction). Now *b1* may well be the earliest formulation of the ontological principle in *Process and Reality*, one which finds its canonical expression in the following statement Whitehead gave to his Harvard students during October 1927:

THE PRINCIPLE OF EXTRINSIC REFERENCE

> *c1*. That every condition to which a process of becoming conforms in any particular instance has its *reason* in the character of some actual entity whose objectification is one of the components entering into the particular instance in question (the ontological principle—or principle of extrinsic reference). (EWM 323f)

We have already seen that this principle is not yet sufficiently generalized to apply to acting entities. To be sure, this limited version is nowhere explicitly mentioned in *Process and Reality* either. Yet it governed Whitehead's thinking for a long time while formulating his system, and laid behind his references to "the ontological principle" during the composition of the Giffords Draft. Thus, we see it as implicit in all of Whitehead's earlier references (*c-d*).

Because the mature Whitehead places the primary ontological weight on concrescence (as reflected in Leclerc's concern for acting entities), it is instructive to see why there is no mention of the coming into being of an actuality in *c1*. There is a major shift in Whitehead's thinking during the composition of *Process and Reality*, after which Whitehead identifies (positive) feelings with prehensions, conceiving of concrescence as the unification of many physical feelings. Apart from that unification the occasion has no being of its own, only the beings of the many it prehends. Thus, concrescence comes to be conceived as becoming in the sense of the coming into being of a new actuality: the becoming produces the being. Beforehand, that shift intensifying the meaning of becoming, the concrescence was assumed to be a being, although a very dynamic being.[9]

Thus, in his earlier formulations in *Science and the Modern World*, process is the reality (put in other terms, becoming is being), whereas in *Process and Reality* these are contrastive terms. Earlier an occasion was conceived to be a portion of the underlying substantial activity, a bit of process conceived as being. Reasons would be grounded in this being-process, which is accessible to supervening occasions in terms of its objectifications. For it is by means of their prehensive relations of other's objectifications that occasions are what they are. Those past actualities form its reasons.

Other statements which may depend only upon this restricted version of the ontological principle are:

> c2. The two doctrines [of the 'ingression' of eternal objects into actual entities, and of the 'objectification' of actual entities] cannot be explained apart from each other: they constitute explanations of two fundamental principles—the ontological principle and the principle of relativity. (PR 149 [226f])

Eternal objects are ingredient in actualities because they cannot exist apart from them, and any actuality is objectified, i.e. available for being part of any supervening concrescence because this is a feature of all entities. Here, the two principles are intimately associated, as in another statement:

> c3. The ontological principle, and the wider doctrine of universal relativity...blur the sharp distinction between what is universal and what is particular. (PR 48 [76])

No reference, however, to the internal concrescence of any occasion is called for in either principle. Here actuality is explained, not in terms of concrescence, but composition. This allows actuality to pertain to the composite, whether or not it is the outcome of concrescence.

> c4. In the philosophy of organism it is assumed that an actual entity is composite. 'Actuality' is the fundamental exemplification of composition; all other meanings of 'composition' are referent to this root-meaning. But 'actuality' is a general term, which merely indicates this ultimate type of composite unity: there are many composite unities to which this general term applies. There is no general

fact of composition, not expressible in terms of the composite constitutions of the individual occasions. (PR 147 [223])

(This passage comes from the same section of text as *c2*. It does not mention the ontological principle, but it is directly followed by *d3* and *d1*, which do.)

Whitehead also defined 'actuality' in terms of [objective] 'decision', thereby allowing the primordial decision which functioned as the principle of concretion or limitation also to be actual, even though it was not yet conceived as concrescent. 'Decision' for Whitehead did not have the subjective sense of 'deciding' until after God also was conceived as concrescent.

c5. The ontological principle declares that every decision is referable to one or more actual entities, because in separation from actual entities there is nothing, merely nonentity—"The rest is silence."(PR 43 [68.16])[10]

This passage will be explicitly qualified by a later insertion (*f2*). The final turn of phrase anticipates the way Whitehead later formulates the revised subjectivist principle: "Finally, the revised subjectivist principle must be repeated: that apart from the experiences of subjects there is nothing, nothing, nothing, bare nothingness" (PR 167 [254]). (See *i*.)

In the earlier texts, reasons are implicitly restricted to the outcomes of compositional process and not extended to the processes themselves:

c6. But according to the ontological principle... a reason is always a reference to *determinate* actual entities. (PR 256.32 [391]: III, chap. 4, sec. 1; emphasis added)

(This quotation is from part III of *Process and Reality*, but there is strong evidence that at least part of the chapter on propositional feelings (part III, chap. 4)was composed in conjunction with the Giffords Draft. At any rate, *c6* antedates the augmented version of the ontological principle (*i2*) because it restricts reasons to *determinate* actualities, implicitly excluding actualities in process of determination.)

ANTICIPATIONS OF THE DOCTRINE THAT "EVERYTHING MUST BE SOMEWHERE"

If actual entities are the only reasons, then whatever is can be referred to some particular actuality. Each actual entity is constituted out of its particular past actual world; therefore, its situation vis-à-vis that world and its constitution are intimately associated. "In other words the actual entity, in virtue of being *what* it is, is also *where* it is. It is somewhere because it is some actual thing with its correlated actual world" (PR 59 [93]C); *d1* and *d2* apply this idea solely to actual entities, although it is soon to be applied to other entities.

> *d1.* It follows from the ontological principle, thus interpreted, that the notion of a 'common world' must find its exemplification in the constitution of each actual entity.... For an actual entity cannot be a member of a 'common world, except in the sense that the 'common world' is a constituent of its own constitution. It follows that every item in the universe, including all the other actual entities, is a constituent in the constitution of any one actual entity. (PR 148 [224] C) [follows upon *c4* and *d3*]

> *d2.* This amounts to the assumption that each actual entity is a locus for the universe. (PR 80 [123])

It is extended also to propositions, but not yet to eternal objects, probably because of uncertainty with respect to unrealized ones:

> *d3.* Every proposition is entertained in the constitution of some one actual entity, or severally in the constitutions of many actual entities. This is only another rendering of the ontological principle. (PR 147f [223f]) [forms the beginning of *d1*.]

> *d4.* In a proposition the various logical subjects involved are impartially concerned. The proposition is no more about one logical subject than another logical subject. But according to the ontological principle, every proposition must be somewhere. The 'locus' of a proposition consists of those actual occasions whose actual worlds include the logical subjects of the proposition. (PR 186 [283] C)

Later, Whitehead generalizes and deepens the meaning of this principle: see *g, f1, h2,* and *i2*.

A TRANSITIONAL PASSAGE

All of the passages cited previously belong, by my reckoning, to what Whitehead wrote through the summer of 1927, when he conceived concrescence as originating from a unified datum (EWM 177–210, esp.189–91). See, for example, the discussion of 'datum' in the systematic contrast of "datum, process, satisfaction, decision" (PR 150f [227f]C). With part III of *Process and Reality* Whitehead launches a new conception of concrescence as initiating from a multiplicity of simple physical feelings (EWM 211–217). This is achieved in part by correlating the feelings initially devised in the Giffords draft as applying solely within concrescence with the extraconcrescent prehensions (of SMW). Some prehensions cannot be identified with feelings, however, so Whitehead introduces the distinction between positive and negative prehensions so that only positive prehensions can be regarded as feelings.

Whitehead proposes six factors in all which explain the importance of negative prehension, but only the second need concern us here:

> *e*. (2) that by the ontological principle every entity is felt by some actual entity. (PR 41 [66] *D* in II.1.1 *C*)[11]

In context, Whitehead is concerned with past actualities, using the principle of negative prehension to achieve perspectival elimination. The principle is formulated more generally; not only 'every actuality' (so *d1*) but 'every entity' is felt. This formulation is close to the principle of relativity, by which every entity is potentially felt by every actuality (PR 22 [33]).

I believe we must see this as the ideal ontological principle Whitehead is aiming at. It may be questioned whether he is (as yet) prepared to apply this to all eternal objects. Realized eternal objects are all felt by those actual entities which exemplify them, but what about unrealized ones which have not yet become relevant to the creative advance? God is still conceived simply as a principle, and it is difficult to conceive how a principle can house this multitude.

Steps in the direction of a solution have been taken. Just as the original datum from which concrescence springs has dissolved into many actual data, so the single realm of eternal objects, as formally conceived in *Science and the Modern World,* appears to have dissolved into a "multiplicity of Platonic forms" (PR 43 [69]).

THE GENERAL ARISTOTELIAN PRINCIPLE

Thus far, there has been no claim that eternal objects derive their existence from actualities, nor has Whitehead made any reference to Aristotle's principle. He seems to have made only *one* explicit reference, in the following passage. It appears as an addition to an early Giffords draft text (II.1.1 *C*).[12] Because the argument here transforms Whitehead's understanding of God and of actuality, it would appear to have been formulated after the categoreal obligations of conceptual valuation and reversion. In the category of conceptual valuation, God is (indirectly) referred to in terms of "eternal principles of valuation" (PR 248 [380] *F*), thus still as a principle. In this passage the nontemporal divine principle is reconceived as a nontemporal concrescence of conceptual feeling.

f1. The two sets [actual occasions and eternal objects] are mediated by a thing which combines the actuality of what is temporal with the timelessness of what is potential. This final entity is the divine element in the world, by which the barren inefficient disjunction of abstract potentialities obtains primordially the efficient conjunction of ideal realization. This ideal realization of potentialities in a primordial actual entity constitutes the metaphysical stability whereby the actual process exemplifies general principles of metaphysics, and attains the ends proper to specific types of emergent order. By reason of the actuality of this primordial valuation of pure potentials, each eternal object has a definite effective relevance to each concrescent process. Apart from such orderings, there would be a complete disjunction of eternal objects unrealized in the temporal world. Novelty would be meaningless, and inconceivable. We are here extending and rigidly applying Hume's principle, that ideas of reflection are derived from actual facts.

By this recognition of the divine element the general Aristotelian principle is maintained that, apart from things that are actual, there is nothing—nothing either in fact or in efficacy.... This general principle will be termed the 'ontological principle.' It is the principle that everything is positively somewhere in actuality, and in potency everywhere. In one of its applications this principle issues in the doctrine of 'conceptualism.' Thus, the search for a reason is always the search for an actual fact which is the vehicle of the reason. The ontological principle, as here defined, constitutes the first step in the description of the universe as a solidarity of many actual entities. (PR 40 [64] *F* in II.1.1 *C*)

The general Aristotelian principle is explicitly identified with the ontological principle, but it is both more and less than that principle. Whitehead has identified them because he had previously been unable to make connection between he eternal objects and his ontological principle (that actualities are the only reasons) while Aristotle's principle expresses this most centrally. Aristotle's principle, however, is less than Whitehead's in that it is a specialization of the ontological principle. If the reasons for things are to be found solely in actual entities, then the reason for their existence must also be found there as well. (The ideal of the ontological principle has not been achieved, however, until the nature of eternal objects can be explained in terms of actualities.)

Aristotle's principle was more than the ontological principle as long as God was conceived as a pure principle, for then Whitehead had no adequate way of placing unrealized eternal objects within any actuality. *f1* transforms

God as nontemporal principle into nontemporal concrescence, and the totality of eternal objects, whether realized or not, forms the atemporal multiplicity for this nontemporal concrescence (as yet God is the one nontemporal actual entity, having no temporal or everlasting aspect). Without or before God's concrescent reconception, Whitehead could not affirm the Aristotelian principle. Thus, formulations of the ontological principle after *f1* imply the Aristotelian principle, Whitehead's systematic philosophy before *f1* could not live up to such aspirations with respect to unrealized eternal objects.

God as principle could not contain all the eternal objects unless it were the class of them all, a notion he rejects (PR 46 [73]). So we must think of them as free-floating, needing no ontological grounding, somewhat like Platonic forms. To be sure they are merely possible, not as fully real as actualities, but they were not conceived to be dependent upon actuality for their existence.

Then the reason for their existence would not have been given by actualities. I think this simply means that Whitehead had (as yet) been unable to give meaning to the full scope of his ontological principle. At least it appears so to us from the vantage point of his completed work. Yet, the *nature* of eternal objects has not been accounted for in terms of actualities. They are simply said to be uncreated (PR 257 [392]).

Note that the penultimate sentence of *f1* about "the search for a reason" presupposes the principle of extrinsic reference (*c1*), not the final version of the ontological principle, for only (past) actual entities, and not occasions in concrescence, can (as yet) serve as reasons. That notion changes rather dramatically with *f5*, as Whitehead reconceives the nature of actuality. First, however, we should consider some passages which do not appear to presuppose this reconception.

> *f2.* The scope of the ontological principle is not exhausted by the corollary that 'decision' must be referable to an actual entity. [So *c5.]* Everything must be somewhere; and here 'somewhere' means 'some actual entity.' Accordingly the general potentiality of the universe must be somewhere; since it retains its proximate relevance to actual entities for which it is unrealized. This 'proximate relevance' reappears in subsequent concrescence as final causation regulative of the emergence of novelty. This 'somewhere' is the nontemporal actual entity. (PR 46 [73] *G* in II.1.3 *G*)

These two passages on divine existence include and expand the earlier argument (in SMW) for God as the ultimate source for order in the cosmos. Earlier God is conceived as providing a limit upon otherwise unlimited multiplicity of eternal objects, thereby restricting their relevance for ingression.

Only those which conform to a general metaphysical order are allowed to be actualized.

The original argument, however, assumes that eternal objects by nature are relevant for ingression in our world, and God is needed to keep out unactualizable ones which would only cause chaos. That eternal objects are naturally available for actualization would be in keeping with Whitehead's earlier philosophy of nature, which saw no difficulty with objects immanently characterizing events. After God was introduced as the principle of limitation, there was no reason to modify this understanding, either then or later in *Religion in the Making,* or still later in the Giffords draft.

Although Whitehead is silent on the issue, there is no reason, particularly in the light of his great admiration for Plato, for not ascribing a theory of extreme realism to him. In that case the eternal objects could exist by themselves, requiring no actuality for their existence, with a natural relevance for ingression, except as restricted by actualities, either generically by God or particularly by finite occasions. To be sure, Whitehead vastly democratizes the realm of forms and recognizes that as possibilities they are less real than actualities, but he could still affirm their independent status with respect to existence. The adoption of nontemporal concrescence, however, transformed such Platonic realism into Aristotelian conceptualism.

Placing all unrealized eternal objects in God provides the basic reason for Whitehead's decision to abolish the category of reversion (PR 249f [381f]; cf EWM 236f).[13] As long as eternal objects constituted a fixed realm of interrelated forms, the nascent occasion would have to extrapolate alternative relevant forms, given the forms it was able to derive conceptually from its physical prehensions. Since the "primordial valuation of pure potentials, each eternal object has a definite, effective relevance to each concrescent process" (PR 40 [64]), there is no longer any need for this. The occasion can prehend any eternal object directly, and the category of reversion is no longer necessary.

> f3. [The relevance of unrealized eternal objects] is left unanswered by this Category of Reversion. In conformity with the ontological principle, this question can be answered only by reference to some actual entity [in this case, God]. (PR 250 [382] *F*)

Rather than revise his manuscript to eliminate all reference to reversion, Whitehead took the rather bold (and often misunderstood) step of "abolishing reversion," thereby informing his readers that a revised understanding of God with respect to the unrealized eternal objects renders the Category of Reversion superfluous. Whitehead also recognizes that his theory had been hitherto incomplete, for reversion only explains the availability of near alternatives, not why one alternative should be deemed relevant rather than another. Such reasons, by the ontological principle, had to be vested in some actuality, hitherto unspecified.

The implication that *f1* entails the distinction between primary and derivative existence can now be made explicitly and more generally than simply with reference to eternal objects:

> *f4*. Thus, the actual world is built up of actual occasions; and by the ontological principle whatever things there are in any sense of 'existence,' are derived by abstraction from actual occasions. (PR 73 [113] *F* in II.2.4 *C*)[14]

It looks like existence can thus be derived from past occasions; at least this is not explicitly ruled out, and it is in accordance with the principle of extrinsic reference (*c1*). If so, it might even seem that only past occasions (or present occasions insofar as they had achieved final being) could have primary existence in themselves. This is not Whitehead's final view, but it may well have been his original view.

Later, though not in *Process and Reality*, we will see that he tends towards the view that only concrescing actual entities exist in the primary sense, and that past occasions are dependent for their existence on such concrescing actualities just like all other entities (see *j2* in AI). This is Leclerc's interpretation, as his final formulation indicates: "...by the ontological principle, an 'entity' can exist only *either* as itself 'actual' (i.e. acting), *or* as implicated in the activity of some actuality" (WM 102). That view is also transitionally held by Whitehead in the next passage.

> *f5*. The ontological principle can be expressed as: All real togetherness is togetherness in the formal constitution of an actuality. So if there be a relevance of what in the temporal world is unrealized, the relevance must express a fact of togetherness in the formal constitution of a nontemporal actuality. (PR 32 [48])[15]

Whitehead here reiterates the identification of actuality with composition (*c4*), but with a shift of ontological gravity. In the earlier theory, being is the basis for all becoming, but the later theory of concrescence does away with that requirement (EWM 213–17). Now being is the derivate outcome of becoming, so the source of all togetherness must be found in the becoming or concrescence of an actuality, which is its formal constitution (as contrasted with its objective character, its being).

In line with the general Aristotelian principle (*f1*), that forms exist only as ingredient within actualities, this statement denies existence to unrealized forms unless envisaged by the only nontemporal actuality there is, namely, God. By extension, past actualities only have existence as ingredient in present concrescence. This could mean that past actualities are not reasons in their own right, yet more probably that Whitehead's immediate concern with formal actuality (the role of becoming in concrescence) led him to neglect the claims for past actualities, as expressed by the principle of extrinsic reference (*c1*). As we shall see, their role is reasserted in *i2*, Whitehead's first occasion to restate the ontological principle in terms related to the principle of extrinsic reference, and also in the definitive statement of the augmented ontological principle (*i3*).

Actuality's basic meaning was originally given in terms of decision, understood as the objective determinateness that excludes other alternatives. "Just as 'potentiality for process' is the meaning of the more general term 'entity,' or 'thing'; so 'decision' is the additional meaning imported by the word 'actual' into the phrase 'actual entity.' 'Actuality' is the decision amid 'potentiality.' It represents stubborn fact which cannot be evaded" (PR 43 [68] *C*).[16] Then with the adoption of pansubjectivity, the subjective meaning of 'decision' accrued to 'actuality' as well.

Whitehead's reconception of God as a nontemporal concrescence now enables him to reconceive 'actuality' as concrescence (PR 211 [321]). As long as God was not so conceived, concrescence could not serve as a general definition because it would not apply to the divine actuality. It may be at this time, following the principle that actualities are the only reasons, that Whitehead modified his interpretation of the ontological principle to fit this new understanding of actuality. Thus, all reasons are referent to actuality in concrescence. It would have been left open, however, whether there were any postconcrescent objectifications which should also be designated actualities.

Before considering Whitehead's answer, we should take up four intermediate passages.

PASSAGES DEPENDENT UPON 'SUBJECTIVE AIM'

Two passages depend upon 'subjective aim,' which was probably not introduced until Whitehead had nearly completed his elaboration of the categoreal obligations and saw that they were not sufficient to bring about the unification of concrescence (EWM 221–24). One is an insertion into "The Extensive Continuum" (II.2.2 *C*). Whitehead notes that the subjective aim does not share in the coordinate divisibility of an occasion, for the evolution of its subjective forms would be lost in such a division. Were this to happen,

> *g*. The ontological principle has been violated. Something has floated in from nowhere. (PR 69f [108] *G* in II.2.2)[17]

The other passage is very similar, particularly in its opening sentence: "According to the ontological principle there is nothing which floats into the world from nowhere" (PR 244 [373] *L*). It will be considered under *i2*, but it may well belong here. If so, *i2* should really be *g2*.[18]

PASSAGES DEPENDENT UPON THE INTRODUCTION OF 'THE CONSEQUENT NATURE OF GOD'

Heretofore, the consequent nature of God had not been introduced. Once it had been introduced, the exigencies of the ontological principle required Whitehead to place truth and the impartial nexus within it:

> *h1*. The truth itself is nothing else than how the composite natures of the organic actualities of the world obtain adequate representation in the divine nature. Such representations compose the 'consequent nature of God.'(PR 12f [18f])

These sentences appear as part of the only insertion[19] in "Speculative Philosophy" (I.1 *C*).

> *h2*.Thus, just as the 'feeling as one' cannot bear the abstraction from it of the subject, so the 'data as one' cannot bear the abstraction from it of every feeling which feels it as such. [Particular objectified nexuses are felt by finite subjects, but this cannot be true for the 'impartial nexus,' whatever nexus there might be which is not so particularized so as to be appropriate to finite occasions.] According to the ontological principle, the impartial nexus is an objective datum in the consequent nature of God, since it is *somewhere* and yet not by any necessity of its own nature implicated in the feelings of any determined actual entity of the actual world. (PR 231 [352])

Every other nexus as felt is felt from a particular finite standpoint and bears the marks of perspectival elimination. It cannot function as the final truth which must be free of such limitations, which only an impartial nexus can provide, and that is possible only in God's experience.[20]

THE AUGMENTED ONTOLOGICAL PRINCIPLE

I use this designation to specify the Eighteenth Category of Explanation (*i3*), which appears to be the most definitive formulation of the ontological principle because it is prominently displayed in the categoreal scheme. Unlike the principle of extrinsic reference, Whitehead's primary early formulation (*c1*), it can also serve as a basis for Leclerc's claim that only acting or concrescing entities have full or primary existence—but only if its reference to past actualities is neglected. Yet, it is remarkable that this augmented version seems first to appear in Whitehead's revisions of his Gifford lectures for publication. While it might be thought to be simply a restatement of *i2*, which introduces the subjective aim as an additional reason, it is really a generalization applying to all activities of the subject. It appears to have been formed under the influence of Whitehead's growing appreciation for the reformed subjectivist principle.

This principle asserts that the only real togetherness is togetherness in experience. It seems to be an application of *f5*, locating all real togetherness in the formal constitution of an actuality, to the situation of modern philosophy generally (II.9.2) and to what he specifies as the 'subjectivist principle' specifically (II.7.5). The Giffords draft had described an original datum from which concrescence starts, and this datum could only be a togetherness achieved by means foreign to experience. In his revised theory, the experience of concrescence begins with the prehension of the many data comprised by the many actualities in that world. Togetherness becomes Whitehead's most general word for concrescence and reappears in the analysis of the Category of the Ultimate.

Yet, the reformed subjectivist principle is mentioned in only a very few passages (PR II.9.2; II.7.1; II.7.5).[21] All appear to come from Whitehead's final editing, although the basic insight could have been derived from the beginnings of his shift to concrescence from data (PR III.1 *D*). However, Whitehead may have avoided any sweeping assertions of this idea until he was certain in his own mind that God was necessarily subjective.[22] Otherwise, the togetherness of eternal objects in the nontemporal actuality would not be in experience.

A late mention of a revised subjectivist principle in these editings associates it with the ontological principle:

> i1.The subjectivist principle is that the whole universe consists of elements disclosed in the analysis of the experiences of subjects. Process is the becoming of experience. It follows that the philosophy of organism entirely accepts the subjectivist bias of modern philosophy. It also accepts Hume's doctrine that nothing is to be received into the philosophical scheme which is not discoverable as an element in subjective experience. This is the ontological principle. (PR 166 [253f])[23]

Why should the reformed subjectivist principle be mentioned so rarely? I suspect it was primarily an epistemological application of the ontological principle introduced in those contexts in which it was necessary for Whitehead to introduce his own alternative to other alternatives in modern philoso-

Perfecting the Ontological Principle

phy. Moreover, the reformed subjectivist principle simply expresses the present facet of the larger truth that is the ontological principle, for the reformed principle says nothing about past actualities which also function as reasons.

While Whitehead here accepts Hume's principle, there is considerable evidence that he had resisted it in the earlier Giffords draft (EWM 220). In his first formulation of the origination of physical and conceptual feelings all mention of any derivation of the second from the first is studiously avoided (see PR III.2.2). Evidently Whitehead had not yet devised any theory of reversion, for without this Hume's principle would have precluded the emergence of any novelty.

With reversion, Whitehead could not only accept Hume's principle, but identify it with the ontological principle (PR 40: fl), which then was still the principle of extrinsic reference (*c1*). In that sense it applied only to that which is experienced. With this reformulation of the subjectivist theory, Whitehead shows how Hume's principle applies also to the subjective experience itself.

The next passage stems from the opening section of "The Transmission of Feelings" (III.3), where Whitehead for the first time traces the origin of the subjective aim to God:

> *i2*. According to the ontological principle there is nothing which floats into the world from nowhere. Everything in the actual world is referable to some actual entity in the past, *or belongs to the subjective aim of the actual entity to whose concrescence it belongs.* (PR 244 [373]; emphasis added)

The words italicized indicate the most important revision Whitehead makes in the principle of extrinsic reference (*c1*). It is not required in order to derive subjective aims from God because God could function as an actual entity for such reasons according to the older formulation. There is no way, however, of treating modifications of aim as reasons unless the concrescence is taken into account. To be sure, the occasion is objectified in terms of the past actualities it prehends, but also in terms of the way it has unified them and the way in which its autonomous modifications have affected that unification. These additional elements require reference to the subjective aim. For this reason Whitehead here broadens the scope of the ontological principle.

In the preceding paragraph we have ignored the shift in the meaning of actuality. Whitehead first identifies actuality with determinateness, then with concrescence, and now seeks to work out a synthesis based on the principle of extrinsic reference (*c1*) as his model. This is even more evident in:

> *i3*.(xviii) That every condition to which the process of becoming conforms in any particular instance has its reason *either* in the char-

acter of some actual entity in the actual world of that concrescence, *or in the character of the subject which is in process of concrescence.* This category of explanation is termed the 'ontological principle.' It could also be termed the 'principle of efficient, and final causation.' This ontological principle means that actual entities are the only *reasons;* so that to search for a *reason* is to search for one or more actual entities. It follows that any condition to be satisfied by one actual entity in process expresses a fact either about the 'real internal constitutions' of some other actual entities, or about the 'subjective aim' conditioning that process. (PR 24 [36])

This formulation says nothing explicitly about that which many take to be the very core of the ontological principle: that the existence of nonactual entities is dependent upon [the experience of] actual entities. Rather than being assimilated to the general Aristotelian principle (*f1*), or the reformed subjectivist principle (see *i1*), the eighteenth Category of Explanation seems to be more of a descendant of the principle of sufficient reason: Every feature of the present actuality (translated in process terms as every condition to which the process of becoming conforms) must have sufficient reason why it is so and not otherwise. Whitehead avoids Leibniz' conclusion that this is the best of all possible worlds by not locating all reasons in the divine decision, but in the decisions of prior actualities, both divine and finite. However, the principle of extrinsic reference by itself does not avoid the determinism inherent in external causal explanation. The other side of Leibniz' use of sufficient reason is avoided then by the way it is augmented: the causes for an actuality are not exhaustively given by past circumstances but also by that actuality's own self-causation.

It might be thought that the general Aristotelian principle (*f1*) could be explicated from the eighteenth Category of Explanation by construing "reasons" to include the reasons for the existence of some entity or other. However, the augmented ontological principle is a broader principle, speaking of reasons not only for existence but also for the nature of things. Moreover, while it provides reasons for the existence of eternal objects, could it give reasons for the existence of the actuality itself? Would this mean that our claim would have to be interpreted precisely backwards?

Then past occasions would become the reasons for the existence of the present concrescence, and not vice versa, according to the earlier principle of extrinsic reference (*c1*). Or the decision of the present concrescence is the reason for its existing, rather than the existence of the concrescence as being the ground for the occasion's decision making.

On the other hand, there could be a reciprocal relationship, whereby the reasons, themselves grounded in both past and present actualities, account for the precise character of the present actuality, while it in turn accounts for the existence of those reasons (actualities). This is all the more probable in the light of the close association of the fourth and eighteenth Categories of Explanation (see *c2*). If by the principle of relativity every entity is a potentiality for being an element in a concrescence, then every entity that functions as a reason for that concrescence actualizes such a potentiality. To function as a reason it must itself be actual (or ingredient in something actual). It exists as actual because it is one of the many factors taken up into the creative synthesis. Ultimately, creativity as rhythmic unification is the final ground of justification; every concrescence as a specific instance of creativity grounds the existence of the many factors which it unifies.

According to the ontological principle, however, actualities are the only reasons. How can creativity, itself not an actuality, be a reason for anything? William J. Garland has provided an illuminating response: By the ontological principle actualities provide the "ordinary explanations" for things, but creativity provides the "ultimate explanation" for why the ontological principle itself should be so.[24]

Just as Heidegger seeks to ground the principle of sufficient reason in something more fundamental, Being,[25] so Whitehead grounds the ontological principle in creativity. Actual entities are finally the only reasons because everything whatsoever is constituted by them, and they are constituted out of past actual entities as these are appropriated by the present actual entity in its process of self-constitution. These are the fundamental elements of the Category of the Ultimate. The past actualities form the 'many' to be unified, while their appropriation is the present exemplification of creative unification. Moreover, each past actuality was in its own emergence the embodiment of creativity. Actual entities are the only reasons because they alone are the exemplifications of creativity.

They can function as reasons only if existent; so the creativity characterized by these reasons provides their basis of existence.

From a systematic perspective, ignoring all generic differences, the augmented ontological principle appears to logically entail the general Aristotelian principle, the reformed subjectivist principle, and Hume's principle, while Whitehead does not appear to have endorsed any of these principles in the Giffords draft.

One clue may be found in the way the principle of extrinsic reference *(cl)* is expressed. It speaks of an item of the occasion's actual world as an "actual entity whose objectification is one of the components entering into the particular instance in question" (EWM 323f). This is broad enough to apply to those actualities which, according to the earlier theory of the Giffords draft (EWM 189–91), are brought together by the process of transition to form the original datum from whence concrescence flows. If so, the language of "the process of becoming" in the original formulation *(c1)* would here refer both to transition and to concrescence. While this phrase is brought over verbatim into the augmented ontological principle, Whitehead now restricts himself more narrowly to "the actual world of that *concrescence*," which restricts "the process of becoming" simply to its concrescence, excluding any prior process of transition, as this was understood in the Giffords draft. This qualification makes all the difference. If entities exist only in the experience of subjects, they can exist only in concrescence, not also in some process of transition taking place outside of experience.

CONTINUATIONS IN *ADVENTURES OF IDEAS*

None of our three designations, ontological principle, reformed subjectivist principle, or general Aristotelian principle, seem to be explicitly named, which makes it more difficult to trace the furtherance of these doctrines in *Adventures of Ideas*, but the ideas continue to be effective:

> *j1*.The Aristotelian doctrine, that all agency is confined to actuality, is accepted. So also is the Platonic dictum that the very meaning of existence is 'to be a factor in agency' or in other words 'to make a difference.' Thus, 'to be something' is to be discoverable as a factor in the analysis of some actuality.... it is necessary that it be discoverable somewhere, realized [physically or conceptually] in some actual entity. (AI 253f)

> *j2*. Every meaning of 'together' is to be found in various stages of analysis of occasions of experience. No things are 'together' except in experience; and no things *are*, in any sense of 'are', except as components in experience or as immediacies of process which are occasions in self-creation. (AI 304)

III

Now that we have the relevant data before us, ordered as much as possible in accordance with Whitehead's process of composition, we may trace an unfolding trajectory of meaning, as he revises the principle for greater universality or traces out its implications. At the outset it is simply a statement about the [reasons for] the specific nature of creativity *(a)*, but this is quickly generalized into the reasons for all things *(b)*. As formulated at this time, the ontological principle vests these reasons solely in past objectified actual entities *(c1)*.

The general Aristotelian principle, that potentialities are grounded in actualities, or in Whitehead's terms, that eternal objects derive their existence from actual entities, was not mentioned until after he had reconceived the nature of God. Initially God was conceived as the principle of limitation or concretion, and he did not modify that conception until after the major shift in *Process and Reality* which acknowledged that finite concrescence started from a multiplicity of prior actual occasions. In like manner God was reconceived as a nontemporal concrescence unifying a multiplicity of eternal objects.

Even so, the general Aristotelian principle should be recognized as a particularization of the ontological principle, here restricted to eternal objects and applying only to their existence and not to their natures *(f1)*. At this juncture, moreover, the version of the ontological principle, which he has at his disposal for deriving the general Aristotelian principle, applies only to objectified actual entities and does not extend to concrescing or acting actualities, let alone to them exclusively. However, that was soon to change *(f5)*, as his understanding of 'actuality' changed to include 'concrescence.'

If all reasons are vested in actualities, then every factor requiring a reason will be located in some actuality. Everything must be somewhere, i.e. in some actual entity *(f2)*. This must apply to unrealized eternal objects; if they are to be anywhere, it must be in the one primordial actual entity, God *(f5)*.

The introduction of 'subjective aim' brought Whitehead to the recognition that it (and its modifications) could not be exclusively derived from other actual entities, so he qualified the principle of extrinsic reference *(c1)* by the addition "or belongs to the subjective aim of the actual entity to whose concrescence it belongs" *(i2)*. Once revised in accordance with the reformed subjectivist principle, *(i2)* leads to the definitive revision in Category of Explanation (xviii) "That every condition to which the process of becoming conforms in any particular instance has its reason *either* in the character of some actual entity in the actual world of that concrescence, or in the character of the subject which is in process of concrescence" *(i3)*.

In the light of this history, we see that Whitehead himself has no fixed meaning for the ontological principle, but provides a series of meanings as he strives to improve and perfect his own formulations in order to obtain greater coherence with his evolving system. Rather than one meaning, we have a trajectory of meanings. Is it possible to improve upon this account by speculating about further extensions of the trajectory?

One possible course for this trajectory would be to stress the way the principle has been augmented *(i3)* at the expense of its original form as the principle of extrinsic reference *(c1)*. Then our claim might be that "all being is dependent upon becoming for its existence." This would apply to eternal objects as well as actualities, thus affirming the general Aristotelian principle. In this version the ontological principle basically concerns existence, contrasting primary and derivative existence. All secondary existents (beings) derive their existence from that which fully exists, i.e. becoming. This is Leclerc's principle, but it is justified quite differently

Then past actualities would exist only insofar as they are ingredient in present concrescing actualities. Whitehead may not be fully explicit on this point, but it is the common assumption of William A. Christian and Donald W. Sherburne. Christian argues that the past has being only as part of God's experience,[26] while Sherburne counters by claiming that because the entire past is not part of finite experience (there being no God), the total past no longer exists.[27] They both assume the past exists only as ingredient in (becoming) experience, thereby extending the Aristotelian principle to apply to past actualities as well as to eternal objects.

Whitehead, however, recognized that the question of the nature of actuality as well as its existence was embraced in the ontological principle and that, therefore, a wider designation was necessary. In perhaps the final formulation of the ontological principle, he points out: "The eighteenth category asserts that the obligations imposed on the becoming of any particular actual entity arise from the constitutions of other actual entities" (PR 28 [43]). Although Whitehead had already augmented it, this statement by itself is a clear expression of the principle of extrinsic reference. It indicates that when Whitehead reformulated the ontological principle, he did not reject the earlier principle but saw both as different facets of a larger ontological principle.

Moreover, if the ontological principle were limited to matters of existence, it could not apply to matters of efficient causation. Efficient causation seeks to account for features of present actuality in terms of the past actualities which impinge upon them. While other philosophies may derive both existence and nature of present actualities from efficient causation, Whitehead derives only their nature, because each occasion has its creativity inherent within itself. (Otherwise put, past actualities lack any creativity to bestow upon present occasions.) Their nature does come from the past, however, there would be an important loss of explanatory power if the principle were restricted to matters of existence alone. Efficient causation is the basis of scientific insight, which would be without any ultimate account apart from an enlarged ontological principle.

On the other hand, it may be possible to generalize the eighteenth category by something like the following: "That every condition to which *a being* [instead of: "the process of becoming"] conforms has its reason either...or..." This intends to apply the principle not only to questions of existence but also to questions of nature, and to apply it to all beings, not simply to actualities.

The general Aristotelian principle explains the derivative existence of eternal objects, but my proposal would require that the nature of these particular objects be accounted for as well. That would require that eternal objects have a process of emergence which would be the reason for their being thus and so. Then the ninth category of existence, appropriately generalized, would clearly be cognate: "That how *a being* [instead of: 'an actual entity'] becomes constitutes what that *being* is" (PR 23 [34]). Clearly, this is unthinkable within the present Whiteheadian economy, where the atemporality of the eternal objects plays such a large role.

Suppose there were "emergent objects," objects which had the same objective features as their counterpart eternal objects had but which resulted from some temporal process of origination. How would the prehension of an emergent object differ from its counterpart eternal object? For in objectification the process of origination would have been abstracted from. The emergent object so abstracted would *appear* to be just the same and just as atemporal as the real eternal object. How could we ever know that any eternal object was really atemporal and not simply an apparent one whose origination has been forgotten?

Now we do have a process whereby processes of origination can be ignored by abstraction, namely, the conceptual evaluation whereby the past actuality is felt only in terms of one of its eternal objects. Perhaps it might be possible to conceive of Whitehead's whole theory of eternal objects in terms of such conceptual derivation.

Unless such a theory could account for novelty, however, it would be inferior to Whitehead's proposal. Whitehead needed to appeal to either the category of reversion or to God to introduce novelty, and it seems passing strange that it might be possible to derive the new from the old, i.e. past actualities. For the sake of novelty, the question of unrealized eternal objects is deemed important, vesting them in God's primordial nature. The question of novelty is on the cutting edge of any satisfactory systematic philosophy and clearly requires further study, possibly in terms of divine lures that have not yet been objectified.

My purpose here is not to settle the issue of whether Whiteheadian philosophy can or should dispense with the atemporality of the 'eternal objects.' My point is only to show how the ontological principle might be perfected in the direction of greater internal coherence *were it possible* for the forms to emerge, so that how they become might constitute what they are. Here we would be simply following the master's own advice: "There is no justification for checking generalization at any particular stage" (PR 16 [25]).

NOTES

1. Ivor Leclerc, *Whitehead's Metaphysics: An Introductory Exposition* (London: George Allen and Unwin, 1958); cited hereafter as WM.

2. References in lower case letters (italicized) such as this specify particular formulations of the ontological principle which will be introduced seriatim in part two of this essay. Those italicized in capital letters refer to the compositional strata of *Process and Reality: An Essay in Cosmology*, cited hereafter as PR, eds. D. Griffin and D. Sherburne, (New York: Free Press, 1978), as I have best been able to determine them. See my *The Emergence of Whitehead's Metaphysics* (Albany: State University of New York Press, 1984), chapters 8 and 9; cited hereafter as EWM.

3. At the time this passage was composed (see note 6), Whitehead thought of 'decision' in purely objective terms, as the determinate character of the satisfaction as it affected supervening occasions. Any subjective interpretation of 'decision' would have to come later. See note 10.

4. This presupposes a univocal understanding of 'actuality' and 'primary existence' such as Whitehead and many others champion. We may find reason to modify this if we adopt diverse meanings dependent on difference temporal modalities. See my "The Modes of Actuality," *The Modern Schoolman* 67 (May 1990): 275–283.

5. For *c1*, see p. 127.

6. See my essay on "When Did Whitehead Conceive God to Be Personal?" *Anglican Theological Review* 72 (Summer 1990): 280–291.

7. The actual lectures turned out to be quite different than originally intended, as the prospectus indicates: EWM 325–27.

8. The designation "I.1.1" is used throughout to refer to the part.chapter.section structure of PR.

9. This is argued in *The Emergence of Whitehead's Metaphysics*, chapters 8 and 9.

10. That 'decision' is objectively meant, in terms of "a determinate condition [an occasion contributes] to the settlement for the future beyond itself," and does not yet mean the subjective deciding in concrescence, is clear from the discussion of datum, process, satisfaction, decision, also part of the Giffords draft (PR 150 [227]).

11. To be sure, this is found in the first section of "Fact and Form" (II.1) which on the whole belongs solidly to the Giffords draft. However,

Perfecting the Ontological Principle   147

negative prehensions make no sense without subjective forms, a later notion; we suspect that the final paragraph of this section is a later insertion.

It is also possible that the last sentence of this paragraph (PR 41.34–42.4) is a still later insertion (F+), after *f1* or *f5*, at least. This is really a description of the solidarity of relevance among entities, with 'negative prehension' playing a subordinate role, which is attached to the negative prehension paragraph by the opening transitional phrase "The importance of negative prehensions arises from the fact..." If so, *e* merely expresses Whitehead's conviction, achieved by *f1* or *f5*, that unrealized eternal objects, as well as other entities, must be felt by some actuality.

12. The rest of II.1.1 probably consists of two additions: p. 41f appears to be the very first description of concrescence after Whitehead's basic shift from a single datum to many data as the initial situation for concrescence. II.1.2 (on decision), II.1.3 (on the *multiplicity* of Platonic forms) may have been added, and certainly II.1.4 (on the ninth categoreal obligation, when part III knows only 8). Thus, originally the text may have gone from II.1.1 to 1.5, from 40.3 to 48.6: "The things which are temporal arise by their participation in the things which are eternal.... The antithetical terms 'universals' and 'particulars' are the usual words employed to denote respectively entities which nearly, though not quite, correspond to the entities here termed 'eternal objects,' and 'actual entities'."

13. Earlier I classified the abolition of reversion (PR 249.41–250.11) as *L* in EWM, primary because of its reference to 'hybrid physical prehension'. The key sentence reads in part: "Thus, a more fundamental account must ascribe the reverted conceptual feeling in a temporal subject to its conceptual feeling derived...from [the hybrid physical feeling of] the relevancies conceptually ordered in God's experience." If we omit the bracketed words as *L*, the rest of the sentence and paragraph can be much earlier (*F*). Yet the whole passage may be early (*F*), as evidenced by its lack of any relevant intermediary conceptuality such as 'primordial nature'.

14. The probable insertion (PR 73.14–22) can be discerned in terms of the context, which is about motion. "Thus an actual entity never moves: it is where it is and what it is.... It is quite obvious that meanings have to be found for the notions of 'motion' and of 'moving bodies'." The omitted passage discusses actuality, the ontological principle, and event, but not motion.

15. Elements of "Some Derivative Notions" (PR I.3.1) are quite early. It has been subject to heavy editing in the light of the distinction between the primordial and the consequent nature (*I*) as well as several later additions.

The designation of God as "a non-temporal actuality" suggests that this passage is early, even part of the original section.

The present arrangement presupposes that the sixth paragraph (in which *f5* appears) is an integral part of the original passage (PR I.3.1). It is possible, however, that it (PR 32.27–40) was an even earlier passage subsequently inserted into I.3.1. If so, *f5* may be earlier even than *f1*.

16. This "objective" meaning of decision may also be seen in the discussion of the four terms, 'datum', 'process', 'satisfaction', 'decision' (PR 150f [227f] C). Decision is *not* part of the process.

17. The probable insertion runs from 69.27 to 70.4.

18. See my essay, "Subjectivity in the Making," *Process Studies* 21 (Spring 1992): 19.

19. PR 12.38–13.6. Because this is an insertion, it was probably made during Whitehead's general editing, when he also inserted the reformed subjectivist principle (see *i1*) and the augmented ontological principle *(i3)*. While it makes better sense for the reformed subjectivist to precede *i3*, there seems no easy way to order either with respect to *h1*.

20. This is part of an *I+* insertion (230.45–231.18) in III.1.9 *D*. Though these insertions are dependent upon the introduction of the consequent nature, and hence are after *A-G*, there does not seem to be a sufficient means of determining whether they are before or after *i1* or *i2*.

21. The passage in II.9.2 comes in an insertion, from the middle of the first paragraph (PR 189.30 [288.16]) to the seventh paragraph (PR 191.11 [290.30]). All those mentions of the reformed subjectivist principle in II.7.1 and II.7.5 may also be additions. In addition, while the reformed subjectivist principle is clearly a subjectivist principle, it does not seem to be a revision of Whitehead's own subjectivist principle. See my companion essay, "The Reformed Subjectivist Principle Revisited," *Process Studies* 19 (Spring 1990): 28–48.

22. See my essay, "When did Whitehead Conceive God to be Personal?", cited in note 6.

23. The "Reformed Subjectivist Principle Revisited" distinguishes between the subjectivist principle Whitehead rejects, and two principles he accepts: a revised principle (*i1*) and the final reformed subjectivist principle.

I am now not sure whether the "togetherness" insight affects solely the final principle or both of the last two principles.

24. "The Ultimacy of Creativity," in *Explorations in Whitehead's Philosophy*, edited by Lewis S. Ford and George L. Kline (New York: Fordham University Press, 1983), 212–238.

25. For an account of this endeavor, see the fourth chapter of John D. Caputo, *The Mystical Element in Heidegger's Thought* (Athens: Ohio University Press, 1978).

26. "God and the Givenness of the Past," *An Interpretation of Whitehead's Metaphysics* (New Haven: Yale University Press, 1959), 319–330.

27. "Whitehead Without God," *Process Philosophy and Christian Thought*, ed. Delwin Brown, Ralph E. James, Jr., and Gene Reeves, (Indianapolis: The Bobbs-Merrill Company, 1971), 305–328.

8

The Systematic Ambiguity of Some Key Whiteheadian Terms

George L. Kline

In an earlier paper, I argued that Whitehead is a more thoroughgoing process philosopher than Hegel (because his position is a "relational *atomistic* ontology of process" in contrast to Hegel's "relational *substantialist* ontology of process") but admitted that Hegel's *language* more adequately expresses the processive and dynamic character of things than Whitehead's language does.[1] I wish to begin the present paper by considering the second point in greater detail.

I

Various commentators have noted the relative paucity of verbs, adverbs, and gerunds and the relative abundance of nouns and adjectives in Whitehead's philosophical prose. This trait—surprising in a process thinker—becomes even more striking when Whitehead's texts are compared to Hegel's. Hegel uses such key verbs (in his own speculative lexicon) as *bestimmen* [determine], *vermitteln* [mediate], and *vorstellen* [represent] much more often than Whitehead uses the key verbs in *his* speculative lexicon, such as 'appropriate', 'decide', and 'prehend'. Whitehead uses nouns like 'actuality', 'concrescence', and 'prehension' much more often than the corresponding verbs ('act', 'conscresce', 'prehend'). What is at least equally important is the fact that Hegel was careful, as Whitehead was not, to disambiguate the German nouns ending in "-*ung*," which correspond to English nouns ending in "-tion" or "-sion."

Words like 'decision' are ambiguous in a way that might be called functional or perhaps syntactical, and such ambiguity, being more than casual or episodic, I have chosen to call systematic. 'Decision' can mean either "the *act* or *process* of deciding"—which I designate, accurately[2] but inelegantly, as 'decision$_1$'—or "the *state* or *condition* of having been decided"—which I call 'decision$_2$'. 'Decision$_1$' occurs in such sentences as "The decision$_1$ which

I am now making (or am about to make) is a difficult one." 'Decision$_2$,' occurs in such sentences as "I now regret the decision$_2$ which I made last week" or in comments about "the 1964 decision$_2$ of the Supreme Court."

Hegel, without alerting the reader to what he is doing,[3] carefully disambiguates a series of important nouns ending in "*-ung*" (and certain other nouns such as *Arbeit* [work] and *Kampf* [struggle], which I shall not undertake to discuss here). Thus, (*die*) *Bestimmung* [determination] can mean either (*das*) *Bestimmen* [the act or process of determining] or (*ein*) *Bestimmtes* [the state or condition of having been determined]. Similarly, (*die*) *Vermittlung* [mediation] can mean either (*das*) *Vermitteln* [the act of mediating] or (*ein*) *Vermitteltes* [the state of having been mediated]. In both the *Phänomenologie des Geistes* and the *Wissenschaft der Logik* Hegel frequently uses all three forms of such nouns in a single passage, often with the addition of the more abstract forms of (*ein*) *Bestimmtes* such as (*die*) *Bestimmtheit,* and more abstract forms of (*ein*) *Vermitteltes* such as (*das*) *Vermitteltsein.*

The distinction between 'decision$_1$' and 'decision$_2$', or between (*das*) *Bestimmen* und (*ein*) *Bestimmtes*, may be called an "-ing/-ed" or "process/product" distinction. The "-ing/-ed" distinction was made current by John Dewey during the 1920s, with primary application to the verb 'experience'. Dewey distinguished between 'experien*cing*' and the 'experien*ced*' (which he also called funded experience). He held that the former was an active unit-process of which the latter was the cumulative result or product.

However, this distinction was not entirely original with Dewey. An analogous distinction can be traced back at least to Descartes, whose dualism of mind and body is expressed at least as much in the distinction between activity and passivity as in that between thought and extension. *Cogitatio* and *extensio* are both nouns and thus offer no syntactical contrast. Descartes's characteristic expressions for thought and extension, *res cogitans* and *res extensa*, involve a contrast between the *present active* participle *cogitans* [thinking] and the *past passive* participle *extensa* [extended, literally, having been extended]. For Descartes it is the act (strictly, a continuing series of acts) of the supremely active, non-extended Thinking Substance or God which extends, or conveys extension upon, passive matter. Note that the switching of the *kinds* of participles—the rendering of 'mind' as *res cogitata* and of 'matter' or 'extension' as *res extendens*—would seriously distort Descartes's position, even though the semantically appropriate verbs, *cogitare* and *extendere*, are retained.

Precisely what kind of ambiguity are we dealing with here? It seems not to be a primarily semantic ambiguity. The meaning of 'decision' and 'decide' is the same for both 'decision$_1$' and 'decision$_2$,'—for both the "act of deciding" and the "state of having been decided." Yet—as the example of

Descartes shows—the syntactical difference between present active participle and past passive participle entails a general semantic distinction between activity and passivity. (This also applies to the difference between the adjectives 'actual$_1$' and 'actual$_2$'.) The difference between *cogitatio* and *extensio*—as the respective participles *cogitans* and *extensa* make clear—is a difference between that which is (by nature) active and that which is (by nature) passive. Since the syntactical difference involves a difference of meaning, perhaps the most appropriate expression would be the awkward "syntactico-semantic distinction."

In any case, for Whitehead, who takes time seriously, i.e., categoreally, though not for Descartes, who doesn't, the active/passive distinction is also a *temporal* distinction. Activity is confined to *present* (concrescent) *subjects*; passivity characterizes *objects* of two kinds: *past* actual$_2$ entities (what I have called concreta) and timeless forms (what Whitehead calls eternal objects).

II

Before turning to a more detailed examination of Whitehead's use of "-tion/-sion" words, it will be appropriate to mention a few exceptions to the rule of "-tion/-sion" ambiguity, words that end in either "-tion" or "-sion," but which are *not* subject to disambiguation into "-ing" or "process" forms, on the one hand, and "-ed" or "product" forms, on the other. I shall mention only three such words, though there are others, and will pay special attention to the third of them.

As Whitehead uses it, the word 'condition' means "status" or "circumstance"; it cannot be analyzed into "act of conditioning" and "state of having been conditioned." Its connection with the verb 'to condition' has been lost or at least submerged. This contrasts with Hegel's use of *Bedingung* [condition], which has *not* lost its connection with the verb *bedingen* and thus can be analyzed into the process form, *(das) Bedingen* [act of conditioning] and the product form *(ein) Bedingtes* [state of having been conditioned].

Similarly with the term 'precision': it means simply "preciseness," contrasted with "vagueness." Here the relevant contrast is with the French noun *précision* [act of making precise], which has retained its connection with the verb *préciser* [to make precise].

By far the most troublesome of the exception words is 'ingression', the term which Whitehead introduced in *Science and the Modern World* (1925) to designate the passive relation of form or eternal object to actuality—both actuality$_1$ and actuality$_2$. The term occurs very frequently in *Process and Reality* (1929), but there, as earlier in *Science and the Modern World*, Whitehead also uses the less misleading adjective (and noun) 'ingredient' and the expression 'have ingredience' to designate the relation of eternal objects to actual occasions (cf. SMW 106, 244; PR 240/367, 251/385-386, 316/482, 323/493).[4] Whitehead's more usual way of expressing the relation, in both books, is to say that eternal objects "have ingression" in actual entities. He is scrupulously careful *never* to use the verb 'ingress'.[5]

Many commentators have disregarded the example of Whitehead's scruple and Christian's explicit warning, and have treated the verb 'ingress' as the counterpart of the verb 'prehend', on the analogy of the relation of the noun 'ingression' to the noun 'prehension'. One of Whitehead's earliest commentators, Everett Hall, writing in 1930, set an unfortunate precedent by asserting that, according to Whitehead, an eternal object, "by *ingressing* into any one occasion, *ingresses* into all."[6] Dorothy Emmett, in 1966, incautiously declared that Whiteheadian eternal objects "*ingress* into actual entities."[7] Donald Sherburne was equally careless in 1961, stating that "Not all of the...eternal objects could...*ingress* fully into actual entities." He added that "Beauty is...an eternal object...which *ingresses* into...a concrescence," and that an actual entity decides "which eternal objects it will allow...to *ingress* into its concrescence."[8] Jorge Nobo, who is careful not to use the noun 'eternal object' as the grammatical subject of the verb 'ingress', nevertheless repeats the curious passive construction "eternal objects are ingressed" (by actual$_1$ entities) and the equally curious expression "ingressed eternal objects" and, in at least one place, "reingressed eternal objects." Nothing like these expressions appears in Whitehead's own text (Whitehead says that eternal objects are "realized" or "objectified" by actual$_1$ entities), despite Nobo's incautious claim that, "An eternal object instantiated in a particular actual entity is said [the clear implication being 'by Whitehead'] to be *ingressed* in the actuality in question."[9]

In general, the use of 'ingress' as an active verb is not just a matter of inexact formulation or stylistic infelicity; it is seriously misleading, strongly suggesting—against Whitehead's clear intention—that timeless objects are *active*, function as *agents*. Eternal objects do indeed function, providing potentials for the definiteness of actual entities, but their functioning is *passive*, not *active*.[10]

III

Although Whitehead's philosophical lexicon is lamentably deficient in verbs and he makes no systematic distinction comparable to Hegel's distinction between "-ing" or process forms and "-ed" or product forms of key nouns, he does make use of two significant devices which serve to suggest that for him the process senses of "-tion/-sion" nouns predominate.

(1) He uses two kinds of prefixes: the expression "process of...," and a series of qualifying adjectives such as 'concrescent', 'originative', and 'sub-

jective', to suggest the process meaning of such nouns as 'decision', 'integration', and 'transition'.[11] (Further examples are given below, pp.155–156.)

(2) In a number of cases—most strikingly in the case of such frequently used key terms as 'determination', 'elimination', 'integration', 'origination', 'realization', and 'transition'—close examination reveals that the ratio of process to product senses is between 30 to 1 and 50 to 1. (Details are given below, pp. 156–157.)

Perhaps Whitehead assumed that these two devices—neither of which he explicitly mentions—would be sufficient to convey his vivid sense of the processive and dynamic nature of reality. His readers would have been greatly helped if he had done two other things: (1) called explicit attention to these devices and explained their purpose; (2) taken greater pains to disambiguate such particularly troublesome terms as 'decision' and 'constitution' where, in any case, the number of product senses of the terms appears to be relatively *large*.

IV

As we have seen, Whitehead generally uses "-tion/-sion" nouns in their "-ing" or process senses much more frequently than in their "-ed" or product senses. In this respect he is like Hegel, except that, in disambiguating German nouns ending in "*-ung*" (and certain other nouns), Hegel makes clearer than Whitehead does just where he intends the active or process sense. Thus, in both the *Phenomenology* and the *Logic* he uses (*das*) *Aufheben* [the act or process of sublating] much more frequently than (*die*) *Aufhebung* [sublation]. 'Sublation' is of course a Latinate term; it has been adopted by recent translators of Hegel to suggest the triple meaning of *Aufhebung*, namely, "canceling, preserving, and raising to a higher [dialectical] level." This ambiguity is clearly semantic, in contrast to the syntactical ambiguity of both "*-ung*" and "-tion/-sion" words.

This predominance of "process" forms is not consistent in Hegel's writings. For example, the noun (*die*) *Vorstellung* [representation] appears in this form—in both the *Phenomenology* and the *Logic*—about as often as the process form (*das*) *Vorstellen* [the act of representing]. (*Die*) *Wahrnehmung* [perception] appears about as often as (*das*) *Wahrnehmen* [the act of perceiving]. And some key terms appear in the opposite proportion: (*die*) *Vermittlung* [mediation] appears—in both the *Phenomenology* and the *Logic*— much more frequently than (*das*) *Vermitteln* [the act of mediating].

As we have noted, Whitehead provides clues of two kinds to suggest that he is using a given "-tion/-sion" noun in the "-ing" or process sense. The first and most explicit of these, as we have seen, is the placing of the expression "process of..." before the noun in question. Thus, in the case of Whitehead's

The Systematic Ambiguity of Some Key Whiteheadian Terms   155

relatively infrequent terms we find, for example, "process of acquisition" (164/249), "...appropriation" (219/335), "...generation" (60/94 [twice]), "...production" (215/327, 224/342), "...selection" (340/517), and "...super-session" (46/72). Although these are all helpful clues, Whitehead would have been even more helpful to his readers if he had used the formula "process of acquiring" more often. (He did, at least, use the formula "process of realizing." See below.)

A second set of clues, applied to these same, relatively infrequent, terms, is the prefixing of qualifying adjectives that strongly suggest the process sense of a given noun. Examples are: "immediate absorption" (177/269), "originative amplification" (117/179), "subjective appropriation"(177/269), "emergent evolution" (30/45, 229/349—this, of course, in reference to Bergson's celebrated book), and "direct mediation" (141/214 [twice]).

In the case of Whitehead's more frequently used terms, the same two kinds of clues are supplied as with the less frequently used terms.

First, there is the prefixing of "process of...." For example, "process of completion" (345/524), "...constitution" (AI 328), "...creation" (25/38, 344/522), "...integration" (eleven occurrences, the first at 58/91, the last at 312/476), "...origination" (232/354, 271/413, 273/417 [three times]), "...production" (215/327, 224/342), "...transition" (45/72), and "...transmission" (288/441). In the case of the much-used term 'realization' the expression "process of..." does not occur in *Process and Reality*, but—as already indicated—the more adequate expression "process of realizing" does (129/196). In an earlier work Whitehead had in fact written precisely "process of...realization" (cf. PNK n.1).

The more frequently used and important terms are also provided with clues of the second type. Thus, we find "internal constitution" (fifteen occurrences, the first at 24/37, the last at 291/446). Of course this is a special case—see p. 159 below—because the entire expression "real internal constitution," borrowed from Locke, is used repeatedly by Whitehead, mostly in the sense of 'constitution$_1$,' but sometimes in Locke's sense ('constitution$_2$,') (cf. 24/37, 41/66, 291/466). In this latter sense the German (*die*) *Beschaffenheit*[12] is an appropriate rendering, but quite inappropriate when it is used (frequently) to render 'constitution$_1$,' as well, because it fails to convey the active process sense of 'constitution$_1$'. 'Internal' and 'creative' are also used with 'determination', the former at 28/41, 46/74, and 47/74 [twice], the latter at 102/156. 'Decision' is prefixed by a number of related adjectives: 'concrescent' (56/88), 'immanent' (63/248, 164/249), 'immediate (248/436 [three times]), and 'originative' (86/131, 232/354). We also find 'concrescent integration' (56/88) and 'direct mediation' (141/214 [twice])—the latter expression would have puzzled Hegel. Both 'direct' and 'immediate' are used with 'objectification': the former at 63/98, 112/171, 284/435, and 308/469, the latter at 307/468 [twice] and 308/469 [twice]. Both 'immediate' and 'subjective' are used with 'transition, the former at 129/197, the latter at 174/264. We also find "immediate transmission" (307/468) and, a less frequently used kind of clue, "act of transmutation" (313/477). Although Whitehead offers none of the more familiar clues in connection with 'valuation', he does provide other, perhaps more subtle, but in the end equally persuasive clues, e.g., putting 'renewed' before 'valuation' and adding the verb 'arises' after 'valuation' (both 313/477). In a later work he added a vivid clue by using the expression "ferment of valuation" (AI 269).

As I have indicated, the ratio of "-ing" or process senses to "-ed" or product senses of "-tion/-sion" nouns in Whitehead's texts is on the order of between 30 to 1 and 50 to 1. Here are some rough figures: all three occurrences of 'atomization' are 'atomization$_1$', i.e., "the act of atomizing." Out of nine occurrences of 'completion' at least seven are 'completion$_1$', i.e. "the act of completing." Of the more than sixty occurrences of 'constitution' about fifty are 'constitution$_1$' (the act of constituting or creating), and only about a dozen are 'constitution$_2$' (the state of having been constituted or created).

All of the dozen or so occurrences of 'creation' appear to be 'creation$_1$' (the act of creating). This also holds for occurrences of the term in Whitehead's later works (cf. AI 248 [four times], 249 [twice], 254; MT 120). In the case of 'decision' the ratio is closer to fifty-fifty: there are more than thirty cases of 'decision$_1$' (the act of deciding) and more than two dozen of 'decision$_2$' (the state of having been decided). This is one of the few terms in connection with which Whitehead makes an explicit distinction that meshes with my distinction between 'decision$_1$' and 'decision$_2$'. He calls the former "immanent decision" (though not in all cases) and the latter "transcendent decision" (though in relatively few cases). (Both terms occur at 164/249.)

Some twenty-eight occurrences of 'determination' appear to be 'determination$_1$' (the act of determining) and only eight or ten 'determination$_2$' (the state of having been determined). In the case of 'division' the ratio is closer to Whitehead's norm—about eight cases of 'division$_1$' (the act of dividing) and only about three of 'division$_2$' (the state of having been divided). 'Elimination' appears more than twenty times as 'elimination$_1$' (the act of eliminating) and only once or twice as 'elimination$_2$' (the state of having been eliminated).

All five of the occurrences of 'exclusion' which I have noted appear to be 'exclusion$_1$' (the act of excluding). This is also true of all four cases of 'generation'. All three cases of 'individualization' are 'individualization$_1$' (the act of individualizing), as are more than a dozen cases of 'inhibition'. With the term 'integration' the ratio is maximally one-sided in favor of the process sense: there are nearly eighty occurrences of 'integration$_1$' and none, so far as I can see, of 'integration$_2$'. 'Integration$_1$' also appears at AI 298 and 327.

All eight occurrences of 'intensification' appear to be 'intensification$_1$'. Similarly with the seven cases of 'intervention'; all are 'intervention$_1$', i.e., the act of intervening. In the case of 'operation' all of the nearly thirty occurrences appear to be 'operation$_1$', except for the idiomatic expression "in operation," referring to the laws of nature, which does not fall clearly under either the process or product sense of the term (cf. 204/311). 'Origination' in all of its more than fifty occurrences appears to be 'origination$_1$'. All of the dozen cases of 'production' are 'production$_1$'.

'Realization' occurs some forty-five times as 'realization$_1$' and only once or twice as 'realization$_2$' (cf. 233/356). In the case of 'selection' all but one of the eight occurrences (that at 15/22) appear to be 'selection$_1$'. The one exception refers to the selective emphasis of earlier philosophers, and thus does not count as a systematic use of the term. All twenty occurrences of 'transition' appear to be 'transition$_1$' and all fifty occurrences of 'valuation' to be 'valuation$_1$'. Thus, in the case of such frequently used terms as 'determination', 'elimination', 'integration', 'intensification', 'operation', 'origination', 'realization', 'transition', and 'valuation' the ratio of process to product senses averages out at almost 50 to 1.

V

The "syntactico-semantic" ambiguity identified above (section I) is especially troublesome in the case of the nouns 'decision' and 'constitution', the adjective 'actual', and the verb 'constitute'. Without explicitly noting the sharp contrast in the meanings of actual,[13] Whitehead regularly uses the term both in the sense related to the "-ing" or process sense of 'decision', namely, "active and self-significant,"[14] what I have called 'actual$_1$', but also, and often in the same phrase, in the quite different sense, related to the "-ed" or product sense of 'decision', namely "efficacious and other-significant," what I have called 'actual$_2$'. For Whitehead only present (concrescent) subjects are actual$_1$; it is past objects (concreta) that are actual$_2$. However, entities that are passively or non-actively efficacious share with entities that are active the character or quality of "making a difference," and perhaps this common character provides some justification for Whitehead's otherwise puzzling use of the same term for both. (See his discussion of "making a difference" at AI 254.)

Process and Reality bristles with sentences like the following two: "[T]he process, or concrescence, of one [present] actual$_1$ entity involves the other [past] actual$_2$ entities among its components" (7/10). "Each [present] actual$_1$ entity defines its own [past] actual$_2$ world from which it originates" (210/321).[15] Substituting the meanings of 'actual$_1$' and 'actual$_2$' for the terms to which I have added subscripts, we might write, for the first sentence: "[T]he process, or concrescence, of one [present] active, self-significant entity involves the other [past] efficacious, other-significant entities among its components." For the second sentence such a reformulation might read: "Each [present] active, self-significant entity defines its own [past] efficacious, other-significant world from which it originates."

The noun 'decision' is comparably difficult to disambiguate, for example in the sentence "This concrete finality of the individual is nothing else than a decision referent beyond itself" (60/94). This could have two quite different meanings. (1) If 'decision' is 'decision$_1$,' then 'concrete' is what I have called 'concrete$_1$', i.e., concrescent', and characterizes the present concrescent occasion. (2) But if 'decision' is 'decision$_2$,' then 'concrete' is 'concrete$_2$', i.e., 'post-concrescent', and characterizes the past concretum.[16] There are related ambiguities in Whitehead's use of the term 'finality' and the expression "referent beyond itself." On a process interpretation, 'finality' would mean purposiveness (a meaning standard in the Thomist tradition and in such French thinkers as Bergson and Merleau-Ponty). On a product interpretation, 'finality' would mean simply conclusiveness or definitiveness. Similarly, on a process interpretation, the expression "referent beyond itself" would apply to the present occasion's anticipation of the subsequent occasions, "future" to it, which are now only possible, but which, once they are present, will be actual$_1$. In other words, 'beyond' is "from present to anticipated future." On the product interpretation "referent beyond itself" would apply to the relation of the past actual$_2$ entity to the present actual$_1$ entity, which is, in a sense, in "its future." Here, 'beyond' is "from past to present." This is the function of "providing unrefusable data," the passive functioning of (past) actual$_2$ entities with respect to (present) actual$_1$ entities, which makes a significant difference to the present entities' processes of concrescent self-creation or self-completion.

In the case of this short but enormously difficult passage, I tend to favor the process interpretation, but I see no way in which the product interpretation can be definitively excluded.

As Jorge Nobo has shown, Whitehead sometimes uses the verb 'to constitute' in the active sense of "to form" or "to create."[17] Here are a few examples of such usage, intended to convince skeptics (like Sherburne), who claim that 'constitute' in Whitehead *always* means just "comprise" or "amount to"—is always, in my terms, 'constitute$_2$'. Referring to the actual entity, Whitehead declares, in a celebrated and much disputed passage: "Its being is constituted$_1$ by its becoming" (23/34–35; here and hereafter I add my subscripts to Whitehead's terms). I take this to mean: "the being of the actual$_2$ entity is produced or created by the becoming of the actual$_1$ entity of whose concrescent (concrete$_1$) process it is the concrete$_2$ product." Again: "The subjective forms of the feelings...constitute$_1$ [i.e., shape] the eternal objects into...lures of feeling" (88/134). In another place Whitehead refers to the "already-constituted$_1$

The Systematic Ambiguity of Some Key Whiteheadian Terms 159

[i.e., created or produced] actual$_2$ entities" (219/235) and says that "the process constitutes$_1$ [i.e., shapes] the character of the product" (255/390). In a later work he added: "There are no actual$_2$ occasions in the future, already constituted$_1$ [i.e., created, produced]" (AI 251).

In other cases, sometimes on the same page, Whitehead uses the verb 'constitute' in the non-active or copulative sense, meaning "to comprise" or to "amount to." Here are a few examples: "the actualities$_1$ constituting$_2$ [i.e., comprising] the process of the world" and eternal objects "constitute$_2$ [i.e., comprise]...potentialities of definiteness" (39-40/63; "the actual$_2$ entities constituting$_2$ [i.e., comprising] the antecedent [i.e., past] environment" (68/105); "an actual$_1$ entity...may...constitute$_2$ [i.e., amount to] an instance..." (161/244); an actuality$_2$'s "public side is constituted$_2$ by [i.e., is made up of or comprises] the...datum prehended"; an actuality$_1$'s "private side is constituted$_2$ by [i.e., is made up of or comprises] the subjective form" (290/444).

In a particularly puzzling passage Whitehead refers to the "becoming, the perishing, and the objective immortalities of those things which jointly constitute stubborn fact" (xiv/ix). Things in the sense of concrescences, constitute$_1$ in the sense of actively creating "stubborn fact," i.e., the concreta in their aggregate, that is to say, the past actual$_2$ world. Things in the sense of concreta constitute$_2$ in the quite different sense of passively comprising or amounting to precisely this aggregate or this world. To put the point in slightly different terms, active things, i.e., concrescences, "become and perish"; passive things, i.e., concreta, "enjoy objective immortality."

Here again I favor the process interpretation, but find it difficult if not impossible to exclude the product interpretation of this key passage.

As we have seen, the noun 'constitution' in the Lockean phrase "real internal...constitution," which Whitehead regularly uses to characterize actual$_1$ entities, is 'constitution$_1$', i.e., "the act of [self-]constituting or [self-]creating," when applied to present concrescences (actual$_1$ entities) but 'constitution$_2$', i.e. "state of having been constituted [or created]" when applied to concreta (actual$_2$ entities). This second sense, equivalent to "static structure or make-up," is close to what Locke himself intended, since he used the expression "real internal...constitution" as a definition of *essence*.[18]

When Whitehead writes: "The process...is the constitution$_1$ of the actual$_1$ entity; in Locke's phrase, it is the 'real internal constitution$_2$,' of the actual$_2$ entity" (219/335), the first half of the sentence expresses unexceptionable Whiteheadian doctrine, but is entirely at variance with the second half of the sentence, in which the active or process sense of 'constitution$_1$' is quite gratuitously attributed to Locke himself.

Consider Whitehead's parallel claims, in a single passage, that (a) the "[categoreal] obligations imposed on the becoming of any particular actual$_1$ entity arise from the constitutions$_2$ [i,.e., the 'states or conditions of having been constituted'] of other actual$_2$ entities" (28/43), and (b) "the term 'subject' will be...employed when the actual$_1$ entity is considered in respect to its own internal constitution$_1$ [i.e., act of constituting (itself)]" (29/43). At the very least, it will be evident to any alert reader that the word 'constitution' like the word 'actual', is being used in these neighboring passages in sharply contrasting senses. The product sense of 'constitution' ('constitution$_2$') also appears at 24/37, 72/112, 149/225, 185/281, 213/325, 274/419, and 291/446. The process sense of 'constitution' ('constitution$_1$') occurs, as I have already indicated, more than forty times. The first of these occurrences is at 25/37 [twice], the last of them at 291/446.

VI

Whitehead the accomplished mathematician was for decades comfortably at home with technical symbols and complex display formulas. Almost any page of the monumental three-volume *Principia Mathematica* (which he wrote jointly with Bertrand Russell) would supply examples of what I have in mind. So perhaps he would not object too strenuously to the introduction into his texts in speculative philosophy, and in the first instance the text of his magnum opus *Process and Reality*, of the somewhat obtrusive and inelegant subscript numerals which I have used in my attempts to disambiguate some of his key terms. My "modest proposal," which is certain to meet with resistance from editors and publishers, would be to produce a student edition of *Process and Reality* in which the process sense of key terms (verbs and adjectives as well as nouns) would be marked by subscript$_1$, the product sense by subscript$_2$, the cases in which, on reflection, it appears that Whitehead intended *both* senses by subscripts$_1$ and $_2$, and the (relatively few, one would hope) undecidable cases by subscript question mark.

This would, I submit, be a valuable first step in the ambitious project of disambiguating the most important of Whitehead's technical terms, a project which—though largely neglected up to now—would be an essential precondition for the eventual rigorous reformulation of the central doctrines of Whitehead's powerful speculative system.

NOTES

1. See my "Concept and Concrescence: An Essay in Hegelian-Whiteheadian Ontology" in *Hegel and Whitehead: Contemporary Perspectives on Systematic Philosophy*, ed. George R. Lucas, Jr. (Albany: State University of New York Press, 1986), 133–151; esp. 136–137 and 142–144.

The Systematic Ambiguity of Some Key Whiteheadian Terms   161

2. It is "accurate" in the sense of corresponding closely to the senses I have previously distinguished of 'actual', namely 'actual$_1$' = "active and self-significant"; 'actual$_2$'= "efficacious and other significant." For details see my "Form, Concrescence, and Concretum" in *Explorations in Whitehead's Philosophy*, ed. Lewis S. Ford and George L. Kline (New York: Fordham University Press, 1983), 104–146; esp. 104–105, 115, and 119.

3. As he *does* explain the semantic ambiguity of his key term *aufheben* (viz., "to preserve, cancel, and raise to a higher [dialectical] level"). Cf. *Wissenschaft der Logik*, ed. Georg Lasson (Hamburg: Meiner Verlag, 1934), I, 94.

4. In this essay I use the following abbreviations (sigla) to refer to Whitehead's works:

AI - *Adventures of Ideas*, (New York: Macmillan, 1933)
MT - *Modes of Thought*, (New York: Macmillan, 1938)
PNK - *An Inquiry Concerning the Principles of Natural Knowledge*, (Cambridge: Cambridge University Press, 1919)
PR - *Process and Reality*, (New York: Macmillan, 1929). In quotations from *Process and Reality* I shall use *two* page numbers, the first will refer to the Corrected Edition (New York: Free Press, 1978), ed. David R. Griffin and Donald W. Sherburne, the second, following a diagonal, to the 1929 edition. No other references will have such double numbering, therefore, I shall in most cases omit the "PR."
SMW - *Science and the Modern World,*. 2nd ed. (New York: Macmillan, 1926)

5. William Christian made this point early and well, but overstated his case when he claimed that Whitehead "nowhere uses the word 'ingress' either as a verb or as a *noun*" (*An Interpretation of Whitehead's Metaphysics* [New Haven: Yale University Press, 1959], 185; italics added). He is right about the verb 'ingress' but wrong about the noun because Whitehead at least once uses the odd expression "has ingress" (240/368).

6. Everett W. Hall, "Of What Use are Whitehead's Eternal Objects?" originally in the *Journal of Philosophy*, 27 (1930), 29–44, as reprinted in *Alfred North Whitehead: Essays on His Philosophy*, ed. George L. Kline (Englewood Cliffs, New Jersey: Prentice Hall, 1963; corrected reprint Lanham, Maryland: University Press of America: 1989), 103; italics added.

7. Dorothy Emmett, Preface to the Second Edition (New York: St. Mar-

tin's Press, 1966) of *Whitehead's Philosophy of Organism* (London: Macmillan, 1932), xx; italics added.

8. Donald W. Sherburne, *A Whiteheadian Aesthetic* (New Haven: Yale University Press, 1961), 31, 155, 25; italics added.

9. Jorge Luis Nobo, *Whitehead's Metaphysics of Extension and Solidarity* (Albany: State University of New York Press, 1986), 25; italics added. The German translation of 'ingression' as (*das*) *Eintreten* is thus seriously misleading. It appears to have been modeled on the use of (*das*) *Erfassen* for 'prehension', the latter term being quite appropriate. A (present) prehension *is* an "act of prehending" but a (timeless) ingression is *not* an "act of ingressing," as the German term suggests. Cf. *Prozess und Realität*, trans. Hans Günter Holl, 2nd rev. ed. (Frankfurt/Main: Suhrkamp, 1984), 64, 66, and *passim*.

10. Thus, *Wirken* is appropriate for the active functioning of actual$_1$ entities, but highly misleading as a rendering of the passive functioning of eternal objects. Cf. *Prozess und Realität*, 292 and *passim*.

11. In an earlier essay I made the overhasty claim that *all* cases of Whitehead's technical term 'satisfaction' are cases of 'satisfaction$_2$'. (See "Form, Concrescence, and Concretum," 107.) Nobo has convinced me that Whitehead in fact uses the term in two quite different senses, which Nobo calls "subjective satisfaction" and "superjective satisfaction," the former being experienceable, the latter *not* experienceable, by the subject of the satisfaction. The subjective satisfaction corresponds to my satisfaction$_1$, the superjective satisfaction to my satisfaction$_2$. Cf. Nobo, *Whitehead's Metaphysics of Extension and Solidarity*, 29.

12. Cf. *Prozess und Realität*, 76, 283, and *passim*.

13. An actual$_1$ entity, or concrescent occasion, is characterized by subjectivity, activity, and ontological "privacy"; an actual$_2$ entity, or concretum, is characterized by objectivity, passive efficacy, and ontological "publicity."

14. Ivor Leclerc was the first to make the important point that an actual$_1$ entity is an *active* or *acting* entity. He added the significant corollary that an actual$_1$ entity is also a *deciding* entity. See his *Whitehead's Metaphysics: An Introductory Exposition* (London and New York: Allen and Unwin, 1958), 100.

15. The German translation of *Process and Reality* renders both 'actual$_1$' and 'actual$_2$', in this passage and elsewhere, as *wirklich*. This is

appropriate for 'actual$_1$', but quite misleading for 'actual$_2$'. Cf. *Prozess und Realität*, 38, 389, and *passim*.

16. See my "Form, Concrescence, and Concretum," esp. 107–109.

17. See Nobo's article, "Whitehead's Principle of Process," *Process Studies*, 4 (1974), esp. 276–277. This discussion is now included in his book *Whitehead's Metaphysics of Extension and Solidarity*, esp. 142–143.

18. See "Form, Concrescence, and Concretum," 106, 133.

9

To Be Is To Be Substance-In-Relation

W. Norris Clarke, S. J.

The aim of this paper is to operate a double retrieval. It is first to retrieve the classical (pre-Cartesian) notion of substance as dynamic, as an active nature, i.e., an abiding center of acting and being acted upon—one of the richest insights of ancient and medieval thought; and secondly, to integrate it more closely with the notion of relation as an intrinsic dimension of being, which has become one of the most characteristic and highly developed instruments of later modern and contemporary thought. The two belong together in any adequate metaphysics, I submit, as intrinsically complementary aspects, distinct but inseparable, of what it means to *be*, to be a *real being* in the full and proper sense of the term.

Unfortunately the two notions, originally joined together, have become sundered and more and more opposed to each other as modern philosophy has unfolded since Descartes, partly due to the pressure of modern mathematized science, with its almost exclusive focus on relations as the locus of intelligibility in nature. On the one hand, the classical notion of substance as active nature imbedded in a network of relations resulting from its acting and being acted on has been gradually distorted in successive stages throughout the history of post-Cartesian thought. I like to call this chapter in the history of substance "The Sad Adventures of Substance in Modern Philosophy from Descartes to Whitehead."

The three successive phases of this distortion can be summed up as (1) the Cartesian self-enclosed substance; (2) the Lockean inert substance as unknowable substratum; and (3) the Humean separable substance, rejected as unintelligible—which it indeed is as so understood. All of these have been repudiated—and rightly so—by the majority of late modern and contemporary thinkers. Nothing adequate has replaced them; the authentic classical notion has apparently slowly sunk out of sight (save in the contemporary Aristotelian and Thomistic traditions, which themselves have remained somewhat isolated from the main streams of modern philosophy). As a result, real being tends to be reduced to nothing more than a pattern of relations with no subjects grounding them, or a pattern of events with no agents enacting them. The fundamental polarity within real being between the "in itself" and the "toward others," the self-immanence and the self-transcendence of being, collapses into the one pole of pure relatedness to others.

On the other hand, one can overstress the other side of the polarity, focusing exclusively on the notion of substance as in itself, unchanging substratum, the ground of all attributes and relations and thus the primary instance of being. Then relations become second-class citizens in the hierarchy of being, not only ontologically posterior to substance in the order of being—which they must be—but also of secondary importance compared to it. This danger is latent from the beginning in the classical notion of substance, especially in its originator, Aristotle, insofar as the substantial forms that were the intelligible core of substances were necessary and eternal, whereas relations to others were (for the most part) contingent and changing. The priority of substance, which Aristotle is so justly proud to have discovered, tends to push too much into the background the complementarity of relations as equally intrinsic to being.

The medievals, especially St. Thomas, restored in principle the complementarity between substance and relation by their doctrine of real being as intrinsically ordered towards action and self-communication; for all action necessarily generates a web of relations between agents and recipients. Christian revelation, through the medium of theological explication, also had a significant philosophical input on the meaning and importance of relations. This came principally through the doctrine of God as Triune, where the personhood of the three Persons, Father, Son, and Holy Spirit, is constituted entirely through relations. The analysis of human being as intrinsically social, hence as imbedded in a web of relations to others in the social and political community, also clearly implied the key role of relations. This aspect is quite explicit in Aristotle, too.

Nonetheless, in fact when St. Thomas and the other medievals worked out their technical philosophical analysis of what it means to be a person, their principal focus was on identifying precisely the root of the "incommunicability" or uniqueness of the person, human or divine, as distinct from every other. This was important for theological reasons, e.g. for understanding the distinction of the divine Persons within the unity of the divine nature, as well as why the human nature of Christ was complete as a nature but was not a person on its own as distinct from the divine Person who assumed it as its own. As a result, although the aspect of person (and hence of substance) as intrinsically relational was explicitly affirmed in the case of the divine Persons and clearly implied for all persons and substances in terms of the underlying Thomistic metaphysics of being as by nature active and self-communicative, still this relational aspect of all substances as actual existents did not receive the same explicit full-dress philosophical analysis as the in itself aspect of substance, existing as *distinct* from all others. The full implications of his own metaphysics of existence as act had not yet been drawn fully into the light by Thomas himself, nor perhaps fully even by his followers to this day.

Hence what is needed, it seems to me, is first to retrieve the classical notion of substance as *active* and *self-communicative*. This would be a corrective of the principal distortions of substance that have become endemic to modern thinking about it. Secondly, it is necessary to retrieve the full value of the *relational* dimension of being, as intrinsically complementary to substance and of equal importance with it. This dimension, left too much in the shadow in classical thought, has been one of the most brilliant and fruitful contributions of modern thought, but by losing its roots in substance, in the "in-itself" of being, has become overdeveloped in a one-sided way and upset the dyadic balance of being. In summary, to be real is to be a *dyadic synthesis* of substance and relation; it is to be *substance-in-relation*. This is true both of God and of all other beings, in analogously different ways. It belongs to the very nature of being itself, both in its supreme instance and in all the finite images thereof.

RETRIEVAL OF THE CLASSICAL NOTION OF SUBSTANCE

The main point here is to retrieve the aspect of substance as active and self-communicative, thus generative of relations. I shall draw principally on the thought of Aquinas, because of the richness of his underlying metaphysics,[1] in particular his notion of being as active and self-communicative. The primary instance of real being is the individual existent as a nature, i.e., as an abiding center (no matter for how long) of its own characteristic actions and the ultimate subject of which attributes are predicated, but which itself is predicated of no other subject as an attribute or part. This power to exist *in itself* as an ultimate subject of action and attribution and not as a part of any other being is what it means to be called a *substance* (from the Latin *substans*: that which "stands under" all its attributes as their ultimate subject). To stand thus "in itself" does not mean that the entity thus characterized is not *related* to others. As we shall see, the intrinsic orientation toward self-expressive action that is also characteristic of all natures—hence of all substances—implies that all substances will be related at least to some others. But it does mean that no substance, no real being in an unqualified sense, can be nothing but a pure *relation*. A relation in the real order must relate something, making it a relat*ed* or the relation itself self-destructs. As the Buddhists have long insightfully argued, if all beings are nothing but relations, such that A is nothing but a relation to B, and B is nothing but a relation to A, then neither one has its "own being" and both disappear into "emptiness" (*sunyatta*)—a point often naively overlooked, it seems to me, by many modern Western philosophers who cavalierly dismiss substance for relation as the primary mode of being.

Thus, wherever there is any real being at all, there must be substance, or being in a substantial mode, either within the being itself or grounding it as its ultimate subject of inherence. The basic classical argument for the necessity of substance wherever there is real being runs as follows: It is impossible that every instance of real being should be a part of, inhering in, some other being, which in turn inheres in some other and so on to infinity. An infinite regress is not possible here because the necessary fulfilling conditions for any being to exist would be endlessly deferred, never in principle fulfilled. Nothing could ever get going in reality at all. Hence, there must always be substance somewhere in being to ground whatever else is there. (In this basic sense, it seems to me, even the Whiteheadian actual entities must be considered as substances because they exist somehow as subjects in themselves, not merely as parts of others, even though they subsist only for a moment. His own reason for rejecting substance derives, as we shall see, from the Cartesian distortion of substance as self-enclosed.) As Bernard Lonergan sums up aptly the classical doctrine: substance is that which makes a being to be a "unity, identity, whole."

There are four basic points to note about this conception of substance as the primary instance of real being: (1) it has the aptitude to exist *in itself* and not as a part of any other being; (2) it is the unifying center of all the various attributes and properties that belong to it at any one moment; (3) if the being persists as the same individual throughout a process of change, it is the substance which is the abiding, unifying center of the being across time; (4) it has an intrinsic dynamic orientation toward self-expressive action, toward self-communication with others, as the crown of its perfection, as its very *raison d'etre*, literally, for St. Thomas. It is this last aspect that we shall give most stress to and develop more fully in this paper, precisely because it is the one that has been most frequently downplayed, ignored, or denied in the modern Western philosophy since Descartes. Let us listen to St. Thomas on this intrinsically active aspect of every being, hence of every substance:

Every substance exists for the sake of its operation.[2]

Each and every thing shows forth that it exists for the sake of its operation. Indeed operation is the ultimate perfection of each thing.[3]

And since all action proceeding from a being is in some way a self-communication of that being, it follows that:

It is the nature of every actuality to communicate itself insofar as it is possible. Hence every agent acts according as it exists in actuality.[4]

It follows upon the superabundance proper to perfection as such that the perfection which something has it can communicate to another.[5]

Communication follows upon the very intelligibility (*ratio*) of actuality.[6]

For natural things have a natural inclination not only toward their own proper good, to acquire it, if not possessed, and, if possessed, to rest therein; but also to diffuse their own goodness among others as far as possible.... Hence if natural things, insofar as they are perfect, communicate their own goodness to others, much more does it pertain to the divine will to communicate by likeness its own goodness to others as far as possible.[7]

This is a far cry from the Lockean and other modern conceptions of substance as inert, static, unknowable substratum. Action is precisely the way an existing substance manifests its inner being, both its existence and its essence. As St. Thomas puts it:

The operation of a thing manifests both its substance and its existence.[8]

The operation of a thing shows forth its power, which in turn manifests (*indicat*: points out) its essence.[9]

The substantial forms of things, which, according as they are in themselves, are unknown to us, shine forth to us (*innotescunt*) through their accidental properties.[10]

Every real substance, therefore, is highly dynamic. The whole point of its being is to express itself, to fulfill itself, to share its riches, through action appropriate to its mode of being (its essence). The substance of a being, accordingly, is its perduring autonomous self-identity, as manifested and fulfilled through activity. It is a serious misunderstanding, then, to describe substance, as has so often been done after Locke, not only as inert but as unqualifiedly *unchanging*. It is an essential ingredient of the classical understanding of substance that the substance *itself changes* in every accidental change. Of course it does; otherwise the change would make no difference at all to the being which undergoes the change, which is absurd. The exact technical formula runs as follows: *In every accidental change the substance itself changes, but not substantially, only accidentally*. It does not become another being, essentially different from what it was before. Being substantially *self-identical*, therefore, is not at all equivalent to being *unchanging*. Real self-identity is dynamic and accommodates a wide range of changes within it, but always within limits. If these are broken down by too extreme a change, its essential self-identity can no longer maintain itself and dissolves into something else.[11]

This notion of substance as dynamic self-identity expressing itself in action—and, therefore, undergoing accidental change in our finite, material world—is rooted, for Aquinas, in his most significant contribution to metaphysics, the notion that the core of every real being is constituted by its (*esse*) or act of existence, conceived not as form or whatness or essence but as active presence—power-filled presence, if you will (*virtus essendi*). This active presence is limited, indeed, in all beings outside the pure unlimited act of divine existence, by its distinctive limiting essence. But because of this dynamic inner core, every being, by its very nature as existing being, as being in act, tends naturally to flow over into action according to its essence. And since all action is not only self-manifestation but self-communication in some way; every being is by nature self-communicative, oriented toward presenting itself through action to the community of other real existents and reciprocally receiving their self-communications in its own being. Action is thus the dynamic bond between beings, which, without dissolving them into each other, binds them together to make a *universe (universum*: turned toward unity). In his doctrine of existence as self-communicative act Aquinas has integrated the whole dynamism of the self-diffusiveness of the Good from the Platonic tradition into his own metaphysics of being, with appropriate modifications.[12]

The immediate corollary of this notion of dynamic substance is that every substance, as active, becomes the center of a web of relations to other active beings around it. For action by its very nature generates relations with those on which it acts and from which it receives action in turn. Action, in fact, is the primary generator of real relations within the community of real beings. An existing substance, therefore, in St. Thomas's universe, as active, self-communicating presence, cannot *be* what it is without *being related* in some way. To be a substance and to be related are distinct but complementary and inseparable aspects of every real being. The structure of every being is indissolubly dyadic: it exists both as in itself and as toward others.

Is this true of God also? From the philosophical viewpoint, St. Thomas, with the other Christian thirteenth-century thinkers, speaks cautiously here, more cautiously than some before him in the twelfth century. He does not want to say that reason alone can deduce that the divine nature is necessarily self-communicative within itself. The fact that this is so can be known only through the free divine revelation of the mystery of God as Triune, three Persons in one nature. Nor does he want to say that God *necessarily* pours over to share his own goodness in a created universe, as did Plotinus and the Neoplatonic schools; the freedom of creation was a central Christian doctrine, which all Christian thinkers were intent to defend against the necessitarian emanationism of the great Arabic metaphysicians of the time. So he argues by analogy that if all the creatures we know in fact manifest this self-communicativeness of their own goodness, it is necessary that the divine nature, the exemplar of all creatures, should have this same *aptitude* in the highest degree and most "fitting" that it should exercise it.

St. Bonaventure, for whom the fecundity of the divine goodness is a central pillar of his whole philosophy, speaks at times a little more daringly, and I think myself that St. Thomas should have, too. They could, for example, have moved further in the direction of Hegel by saying that it is according to the divine nature—inevitable, if you will (*necessity* is perhaps too strong a word, with misleading implications of impersonal compulsion)—to communicate its goodness to *some* finite created world, but to *which particular* finite universe would have to be determined by a free choice because there is no proportion between any finite universe and the infinite perfection of God such that we could deduce the first necessarily from the second. An infinite number of other finite universes always remain possible for the infinite divine power. The determination of *this* one would have to be the result of free choice and not of nature or necessity.[13]

But although philosophical reason by itself cannot determine the actual mode of the divine self-communication, Christian revelation fills in the picture magnificently, thus shedding brilliant new light on the philosophical explanation of the universe itself. For according to this revelation, although the creation of this finite universe is a free act of God, the inner being of God is by the very necessity of its nature *self-communicating love* which flowers out into the internal procession of the three Persons within the unity of the divine nature. It is constitutive of the very personality of God as Father that he communicates the whole fullness of the divine perfection (or nature) without remainder to the Son, and that both together, in a mutual act of love, communicate the identical fullness of the same divine nature to their love-image the Holy Spirit. It is thus of the very nature of being at its supreme intensity to pour over into self-communicative relatedness. God is the ultimate paradigm of being, of which all creatures in their distinctive ways must somehow be images; therefore, it follows that self-communication and relatedness to others must belong to the very nature of all being as such, and especially to persons as such. This does not mean that a person is *nothing but* a relation to others, as seems to be the case in most contemporary phenomenology and personalist existentialism with their customary denials of person as substance. A relat*ed* is not identical with the relation which makes it related, but neither is it separable from it. Every person must bear within it the dyadic structure of in-itself interiority and self-transcending relatedness toward others. All the above is contained implicitly in the very structure and dynamism of St. Thomas's metaphysics of being as self-communicating act, although unfortunately, for various accidental historical reasons, I believe he did not highlight as explicitly as I have the intrinsically relational aspect of being.

DISTORTIONS OF SUBSTANCE IN MODERN PHILOSOPHY

The Cartesian Self-enclosed Substance

Descartes is mainly responsible (although there were slippages toward it in the late scholastic thought just before him) for the introduction of a new definition of substance, carrying with it a significant shift in its meaning. Substance for him is "that which exists by itself, that which needs nothing else but itself to exist."[14] When it was pointed out to him that strictly speaking this can apply only to God, he quickly modified it, when applied to creatures, to "that which needs nothing else save God to exist." Arrived at by his experience of himself as nothing but pure thinking substance, substance is here conceived as related vertically to God, but horizontally independent of other creatures, self-contained and self-sufficient. Later, of course, relations to other things did come in, but they remain adventitious. In its core, substance is radical autonomy, a self-enclosed monad, unrelated and self-sufficient. Even its clear and distinct knowledge of the rest of the world is ideally to be deduced from its own innate ideas, not received by action from without.

Note the radical shift in meaning introduced by the apparently innocent change of a single word in the definition. The "in itself" of the classical definition becomes the "by itself" of the Cartesian. "In itself" by no means denies relatedness to others or dependence on others as causes; it implies only that its subject is not a *part* of any other being but is an original center of action. "By itself" implies more: self-sufficiency, self-enclosure (at least toward other creatures), essential unrelatedness—or at least the assigning of real relations to a distinctly lower, more adventitious level of existence.

Whether Descartes was fully aware of the significant shift in meaning he had introduced and fully intended it, is not clear (there some indications to the contrary because he occasionally proposes another more traditional definition). In fact it is this aura of self-enclosure and essential unrelatedness that got attached to the notion of substance from now on in the history of modern philosophy, and is one main reason why so many have later rejected it. Whitehead, for example, bases his whole rejection of substance explicitly on this Cartesian definition. According to Descartes, Whitehead tells us, substance is that which exists by itself, that which needs nothing else save God to exist. For Whitehead himself the opposite is true. "Actuality is through and through togetherness." Every actual entity is related to and influenced by every other actual entity in the world. Hence it cannot be a substance. Such a notion of substance has no relevance in the real world of intrinsically interrelated process.[15]

After rightly rejecting the Cartesian notion of substance as isolated and self-enclosed, however, Whitehead goes on to reject substance entirely, with no further discussion, as though this were the only available meaning of the term. He seems quite unaware of the whole classical notion of substance as intrinsically dynamic, self-communicative to others, and imbedded in a web of relations generated by action and interaction. I do not blame Whitehead that much for this misunderstanding. He knew Plato well but not Aristotle and certainly not Aquinas. I do object to contemporary Whiteheadians continuing to argue in the same way: first setting forth the Cartesian notion of substance, then demolishing it—correctly—and then concluding that the case in closed against substance. There may have been some excuse for Whitehead's doing this, coming late as he did to metaphysics, but not for perpetuating the same misunderstanding today.

The Inert, Unknowable Substratum of Locke

Another quite different notion of substance comes in with Locke. This is the identification of substance as the inert, unknowable substratum of accidents, which are alone known to us. These accidental properties need substance as an ontological support, but seem too much like pins stuck in a pin cushion, which is itself inert, static, without dynamic, self-communicative relationship with them and through them to the outside world. Although Locke speaks somewhat differently of the self, and seems to have started out with a more traditional notion of substance as agent, his growing interest in science and Newtonian physics gradually drew him towards assimilating the philosophical notion of substance to the scientific notion of underlying material substratum, on the model of Newton's atoms, that were themselves not active but moved from without.[16]

This notion of substance as essentially inert, passive substratum, unchanging in its being, became deeply imbedded in subsequent Western thought and is one of the main reasons why so many later thinkers to this day reject substance as opposed to activity, development, relationship. For this reason, Hegel, for example, felt he had to substitute "subject" for "substance" as the primary instance of being because the aura of inertness, passivity, and other materialistic connotations that had begun to infect the notion of substance through Locke rendered it inapt to express the dynamic activity and creative self-unfolding proper to the life of spirit. There is much to be learned from Hegel's critique, once substance is understood in the Lockean sense. (His solution, however, brought with it its own difficulties: the subject takes on an epistemological dimension in which it tends to become totally productive of its own object.)[17]

For a similar reason, many phenomenologists—and psychologists, in their philosophical moments—reject substance, on the grounds that what is really significant in the study of human beings is their activity, their behavior, their dynamic development, their relatedness, not their static, unchanging substance or essence. The retriever of classical substance would, of course, answer that substance is precisely the dynamic principle of all such activity and development, expressing its own self through them.

The Separable Substance of Hume

Still a different—and perhaps the most destructive—distortion is brought in by Hume, with strong roots in the nominalist tradition of William of Ockham. Hume, as is well known, rejects outright the notion of an abiding, self-identical substance, as an invention of the metaphysicians with no grounding in reality. The real (at least as regards our knowledge of it) is nothing more than a succession of discrete sense impressions, bound together in bundles. But the important point for our purposes is *what kind* of substance he rejects and why. It is clear from his arguments and those of his empiricist followers, like Bertrand Russell, that substance is something which, if it existed, would have to be found *separate* (or separable) from its accidental properties, existing in a kind of naked, indeterminate state. Since that is obviously impossible, indeed absurd—there can be, for example, no real human nature that exists as neither old nor young, black or white, fat or thin, wise or ignorant, a pure indeterminate blob without attributes—it follows that no such thing as substance exists as really distinct from its accidents or attributes.

The key to Hume's argument is that whatever exists as really *distinct* from something else must also be *separable* from it—at least in our imagination and, as far as we know, in reality. Thus, substance is a metaphysical mirage, a linguistic accident based on our Western subject-object languages and illegitimately projected into the real, as Bertrand Russell has put it.[18] This notion of substance as something not only distinct but *separable* from its accidents, that must be discovered *apart* from them, has been deeply imbedded in empiricist thought ever since, and is simply taken for granted as the only notion there is. The metaphysical principle upon which it is based, that all real distinction necessarily implies separability, is again simply taken for granted by Hume as obvious, never explicitly justified or argued for.

According to the classical understanding, on the contrary, a substance is indeed really *distinct* from (i.e., objectively irreducible to) its accidental attributes, but never *separable* from the whole body of them. As center of activity and relations, it must always possess some accidents, though particular ones may come and go. It is immanent in each of them, expresses itself through them, but transcends them all; it is never *reducible without remainder* to any or all of them. I must always have some particular height and weight, but I am not stuck permanently in the present one.

The association of substance with separability from all its accidents, especially from its relations to others, seems to be one of the main reasons why most, if not all, existentialists—with surprising unanimity on this point despite their other differences—and most phenomenologists reject substance as applying to the human person.[19] For them the person is so inseparable from I-Thou relations to others that its very being is constituted by relations; hence, they believe, it cannot be a substance. Thus, for Heidegger the human *Da-sein* is not to be identified with substance, the reason being that its very being is intrinsically constituted by its relation to Being as the receiver, interpreter, and spokesman of the latter's self-revelation. With the denial of substance, the "in-itself" dimension of being, the personal subject tends to dissolve into its relations, to become *nothing but* its relations to others. This culminates in the explicit rejection by the postmoderns and deconstructionists of all interiority, of all selfhood as nothing but the creation of literary texts.

What thinkers of this persuasion do not seem to be aware of is that by reducing beings to their relations they fall right into the trap of the Buddhists, based on the identical Humean principle that all real distinction necessarily implies separability. Whereas Hume used it to deny the reality of relations, the Buddhists turn it in the opposite direction to show the total reducibility of all beings to pure mutual relations. They then show that in such a system there is no ontological support for anything—nothing has "own-being," as they say—and the whole collapses into "emptiness" (*sunyatta*). Only nonrelated being can be truly real, and this is beyond access to concepts and language.

THE REINTEGRATION OF SUBSTANCE AND RELATION

We are now in a position to retrieve creatively the full richness of what it means to be, drawing on the resources of both classical and modern thought. We do not have to choose between substance and relation, between the in-itselfness of being and its transcendence toward others, as though they were opposed to or excluded each other. The intrinsic structure of all being is irreducibly dyadic: *substance-in-relation*. The dichotomizing of being into one or the other is due to one or more of the successive distortions of the original meaning of substance: the self-enclosed substance of Descartes, the inert, unknowable substance of Locke, or the separable substance of Hume— with numerous variations and interweaving of these themes. Once substance has been reconceived as the in-itself dimension of being that is also by its very nature oriented toward self-transcending, self-communicative action reaching out to others, and thus necessarily generative of a web of relations all around it, we can also integrate with it all the rich developments of the relational dimension so characteristic of later modern and contemporary thought, so deeply influenced by the relational structure of modern scientific thought. By the very nature of being as active presence, substance and relation are intrinsically complementary to each other, distinct but inseparable. *To be* in the world of real existents is to be *substance-in-relation*.

An important qualifying note must be added. Substance, like all the major metaphysical concepts, must be understood *analogously*. Like being itself as active presence, it is realized in different degrees of intensity and perfection on different levels of being. Thus, the human substance stands out from the common matrix of nature with a fairly strong individuality, autonomy, and self-possession. As one goes down the scale of being, this in-itselfness, which is a function of the immanent energy of existence as active presence, becomes weaker, less intense, more deeply dependent on the environmental matrix around it, less distinguishable from the fields which envelop it. When we reach the level of subatomic particles, they become interwoven so deeply with these developing fields that it is hard to identify where their individuality begins or ends. They exist only minimally as substances. There is more "outside" to them than "inside," we might say.

It remains an open question scientifically—perhaps even metaphysically—whether this in-itself dimension, this "interiority" aspect of being could ever fade out entirely and become pure relational field with no particles or centers of action at all. Here my reflections come to touch more closely the recent work of Ivor Leclerc, in whose honor these essays have been gathered, whose life's work has been to revitalize the philosophy—or perhaps more precisely the metaphysics—of nature. On one hand, contemporary metaphysicians have wisely become more cautious, in the light of the very strange phenomena uncovered at the fringes of nature by quantum physics, about legislating on a priori philosophical grounds what can be real and what not. Metaphysicians in the past have tended to ground their analyses of being a bit too exclusively on the middle levels of reality more immediately accessible to us in our direct human experience, in particular living things and persons. Thus, Aristotle's metaphysics of nature, substance, final causality, etc., find their clearest application on the levels of being from living organisms upwards, but become fuzzy when applied below this level. It is not clear in him whether the primal elements, earth, air, fire, and water, are to be classified as primary substances or not. The fringe phenomena of the subatomic world are also an authentic revelation of what it means to be, difficult as it may be for us at present to decipher and articulate just what they are revealing.

Despite this methodological caution, it does seem to me, as I think it does to Prof. Leclerc, more solidly plausible to hold that pure relational field theories of material reality as more primordial than particles are not adequate, either scientifically or metaphysically. Scientifically it does seem at present that it is not possible to substitute pure fields of energy for particles. Particles are always needed as correlative with fields, if not as primordially generative of fields. (A metaphysician, of course, cannot settle such questions scientifically.) Metaphysically speaking, it does seem to me that particles of some kind, which at least give the appearance of being more centered and unified, are the more plausible candidates for being the primal individual substances or natures which stand "in themselves" as original centers of action that generate relational fields out of their actions. Could it be, though, that energy fields themselves could have their own form and matter and thus somehow have enough of a unified action of their own to qualify as substances or basic entities in their own right? I am not sure whether or how a metaphysician could in principle rule this out. So I had better take the more prudent path of not trying to settle it with our present state of knowledge but leaving it rather as a question mark still enveloped in mystery. If particles, once paired, now seem to be instantaneously present to each other across space, why could there not be some space-and-time-transcending unity enabling a field to have some centered unity of action?

As we go up the scale of being, on the other hand, the inner intensity and autonomy, the in-itself aspect of substances, would gradually increase, so that they would stand out more and more distinctively and autonomously from their surrounding and supporting environments, finally attaining the level of self-initiating freedom in their actions such as we observe in human persons, partially limited though this still remains by outside influences. As we ascend still higher, the autonomy and freedom grows stronger, so that finally in the supreme being the in itselfness becomes total autonomy and self-sufficiency with all relations to the outside purely the result of its own free gratuitous initiatives. But at all levels real being would always remain dyadic, a polarity of active substance and relation, of in-self interiority and self-transcending outreach toward others.

APPLICATION TO THE HUMAN PERSON

It seems to me especially illuminating to apply this basic metaphysics of being to the level of reality closest and most significant to us, that of the human person. Let us begin with the theme of the proportionate correlativity of substance and its field of relations, in St. Thomas. For him, the higher one ascends on the ladder of being and the more immaterial a being becomes, the more its depth of interiority and self-possession increases, while at the same time in direct proportion the field of its relations broadens in scope and deepens in intensity and perfection. As St. Thomas puts it in one of his sweeping synoptic statements:

The higher a power the more comprehensive is the sphere of objects toward which it is ordered. The entire range over which the soul's activity extends can be ordered into three levels. One of the soul's powers concerns only the body to which the soul is joined; this kind of power is called the vegetative faculty, and its activity affects only the body to which this soul is joined. Then there is in the soul another kind of power that relates to a wider sphere, namely, to all material objects accessible through the senses and not just relating to the body to which the soul is joined. And a third kind of power in the soul is directed toward an even more comprehensive sphere of objects: not only toward all material things but toward all that exists.[20]

Josef Pieper, commenting on this text, sums the point up beautifully:

To sum it up then: to have (or to be) an "intrinsic existence" means "to be able to relate" and "to be the sustaining center of a field of reference." The hierarchy of existing things, being equally a hierarchy of intrinsic existences, corresponds on each level to the intensity and extension of the respective relationship in their power, character, and domain. Consequently, the spirit-based self, the highest form of being and of intrinsic existence as well, must have the most intensive power to relate and the most comprehensive domain of relatedness: the universe of all existing things. These two aspects combined—dwelling most intensively within itself and being *capax universi*, able to grasp the universe—together constitute the essence of the spirit. Any definition of "spirit" will have to contain these two aspects as its core.[21]

St. Thomas develops in detail the intellectual aspect of this comprehensiveness of relations as one of his favorite themes: "It has been said that the soul is in a certain sense all in all; for its nature is directed toward universal knowledge. In this manner it is possible for the perfection of the entire world to be present in one single being."[22] The same is true of the will, with its corresponding power to relate to and love all beings in the universe as good. As we have seen earlier, "Every substance exists for the sake of its operations"; it follows that the authentic life of the soul, the full flowering of perfection of the human person as such, consists of the fullest and broadest possible self-transcendence toward loving relationships to others. To *be* authentically for a human person is to *live in love*, to express itself by loving, in the broadest sense of the term, to make itself the center of the widest possible web of relationships to all things, and especially to all persons, through our two major self-relating and self-transcending powers, knowledge and love. To live as a person is to live in relation.[23]

St. Thomas has laid down clearly the metaphysical underpinnings of this relational dimension of the person as spirit. The full phenomenological development of the point had to wait for the rich descriptive analyses of the personalist existentialists and phenomenologists of our own day, such as Martin Buber, Gabriel Marcel, etc. St. Thomas would have been delighted with them, I am sure. But despite all their richness, these descriptions tend too often to stress the relational side of the person so exclusively that the correlative pole of indepth interiority and self-possession, the in-itself dimension of the person, becomes obscured or even wiped out. The extreme of this tendency has revealed itself in the various forms of postmodernism, with their openly declared "war against interiority." For St. Thomas there is no need to play down the substance pole of a being in order to safeguard the relational: the substance itself is the active source from which flow the relations as its own self-expression. To absorb the person entirely into its relations, into its "toward-others," is to empty it of anything truly belonging to it that is worth expressing to others. There is no merit in giving oneself totally to others unless one has something to give.

In connection with this notion of the person as intrinsically relational, it is interesting to note that Cardinal Josef Ratzinger, in his often remarkably insightful and creative earlier theological writings, makes the point that the Christian theological tradition did not have to wait for contemporary phenomenology to discover the relational dimension of the person. It was already deeply imbedded in its own Gospel revelation and theological explication of the Trinity, though this has never, he feels, been adequately developed and exploited in the Christian philosophical tradition. The very notion of person in the doctrine of God as three Persons in one divine nature is a totally relational one. Each Person is distinguished from the others solely by its relational character, by "the opposition of relations," as it is technically called; all else in the divine nature is held in common. Thus, the Father knows himself *as Father* only in communicating the whole "absolute" perfection of his divine nature to the Son, that is, as Giver; whereas the Son knows himself *as Son* only in receiving this same nature from the Father, that is, as Receiver; so too the Holy Spirit is known only as the love image breathed forth by both Father and Son as the expression of their mutual love. The whole personality of Jesus as expressed in the Gospels is also totally relational, dialogical, *toward the Father*: "All that I have I have received from my Father...all that my Father has he has given to me...my food is to do my Father's will," etc. So we, too, come to know ourselves, what we are and who we are, only by looking in the eyes of another, through the loving (or hating) look in the eyes of another person, the "I" through the "Thou" and vice versa.

The notion of the self, the person, as primordially an isolated, atomic individual, only accidentally related to others, came in much later with

Descartes and Locke. It is as alien to the classical and medieval Christian tradition, both theological and philosophical, as their notions of substance are to the classical and medieval one of substance as active relation-generating center. The human person, in fact, comes into existence enveloped in a web of relations of dependence on others even before it can begin to generate its own relations actively: dependence on God as the ultimate source of its being, on its parents for the gift of its nature, on the surrounding environment for the necessary conditions for its survival and growth (air, temperature, good, etc.). Its whole development will consist in relating itself appropriately, both actively and responsively, to the world around it and especially to other persons, both human and divine. The Christian *philosophical* tradition, however, at least in its medieval scholastic—and even Thomistic—forms, although it had laid down well the metaphysical foundations for the notion of person as intrinsically relational, in fact got so preoccupied in its technical analyses with determining in just what consisted the "incommunicability" or distinctness of persons from each other that it failed to develop and highlight with full explicitness the relational pole, equally intrinsic to all persons, that was already so richly imbedded in its own theological sources.[24]

CONCLUSION

In our own time, however, there is no longer any need for us to get stuck exclusively in one or other of the two correlative poles of real being, substance *or* relation. It is high time to retrieve the full richness of the classical notion of substance as active center generative (and receptive) of relations, and restore the full polarity of the real which flourishes only in the vital tension and mutual complementarity of substance *and* relation. In sum, *to be is to be substance-in-relation*. And the ultimate reason for this is, in what to my mind is the essence of St. Thomas' metaphysical vision, that the *esse* (the "to be") or act of existing that is the deepest core of every real being is of its very nature not just presence but *active presence*: presence both in itself and actively presenting itself to others. "It is the nature of every actuality to communicate itself insofar as it is possible. Hence every agent acts according as it exists in actuality." "Communication follows upon the very intelligibility (*ratio*) of actuality." (See notes 4 and 6.)

NOTES

1. One of the best expositions of the Thomistic doctrine of substance can be found in L. De Raeymaeker, *The Philosophy of Being* (St. Louis: Herder, 1954), chap. 7.

2. *Summa contra Gentiles*, Bk. III, chap. 26.

3. *Sum. c. Gent.*, Bk. I, chap. 45.

4. *Sum. c. Gent.*, Bk. III, chap. 113.

5. *De Potentia*, q. 2, art. 1.

6. *Expositio in Libros Sententiarum*, Bk. I, dist. 4, q. 1, art. 1.

7. *Summa Theologiae*, I, q. 19, art. 2.

8. *Sum. c. Gent.*, Bk. II, chap. 79.

9. *Sum. c. Gent* Bk. II, chap. 94.

10. *Sum. Theol.*, I, q. 77, art 1 ad 7.

11. Cf. De Raeymaeker, *Philosophy of Being*, 174–177.

12. W. Norris Clarke, "Action as the Self-Revelation of Being: A Central Theme in the Thought of St. Thomas," in L. Thro, ed., *History of Philosophy in the Making: Essays in Honor of James Collins* (Washington: Univ. Press of America, 1982), 63–80.

13. For the discussion of this whole question of the self-diffusiveness of the good and the freedom of creation, cf. M. J. Nicolas, OP, "Bonum est diffusivum sui," *Revue thomiste*, 55 (1955): 363–376; Kevin Keane, "Why Creation? Bonaventure and Thomas Aquinas on God as Creative Good," *Downside Review* 93 (1975): 100–121. The consistency of the two notions was given a famous challenge by Arthur Lovejoy in his *Great Chain of Being* (Cambridge, Mass.: Harvard University Press, 1942). Henry Veatch's and Anton Pegis's answers and Lovejoy's response to each can be found in *Philosophy and Phenomenological Research*, 7 (1946). Norman Kretzmann has reopened the question in his "Goodness, Knowledge and Indeterminacy in the Philosophy of Thomas Aquinas," *Journal of Philosophy*, 80 (1983): 631–649.

14. *Replies to the 4th Series of Objections* in Haldane & Ross, eds., *Philosophical Works of Descartes* (Cambridge Univ. Press, 1931), vol. 2: 101.

15. See the fine discussion of Whitehead on substance: James Felt, "Whitehead's Misconception of Substance," *Process Studies*, 14 (1985): 224–236.

16. For a useful study of Locke on substance, see Gregory Reichberg, "Nominalism and the Inscrutability of Substance in Locke's *Essay Concerning Human Understanding*," *Proc. of Amer. Cath. Phil. Assoc.*, 61 (1987):132–142.

17. Cf. the fine study of Kenneth Schmitz, "Substance Is Not Enough. Hegel's Slogan: From Substance to Subject," *Proc. Amer. Cath. Phil. Assoc.* 61 (1987): 52–68.

18. *A History of Western Philosophy* (New York: Simon & Schuster, 1945), 201–202.

19. Cf. William Shearson, "The Common Assumptions of Existentialist Philosophy," *Internat. Phil. Quarterly*, 15 (1975): 131–147.

20. *Sum. Theol.*, I, q. 78, art. 1.

21. Josef Pieper, *The Truth of All Things*, reprinted in *The Living Truth* (San Francisco: Ignatius Press, 1989), 83.

22. *De Veritate*, q. 2, art. 2.

23. As Maritain beautifully expresses it: "Thus it is that when a man has been fully awakened to the sense of being or existence, and grasps intuitively the obscure, living depth of the Self and subjectivity, he discovers by the same token the basic generosity of existence and realises, by virtue of the inner dynamism of this intuition, that love is not a passing pleasure or emotion, but the very meaning of his being alive." *Existence and the Existent* (Garden City: Doubleday, 1957), 90.

24. Cf. Josef Ratzinger, *Introduction to Christianity* (New York: Crossroad, 1969), 102–103; and the more fully developed exposition of his position in "Zum Personverständnis in der Theologie," ["Theology's Understanding of the Person"] *Dogma und Verkündigung* (Munich: Wewel, 1973), 205–223. The author includes St. Thomas in his criticism. A translation into English of this creative and challenging essay has been completed by Rev. M. J. O'Connell, *Dogma and Preaching* (Chicago: Franciscan Herald Press, 1985), and another by Michael Waldstein in *Communio*, 17 (1990): 439–454.

Section Three
The Subject as Foundation

10

Temporality and the Concept of Being

Albert Shalom

If the object of an inquiry is a constituent of the physical world, such as a physical force or a chemical substance, it is not incumbent on the inquirer to raise the prior question of the basis of the inquiry itself. This is also true of the bodily functions of organisms endowed with subjective capacities because the body is also constituted of such physical forces and chemical substances. This situation no longer holds when the object of inquiry refers primarily to the nature of subjectivity itself, rather than to the elements and processes of the spatio-temporal world from which subjects have emerged. The physical universe is a process of cosmological and biological evolution which stretches back for billions of years prior to the appearance on this planet of any sort of subject, nonhuman or human. Subjects did emerge in the course of that evolution. Therefore, it follows that if we are to attempt an analysis of any concept which does not refer primarily to the physical world itself, but rather to the implications of subjectivity, then it is necessary to begin by situating subjectivity relatively to the evolutionary process.

By virtue of its very generality, the word 'being' does not refer to any specific element or reaction of the spatio-temporal process. It does not even refer to the constituents involved in the very process referred to by the expression "spatio-temporal process." The word 'being' is not meant to be limited to the realities referred to by the terms 'space', 'time', and 'process', but is meant to encompass all of these and much else besides. This means that any analysis of the concept of being must also refer to the way we conceive things in general, including space, time, and process. The consequence of this is that it would be misleading to try to elucidate the significance of this word 'being' without a reciprocal analysis of the foundations which can allow for such signifying to occur, that is to say, conceptual thinking. In other words, before trying to elucidate the word 'being', it is necessary to sketch out a theory of how significant discourse became possible at all: the problem of the concept of being is correlative to that of the being of concepts. For the very fact that conceptual thinking is an activity characteristic of an entity which has emerged in the course of cosmological and biological evolution, is a clear statement that the possibility of conceptual thinking is itself grounded in some aspect of that evolutionary process which has, in fact, given rise to entities possessed of such capacities.

At this point it is necessary to refer to a conceptual framework which is the spontaneously natural framework of common-sense thinking. The framework constituted by the physical and the mental, treating these two concepts as basic or ultimate, is perhaps the oldest framework in the history of philosophy. It is a framework which gave rise to the first great systematic analysis of fundamental philosophy, namely Plato's system based on his familiar theory of Ideas. In terms of this system concepts are viewed as the recollections in individual psyches of these Ideas postulated as eternal existences of an intelligible world of true being. These objectively existing Ideas serve as the intellectual foundation on the basis of which the physical universe is held to be organized. The point which concerns us here is that Ideas and psyche are postulated as both irreducible and as the formative principle of the physical world. Clearly, such a theory is not compatible with a theory of the emergence of conceptual thinking, or mind, in the course of cosmological and biological evolution.

If we are to take evolution seriously, what can be said of Plato's theory and of the many variations on this theory is that because the antiquity of the evolutionary process was not known, it could not be taken into consideration. Therefore, there could be no query regarding the *emergence* of entities endowed with subjective capacities in the course of the evolutionary process itself. Only the later results of evolution could be taken into account, and these results pointed to the reality of a physical world and to the reality of a mental world which appeared to be of an entirely different nature. It is no doubt in this manner that the physical/mental framework came to be constituted. Constituted against the background of a long period of religion and mythology, it was quite natural that the mind component of this framework came to be directly related to the divine, if not identified with it. This quasi-divinity and quasi-autonomy of the mind-component of the physical/mental framework is, of course, one of the major themes of the history of philosophy. Thus, even in Aristotle's more realistic approach to philosophy, the platonic Ideas are maintained under a different modality. The Ideas are simply transposed into "forms" held to constitute the inner or immanent essences of particular objects, defining them as what they actually are. These same forms now become the direct object of knowledge for the passive intellect of the human being which can identify with these forms by virtue of its illumination by a god, itself conceived as the active intellect of self-reflexive thinking.

The dominance of the mind component of the matter/mind framework became even more absolute as a result of the Cartesian revolution. Paradoxically, the source of Descartes' philosophy lies in the extrusion of any mind factor from the physical world. The requirements of the new physics which was coming to a head in the seventeenth century constitute, in my view, the primary *raison d'être* of Descartes's philosophy. One of those requirements was a conception of matter which would be purified of all Aristotelian and scholastic "substantial forms." The metaphysical correlate of this new physics was a return to the Platonic assertion of a pure mind, an assertion rendered more radical by Descartes's prior assertion, around 1632, of matter as pure material extension. However, the price which had to be paid for this radical matter/mind dichotomy was, precisely, a separation which could not be taken as literally true. This is not the place to do more than simply mention the long history of the endeavor to transform the physical into a phenomenological manifestation of a mental conceived as transcendental subject or absolute spirit. From Malebranche's reinterpretation of Cartesian extension as an intelligible extension grasped through human participation in the creative ideas of God, to Berkeley's "immaterialism" transforming the physical world into perceptions of the ideas of God, and thereby concluding that "being" is, in effect, "to be perceived"; from Kant's transformation of the physical world into a "phenomenal" world structured by virtue of a transcendental synthesis, to Fichte's conception of the world as a "not-self" posited by an absolute self, or to Hegel's conception of being as the self-explicating dialectic of an absolute spirit: this endeavor to integrate the physical into a transcendental version of the mental has, surely, been one of the main drives of philosophy since the seventeenth century.

That this idealist drive should have engendered the purely materialist reactions of a Freud, for instance, is not only a consequence of the developments of the physical sciences but also a consequence of the spontaneous use of the matter/mind framework as ultimate. If the physical cannot be interpreted in terms of a transcendental version of the mental, then it is natural to suppose that mind must be explicable in terms of the physical. That, at any rate, is the presupposition of a thinker like Freud, as well as that of a number of contemporary philosophers and neurologists. However, the supposition that subjective experience is a direct emanation of neurochemical reactions is, it would seem, necessarily nullified by the fact that there are no such things as neurochemical reactions of this sort which do not already presuppose the presence of a subject of experiencing. If it is the case that subjective manifestations are derived from the physical, then it must be, as I shall attempt to argue, from an aspect of the physical which is not amenable to physical and chemical analysis.

There is one final preliminary point which needs to be made. There have been a number of recent approaches, on the part of both philosophers and scientists, in terms of the self-differentiating processes of a holistic universe explicating itself by virtue of an immanent principle of organization and of differentiation, suggesting the idea of a sort of *anima mundi* or *god-universe* in the making. Such approaches do not use mentalistic language but aim at encompassing the physical and the mental by the use of a terminology which is sufficiently general to be apparently applicable to both. The word 'process' is itself one of these general terms, as are the expressions 'adaptation', used by Max Delbrück, or 'universal programme', used by the adherents of the anthropic principle, or 'self-differentiation of the whole', used by some metaphysicians. The principal difficulty of these approaches is that in their formulations, the analyses of these approaches seem to slide over from the physical to the sentient and then to the conceptual without any clear explanation of how manifestations so different from each other can, in fact, have derived from an initial physical which is frequently simply taken for granted. To simply point to adaptation, for instance, or to use an expression like 'organizational *integration*', tells us nothing at all about the actual fact of sensation or of thinking, and does not relate these manifestations to the physical world in any intelligible manner.

To set the framework of the ensuing analysis, I will refer to what seem to me to be two incontrovertible but related facts, the one concerning the ontogenesis of sentient and thinking individuals, and the other referring to the analogous phylogenesis which has led to the appearance on this planet of organisms capable of sentience and of thinking. In a paper as brief as this one must be, I can only summarize a theory which would require a good deal more elaboration for its full justification. The first of the two facts to which I have referred is that the real beginning of each one of us is neither sensations nor thinking, but the specific fertilized ovum from which each and every one of us has developed. It is precisely because the capacities for sensing and for thinking have emerged from the growth of this or that specific fetus that the Cartesian dichotomy between matter and mind is simply misleading. For the same reason, it is entirely misleading to refer to the physical world as either a phenomenal or a phenomenological world, for there is no such thing as autonomous thinking or autonomous subjectivity. Organisms capable of sentience and of thinking are in direct contact with the physical world, in accordance with their different and specific physiological and nervous structures, because all such organisms are derived from the processes of the physical universe. The second related fact to which I have referred should now be obvious: what is true on the scale of the individual is equally true on the universal scale of cosmological and biological evolution. In a sense, each individual capable of subjectivity is, according to its particular manner, a recapitulation in brief of the universal process of evolution.

Of course, this does not as yet give us any clue as to the emergence of individuals capable of sentience and of conceptualization. It does at least indicate that the temporal process is constitutive in the emergence both of individuals capable of subjectivity and of those subjective capacities themselves. The fact that temporality is constitutive in this way is the essential theme of this theory. We know that organisms capable of subjectivity are latecomers in the course of evolution, and the science of cosmology has taught us that within the framework of cosmological evolution, they are very latecomers indeed. In other words, the processes of temporality have been in operation since the beginning of this universe and long antedate anything we can really call subjectivity. If the theory of "the big bang" has any validity, we can suppose that that high-density and high-temperature explosion of energy constituted, in effect, the beginnings of space, time, and matter. Therefore, these elements must be held as the constitutive factors of the early universe. If we must suppose, as we surely must, that it is from the reciprocal interactions involving these elements that entities endowed with subjective capacities have emerged in the course of evolution, then it is to the operations of these elements that we must look for an explanation of the emergence of subjectivity.

Let us now consider this situation from the reverse side, so to speak, from the side of subjectivity itself. Clearly, time is a fundamental factor in subjectivity, but it is not clear in what sense this is so. I shall argue that subjectivity is temporal in a sense that is very different from the mechanical linear time associated with spatio-temporal activities. The temporality we ascribe to the processes of the physical universe is an abstraction from a reality which physics holds to be indissolubly spatio-temporal. Abstraction is, of course, a function of conceptual thought, but the point of fundamental importance is that even if we consider the most elementary of sensations, we will have to recognize a mode of temporality which is quite other than the temporality we ascribe to the spatio-temporal process itself. For though, as we shall see, the sensations themselves directly relate us to the spatio-temporal events of the physical world, sensing as such, sensing as a manifestation of experience, is a purely temporal event which possesses neither spatiality nor materiality. The sensing of the color "red" has no mass and does not have length, breadth, or depth. Nor is it as *sensing* of the color red: as sensing it possesses no quality other than the fact that it constitutes a purely temporal event. *What* is sensed is described by referring to qualities *and* quantities, but *that* there is sensation is a purely temporal event. As an event it is temporal, as a certain kind of event it is qualitative. The experience of red and the experience of blue are both temporal events, and in that they are identical; as kinds of temporal events they, of course, differ. In the spatio-temporal processes of cosmological and biological evolution, the emergence of entities capable of registering qualities in a purely temporal manner is the emergence of something entirely new.

Temporality and the Concept of Being

If we now relate the operations of spatio-temporality which have been active since the beginnings of the universe with the appearance of organisms capable of subjective manifestations involving a temporality dissociated from mass and from spatiality, we are faced with the essential problem of the metaphysical approach proposed here. Concurrently with this essential problem, and because of it, we are also in possession of the initial sketch of a conceptual scheme which aims at undercutting the Cartesian framework by holding that subjectivity, and therefore mind, are derivative, and therefore cannot constitute irreducible elements of an ultimate metaphysical framework. For the thesis which is being proposed here is the inverse of those theories in terms of which temporality is to be attributed to the constitutive activity of some mode of transcendental subjectivity or to the presence of a so-called *Dasein* whose *da* is supposed to be the locus of differentiations between past, present, and future. From the standpoint adopted here, there is no such thing as "transcendental" subjectivity: it is a concept which came to seem metaphysically necessary only because of the inevitable implications of the Cartesian framework which rapidly became so integral a part of philosophical thinking.

In terms of the conceptual framework adopted here, subjectivity, in any sense in which we can conceive it, does not give rise to temporality: on the contrary, it is the operations of an equivocal temporality, a temporality which is beyond our control, which constitute the source of subjectivity. This, of course, immediately raises the several problems regarding the manner in which temporality can give rise to subjectivity and regarding the implications of a process of this nature. If I suppose my dog to be watching the movements of a neighboring cat, and if I consider the situation in terms of the physical processes involved, I will have to refer to a multiplicity of reactions which together constitute the domain of the physical and the biological sciences. And since I do not believe, as Whitehead did believe, that there is any degree of subjectivity involved at the level of elementary particles, I hold these multiple reactions to be physical, chemical, and biological in the traditional sense of these words. Concretely, this means that there is an actual spatio-temporal scene which will be varyingly accessible according to the structure and processes of the organism concerned. I do not, therefore, have to suppose that a bird, a dog, or a human being is supposed to engage in some sort of phenomenological construction; in terms of phenomenology I do not see how one can avoid supposing such a process for animals as well as for humans. Again, it will also be necessary to refer to a multitude of signals—photons, sound waves and the like—and to the different organs of reception for those different signals, again according to the particular structure of the organism concerned.

The position is, of course, realist in the sense of referring to the physical universe which is common to all of us, animals and humans, but it is not what is referred to as "naive" realism because so much depends on the physiological structure and the temporal processes of the organism involved. Whatever the spatio-temporal scene might be "in itself," it is clear that the differentiations of energy frequencies or signals, and the differentiations of organs of reception, will give rise to a fragmentation of that real spatio-temporal scene. In point of fact, if we pursue the analysis in terms of the physics and the physiology involved, we shall very soon come to realize that this initial fragmentation in terms of signals and of organs of reception for these signals must be pushed much further to become something like a veritable dissolution. For the signals affecting different organs of reception culminate in very complex series of chemical reactions in the different organs involved, and in an even more complex series of electrical and neurochemical reactions in the nervous system. What is there in common, we may be tempted to ask, between this complex of physical and physiological reactions and the scene perceived by my dog or by myself? This, once again, is to view the situation in terms of the Cartesian framework, and it is just this framework which is here being rejected. In terms of the framework adopted in this approach, my beginnings are neither sensations nor thoughts, but a particular fetus to which no subjective manifestations can be attributed in its initial phase. There is no contradiction in accepting the physicalist analysis as a starting point, provided it is possible to move from this starting point to the emergence of sensations and of thought.

Now, given the physical and the physiological background to this general situation, the question which must now be raised is how does all this lead to my dog being able to watch the antics of the neighbor's cat? All the processes collectively referred to as the physics, chemistry and physiology of the situation are spatio-temporal processes, changes which involve matter and which are measurable and reproducible in isolation in the laboratory. As we have seen, such is not the case for the subjective acts of seeing, hearing, smelling, watching, and the like. However frequently the physical and chemical processes involved are reproduced in the laboratory, they will never give rise to the subjective consequences of actual organisms actually sensing. This actual sensing is in the form of purely temporal occurrences involving, in themselves, no component of spatiality or materiality. So the question arises of how such a complex variety of spatio-temporal reactions can possibly give rise to the purely temporal occurrence of sensing. The clue to a possible solution can only lie in the extraordinary occurrence of a purely temporal event, an event dissociated from spatiality and from materiality.

A purely temporal occurrence is something which exists nowhere in nature except in experiencing organisms: which is to say that experiencing organisms must be so structured as to be loci of purely temporal events. The actual locus of a purely temporal event cannot be the body or the brain as such, for these are spatio-temporal organs and can only mediate between the spatio-temporal processes of the world and the spatio-temporal processes of the body itself. We, therefore, have no other alternative but to postulate another sort of locus, but a locus so intimately associated with body that this latter must serve as mediation for the activities of the physical world and of its own internal physicochemical processes. Both subjective experiences and subjective acts are temporal occurrences; therefore, we again have no alternative but to postulate a locus of a purely temporal nature, but a temporal nature of such a kind that it can, in fact, serve as a locus for a series of ephemeral temporal events. Such a locus can only be that of a temporal permanence or a temporal identity; nothing else but some kind of temporal identity can constitute an actual, real, concrete locus for purely temporal events.

There is no separate substance defining the subjectivity of a cat, a dog, or a human being. The subjectivities of these entities are defined by the differing potentialities of temporal identity as these express themselves in the differing physiological structures of this or that organism. The expression "temporal identity" is, of course, an abstract expression, whereas the reality to which such expression refers is anything but abstract. Before completing the summary description of the nature of sensations, it will be as well to situate this concept of temporal identity in the broader framework of cosmological evolution. In terms of our own abstract concept of linear time, cosmologists measure the spatio-temporal processes of evolution in the billions of years. To make sense of the emergence of organisms endowed with subjective capacities, I am postulating a progressive process of the internalization of time itself.

Insofar as we consider the phase of spatio-temporal process prior to the emergence of subjective organisms, the concept of internalization is the equivalent of that of the combination or formation of the successively more and more complex physical and chemical bodies produced in the course of evolution, and progressively establishing the ordered modes of activity which were later to be summarized as the laws of physics, chemistry and biology. With the emergence of organisms capable of subjective experience, we can no longer refer to combinations and to the increasingly complex structures of physical bodies. Neurologists and brain/mind identity theorists repeatedly refer to the extraordinary complexity of the structure and neurochemistry of the brain, as if this should *ipso facto* explain sensory experience. But however complex, physical structure is physical structure and the idea of complexity simply does not provide an explanation for the appearance of something so fundamentally different from physical structure or physical process as the pure temporality of the simplest of sensations. For that reason, the materialist's supposition that sensory experience constitutes a sort of gaseous emanation from neurochemical reactions seems to me conceptually incoherent. Chemical complexity is not commensurate with sensing, as the neurologist, Hughlings Jackson, pointed out a century ago.

Conversely, unless we are to magically introduce an entirely new substance called sensation or mind, we must accept the evidence that organisms capable of sensing emerged in the course of evolution. And this means that we must derive this capacity for sensations from the spatio-temporal process itself. Since we know that the sensing of sensations is a series of temporal occurrences, it seems to me that once again, we have no alternative but to attribute this sensing to something involving the factor of temporality in this spatio-temporal process. Having postulated the necessity of a temporal identity as basis for the occurrence of purely temporal events, I must conclude that in the case of certain entities which have reached a certain stage of anatomical and physiological development, there occurs an inversion or an internalization of the time factor in the spatio-temporal process. This internalization of the time factor itself is the establishment of a temporal identity as locus or foundation of the spatio-temporal growth of the physical organism itself.

Though I'm not here concerned with theological issues, I think it necessary to point out that such a process can have nothing to do with those hypostatized analogues of human thinking called *transcendental* egos or *transcendental* subjects. We are talking about an evolutionary process which long antedates the appearance of any organism capable of any sort of subjectivity. What we are concerned with is just precisely the conditions for the appearance of such entities. We cannot find the source of subjective capacities in chemical reactions per se, or in the body of laws of the physical sciences, nor in such abstract concepts as process itself or a supposed "principle of self-differentiation and self-integration." Instead, we must look for it in the constitutive principles of physical existence itself. It is increasingly recognized that temporality is the most obscure and the most fundamental of these constitutive principles. If the operations of a fundamentally equivocal temporality can indeed explain the emergence of subjective capacities, then what this ultimately points to is not the quasi-god whom philosophers have equated with their own mentalistic capacities, but a God who is the master of time and eternity and, therefore, of the entire evolutionary process.

To return to the argument, how then does sensation occur? We are left with signals from an external world and the transformation and dissolution of these signals into the complex totality of physiological and neurochemical reactions. On the other hand, we now have a locus of temporal identity constituting the ontological foundation of both the particularity of the organism in question and of its subjective capacities. Despite appearances to the contrary, we are almost in possession of an initial sketch for a solution. What we now need to do is to reject one of the most pernicious consequences of the

Cartesian framework: the doctrine of primary and secondary qualities. We know that the founders of the new science believed that objective reality consists of nothing but matter in motion, and in Descartes's system this became the assertion that all the qualitative aspects of the external world are no more than properties of the human mind. With the rejection of the Cartesian framework comes the rejection of this unlikely consequence. In this world of evolution we know that a vast variety of animals function in terms of smell, sight and sound. To interpret such actions as no more than reflex actions consequent on the reception of different energy frequencies is, itself, no more than an attempt to preserve the essentials of the Cartesian framework. A soundless explosion, a colorless flower, are concepts which have no meaning outside the Cartesian framework.

Colors and sounds exist in the physical world—for those entities which have the structure and organs to see them and to hear them—and what we need is a process of transposition to entities capable of subjectivity. Together with temporal identity, the objectivity of qualities gives us the key to the solution of our problem. It also provides a theory as to the essential function of the nervous system. In the spatio-temporal world the color red is manifested by a certain energy frequency or wavelength. The quality is carried by the frequency and in the purely physical world does not exist without it. The frequency and its accompanying qualitative manifestation are carried to an organism possessed of eyes and of a nervous system. The chemical composition of the eye or nervous system may not be affected by this particular frequency, in which case the organism cannot experience the color red. If, on the other hand, the organism's physiological and nervous structure are affected by this particular energy frequency, and if the chemistry of the eye is free from any constantly unusual chemical reaction leading to color blindness, then we can suppose that the regularity of this signal leads to physical and neurochemical reactions which are equally regular. Instead of supposing that it is these physical and neurochemical reactions themselves which give rise to the sensing of red, we on the contrary suppose that these chemical reactions are the termination or the end processes of the space-time signals of frequencies or wavelengths.

But what happens to the accompanying quality of redness? In the spatio-temporal world it cannot be dissociated from the frequency which manifests it. As a quality, as a manifestation carried by an energy frequency, it can in principle be dissociated from spatiality and motion: in itself, and given the appropriate conditions, it is nothing but a qualitative occurrence. Since we are postulating a temporal identity as foundation of the organism capable of sensing, can we not then infer that this potentially purely qualitative occurrence is just precisely of such a nature as to be able to manifest itself as a temporal event in the locus of temporal identity? From this standpoint, experiencing "red" is, in effect, registering, through the locus of temporal identity, a quality of the external world whilst the dynamic frequency which subtends it is being processed and, in effect, absorbed by the chemistry of the body and the brain; it follows that the essential function of the nervous system would be to allow for the transmission of the qualities from the physical world to the locus of temporal identity.

When we consider the springs of animal action—hunger, pain, sexual drive, fear, and so on—their explanation will be of the same kind. By virtue of the temporal permanence as foundation of the living body, these internal bodily drives are to the chemistry of the body what the qualities of the external world are to their associated spatio-temporal processes. When I have a toothache, it would be quite artificial to suppose that certain chemical changes around my teeth affecting certain nerves and bringing about certain neurochemical changes then retranslate themselves into an entirely different form called sensations. What I feel as a pain in my tooth *is* those chemical and neurochemical changes. I feel them as sensations of pain because I *am* my bodily changes by virtue of my spatio-temporal processes, and I *am* the sensory counterpart of these changes by virtue of my quasi-timeless foundation. It is for this reason that the living body is so fundamentally different from the purely spatio-temporal objects of the physical world. And it is for the same reason that however closely the anatomy and the chemical composition of a corpse approximates to that of a living body, the chemical processes of both cannot function in the same way: the quasi-timeless foundation has vanished from the physical, space-time world, and, therefore, the physicochemical processes are no longer directed to the locus of temporal identity.

If I have lingered on the subject of sensations, it is because they constitute the basic elements of subjective life. Their specific nature as this or that type of sensation depends on the physical and chemical functioning of the world and of the body, but their generic nature as a mode of experiencing depends on a foundation of temporal permanence or temporal identity. In other words, consciousness derives from the timeless and is not, as the Cartesian framework holds, an irreducible reality. A sufficient analysis of conceptual thinking would take even longer, but for the purpose of the present paper it is no longer necessary, for the essential point has been made: subjectivity derives from the timeless. This is more fundamentally the case for conceptualization than for sensing because conceptualization is a consequence of a further operation of temporality. But what remains is the essential principle that concepts derive from the timeless, and that therefore timelessness is the fundamental "being" of concepts. It will, therefore, be enough to indicate very briefly what is involved in conceptualization before we turn to the concept of being.

Animals adapt immediately, almost, and spontaneously to the environment in which they are born, but when the human being emerged, what emerged with him was the loss of this paradise of spontaneous adaptation. What was born was a creature with the initial makings of a sense of self over against a world which presented itself to him as other, as alien and, no doubt, as fearsome. It is no accident that religious mythologies are the first mode of human thinking. To see oneself as descended from gods is a way of appropriating an alien world, but what concerns us is the operation underlying this new emergence. If the possibility of sensations depends on the internalization of time, establishing a temporal identity as foundation of the sensing organism, then the possibility of a sensing entity which distinguishes itself as other than the world it senses must depend on an operation bringing that temporal identity itself to its own self-manifestation. This can be most clearly seen if we consider sensations themselves. By virtue of their foundation as temporal identities, sensing organisms can identify differing aspects of the sensory physical world. But when a subsequent operation has brought about the self-manifesting of a temporal identity itself, which is what we call personal identity, then the identification of sensations is experienced as an identification made by the new subjectivity itself. My dog is not aware that it is distinguishing this from that: it simply distinguishes between them. Humans very rapidly do become aware that they are distinguishing between this and that.

Before a year has passed, the human child spontaneously differentiates between itself and its surroundings. As the psychoanalyst and developmental psychologist, David Stern, remarks, the child has a sense of self long before the use of language. I would only add that it is for this very reason that the child can develop the use of language. The foundation for the use of language, in the proper sense of that word, is not Chomsky's Cartesian concept of a "deep grammar," it is the ontological fact of personal identity which naturally leads the child to differentiate between itself and the world around it. This also constitutes the ultimate foundation of conceptualization, followed by the later sense of self-awareness. For this reality of personal identity brings to birth a new type of consciousness. It brings to birth a type of consciousness which is not limited to acts of identification of the varying qualities of the physical world and to the empirical use of such information. It brings to birth a type of consciousness which spontaneously identifies by recognizing that similar sensations are similar, and different sensations different. This has the most far-reaching implications, for it is, in effect, the implicit recognition of order in the universe. To recognize that red is red and that red differs from green, is a different mode of recognition than that which recognizes red and reacts to it one way, whilst recognizing green and reacting to it in another way. The difference lies in the fact that the former mode of recognition is the implicit recognition of the principle of noncontradiction, and that is a conceptual act.

But such a conceptual act is only possible for a creature which can spontaneously differentiate between itself and what it experiences, that is to say which makes the spontaneous distinction establishing the difference between subject and object. The only kind of creature able to make such a distinction is a creature so structured that what it experiences is experienced as being other than itself. This is only possible if the temporal identity at the root of sensing subjects is a temporal identity manifesting its identity to itself, a personal identity. Concepts are, therefore, acts of identification of a creature of this sort, acts which we refer to when speaking of ourselves as acts of the intellect. But if it is clear, from this standpoint, that the source of conceptualization, like that of consciousness in general, is the timelessness of temporal identity and of its special mode called personal identity, what still remains to be clarified is the specific nature of concepts within the context of their generic nature as timeless entities which can be temporally deployed. The clarification of this point should lead us to the problem of being.

I have suggested that the ability to recognize that red is red and not green is the implicit ability to recognize order in the universe. To recognize that there is order in the universe is, in effect, to recognize what is potentially intelligible to us of the universe. But we are particular and ephemeral beings, and it is only through this mode of ephemeral particularity that we are able to discern whatever there is of intelligibility for us in this universe. Whether the universe is or is not entirely intelligible is something which is beyond our ken, for we do not possess the universality of comprehension which would be necessary to render all things intelligible to us. The mere fact of the eventual death of each one of us gives the lie to any philosophy which pretends to universal comprehension. For comprehension is by the individual, and the death of the individual is the nullification of his comprehension, and that in itself should give us the clue to the nature of concepts. Because of our particularity and because of our mortality, the universe can only be fragmentarily intelligible to us. Concepts are, in fact, nothing else but fragments of intelligibility, fragments which we constantly try to integrate into more and more comprehensive conceptual schemes.

From this standpoint, then, concepts are not those absolutes of Platonic theory, but neither are they mere vocal sounds designating empirical experience. Again, concepts are not the inner essences of particular objects, nor the innate manifestations of God. And concepts are not at all those supposed absolutes of a supposed transcendental subject made in our own image. In fact, in themselves concepts have no reality at all. They are the provisional tools of a personal identity to whom it has been given to understand something of the universe from which he has emerged. Conversely, the very manner of our emergence implies that the facts of consciousness and of conceptualization mean more than can actually be expressed by any set of concepts.

For if the very facts of consciousness and of conceptualization are themselves the results of temporal operations which are, by nature, over and above the space-time processes of the physical universe, then clearly any analysis of the concept of being must take into account the possible implications of those operations which have brought about the very possibility of using concepts.

Initially, being was equated with what was intuited as permanence as opposed to change or becoming, as opposed to what Parmenides alluded to as "what is not." The conceptual impossibility of relating this exclusive and exhaustive assertion of "what is" with this changing world of physical reality led to a fundamental distinction. Being or "what is" came to be identified with what is intelligible and with the intellect itself, both assumed to be permanent. In varying modes, this priority of intellect, intelligibility, mind...seemed to become the very hallmark of metaphysical thinking. If the thesis argued for here has any validity, however, then the distinction established by the several modes of Platonism cannot be maintained. If it is the case that understanding is a result of temporal operations which we cannot fully understand because they are themselves the foundation of understanding, then it is not possible to equate being either with intellect or with intelligibility.

Conversely, if we propose defining being in terms of the spatio-temporal processes of the universe, including the emergence of all entities and their activities which are presently integral parts of this universe, we are faced with the problem of the apparently ultimate senselessness of the whole process. This is so even if we add to the schema the concept of transcendental subjectivity, for what would be the ultimate sense of such a transcendental ego to any particular mortal human being, and it is the particular human being who alone raises the question of ultimate sense. One may perhaps be tempted to suppose that there is no ultimate sense for the individual human being, and that that is the answer to the question which may then be regarded as an irrelevant question having nothing to do with the general problem of the nature of being. Therefore, perhaps being simply means no more than this self-differentiating totality orchestrated by a transcendental subject. If intellect and intelligibility are derivative from this process, then that may seem to confirm such a conclusion.

But this way of seeing things does not seem to me to be at all perspicuous. An ultimately senseless universe which is also partially intelligible is very close to being a contradictory position, for we are ascribing both sense and senselessness to one and the same thing. On the other hand, there is an element of truth in this paradoxical position, but it is just this element of truth which, from the present standpoint, must lead us to a very different conception of being. The element of truth I'm referring to is the fact that it is perfectly true that the universe is not completely intelligible to us. It is precisely the paradox of an apparently ultimately senseless existing universe giving rise to entities capable of understanding something of its nature and processes which should persuade us to rethink the concept of being and reconsider a view which has been virtually proscribed in contemporary philosophy. If the preceding analyses have any validity, then the paradox itself is without foundation. For the paradox lies in the juxtaposition of the idea of a spatio-temporal universe which we treat as an ultimate given, and a process of understanding which we assume to be wholly derived from a principle internal to that spatio-temporal process itself. Both these conceptions are incompatible with the analyses formulated above.

An explanation of being which is in terms of an entirely immanent principle, deriving whatever explanatory powers it has from the postulation of a transcendental subjectivity immanently wedded to the spatio-temporal processes of the physical universe, is an explanation which can only mean ultimate senselessness for mortal man, the being who in fact raises such questions in the first place. But if it is the case that understanding derives from the immanent operations of the internalization of time, establishing temporal identities and a well nigh inconceivable operation resulting in the self-manifesting of certain loci of temporal identity, then we are saying that these immanent operations are not self-explanatory and require a ground and explanation which lies outside themselves, which requires an entirely transcendent and not a transcendental ground as explanation. Processes of this nature are a denial of the supposition that the spatio-temporal universe can be conceived as simply given, for it is only in terms of operations performed upon that spatio-temporal reality that one can explain the internalizations of time. There is nothing in space-time process itself which can explain such operations. If there were, the practitioners of the physical sciences would know about it, and they do not know about it.

Correlatively, it follows from this that the emergence of consciousness and of understanding or conceptualization cannot be wholly derived from the spatio-temporal process itself. We can have no conception of how time can be internalized from the spatio-temporal process: all we can see are the results, and the necessity of an explanation along such lines. On both counts, therefore, the apparent paradox of juxtaposing a spatio-temporal universe as given with an understanding as wholly derived from that process itself, is a paradox without foundation. For both suppositions are false suppositions. The spatio-temporal universe must itself have an ultimate foundation, and it is that foundation which can alone constitute the source of the several internalizations of time. That such a source can have nothing to do with anything that can be referred to as a transcendental subjectivity has already been demonstrated by the general theory formulated here: anything we can conceive of as subjectivity is itself the result of temporal operations which precede all modes of subjectivity.

The entire argument points to the metaphysical necessity of using the word 'being' to refer to this ultimate ground of all the forms of existence which are directly accessible to us, either through experience or by means of conceptual thinking. We have appropriated the word 'God' just as if we know what it means, but we do not know what it means, and there is no such thing as a "god in the making." There was a great deal of virtue in the ancient Hebrew tendency to avoid the use of the name of God. It is just for that reason that in metaphysics the only appropriate word is the word 'being', for in our simple-mindedness we tend to assume that the use of a proper name names a kind of entity like Peter or Elizabeth. To say that God is being is to say something that we cannot fully understand, for it is to say that everything which we do understand is either passing or ephemeral. The spatio-temporal universe, ideas, intelligibility, even the loci of temporal identity, are ephemeral and passing, and they cannot be identified with being. For even if there is such a thing as immortality, it is not by virtue of any individual temporal identity in itself that such a state can exist: it would only be by virtue of the grounding of such temporal identities in being itself. This does at least give us one indication of one characteristic of the nature of being: the operations of the internationalization of time would not be possible unless being were eternal.

11
The Metaphor of a Foundation for Knowledge

Edward Pols

THE REALITY-NEED

It was once thought that knowledge as a whole required a foundation and that philosophy could provide it. The metaphor of a foundation has been powerful and ubiquitous in Western thought since Descartes made such dramatic use of it, although it is so natural a metaphor that it would be surprising if hints of it could not be found earlier. It is not the only metaphor that has been used to express the general and persistent need of rationality Descartes wished to satisfy. It is, however, the dominant one, so much so that even today, when that need is commonly thought to be delusive in the sense that it cannot be satisfied, it is the metaphor used to deprecate enterprises designed to satisfy it.

From the vantage point of radical realism, which I discuss in a book just published,[1] I will in the long run recommend that we discard that metaphor. But radical realism purports to illuminate and in some measure satisfy that general and persistent need of rationality, so my purpose in that book is not unlike that of many philosophers who have made use of the foundation metaphor in the past. They make up a very diverse group, and radical realism makes common cause only with those for whom that persistent need is first of all a need for the real in so comprehensive a sense that the reality which working scientists address themselves to, and which most of them take to be cognitively accessible (whatever philosophers of science may say), is but one aspect of it.

Those philosophers did not merely feel a need for the real, for they assumed that the need was to some extent already supplied; their philosophy was accordingly directed towards what still remained unclear about and incomplete in our intercourse with the real. The incompleteness and lack of clarity were thought, in effect, to march together; accordingly, our engagement with the real is perfected, and our need thus progressively more deeply satisfied, only as our insight into our engagement with the real is itself deepened and perfected. Those philosophers of the foundational tradition with whom radical realism makes common cause belong, then, to the metaphysical wing of that tradition. They suppose that an engagement with the real is part of the very birthright of our rationality; and that the birthright is never quite lost, no matter what doubt and obscurity we might sometimes find ourselves in. But they also understood that it must be constantly justified and not merely passively enjoyed; only in that way could it be made secure, and the achievements open to it made more extensive. There is—so they say or at least imply—no first philosophy at all, unless in the doing of it we are able to show that our rationality does indeed have the power to attain the real in the intended sense. It is not surprising that we cannot point to any philosophy that is acknowledged to have achieved this double—and moreover tormentingly reflexive—task.

Philosophers who have felt the need for the real in this comprehensive sense have always looked beyond the science of their day to find a foundation for science. They took science to be concerned with but one aspect of the real; and they supposed that the more comprehensive reality they looked for both expressed itself in and made demands upon the structure of human nature. Upon the whole of that structure, moreover, for if reality concerned us as knowers, it concerned us as practical agents as well. The need for reality was thus taken to be a need for that with which the pattern of our own feelings, valuations, and habits should in the long run be consonant—a need, in short, for our own best completion as persons.

Philosophical reflection about our capacity for satisfying the need has always been colored by the thought that we may nevertheless have to make do with something short of reality. That is an innocuous enough thought if it merely contrasts our aspiration to reality in its deepest and most comprehensive sense with our actual achievements; for the latter, whether in physical science or in any other sphere, are at best progressive and never complete. The thought becomes paralyzing only if it represents our very best rational achievements as not engaging the real in any sense. Let us bring that thought closer to today's controversies by expressing it in the form of a question—a question which raises the possibility that there is something quite spurious about what I have been calling the general and persistent need of our rationality. Can we ever know anything that is real in the sense of being quite independent of our rationality—independent, that is, of any formative, creative, or shaping power it may possess? Many philosophers today suppose that the point of the question can easily be blunted by a negative answer, coupled with the ingenious suggestion that the term 'real' shall henceforth be given a Pickwickian sense, to wit, 'that which is indeed an outcome of the formative, creative, or shaping power of our rationality.'[2]

The question gives rise to others. The most important one has to do with what I called the comprehensiveness and generality of the real we aspire to: if we can indeed know the independently real, how far does our cognitive reach extend? This raises another question, one that seems important to me but might be rejected by many contemporary writers because it supposes a sense of 'know' that they have dismissed in advance: are some few independently real things known *directly*, so that we can in principle use them as fulcrums for knowing *indirectly* many things that are now—and perhaps forever—hidden from us or otherwise inaccessible to us? Still another question is even more remote from today's controversies in academic philosophy: are all real things joined in a unity, and if so is our access to that unifying principle direct or indirect? This last question obviously concerns what Plato called the *ontōs on*—credibly translatable as the really real. The Latin-based term 'reality' has been well established in philosophy for a long time, and it would not be prudent to recommend that we give it up. Still, it is advisable to remember that the term 'being' has precedence: the expression *ontōs on*, for instance, is made up of two forms of the verb 'to be' in the Greek.

So characterized, the last question expresses the need in a form that goes back to the ancients: a need for Being in general, or for Being as Being. It is too facile to suppose that that is merely a need for a very general *concept* of Being or, as Plato might say, a need for the *form* 'Being'. That is perhaps closer to the mark than supposing it to be a need for a collection of particular and utterly discrete beings, but it is clearly not close enough. To say so is to suggest that in making common cause with a perceived tendency in tradition we should not suppose that tradition cannot lead us astray. So I do not hesitate to characterize the need as radical realism would have it, rather than as we find it in this or that tradition. It is a need for Being as one and as universally present—as present in all particular things; which means that it is a need for that on the basis of which we can form concepts and therefore propositions. Many might think that the need is a delusion; but if it is authentic it does not divert us from whatever particular real things—or whatever particular aspect of real things—we may be concerned with. If the need for Being as one and as universally present is authentic, then it is identical with the need for the real nature of any particular thing or any particular aspect of things, for each particular thing is in that case intimately involved with the universality of Being. If it is authentic, we take at least a step towards satisfying it the moment we refuse to pretend that we are starting from the utter discreteness of any particular experience, any particular thing, or any particular act of rational attention—the moment we stop pretending that in principle whatever unity we find in our knowing comes from us as knowers.

That is the nub of the positive relevance of radical realism to the foundational tradition of first philosophy. There is a negative relevance as well, and

The Metaphor of a Foundation for Knowledge

it will eventually lead me to recommend that we give up, not indeed the aspirations of the "first philosophy" wing of the foundational tradition, but just the metaphor of a foundation for knowledge, which does little justice to the profundity of the aspiration it was designed to serve. Before going into that, I propose to sketch the history of the foundation metaphor, for the philosophers who have in the past invoked it still have something to teach us.

SKETCH FOR A HISTORY OF THE FOUNDATION METAPHOR

It was Descartes who first used the metaphor of a foundation for knowledge; but no reader with any sense of history will forget that Descartes has deep roots in late medieval philosophy and, especially by way of St. Augustine, in the philosophy of antiquity. Concerned though he was to justify and enhance our mathematical understanding of the material world, he intended that his new foundation should support the products of a supposed general rational capacity manifesting itself not only in the activity of natural science but in many other quite different rational activities as well. And, like his classical predecessors who did not use the metaphor, Descartes supposed that, all the while reason engaged in these various particular activities, it retained the general and governing task of bringing them all into harmonious relation and establishing their importance and significance relative to one another.

Philosophy, understood as a discipline having as one of its chief missions the providing of a foundation for knowledge in general, must have a paradoxical status before it has accomplished that mission: it is not yet the knowledge that shall serve as a foundation for knowledge, and so neither it nor knowledge in general is yet truly knowledge. The philosophy that was to have performed this feat, emerging, so to speak, into an actuality it did not yet have, has traditionally been known as metaphysics. It was entrusted with other tasks as well, but they do not concern us here. It is a historical accident that gave us the expression *ta meta ta physika* for certain writings of Aristotle—'the [treatises] after the [treatises about] physics'—and though it is in its literal meaning an innocuous enough expression, the notion that the discipline it now names is concerned with something that purports to lie beyond the physical, and indeed beyond experience, is very persistent. A name that would remind not only the unsophisticated reader but even the cultivated one that materialism is also a metaphysics would be better.

There is one at hand for us, as it was there also for Descartes. It is the name Aristotle himself used: 'first philosophy', *protē philosophia*. It suggests all the right things: the most basic kind of philosophy, the philosophy upon which other kinds depend, the philosophy that can provide our foundation—that perhaps *is* our foundation if we can only bring it into actuality. Aristotle's name for it keeps its paradoxical status more vividly before us, especially if we remember that for him too it was still *in potentia*—"the knowledge (or science) we are seeking."[3] It is probably the best name for any philosophy designed to satisfy what I have called the persistent need of reason, and it will remain so even after we discard the foundation metaphor.

First philosophy was still *in potentia* for Descartes as well. He develops the metaphor of a foundation extensively in parts 1, 2, and 3 of the *Discourse on Method*: as philosophers, we must pull down the building of supposed knowledge, which stands upon an insecure foundation, and erect upon it a well-ordered building that shall stand firm.[4] The paradoxical feature of the enterprise is especially salient in his case, since the truly first philosophy purports to emerge not out of some preexisting but imperfect knowledge but rather out of doubt. We are reminded by the full title of another work, the *Meditations on First Philosophy*, in which the foundation metaphor is mentioned[5] again and in which the foundation-directed enterprise is carried out in greater detail, that it is indeed first philosophy which purports to emerge. If it should still make sense today to talk of a first philosophy designed to satisfy the persistent need of reason, it is clear enough that it has not yet emerged.

Descartes's attempt to overcome doubts about reason's powers—doubts that were by no means unique to him at that time—came when there had already been great progress towards an exact science of nature. Its findings were already so impressive and its future so intoxicating that one would have thought that there was every reason for confidence rather than doubt. Nevertheless, the question whether we can know that whose reality is independent of the act of knowing is not to be settled in the affirmative by pointing to the existence of a viable science. Certainly the existence of a science of nature immensely more deep, intricate, and powerful than the first half of the seventeenth century dreamed of has not settled that matter today.

What, precisely, was Descartes aiming at? It is only a small part of the story that he wanted to move from doubt to certainty, or—what amounts to the same thing—that he wanted to know truly and to know that he knew truly. Although, following Augustine, he made ingenious philosophical use of doubt in his quest for certainty, and although he speaks of the doubt as hyperbolical at one point,[6] the doubt itself seems to have been real enough—hardly surprising in an age that was so moved by the revival of ancient skepticism.[7] However impressed Descartes may have been by the case for skepticism, it seems clear that the urgency of the matter must have been brought home to him by the very certainties of one of his own most brilliant discoveries. Analytic geometry promised to bring certainty to our understanding of the physical world, provided only that we have a *right* to apply those certainties to a physical world which, in a *prima facie* sense, is full of uncertainty, and about whose very existence there may be some uncertainty. From the time of Plato the problem inherent in this proviso had often been dismissed by virtue of a philosophic judgment that relegated the commonsense physical world to the subordinate ontological status of mere becoming—something less than being, and therefore in principle the domain of doubt and opinion rather than knowledge. Why should such a realm of mere appearance be worth troubling about, and why should we expect to be able to apply to it mathematical certainties that are associated with being and are therefore accessible to our rationality?

For Descartes this dismissive gesture would not do, and in the long run it apparently would not do for Plato either. The *Timaeus* is there to remind us that in his old age Plato thought the explanation for the regularity observable in (phenomenal) physical transformations was to be sought in the laws that govern the transformation of certain figures of pure mathematics into certain other figures. No doubt we should not push this too far: Plato is merely illustrating a modest shift in his doctrine—a shift towards a more intimate relation between Being and becoming than he envisioned in, say, the *Phaedo* and the *Republic*—and is by no means claiming that he has found the true mathematical transformation laws of physical nature. Descartes, however, is quite clear that it is just those laws that he himself must have: the certainties of mathematics must *be* certainties that rule also in physical nature. Accordingly, in *Meditations* V and VI, he builds on the foundation of the *cogito*, taken together with what he took to be the representative character of the ideas of the thinking being, an argument that purports to demonstrate (a) the real nature (extension) of the physical world (if it should indeed exist); (b) that it does indeed exist, distinct from and independent of the knower; and (c) why it *appears* to us in experience as the world of common sense rather than what it *really* is. We may be reasonably sure about Descartes's motives in shaping this complex argument, even if we feel that there is something fundamentally wrong about the *Meditations* in general and about the arguments of *Meditations* V and VI in particular.

There is another theme of great importance in Descartes's foundational enterprise, one that occurs also in some later philosophers who use the foundation metaphor and in certain earlier philosophers who do not use it but are nevertheless doing first philosophy in a spirit that is roughly consistent with it. Descartes wanted more than a deductively unified mathematics that should be *ipso facto* a deductively unified knowledge of the physical world *as it really is*. He aspired to know reality truly, but he conceived reality to be more ample than what a mathematical science of nature can illuminate on its own. So he sought the deductive unification of all knowledge in something upon which not only a mathematical science but also theology and ethics[8] should be seen to depend. Hence, the *cogito*, which purports to yield the thinker's own existence *qua* thinking being, is also the fulcrum for the demonstration of the existence of the Perfect Being. Those twentieth-century critics of Descartes who suppose that no great man of the past could possibly take seriously what they themselves cannot take seriously dismiss that side of Descartes as hypocrisy motivated by prudence. Prudent he was, but what he has to say about the Perfect Being is crucial to the whole argument of the *Meditations on First Philosophy*. Whatever we may think of that book as a whole, however we may criticize the structure of its arguments, it is, first of all, an exercise in first philosophy, and as such it is different in spirit from the metaphysics of, say, our twentieth-century Antipodean scientific realists.

The theme I have in mind just now, however, is not the interest in first philosophy as such, but rather the ambiguity of the deductive unification that characterizes Descartes's version of first philosophy. In one sense that unification seems to go back to one complex proposition that he expresses (explicitly or implicitly) in a number of ways—*cogito ergo sum, dubito ergo cogito ergo sum, cogito sum, dubito cogito sum*. It might be thought that this proposition, properly understood, should yield all the propositions one needs to accomplish the task of deductive unification. But Descartes does not take the *cogito* as a proposition which, once it is propounded to us, we see to be true independently of ourselves; nor does he proceed by deducing other propositions from it that purport to be theorems of which it is the sole premise. Although he takes the *cogito* to be true, he supposes its truth to be dependent on the entertaining of it in a sense in which the truth of, say, 'if (p then q) and p, then q', on the one hand, or 'snow is white', on the other, does not. In the case of the *cogito*, it is the asserting and entertaining of it that makes it true, for Descartes tells us "that this proposition: I am, I exist, is necessarily true each time I pronounce it, or that I mentally conceive it."[9] So it is the active existence (regarded for the moment as a merely thinking existence) of the thinking being that confers truth upon the proposition by the very act which sees it to be true. The thinking being, in both asserting its existence and responding affirmatively to that same existence, is thus more active, more creative, more vital than its propositional residue. After undergoing many modulations, this theme emerges again in the key of nineteenth-century idealism, where it is heard in perhaps its most complex statement in the three principles (propositions) developed in sections 1, 2, and 3 of Fichte's *Wissenschaftslehre*.

Moreover, Descartes gives many signs that propositions like "I think, I exist," "I think, therefore I am," and—still more—"I doubt, I think, I exist" do not quite express the full depth of the living presence of the thinker to itself that he has in mind. From the *Discourse*, for instance, we learn that the doubt which is present in and yet overcome by the thinker carries with it intimations of a deeper presence, for in that treatise Descartes tells us that doubt and certainty, conjoined in the *cogito*, may be contrasted in terms of imperfection and perfection, and that with this goes an awareness of the dependence of the (imperfect) doubter on the Perfect Being. What is set forth in that proof of the existence of God which is usually called the Cartesian one thus seems to be already present in the *cogito* in an active form, rather than in the form of a proposition given to us and from which we then take the necessary proof steps seriatim.

This, however, is only an intimation, especially with respect to the matter of *presence*, for in the unpacking of the *cogito* Descartes depends upon the alleged representative nature of the ideas the thinking being finds in itself. He thus keeps recurring to the thinking being's consciousness of and affirmation of its own existence, finding each time more empirical content in it. If there is indeed something in Descartes's first certainty that is more active and living than propositional and inert, and if this active certainty should seem a promising mode of access to the real, this realistic promise is at once negated by the representative doctrine of ideas. If we knew in advance that on some occasions we had direct access to something real, and direct access to an idea that did in fact represent it adequately, we could know directly that some ideas do in fact represent realities. We could then no doubt make a persuasive case for indirect access to inaccessible realities by way of certain ideas—or for that matter, certain concepts, certain theories, or certain linguistic items. But if we have only our own existence as thinking beings and our own ideas, together with a merely asserted doctrine to the effect that these ideas are indeed representative, we can make no headway whatever in the direction of realism.

One important lesson for someone who wishes to make a radically realistic gesture is that our hold on the real, if it is to be effective, must in some cases be direct; otherwise the moment doubt is eliminated in one quarter, it will reappear in another. The seeds of the failure of Descartes's foundational enterprise (regarded as a way of assuring us that we have cognitive access to realities other than our own thought) are sown by the same *august geste du semeur* that gave us the so-momentous *cogito*. Another important lesson is the one Descartes often seems to be on the point of teaching us, only to fall off into more static terminology: our foundation, if it is to be effective, should not really be static in the way that both propositions and the foundations of buildings are static. What we need instead is the authority of an *activity*—an activity generative of the propositions that partially express it, and sure of itself in the same active mode that gives rise to propositions.

Although Descartes seems to have been the first to use the metaphor of a foundation for knowledge, there are many earlier philosophical enterprises to which we could legitimately apply it, seeing that they bear a strong family resemblance to at least some philosophical doctrines after Descartes about which their originators used the metaphor as a matter of course. We can say, for instance, without doing violence to what Plato meant, that in his discussion of dialectical progress towards the form of the Good in the *Republic* he was talking about a foundation for knowledge, even though he uses concepts and imagery that turn our attention away from the ground and towards the sun.

One example of the complex and well-known imagery he uses there must suffice. In speaking of hypotheses in *Republic* 511 he exploits the literal meaning of the Greek word—a meaning that tends to be suppressed in our routine use of the word today—by calling hypotheses steps *laid down* and leading upward. It is an interesting oddity, incidentally, that the word 'hypothesis' can also mean foundation in Greek, because even if Plato had been making explicit use of the foundation metaphor, he obviously would not have thought of hypotheses as providing what Descartes would have called a foundation for knowledge. Important as hypotheses are for Plato, they are only preliminaries. Thus, if we manage to climb the steps to where we can see what is not a step laid down—that is, the Sun of the allegory—we shall understand that the whole procedure of building a stairway and mounting it depended upon what we ultimately see, although we did not understand that at first. Plato interprets the imagery with some care: dialectical progress towards the Good itself takes place by means of discourse which, as it frames definitions, accounts, or hypotheses, does so by virtue of the forms. But when we finally see the Good itself and thus understand at last that discourse, dialectical progress, and any deductive system achieved with the help of dialectic all depend upon it, we shall also see that the Good itself lies beyond the other forms and so is not expressible in discourse. The lesson of all this is that the Good is *fundamental* to all sound knowledge—the foundation metaphor springs thus naturally to our modern pens and tongues even while, mindful that the sun metaphor is at odds with it, we concede that it is strange to say that Plato was concerned to lay a foundation for knowledge.

The role of the form of the Good in Plato's doctrine makes it clear that he was not looking for a foundation for what we should today call theoretic knowledge[10] of physical nature only. Although, as noted above, he was interested in the mathematical interpretation of physical regularities at least when he wrote the *Timaeus,* he took the role of the Good in the nature of things to be so *fundamental* that *it* provided the reason why any regularities are as they are. These regularities he takes seriously, at the time of the *Timaeus*, even though he does not seem to wish us to take his instances of transformation "laws" to be the ones that actually prevail in nature. The importance of the Good as the real explanation of such regularities thus makes the question of the good life more *fundamental* for Plato than the physical science of his day; if he knew of the physical science of our own day, he would presumably say the same thing about that. He thus sets a precedent for the completeness of scope of first philosophy that Descartes aspired to. We shall find this comprehensiveness of the foundational instinct again and again in philosophers of the modern era who aspire to first philosophy; indeed, we shall find it even in some philosophers whose foundations are meant to replace those of metaphysics.

If the sun of the allegory (the form of the Good) is thus *fundamental*, it is so in an odd way. The ideal philosopher, when he at last sees the sun, clearly sees no mere proposition, even though, according to Plato, he does indeed see that the deductive unity of all propositional knowledge depends upon the sun. The vital presence of the Good is seen to engender the whole structure of a unified knowledge, but it is also seen to so exceed propositional knowledge as to be itself inexpressible in propositions. I have already suggested that the full reality of the Cartesian thinking being is not adequately expressed in the *cogito*, taking the *cogito* as a proposition merely understood by the knower. It is the active exercise of its own existence on the part of the thinking being (in the entertaining-cum-asserting of the *cogito*) that makes the corresponding proposition true; and this dependence of the proposition on the activity which thinks it does not come through in the proposition itself. Descartes seems on the point of becoming aware of all this, but it would strain the historical record to suggest that the peculiarly fundamental nature of the form of the Good in the Platonic tradition is responsible for this ambiguous status of the *cogito*. On the other hand, the Perfect Being, whose existence is already intimated by the certainty-doubt, perfection-imperfection tension in the *cogito*, adds another dimension to the ambiguity of the *cogito*; and the notion of the Perfect Being does indeed derive from the Platonic tradition. It would thus seem that we are safe in taking Plato as at least a precedent for any later intimations that any authentic foundation cannot be fully expressed in propositional form.

It takes no great ingenuity to show that the foundation metaphor may be applied with as much justice to Aristotle as to Plato, although the setting of Aristotle's first philosophy is usually conceptual rather than imaginative. The first principles *(archai)* of a particular science do not provide the foundation for that science because they themselves go back to the first principles of first philosophy; but the first principles of first philosophy do indeed provide a foundation for the particular sciences. Aristotle's own metaphor, to be sure, is that of a beginning rather than that of a foundation, as the presence of the term *'archē'* reminds us, but the point is much the same as it was for Plato. In both cases there is the paradox that the real beginning is arrived at only at the end of a progress that begins elsewhere.

As we range down through the history of philosophy in the pre-Cartesian period, we can find many other philosophers who are engaged in metaphysics, or first philosophy, and who suppose that other sorts of knowledge depend upon first philosophy, even though they do not use the foundation metaphor to make that point. But after Descartes, his foundation metaphor explicitly dominates both those who profess to be doing metaphysics and those who reject metaphysics and restrict themselves to what later came to be called epistemology. Philosophers as diverse as Leibniz, Locke, Hume, Kant, Fichte, Moritz Schlick, and A. J. Ayer all employ it about their own work.

Few philosophers take the primacy of propositions more for granted than Leibniz does, for he holds that the very foundation of all knowledge consists in principles known to be true.

> As a man who wishes to construct a building on solid ground must continue to dig with his spade until he comes to a solid and stony basis, and as Archimedes required an immovable point in order to be able to lift the universe;—so we are in need of a fixed point as a foundation upon which we may establish the elements of human knowledge. And this starting point is the analysis of the different kinds of truth.[11]

For Leibniz, one fundamental kind of truth is that which we reach with the help of the principle of sufficient reason. He claims, in fact, that a greater reliance on the principle is essential to the sound development of "the *prima philosophia*."[12] The allegedly foundational character of this principle is intimately linked in his mind with the principle of contradiction. I quote the two principles as they appear together in the *Monadology*.

> 31. Our reasonings are founded on *two great principles, that of contradiction*, in virtue of which we judge that to be *false* which involves contradiction, and that *true*, which is opposed or contradictory to the false.

> 32. And *that of sufficient reason*, in virtue of which we hold that no fact can be real or existent, no statement true, unless there be a sufficient reason why it is so and not otherwise, although most often these reasons cannot be known to us.[13]

The principle of sufficient reason, he thinks, has its chief application in the realm of experience: knowing the principle to be true, we must look to the contingent facts of some particular empirical situation to determine the cause or causes of an event—that is, the reasons that explain it. But the principle itself, he thinks, is no more derivable from experience than is the principle of contradiction. Indeed, he claims that we know the principle of sufficient reason to be true on the basis of the principle of contradiction, although he insists that this dependence in no way alters the contingency of the causal connections we look for with the help of the former principle.

I certainly maintain that a power of determining oneself without any cause or without any source of determination, implies contradiction, as does a relation without foundations; but from this the metaphysical necessity of all effects does not follow. For it suffices that the cause or reason be not one that metaphysically necessitates, though it is metaphysically necessary that there should be some such cause.[14]

For a full account of the principle of sufficient reason as Leibniz understands it, we must go to the rest of his system—that is, the rest of the complex of propositions that make up his body of philosophical theory. The main bearings of the principle within the system are familiar enough. Monads, which he also calls substances, can in principle be analyzed in terms of predicates attaching to a subject: they are, in fact, the subjects to which the predicates belong, and a complete knowledge of one of them would thus yield all its predicates. But since all monads are also eternal, a complete knowledge of one of them from that perspective would be both analytic and a priori. An analysis of that kind would, however, be infinite and so could be carried out only by a divine mind. 'Analytic' must thus be taken in an unusual sense in this context, for the attachment of predicate to subject would still (in accordance with the principle) be contingent rather than necessary, seeing that, as Leibniz says, there is no contradiction in imagining the opposite of some particular predicate. Leibniz supposes, moreover, that the ordering of the whole causal chain depends upon God's understanding of what is best or most fitting; so the nature of each particular contingent causal connection must be understood in the same way. In sum: what is true on the principle of sufficient reason is, from God's point of view, contingent, a priori and analytic (but not finitely); from our point of view, however, it is contingent, a posteriori, and (as it is usual to say since Kant) synthetic. In both cases contingency is tied to goodness.

All this makes propositions *fundamental* indeed, for it appears that they are fundamental not only to human knowledge but also to the structure of all monads whatsoever. Is there any ambiguity in Leibniz about the fundamental character of propositions that is analogous to the odd propositional status of the various forms of the *cogito* in Descartes? Perhaps only in the sense that all propositions are in some way innate in each and every monad (the point being of importance only for conscious monads) and so might be regarded as dependent upon the *being* of the monads. But Leibniz does not seem to say anything to that effect. In any event his practical influence on the foundational tradition (both that part which belongs to first philosophy and that part which begins with Hume) makes for the identification of a foundation with a set of propositions.

When Locke describes himself, in that famous passage in the "Epistle to the Reader" at the start of the *Essay,* as an underlaborer helping to clear the ground for master builders, it is true that he does not explicitly speak of a foundation for knowledge, but the image is obviously the same as that of Descartes. But between Descartes and Locke there is a great gulf fixed: we may sum up the vastness of it by remembering that for Locke substance is an "X I know not what." In one important sense reality is thus asserted to be put beyond our reach. The task of the empirical wing of the foundational tradition is thus set for it very early: it must provide a foundation both for science and for human affairs in general that does not purport to be coincidental with the knowing of the real. No doubt Locke himself evades some of the consequences of this principle by a residual reliance on other principles that go back to the metaphysical tradition—principles he holds in common with Descartes.

Hume's attempt to supply a foundation for knowledge reveals the difficulty of empiricism in all its starkness. And Hume *does* indeed use the metaphor of a foundation, although that fact often goes unremarked. He notices, in the introduction to the *Treatise,* the dependence of mathematics, natural philosophy, and natural religion on the "science of man," and he first uses a military metaphor to advocate the proper way of dealing with the basic status of that science: we should not attack castles or villages on the frontier but rather "march up directly to the capital or center of these sciences, to human nature itself." But this image is soon supplemented by the foundation one. "In pretending therefore to explain the principles of human nature," he says, "we in effect propose a compleat system of the sciences, built on a foundation almost entirely new, and the only one upon which they can stand with any security." Later, in section I of *An Inquiry Concerning Human Understanding,* he speaks of himself as engaging, however reluctantly, in "profound or abstract philosophy," or "true metaphysics," whose purpose it is "to undermine the foundations of an abstruse philosophy"—to undermine, that is, the foundation of a false metaphysics.

The tidy picture that seems to emerge when we sort foundational philosophers into those who are metaphysical and those who are antimetaphysical dislimns as soon as we notice that many foundational philosophers who reject the discipline of metaphysics so cherish the term 'metaphysics' that they try to repossess it for their own philosophies. Hume, as we have just seen, tells us that his own antimetaphysical work constitutes true metaphysics. Kant in effect does the same thing. Consider, for instance, the full title of the *Prolegomena,* which posits a true *science* of metaphysics as the eventual goal of critical philosophy: *Prolegomena to any Future Metaphysics that Will be Able to Present Itself as Science.* Those who are interested in the oddities of philosophical terminology will find at least two senses of the term 'metaphysics' in the *Prolegomena*—one for a study Kant rejects and one for the perfected critical philosophy he aims at; and there may well be a third sense. This curious affection for the term 'metaphysics' persists into our own day: at least some influential analytic-linguistic philosophers have called their own work metaphysics.[15]

Ironically, the digging undertaken by Hume with the purpose of undermining metaphysics ended in undermining science as well. In any case, it has been generally perceived that Hume's "science of man," with its internal chasm between relations of ideas and matters of fact, does not in fact provide a foundation for science. It is usual to suppose that Hume's doctrine of causality presents the gravest problem for science, but the diremption between mathematics (understood as concerned with relations between ideas) and the (commonsense) physical world is probably even graver.

Kant's doctrine of the synthetic a priori is designed to overcome both the problem of causality and that of the relation between mathematics and the experienced world. He uses several metaphors about his own critical enterprise, the foundation one being by no means the most prominent. In the preface to the first edition of the *Critique of Pure Reason* (Axii), he says that critique is a "tribunal which will assure reason its lawful claims." Sometimes he says that critique is designed to find a new point of view; sometimes, and rather more often, he tells us that it has the task of setting reason on the secure path of science. But the foundation metaphor is also used early in the *Critique of Pure Reason* (A3/B7), and it occurs again in the introduction to the *Prolegomena*.

As for Fichte, he makes it part of the very title of his most important foundation-directed exercise, *Grundlage der gesammten Wissenschaftslehre (Foundation of the Entire Theory of Science [or Knowledge])*.[16] Those who undertake such enterprises in the German language are reminded by *Grundlage* and *Grundlegung* that the ground itself is much more solid than anything we can erect upon it. In this century that linguistic fact has brought with it more than a little portentous solemnity from the existential wing of the old metaphysical tradition.[17] Fichte, like Leibniz, makes the foundational role of propositions salient, for the three principles presented and discussed in detail in part I of the *Wissenschaftslehre* are, of course, complex propositions. Section 1 deals with what Fichte calls the first, absolutely unconditioned principle; section 2, with the second principle, conditioned as to content; section 3, with the third principle, conditioned as to form. It is a complex story and an important one in the development of idealism. I confine myself here to a few summary remarks on the first principle. (a) Fichte begins in a way that reminds us of the fundamental role the principle of contradiction plays in Leibniz, for the principle of identity, $A = A$, is assumed in order to get under way the reflection that produces the first principle. But in due course it becomes clear that the proposition '$A = A$' is in fact derivable from the *real* first principle, although the assertion of the latter is not warranted unless such logical principles are warranted; Fichte acknowledges this as an unavoidable circle. (b) The real first principle is expressed in several different ways. Either 'I am absolutely' or simply 'I am' will do for our present modest purpose. It is this proposition, then, that is our real foundation. (c) Fichte's foundation, however, is not to be unambiguously located in a proposition as such, no more than it was for Descartes. For according to Fichte, the self *posits* itself in an act, and it is by virtue of the act of self-assertion that the proposition 'I am' is true. In effect the proposition expresses the ground of its own truth, and that ground is the act of self-positing rather than the *particular formulations* (propositions) in which we try to express the whole matter.

I have no brief for idealism of that kind, but it is a useful reminder that there is an ambiguity about the role of propositions within the foundational tradition of first philosophy. Some philosophers of that tradition both propound what purport to be foundational propositions and seek to get at a true foundation that is not so much a proposition as what *produces* the proposition and *exemplifies its existential warrant*. In Fichte's case this "real" foundation is an *act* that is a self-positing.

In this century, the foundation question has been of obvious importance in mathematics and in other special disciplines and no doubt will continue to be so; but the most influential effort to establish a foundation took place in philosophy of science. For much of the period this effort fell well within the traditional bounds of empiricism: the analytic philosophers engaged in it were for the most part unimpressed by Kant's answer to Hume,[18] and so they sought to counter in their own ways the threat posed to the rationality of science by Hume's dichotomy of relations of ideas and matters of fact. Acknowledging that the foundation provided by Hume—his science of human nature—undermined rather than undergirded science itself, they undertook to provide a sound foundation for all of the sciences. Since they took science to be coextensive with knowledge, they assumed that if they were successful they would also have provided a foundation for knowledge in general. The unity-of-science movement, which can be regarded as closely allied with positivism if not always identical with it, was foremost in this foundational effort, but philosophers who were not identified with that movement also played a prominent role.

One promising way of overcoming the Humean diremption of reason and experience was to begin by taking the analytic a priori character of logic as our rational pole and the synthetic a posteriori character of empirical statements as our empirical pole. The two poles, whose superficial distinction and separateness was precisely the problem for science,[19] could then be bound together by the device of transforming traditional logic into what purported to be extensional logic. Logical connections were given a truth-functional interpretation, which meant that their truth value could always be established, in the long run, in terms of the truth or falsity of atomic propositional variables that stood for synthetic a posteriori propositions. This approach, in turn, permitted at least one influential interpretation in terms of *reality*—that of Wittgenstein's *Tractatus*, in which the extensional logic is seen as expressing the conditions under which a plurality of metaphysical ultimates (simples) may exist together—and a variety of phenomenalist interpretations in which the question of reality is avoided. Under both interpretations mathematics can intelligibly say something about experience—at the very least that such and such mathematical truths must hold in all possible worlds (even if 'world' is given a phenomenalist interpretation) and that they are therefore not mere relations between our ideas.

The suspicion that a single foundation could not be provided for science—the suspicion, indeed, that to try to provide one was to misunderstand the nature of the physical sciences—is, however, an old one. Neurath's famous coherentist image of philosophers of science as sailors who must rebuild their ship on the high seas, without ever being able to lay it up in drydock and build it anew out of the best materials, dates from 1932.[20] That image is an attack, in effect, on the notion that what I called the empirical pole in the effort to overcome the Humean diremption can be provided by statements that are *merely* synthetic a posteriori in the sense that their meanings derive only from the particular empirical situation they purport to express. The attack was mounted in the very heyday of the unity-of-science movement, and the heyday also of the search for a foundation for science. Indeed, two years later, in an article entitled "The Foundation of Knowledge," Neurath's colleague Schlick reiterates the importance of providing a foundation. In the course of that article Schlick rejects the coherence theory adopted by Neurath, insists that there is "no reason not to use...the good old expression 'agreement with reality'," and offers what he calls sometimes confirmations and sometimes observation statements as a foundation to serve in place of the protocol statements dismissed by Neurath with the help of that famous image. The so-called confirmations are not so much statements as empirical exclamations like "Here now blue," and in the long run Neurath's position was more persuasive than Schlick's to analytic-linguistic philosophers.[21]

The search for a foundation for the sciences remained urgent for many philosophers in the empirical-analytic community for a long while, and it remained respectable for some time after it had ceased to be urgent. Ayer's *Foundations of Empirical Knowledge*, for instance, dates from 1940.[22] It sums up the foundation-directed nisus of twentieth-century analytic philosophy just when that nisus was about to lose its force. It has the virtue of reminding us—what recent discussion of foundational*ism* tends to overlook—that the tradition which springs from Hume sought for a foundation which should take account of and reconcile two distinct foundational needs—that of the rational factor and that of the empirical factor in knowledge. The tide had clearly turned by 1951, when Quine's "Two Dogmas of Empiricism" was first published,[23] and by the sixties the search had lost respectability among the leaders of that community. Quine's use of Neurath's famous image as an epigraph for *Word and Object* in 1960[24] may be taken as a convenient sign that a new attitude now prevailed.

Though many different foundations had been propounded for many different purposes during the years we have touched upon, foundational*ism* as a general epistemological doctrine has only recently been defined with some precision. Since this definition took place in the atmosphere of a completed revolution on the foundation question, the terms 'foundationalism' and 'foundational', which seem to have become current only in the seventies, have acquired pejorative overtones in spite of the defenders the doctrine continues to have. The tenets common to the several versions of the doctrine appear to be these:

(a) knowledge is a matter of justified true belief;
(b) it consists of a system of propositions, and it is therefore these in which the knower has justified true belief;
(c) the justification of some of the propositions is direct, or immediate, and these are the foundational ones;
(d) the justification of the rest of the propositions is mediated by the foundational ones and so is indirect.

Although some of those who developed the doctrine saw clearly that its significance transcended philosophy of science, the most influential writers within the empirical-analytic community took it for granted that any effort to provide a foundation for knowledge must coincide with philosophy of science because for them only science counted as knowledge. Looking back at the determined effort in the first half of the century to provide a foundation upon which a unified science might rest—an effort in which at least some of them had participated, they concluded that it had failed. They also concluded, on the basis of difficulties which had become apparent to them in the course of the assimilation of Wittgenstein's *Philosophical Investigations*, Quine's "Two Dogmas of Empiricism," and Sellars's criticism of the notion of the empirically given, that in principle this foundation-directed effort had been doomed in advance. It therefore seemed to them that foundationalism could be summarily dismissed. Since science was identical with knowledge, since no foundation could be provided for science, and since the very notion of such a foundation was inappropriate, there could be no remaining point to even the most well-articulated and novel foundationalism. To those who took this line it did not seem to matter much that this long effort to provide a foundation for science had neither employed the term 'foundationalism' nor laid out in detail the tenets listed above. Nor did it matter that some varieties of foundationalism—Chisholm's is a recent example[25]—range beyond philosophy of science into metaphysics. The history of the gradual disillusionment of the analytic community in its search for a foundation for science is of great interest, but it must not detain us further here.

There are difficulties enough with foundationalism in the form stated above, difficulties beginning with the tenet that knowledge is justified true belief. That tenet, however, is probably not essential to foundationalism, and indeed the doctrine might be more plausible if the foundational propositions, at least, were simply said to be immediately *known* in some unanalyzable sense. In any case we must set these difficulties aside as well, since it is not our purpose either to defend or to attack foundationalism, but only to characterize it as a recent approach to the foundation question.

That it is so recent should tell us that few if any of the foundation-directed enterprises that were undertaken before this century can be brought with exactness under the rubric of foundationalism. Not even Descartes's doctrine fits neatly under that rubric, although his doctrine does have some features in common with at least some of the twentieth-century doctrines that do fit under it—not surprising, since Descartes's doctrine is the most distinguished progenitor of contemporary foundationalism. One reason it does not fit is that Descartes demands that knowledge be something more than justified belief. Another is that he places a greater emphasis on the reflective act of the thinker than upon knowledge regarded as a system of propositions. It is true that he identifies the formula '*cogito ergo sum*' as a proposition, but, as noticed earlier, the focus of his interest is much more on the entity who entertains that proposition—indeed it is that entertaining which is central to the proposition's supposed indefeasibility. Chisholm, it is true, also does something of that kind, but most recent defenders of foundationalism do not. As for Descartes, as soon as he has used that initial proposition to certify the existence of the thinking being who entertains it, his interest turns to the ideas, rather than the propositions, which that being is said to entertain. A philosopher of our own century who returned again and again to the foundation question and who invoked the name of Descartes in doing so—Edmund Husserl—also fits uneasily under the rubric of foundationalism and for somewhat the same reasons.

DISCARDING THE METAPHOR

What is negative in the foundational tradition is the static nature of the metaphor itself, which tempts its users into producing, as the counterpart of the metaphor, something that is as static, completed, and unchanging as the stable structures upon which buildings are erected. This counterpart is in practice usually a proposition or group of propositions expressing truths or principles out of which philosophy and the sciences are to follow. There is by no means agreement about what 'follow' should mean in this context, but too often it has meant a logical progress dominated by the ideal of deductive unity. It is no mean ideal, to be sure, but I suspect it is an ideal more appropriate for well-defined branches of knowledge that lend themselves to axiomatization than for knowledge in general.

If we consider not the systematic outcome of so many foundational efforts but rather the effect of the metaphor on the rational powers of the philosopher conducting such investigations, it seems fair to say that the metaphor too often represses certain resources of our rationality whose free play is essential to our seeing clearly and satisfying what I have called the persistent need of reason, and that this is no less true just because the metaphor was invented to help satisfy that need. In this setting then, the most important objection to the metaphor is that it fails to do justice to the active nature of the power or powers by virtue of which we know, and by virtue of which we produce the complex propositional structures in which knowing is expressed, stabilized, and made communicable. These powers then become thwarted; they lose their self-confidence; they fail to grow. Nor do I think that we should be looking for another metaphor; for we must rely on that same activity even to see the force and applicability of this or that metaphor. Why, therefore, should we need a metaphor to make the nature, the prerogatives, and the limitations of that activity vivid and immediate to us? Evidently one of the things we need is a certain kind of self-knowledge: one that does indeed suffuse the judgments we make about the propositional products of our rational activity but whose autonomous vitality is not to be found in those products as such.

As we have seen, the foundational tradition that is concerned with perfecting a first philosophy manifests two conflicting themes. One theme—it is in fact much older than the metaphor, but it is at least implicit in the work of many who use the metaphor—suggests that the real foundation never consists in a set of principles expressed in propositions. Sometimes—especially when the influence of neo-Platonism is felt—it is also suggested that there is something about the real foundation that is not expressible in propositions; sometimes—especially in idealism—merely that the real foundation is to be found in an active power that is capable of expressing things in propositions. The other theme is that a foundation for knowledge must consist of a set of principles—that is, a set of fundamental propositions. This latter theme is by no means limited to the foundational tradition which is concerned with first philosophy; it is indeed more common in the tradition which rejects first philosophy; and it is especially salient in what has come to be called foundational*ism*.

The Metaphor of a Foundation for Knowledge 219

Radical realism calls attention to a function or activity on our part which is not static in the way that propositions and the foundation metaphor itself are static. According to radical realism, the origins of the propositional are to be found in the overlap of the active function of rational awareness with the equally active formative function of rationality. In my own efforts to revive the foundation metaphor—some of them unpublished preparatory studies delivered as lectures—I tried to focus on the activity that *makes* a foundation; I sometimes used the expression 'foundation-directed exercise' to draw attention to it. I now think that the static overtones of the metaphor itself make that a self-defeating maneuver. What we need instead is the authority of an *activity*—an activity that is dynamic and generative of the propositions that partially express it, and sure of itself in the same active and self-confident mode that gives rise to propositions. If radical realism should in due course be persuasive, the foundation metaphor will lose what hold it still has and be displaced by expressions like 'rational authority', 'rational autonomy', 'self-confident rational activity', and 'reason in act'. I call them expressions because I do not think they will be functioning as new metaphors that displace the old one.

If we consider not the systematic outcome of so many foundational enterprises but rather the effect of the metaphor on the rational powers of the philosophers who undertook them, it seems fair to say that the metaphor too often represses certain resources of our rationality whose free play is essential to our seeing clearly and satisfying the persistent appetite for reality that it is at the heart of first philosophy. That the metaphor was invented precisely to help satisfy that need does not alter the matter. In the present setting then, the most important objection to the metaphor is that it fails to do justice to the active nature of the power or powers by virtue of which we know and by virtue of which we produce the complex propositional structures in which knowing is expressed, stabilized, and made communicable. The foundation metaphor—with all those overtones of something that supports because it is static, inactive, and enduring; of something that does not actualize itself in the temporal order—strikes quite the wrong note. It also helps encourage that most hubristic of all aspirations of first philosophy and science: the aspirations to an ideal, complete, and perfect knowledge consisting of a set of propositions bound together in a deductive unity. What we need instead is a confident self-knowledge that is coincidental with our active dealing with the independently real: one that does indeed sustain the judgments we make about the propositional products of our rational activity but whose autonomous vitality is not to be found in those products as such. And we may need a good deal of self-confidence and a good deal of growth if we are ever to understand and satisfy that need.

This brings us back to the question of the relation between reality and the propositional. The point of all this emphasis on activity is by no means that reality is inexpressible. It is rather that what we do succeed in expressing in propositions has precisely the status of a formed and completed group of *propositions*. If we then take them as our foundation, we shall have overlooked, put out of play, or dismissed the rational activity which, in this experiential engagement with the real, formed or produced those same propositions. That activity is never completed; indeed, it is a permanent background activity sustaining those propositions all the while it is itself sustained by what it is engaged with—and of which it is itself an expression in another sense of that word. It sustains those propositions in the very straightforward sense that certain marks or sounds become vehicles for propositions, rather than mere sounds or marks, only in the presence of rational action. Language does not make reality. Language is made by rationality—itself a nonlinguistic reality—when rationality so engages the real as to become aware of some part or feature of it. So our authority lies in the activity of rational awareness in its engagement with the real, an activity which involves language making and language sustaining but is by no means identical with them. These propositions I now enunciate have as their deepest function the calling attention to something in every respect translinguistic.

The corruption of language consists in our substituting it for the real: we seduce ourselves into supposing that something made by the same formative function that makes language—something that is certainly in part linguistic but also something imagined—is in fact the real. I do not mean merely that bodies of false theory are often taken to provide us with knowledge of the real things we are interested in. That, of course, happens more than we like to think. Thus, much of the twentieth century has been dominated by such bodies of theory as human nature as imagined and articulated by Freud, history as imagined and articulated by Marx, the function of language as imagined and articulated by Wittgenstein, human culture as imagined and articulated by Foucault. In contemplating such bodies of theory, large numbers of intelligent human beings have supposed that they were in fact contemplating the realities their interest in which had led them to turn to those bodies of theory in the first place. I mean rather the further seduction of supposing that such formed "realities"—which are, to be sure, in part formed upon the basis of reality—are the only things accessible to us; that the distinction between Pickwickian reality and reality is a false one.

NOTES

1. *Radical Realism: Direct Knowing in Science and Philosophy.* (Ithaca and London: Cornell University Press, 1992)

The Metaphor of a Foundation for Knowledge

2. Chapters 3 and 4 of my *Radical Realism* deal with suggestions like that, together with the general philosophical situation that gives rise to them.

3. Aristotle, *Metaphysics*, 983a 21–23.

4. *Discourse on Method*, in *The Philosophical Works of Descartes*, trans. Elizabeth S. Haldane and G. R. T. Ross, (Cambridge: University Press, 1911, repr. with corr. 1977), vol. 1: 85, 86, 87–89, 95, 99. Descartes's most exhaustive examination and elaboration of the metaphor occurs in his remarkable reply (in this case called Annotations) to the Third Question of Objections VII. See Haldane & Ross, vol. 2: 325–344.

5. *Meditations* I, first para., Haldane & Ross, vol. 1: 144.

6. *Meditations* VI, Haldane & Ross, vol. 1: 198–199.

7. See, for instance, the significant echoes from Montaigne noticed by Gilson. Etienne Gilson, *The Unity of Philosophical Experience* (New York: Scribner's, 1937), 126–129.

8. See for instance, *Discourse on Method*, part I, Haldane & Ross, vol. 1: 85. Anyone who doubts Descartes's sincerity should take note of the profound dependence of his treatise *The Passions of the Soul* on the general epistemological and metaphysical views set forth in the *Meditations*.

9. *Meditations* II, Haldane & Ross, vol. 1: 150.

10. Plato did not suppose that what he called theoretic knowledge was indirect knowledge by way of theories in our sense of that word.

11. *Opuscules et fragments inédits*, ed. Louis Couturat (Paris: Alcan, 1903), 401.

12. "It must be confessed that though this great principle (of sufficient reason) has been acknowledged, yet it has not been sufficiently made use of. Which is, in great measure, the reason why the *prima philosophia* has not been hitherto so fruitful and demonstrative, as it should have been." The Leibniz–Clarke Correspondence, ed. H. G. Alexander (Manchester: Manchester University Press, 1956), 60–61.

13. As translated by Robert Latta in *Leibniz: The Monadology and Other Philosophical Writings* (Oxford: Oxford University Press, 1898).

14. Leibniz to Des Bosses, *Die philosophischen Schriften von G. F. Leibniz*, ed. C. J. Gerhardt, (Berlin, 1875–90; reprint Hildesheim: Georg Olms Verlag, 1978), vol. 2: 420; as quoted by Bertrand Russell, *A Critical Exposition of the Philosophy of Leibniz* (Cambridge: Cambridge University Press, 1900), 35.

15. See, for instance, Peter Strawson, *Individuals: An Essay in Descriptive Metaphysics* (London: Methuen, 1959); John Wisdom, "Philosophy, Metaphysics, and Psycho-Analysis," in his *Philosophy and Psycho-Analysis* (Oxford: Blackwell, 1953).

16. Heath and Lachs use "Science of Knowledge" as the cover and title-page title of this work, but in their table of contents and in their running heads "Foundations of the Entire Science of Knowledge" is used. J. G. Fichte, *Science of Knowledge*, with the First and Second Introductions, ed. and trans. by Peter Heath and John Lachs, (Cambridge: Cambridge University Press, 1982). The book is a reissue, with a few changes, of the edition published in 1970 by Meredith.

17. The philosophic consequences of Germany's disastrous history from the end of World War I to the end of World War II have yet to be adequately examined. The word *Grund* is only one of many words that have been tainted by perversely romantic word play. One philosopher, Heidegger, who—whatever his virtues—was symptomatic of those times, has made the writing of a proper history more difficult by the opportunism with which, after the second war, he labored to persuade us that the more positive note he then struck was what he had intended all along.

18. It should be remembered that both philosophers tell us in their different ways that we cannot *know* a reality that is independent of the formative capacity of our own subjectivity. That way of putting the matter is more Kantian than Humean. Nonetheless, for Hume also, the commonsense world is not an independent reality attained by the would-be knower but rather the outcome of a response on the part of the knower to the atomic impressions that constitute "real" experience.

19. It has not been sufficiently noticed that Kant's expression 'synthetic a priori' expresses a contradiction in a context in which the association between 'analytic' and 'a priori' and between 'synthetic' and 'a posteriori' is taken for granted.

20. Otto Neurath, *"Protokollsätze,"* Erkenntnis, 3 (1932–33).

21. Moritz Schlick, "Über das Fundament der Erkenntnis," *Erkenntnis*, 4 (1934).

22. A. J. Ayer, *Foundations of Empirical Knowledge* (London: Macmillan, 1940).

23. W. V. Quine, "Two Dogmas of Empiricism," in *From a Logical Point of View* (Cambridge: Harvard University Press, 1953), 20–46. The essay first appeared in the *Philosophical Review* in January, 1951.

24. W. V. Quine, *Word and Object* (New York and London: Wiley, 1960).

25. Roderick M. Chisholm, *The Foundations of Knowing* (Minneapolis: University of Minnesota Press, 1982).

12
Collective Guilt

Jude P. Dougherty

I

There are two things which I wish to do in this brief presentation. First, I intend to sketch in a general way the philosophical temperament which has in recent decades influenced the framing of law and, secondly, to single out for special treatment the idea of "collective guilt," which I take to be one of many concepts which first gained currency in the philosophical world before its employment in the law. Particular attention will be paid to the use of the notion of collective guilt in corporate law.

Lord Patrick Devlin, writing in the early 1960s speculated that if a society's laws are based on a particular world-view and that world-view collapses, the laws themselves will crumble.[1] Ronald Dworkin in his work, *Law's Empire*, argues the converse thesis that in a morally pluralistic society it is only the law which can provide the unity required for social order.[2] For Dworkin, law receives its moral force precisely because it provides this unifying function. He recognizes that Western society is ideologically split, with the consequence that its laws no longer flow out of a common view. Law tends to be created as a tissue of compromises between self-interested factions, and consequently provides the only set of agreed upon principles which may serve for concerted action. The open question, of course, is whether law pragmatically created will serve either the common good or foster the noblest of human tendencies.

Alasdair MacIntyre, in *Whose Justice, Which Rationality?* makes the point that theories of justice and practical rationality are but aspects of an allegiance given to a much larger intellectual tradition.[3] He speaks of the illusion of the autonomy of philosophical thought. "Philosophical theories," he argues, "give organized expression to concepts and theories already embodied in forms of practice and types of community. As such they make available for rational criticism and for further rational development those socially embodied theories and concepts of which they provided an understanding."[4]

One can be, suggests MacIntyre, an Aristotelian or Humean but one cannot be both. Furthermore, one cannot be either without appropriate social organization, or without a congenial polis. The conditions of the administration of Aristotelian justice are different from the conditions of Humean justice.

Although such issues are rarely accorded public debate, the forums where they are occasionally aired are those provided by the United States Supreme Court and the Senate Judiciary Committee. It is principally in briefs submitted to the Court that ideas which touch upon the fundamental aspirations of life and which affect the culture of the nation and its modes of governance are contested. No one denies that judge-made law has become a powerful force in shaping the nation's culture, perhaps more so than the enactments of legislative assemblies, either at the national or state level. So-called interest groups with legislative agendas take it for granted that they are more likely to have their aims implemented through the process of judicial review than through the enactments of legislative assemblies. Litigation is instigated with deliberation; forum shopping is standard practice as activist organizations seek judges of like mind. The bench itself tends to reflect the intellectual trends of the very same academy which inspires the interest groups to action. In recent decades most of the moralism has come from the left and has had as its objective the alteration of accepted modes of procedure. Whereas any legislation is apt to be the result of mutual concession, judge-made law often reflects the purely utopian ideas of the academy. Social theory fabricated by intellectuals who are untouched by life in the workaday world is compelling in its clarity and with ease can be translated into law by an activist judiciary. To understand the drift of contemporary courts one has to probe beneath current legal theory and in a MacIntyre-fashion place such theory in a larger cultural, should I say, philosophical context.

MacIntyre is not alone in his judgment that law whether created by legislative or judicial action is but one strand in a single fabric called an intellectual tradition. Peter W. Huber in discussing changing conceptions of "liability" recognizes as much when he identifies a concerted effort on the part of a handful of legal scholars, largely for philosophical reasons, "to repeal the common law of torts."[5] Ted Honderich convincingly shows the legal implication of accepted theories of psychological determinism and their tendency to instantiate liberal rather than conservative policies in the social order.[6] Two other works of interest to both philosophers and lawyers are those provided by Peter A. French and Larry May.[7] French writes on collective and corporate responsibility, providing a systematic rationale for holding corporations not merely civilly but criminally accountable, and Larry May argues that many social groups which lack tight organizational structure can be said to be collectively responsible for the joint actions of their members, and argues similarly that social groups are capable of being harmed even when individual members are not aware of the harm. "In unorganized groups," writes May, "solidarity and other relationships allow the group to have action and interests even though no decision-making structure for the group exists."[8]

These are only a few of many philosophical works which consciously attempt to alter common thinking about the law and the objectives of legislation. One easily forms the impression from a survey of recent legal theory that much discussion is not dispassionate in a professional way but has gone beyond a descriptive stage of theory and of plausible outcomes to one of outright advocacy. The literature is not without its effect. United States corporations are increasingly the victims of the new modes of thought as zealous prosecutors couple philosophical discussion with vague federal statutes to transform civil regulations into criminal law. Countless state and local regulations similarly have been criminalized. In holding corporations accountable for regulatory violations, many prosecutors no longer require evidence of mal intent, the traditional condition of criminal conduct. Dubious or not, the notion of "corporate criminal liability," is one that hands over to an unreasonable prosecutor a powerful capacity for mischief. If a corporation can be exposed to criminal punishment for even a good faith error of judgment, traditional common law in important respects has been abandoned.

With this Chagall-like impression as a backdrop, it is my intention to examine the philosophical wellsprings of certain ideas, particularly the notion of collective guilt, which have crept into legal theory with consequences for civil law. Many examples could be pursued. Need we be reminded that a rejection of the traditional understanding of what it means to be a person was accomplished in the philosophical community before it became the basis of *Roe vs. Wade*. Similarly, the rationale undergirding the use of capital punishment, was eroded in the social sciences before the Supreme Court invalidated most state laws which theretofore had permitted its use. When retribution, for philosophical reasons, ceased to be regarded as a plausible goal, and the deterrent effect of punishment was thrown into doubt by social science, capital punishment became difficult to defend and consequently is rarely employed even where new statutes have been written to make it legally permissible. Interestingly, whereas the retributive purpose of punishment is generally eschewed in criminal law, Peter French is happy to employ it in civil law, at least when it comes to punishing corporations. Tort law is yet another area where shifting philosophical sands have undermined legal structures. Traditional notions of liability depend on the acceptance of the principles of causality and free will. With the ascendancy of various psychological and sociological determinisms, tort law has changed dramatically. There was a time when the law was fairly clear. One had in some way to be causally responsible to be held accountable. Today any loss is thought to demand compensation, and if it is not available from the wrongdoer, then the burden of compensation is thought to be distributable to the community. Notions such as responsibility, causality, and intention obviously do not play the role they once did. Social objectives have become paramount, superseding legitimate accountability or fault. The ancient starting point of tort law, "the loss lies where it falls" has been replaced by "the loss lies with the community." Another example of changing intellectual outlooks influencing the Supreme Court is found if one reviews the opinions of the Court over the last forty years as it has interpreted the religion clauses of the First Amendment. As the academy has become progressively secular, severing its ties with a Christian past, the Court has turned the First Amendment, which was designed to protect religion, into one that handicaps its influence.

This is not to ignore the fact that many changes are the result of the political activism of groups which have effectively lobbied the court, but activism alone cannot account for success. Before judicial change can take place, the intellectual soil first has to be made receptive. It is manifestly easier to change the minds of those associated with the interpreting of law than it is to change the minds of those responsible for legislative enactments. The split between the intellectuals and the people on basic social issues is notorious. Thus, a handful of social scientists by carefully placing in a variety of law journals more or less the same article, with statistics changed to fit the locale, purporting to show the uselessness of capital punishment as a deterrent, managed though sympathetic courts to have the Supreme Court void most state laws. One is forced to make the judgment that in the English-speaking world we have witnessed in the decades since the sixties a concerted effort to change social structures by changing the law. The new law is the product of a "new" way of looking at things. I say *new* guardedly because the new is little more than an Enlightenment way of looking at things. MacIntyre uses the symbols of Aristotle and David Hume to designate the difference between the old and the new.

II

While many of these philosophical underpinnings beg attention, I turn now to the principal theme of the present inquiry, namely the notion of collective guilt. Surprisingly, it goes unexamined in a number of contexts where one would expect the use of critical intelligence. Peoples, generations, classes, races, industries, geographic regions, professions, and religious bodies are held accountable, not in some vague, "public opinion" sort of way, but before courts of law. From tort law to affirmative action policy, blame is often assigned to groups, sometimes to groups no longer in existence, and sometimes to mere conceptual entities. Restitution is not infrequently extracted from groups or from the heirs of groups without any responsibility for harm having been established.

Corporate defendants have been assessed damage even after proving that they could not possibly have caused the harm. Take one case. From the 1940s to 1971, approximately two million women took the synthetic hormone diethylstilbestrol (DES) to prevent miscarriages and morning sickness during pregnancy. The drug had been approved by the Food and Drug Administration (FDA) and marketed by some 300 pharmaceutical companies, often under generic labels. In 1970 researchers reported cancer and other problems among the daughters of DES users. The FDA banned the drug in 1971.

The cases quickly went to court. The mothers of many DES plaintiffs couldn't remember which brands they used. Courts in several states made the assumption that all DES pills were essentially the same and created a market share test so that damages could be assessed against the drug makers in proportion of their share of sales. In *Hymowitz v. Lilly* the highest New York court went further, applying the market share concept of responsibility to a drug manufacturer which could prove that defendant's mother did not use its pill.[9]

The questions forced upon us are these. Can there be collective complicity and therefore, collective liability without personal or corporate guilt? Can a corporation be held liable where there is no evidence that it or anyone else knew of any risks connected with the product?

Broad notions entertained in the framing of law are almost always the byproduct of previous academic discussion. Before the concept of market share became current, certain philosophical discussions of collective guilt, collective responsibility, and punishment had to occur. While this is not the place to examine the history of all of these concepts, little inquiry is needed to show that the notion of collective guilt is an ancient one. Discussions of that notion can be found in ancient and medieval, as well as, in contemporary literature.

The ancients no less than we recognized that societies are generated out of collective beliefs and traditions that are passed unconsciously by individuals. Emile Durkheim, the influential social theorist of the late nineteenth century and student of history, thought that traditions can exist in groups even when they are not instantiated by any individual. In his *Rules of Sociological Method* (1895) he even accords ontological status to social traditions and social relations independent of individual members of the group.[10]

In a now famous article, written shortly after the close of World War II, Karl Jaspers attempted to deal with the guilt of the German people.[11] The horrors perpetrated in the concentration camps were by then generally known. What was suspected had become graphically documented. Jaspers raised the question of guilt in the context of demands for restitution. To what extent were the German people as a whole culpable and to what extent could one expect atonement. The issue which Jaspers raised was not that of the responsibility of the German state. No one questioned national accountability or the requirement of "reparations." Jaspers was probing much deeper. Though his essay was entitled "moral guilt," Jaspers was aware that the vast majority of the German-speaking peoples were not morally responsible for the atrocities committed under the Third Reich. If the vast majority of the German people were neither legally nor morally guilty could the German-speaking peoples yet be held accountable? In an effort to sort things out Jaspers introduced the notion "collective guilt at a psychic level." Insofar as the German people shared a common language and a common culture, and insofar as they were nourished by a common literature, common music, and distinctive patterns of civic behavior, they could be said to be a collective. In Jasper's analysis there existed enough solidarity to produce a national psyche which in some sense could be held accountable such that one generation could make claims to another. Jaspers recognized the difficulty of defending a notion of psychological guilt apart from legal or moral guilt. With Aquinas he could agree "no man can do an injustice except voluntarily."[12] Though he did not, he could in other respects, have appealed to Aquinas for at least partial support of his view.

St. Thomas's position on collective guilt might startle the modern reader. He writes, "When the whole multitude sins, vengeance must be taken on them." He even speaks of the virtue of revenge. The moral virtue of fortitude disposes one to vengeance. Of the two vices opposed to vengeance, cruelty is the excess, being remiss is the defect.[13] The severity of vengeance should be brought to bear upon the few principals if they can be identified. "Sometimes even the good are punished in temporal matters together with the wicked, for not having condemned their sins."[14] St. Thomas enters this qualification: "A man should never be condemned without fault of his own to an inflictive punishment such as death, mutilation or flogging, but he may be condemned...to a punishment of forfeiture, even without any fault on his part, but not without cause," for example, in the crime of high treason, a son loses his inheritance through the sin of his parent.[15] Continuing with St. Thomas, "It is a natural law that one should repent of the evil one has done, by grieving for having done it, and by seeking a remedy for one's grief in some way or other, and also that one should show some signs of grief."[16] Charity demands that a man should both grieve for the offense and be anxious to make satisfaction. "Now amendment for an offense committed against another is not made by merely ceasing to offend, but it is necessary to make some kind of compensation."[17] Clearly, Jaspers is reaching for the same solution. While Jaspers does not use the word 'charity' in his analysis of German guilt and restitution, his analysis leads him to a similar notion. Thomas in many contexts appeals to the principle of charity where modern authors are apt to invoke the concept of 'right'.

For the discussion which follows it is important to lay bare a number of distinctions and assumptions. No one denies that guilt implies responsibility. Responsibility in turn presupposes freedom to act or not to act. In speaking of freedom, it is necessary to distinguish 1) between freedom in a moral sense and freedom under the law, and 2) between the legal sense of guilt and the moral sense. One can be held accountable before civil law without being morally responsible for harm. Civil law itself recognizes this when it takes into consideration motivation and extenuating circumstances which are sometimes allowed to mitigate guilt. The continuity between the moral and civil is so fast that in practice the distinction is often blurred or even ignored. Moral outrage is not infrequently thought to be immediately translatable into law. Appeals for the creation of law typically invoke danger to health, damage to the environment, or cite some other material or social disadvantage if action is not taken, but they are nonetheless appeals to the moral order.

Another insight which must be kept in mind is that action follows judgment and judgment is made necessarily within a cultural context. How one views a proposed course of action is in part dependent upon one's education, i.e. the distinctions one has learned to make and the principles one invokes habitually. Certain courses of action may be accepted in the West which are unthinkable in the East. In the West some may see nothing wrong with the merchandising of pornography, with divorce, or with abortion. The same is not true of Islamic society. It would be precarious to attribute moral guilt to those who act in the light of conscience, even if that conscience judged by a time-transcending moral code seems to be ill-informed, but this does not mean that holders are unaccountable for their beliefs in all respects. From any viewpoint, one has the obligation to form a correct conscience.

Also recognized is the principle that not all law binds in conscience. Good civil law tends to explicate or elaborate the moral order. Thus, building codes, traffic regulations, and rules governing securities trading are in some sense moral dictates before they become statutes. Law which flaunts common perception of right and wrong is not regarded as moral. This distinction between civil law and moral law, though sometimes challenged from the academy, is universally recognized. The distinction cuts both ways. A corporation which operates wholly within the law may yet be guilty of moral infraction. The sale of pornography, the creation of advertising that deliberately manipulates the truth, or media distortion on behalf of partisan causes are examples to the point. One can make the claim that the manufacturing of shabby merchandise which mimics the genuine article and is marketed to the ill-educated or unsuspecting is a kind of moral infraction. Some would extend moral guilt to those who manufacture tobacco products and distilled spirits, or make clothing from animal pelts. No one would hesitate to attribute moral guilt to a corporation that knowingly manufactures a defective and potentially dangerous product, quite apart from any civil penalty which might be inflicted.

Granted immorality on the part of a corporation where does moral guilt lie? Are all associated with the corporation collectively guilty? If not, how far down the corporate ladder does responsibility extend? To the worker on the assembly line? To the wholesaler? To the retailer? To the shareholder? If guilt follows knowledge, it may be that only a few in the testing laboratory or in the executive suite are privy to the information that a given product is potentially troublesome or could be modified with additional cost to diminish risk. Although the corporation, before the law, can be held accountable for negligence, it is difficult to believe that the average worker in the plant or billing office, unless the company has a record of dubious performance, has the knowledge which would imply criminal complicity. There are exceptions of course. We have all read stories of whistle-blowers who have brought to light questionable practices, sometimes to the gratitude of management. Where corporate guilt is determined, it is not likely that all workers would be held accountable either by an irate group of stockholders or before a court of law. When a specific individual, in violation of corporate policy, has been guilty of harm, it makes little sense to hold the corporation criminally liable, subject to punitive damages, which ultimately are collectively shared by innocent shareholders.

Readiness to accept the notion of collective guilt, no doubt, stems from the number of egregious cases where societies taken as a whole seem accountable. The twentieth century provides numerous examples of societies acting, if not as whole, at least with sufficient unity to implement morally unacceptable policy, i.e. Germany under Hitler, the Soviet Union under Stalin, both governments systematically eliminating so called enemies of the state. One also thinks of South Africa limiting full civic participation to whites, the antebellum American South enslaving the black, and the postbellum South enacting segregation laws. To what extent are we willing to blame German or Soviet peoples for the atrocities committed within the borders of their nations? Can the nineteenth century immigrant cooper working within his shop in Minneapolis be blamed for slavery or for postbellum statutes enacted within the South? The way we talk about these matters is often misleading. We speak of "sharing in the greatness of a nation" or we may say that we "take pride in belonging to a scholarly family," but we must be careful not to hypostatize abstractions or make them bearers of value. As H. D. Lewis pointed out in his seminal article, "Collective Responsibility," linguistic devices which make for succinctness of expression are to be recognized for their metaphorical and elliptical meaning and not taken as literal truth.[18]

A family group or a nation, I am willing to argue, cannot be the bearer of guilt; in neither is there sufficient unity or participation in the deliberative process to warrant accountability.

Corporations are different. They are not mere aggregates of people but have a metaphysical-logical identity. Otto van Gierke has suggested that the law in conferring on the corporation the status of a legal person is merely recognizing a prelegal social condition. The corporation is the offspring of certain social actions and possess a *de facto* personality which the law declares to be a juridical fact.[19] Brian Tierney traces the notion of corporate personality to medieval canon law and its doctrine of agency. "In Roman law," writes Tierney, "an individual or group could appoint an agent to negotiate with a third party, but the result of the transaction was to establish an obligation between the third party and the agent, not directly between the third party and the principal. In canon law, when a corporate group established a representative *plena potestas* the group was directly obliged by the representative's acts, even when it had not consented to them in advance."[20] The ancient Roman principle *quod onmes tangit ab omnibus approbator* (what touches all is to be approved by all) was replaced by one that allowed a representative to act on behalf of all. Thus, commitments made in the name of an organized group may persist even after the composition of the group and its "will" changes. If a group reneges on a commitment, the fault may be that of no individual member, yet the liability for breach of contract, falling on the group as a whole, will distribute burdens quite unavoidably on faultless members.

Peter A. French, in his extended analysis of corporate responsibility maintains that for a corporation to be treated as a moral person, it must be possible to attribute to it a corporate intention. This is different from attributing intentions to the biological persons who comprise its board of directors or its top-level management.[21] Corporations, at least major corporations, have internal decision-making structures, and this is reflected in their organizational charts and in their established methods of reaching corporate policy. In many cases, one can even describe the basic beliefs of a corporation from which specific actions flow. The moment policy is sidestepped or violated, it is no longer the policy of the company. Maverick acts can not be described as having been done for corporate reasons. Thus, it is possible to distinguish between individual staff negligence and corporate negligence. Executives voting to adopt certain objectives when required by the corporate structure to vote, in fact, constitute the corporation deciding to do something. A corporate officer who ignores corporate policy, possibly in the name of expediency, may be morally accountable without moral blame being attached to the corporation, although corporate civil accountability may be unavoidable.

The *Exxon Valdez* oil spill provides a case study. The question yet to be answered is, is the poisoning of Prince William Sound a simple matter of a captain and his ship or of a corporation and its policies? The former skipper of the Valdez was criminally charged, but normally, in spite of the National Wildlife Federation urging federal prosecutors to "go after the individual who is responsible at the top,"[22] one would not expect Exxon to be charged with criminal wrongdoing, but, of course, it has. The law offers a way to punish corporations through liability suits. It is usually thought that the possibility of a large judgment against the malfeasance of a company is adequate inducement to establish operational policies sufficient to minimize risk. In the *Valdez* case evidence is yet to be produced that Exxon as a corporation was remiss. Its criminal prosecution may be more a political move than one dictated by legal principle. The *Valdez* oil spill and its aftermath also illustrated a willingness on the part of some to extend blame beyond the principals at hand. This is seen in the suggestion that the Coast Guard be held accountable for not warning the ship that it was heading for a reef. While hasty finger pointing is not evidence of the collapse of law, the readiness to attribute guilt apart from any causal connection has to be confronted. One is amused how outdated is the off quoted remark of Baron Thurlaw. The once Lord Chancellor of England is reputed to have said, "Did you ever expect a corporation to have a conscience, when it has no soul to be damned and no body to be killed?" Times have changed, however. Corporations are expected to have souls, and can be sentenced to death by juries.

Although responsibility belongs essentially to the individual, responsibility can be shared, both morally and before the law. To the extent that one shows the mind set and objectives of the group one participates in its guilt. If one subscribes to a doctrine of natural slavery and is in full sympathy with segregationist laws, one is intellectually united to others of like mind and can be accused of moral failure, but to be held legally accountable is another matter. Here we must distinguish between active and passive participation. Active participation entails full responsibility, passive participation less. It is possible to be part of a community which through its leadership is bent upon injustice of one sort or another and in no way be responsible.

In a democracy it is necessary to distinguish between the nation, the body politic, and the state. A nation is created by a common language and culture and may be broader than the political boundaries which demarcate countries. A body politic is coextensive with geographical boundaries although suffrage may not be universal within those boundaries. The state is the topmost governing body, and even though it must ultimately receive its authority from the people, it may not at every turn reflect the desires of the majority let alone the people as a whole. A nation is more like an aggregate and there is reason to argue that moral responsibility predicates cannot rightfully be ascribed to aggregate collectives. An aggregate may act, but without a decision making organization it can neither be aware of its action nor of the moral nature of the action.

Even where representative government prevails there are severe limitations on the power of the individual to modify the actions of the state. It is easy to envisage a situation where dissent or protest would result in severe penalties. The obligation to work for change in policy varies from situation to situation and depends upon one's station in life. Mental reservation is always possible, but active resistance may be self-defeating. It is idealistic in the extreme to attribute guilt to the whole though sanctions may unavoidably be imposed on the whole from without and indiscriminately affect guilty and nonguilty. The sanctions that one country may morally inflict on another depend upon the gravity of the matter. They range from war to tariffs and import to quotas.

With respect to the ontology of groups, a group is created by a common final cause. A group has no being except in the intentional order. Ends may be shared to varying degrees. Personal responsibility follows interior assent to the end and may not be coextensive with legal accountability. While one may not have options with respect to membership in a nation or in a body politic, one does exercise choice with respect to the organizations one joins or to which one lends one's name. Again, accountability follows intention.

If this analysis is correct, one can speak of collective guilt only if certain conditions are met, that is, only if one can identify a common intention, a common purpose which is the product of a deliberative mechanism, and only if one is successful in enumerating those who belong to the collective. One can allow for differentiating degrees of accountability, but accountability must be demonstrated. Tenuous connections are connections, but they are nevertheless tenuous. They may be both morally and legally compelling, but on the other hand, they may not. Circumstances dictate our judgment. The collective need not be a person in a legal sense.

I find inconsistent deterministic approaches, psychological and sociological, which on the one hand seem to deny personal responsibility but on the other insist on collective responsibility. Deterministic approaches usually fail to recognize the subtlety of decision making. Decisions are always made within a context, but how that context is presented or is allowed to influence decisions is self-determined. This is seen negatively in our ability to opt out of a distasteful milieu, if not physically, at least psychologically. In a pre-Solidarity address to his fellow country men, Karol Wojtyla warned of the dangers of a psychological migration, a failure to engage oneself politically.[23] His admonition may be taken as a recognition that one can be remiss with respect to an obligation to influence the collective and being remiss share responsibility for the harm which may ensue from its action. His analysis also points to a fundamental freedom. We control how things are presented to us. We choose to be engaged by putting the matter at hand in a certain light; appetency follows cognition.

One has the impression that the notion of collective guilt like the notion of right is used principally to extract concessions or reparations from groups judged to be guilty. This is particularly onerous when one generation is charged with the wrongs of another and is confronted with demands to compensate members of generation who were not born when the wrong occurred. Claims may be made across generations if lineage and causality can be established. If an individual can inherit both positively and negatively, something similar is true with respect to natural structures such as family and country and artificial constructs such as corporations, but most of the time what is inherited is a melange. While egregious fault cannot be ignored, nor attendant hardship dismissed, the social milieu is rarely black or white. Reason must prevail in sorting out responsibility and, therefore, accountability. One cannot be guilty either before civil law or the divine throne for infractions not committed. One cannot be part of a collective without intent. When collective guilt is invoked, whether it be called market share or corporate accountability, prudence dictates that one examine not only the causal record which will determine responsibility but the motives of the accuser. The concept of collective guilt may be more a political or distributionist banner than a useful moral insight.

NOTES

1. Lord Patrick Devlin, *The Enforcement of Morals* (London: Oxford University Press, 1965).

2. Ronald Dworkin, *Law's Empire* (London: Fontana, 1986).

3. Alasdair MacIntyre, *Whose Justice, Which Rationality?* (Notre Dame, Indiana: University of Notre Dame Press, 1988).

4. *Whose Justice, Which Rationality?*, 390.

5. Peter W. Huber, *Liability: The Legal Revolution and Its Consequences* (New York: Basic Books, Inc., 1988).

6. Ted Honderich, *A Theory of Determinism: The Mind Neuroscience and Life Hopes* (Oxford: The Clarendon Press, 1988).

7. Peter A. French, *Collective and Corporate Responsibility* (New York: Columbia University Press, 1984); Larry May, *The Morality of Groups: Collective Responsibility, Group Based Harm, and Corporate Rights* (Notre Dame, Indiana: University of Notre Dame Press, 1987).

8. *The Morality of Groups*, 180.

9. *Hymowitz v. Lilly & Co.*, 73 N.Y. 2nd 487, 539 N.E. 2nd 1069, 541 N.Y.S. 2nd 1941 (1989).

10. Emile Durkheim, *Rules of Sociological Method* (1895), trans. S. Soloway and J. Mueller, ed. E. Carlin (New York: Free Press, 1964), 7.

11. Karl Jaspers, "Moral Guilt," reprinted in *Crimes of War*, ed. R. A. Falk, G. Kolko and R. J. Lifton (New York: Vintage, 1971), 476 ff.

12. St. Thomas Aquinas, *Summa Theologica*, trans. The Fathers of the English Dominican Province, (New York: Benzinger Brothers, Inc., 1947), II–II, Q. 59, a. 3.

13. II–II, Q108, a. 1 ad. 5.

14. II–II, 108, a. 4.

15. II–II, 108, a. 4, ad. 2.

16. III, 84, a. 7, ad. 1.

17. III, 85, a. 3.

18. H.D. Lewis, "Collective Responsibility," *Philosophy* 23, 84 (January, 1948): 47. See also Joel Feinberg, "Collection Responsibility," *The Journal of Philosophy*, 65, 2 (November, 1968): 674–688; and Virginia Held, "Can a Random Collection of Individuals Be Morally Responsible," *The Journal of Philosophy*, 67, 14 (July, 1970): 471–481.

19. Otto van Gierke, *Political Theory of the Middle Ages*, trans. F. W. Maitland (Cambridge: Cambridge University Press, 1900).

20. Brian Tierney, *Religion, Law and the Growth of Constitutional Thought* (Cambridge: Cambridge University Press, 1982), 23.

21. *Collective and Corporate Responsibility*, 39.

22. *New York Times* (February 11, 1990) Sec. E, 6

23. *Sollicitudo Rei Socialis*, promulgated December 30, 1987. *Origins*, 17, 38 (March 3, 1988): 656–657.

Section Four
Science, Interaction, and the Philosophy of Nature

13
Metaphysical Systems and Scientific Theories: A Structural Comparison

Friedrich Rapp

DIVERGENT VIEWPOINTS

Wittgenstein was concerned with the problem of certainty until just before he died. On the 3rd of April 1951, a month before his death, he noted: "I am sitting with a philosopher in the garden; and he says again and again, 'I know that's a tree', pointing to a tree that is near us. Someone arrives and hears this, and I tell him: 'This fellow isn't insane. We are only doing philosophy'." Five days later he will add: "It is as if 'I know' did not tolerate a metaphysical emphasis."[1]

This note is indicative of the problem of all metaphysical statements: in spite of their weight they possess a certain fragility; it is even questionable whether they can satisfy stringent conditions of proof. The different philosophical systems that have been constructed in the course of the history of philosophy contradict each other and none of them can be shown conclusively to be the only "true" one. It is nevertheless obvious that we must have recourse at least to implicit, rudimentary theses about the final, basic, a priori, i.e. metaphysical, determining elements of the world in order to be able to put forward philosophical arguments. If a final and consistent philosophical interpretation is to be provided which covers all aspects of human existence, of history, and of the universe, it is necessary to construct metaphysical systems.

Let us briefly consider the positions encountered in discussion of these issues. At the end of his *Enquiry Concerning Human Understanding*, Hume formulated the classic program of empiricism, the basics of which are still valid today. He answered a rhetorical question about the value of the books in a library as follows: "If we take in our hand any volume; of divinity or school metaphysics, for instance; let us ask, 'Does it contain any abstract reasoning concerning quantity or number?' No. 'Does it contain any experimental reasoning concerning matter of fact and existence?' No. Commit it then to the flames: for it can contain nothing but sophistry and illusion."

Logical positivism has taken over Hume's program and has refined its methodology.[2] Put in modern terms, the central claim is that: "Statements are only meaningful if they are either analytic or verifiable. That is to say, they must be true either in terms of their formal structure (as in logic and mathematics), or they must be open to direct or indirect inspection by means of the senses (as the statements of the natural sciences)."[3] Now, since the statements of metaphysics claim to say something about the world without being empirically verifiable, they must be rejected as meaningless when the empiricist criterion of meaning is applied.[4]

One way of preserving metaphysics consists in confining it exclusively to the a priori, metatheoretical knowledge which explains the possibility of attaining empirical knowledge. Kant chooses this means of saving metaphysics in the *Critique of Pure Reason*.[5] By restricting its scope, the possibility of confrontation between metaphysics and concrete sense experience is excluded in principle—though not necessarily in practice. Another, more moderate, solution to the problem of avoiding a conflict consists in taking language as the unchallengeable, ultimate point of reference for philosophical understanding. In this approach, which has a number of variants, philosophy has the task of investigating the use of everyday language (the later Wittgenstein, and Austin), logical structures (Carnap), or the language of the natural sciences (Hempel, Stegmüller). Understanding philosophy as a means of revealing and analyzing differences in language use is also crucial for Ryle's taxonomy of category mistakes and for Strawson's descriptive metaphysics.[6]

To accept a stringent and empiricist criterion of verification is to assign to philosophy a merely derivative, essentially analytic function. In this view, philosophy must restrict itself to the investigation of specific, relatively isolated problems. Any independent philosophical synthesis (such as can be found in the philosophies of Aristotle, Spinoza, Leibniz, Kant, Hegel, Whitehead), which goes beyond everyday experience or beyond the integration of the findings of the sciences, must then be rejected as a meaningless rhapsody.

Apart from such epistemological arguments pragmatic considerations can also be adduced against metaphysics. In particular, the success of the natural sciences and of the technology based on them has strengthened confidence in the empiricist understanding of nature. Since today's society places its priority on usable, discernible results, interest in an ultimate, comprehensive synthesis—and that is to say the interest in philosophical systems—is placed in the background. Just as the amount and variety of information we have gained about man, history, and the universe has increased enormously, so too the gap between scientific knowledge and metaphysical theses has become even greater than it used to be, for example, for Leibniz and Kant. Today it seems as if metaphysical systems are detached from reality to such an extent that they can provide only a nonbinding and, hence, dispensable speculative synthesis. If this is accepted, then the thesis which Hegel put forward in the preface of his *Phänomenologie des Geistes*, namely that: "The true form in which truth exists can only be its scientific [i.e. comprehensive and rigorously developed] system,"[7] would no longer be valid.

Thus, when discussing the question of the relation between metaphysics and experience systematically, a middle path must be found between the extremes of Hegel's optimistic attitude towards philosophical speculation and Hume's sceptical empiricism. Appealing to the dictum that it is a sign of maturity to be able to live with an open conception of the world, one can make do without the benefit of closed and comprehensive metaphysical constructions; this is a logically consistent and factually legitimate position. This holds good irrespective of the fact that the self-understanding of an epoch, including the dominant conceptions of science, is determined by tacit metaphysical presuppositions. Furthermore, the pragmatic decision, whether a philosopher is to devote himself to the analysis of specific problems, or whether he is more interested in an inevitably more general and abstract synthesis, is a legitimate personal choice. As a result, two aspects concerned with the verifiability of philosophical systems can be distinguished: The scope of individualistic, voluntaristic choice is the first aspect, the second aspect is the question, whether metaphysical systems, such as those exemplified by Aristotle's *Metaphysics*, Spinoza's *Ethics*, Leibniz' *Monadology* and the systematic parts of Kant's three *Critiques,* Hegel's *Phenomenology* or Whitehead's *Process and Reality,* are meaningful enterprises at all. What is said in the following is of relevance only to those who are interested in the construction of such systems. The question is whether and to what extent the verifiability criterion means that metaphysical systems are without objects.

VARIANTS OF METAPHYSICS

It must be taken for granted that the intention of verifying metaphysical systems is a meaningful endeavor. Only when this is presupposed does it make sense to understand the question as a question and in this sense meaningful. Dealing with the problem of verifying metaphysical systems involves at least an intuitive understanding of the direction the search for a possible solution will take. It is, of course, still unclear, whether the search will be successful.[8] Thus, the question about the existence of unicorns still makes sense although it will eventually be answered negatively. Taken in this broader sense, all philosophical systems are meaningful in view of their intention because they aim at giving closed, final, and comprehensive philosophical interpretation.

The real problem is to find out whether this intention can really be fulfilled, i.e. whether the system in question has a factual basis or whether it is only a fairy tale.

Whoever is involved in philosophical questioning, i.e. in reasoning with arguments, enters an open area in which every step he takes and every position he may put forward is itself philosophical. Transcending philosophical reasoning by silence (as suggested by the early Wittgenstein)[9] or meditative listening to Being and acceptance of what happens (something which the later Heidegger pleads for)[10] are not counter examples because in these cases one leaves the realm of discursive arguments behind. Every form of philosophical argumentation that is directed towards the clarification of a certain problem implies an implicit but real connection between the individual theses involved in the argumentation and, hence, presupposes a philosophical system, which may however be very loosely constructed and fragmentary. Whoever denies the verifiability of philosophical systems will still have to make use of such systems, however rudimentary they may be. However, such loose and partial conceptual structures must be distinguished from the universal, coherent, and final synthesis which philosophical systems claim to provide. In the final resort, each philosopher gives a different answer to the question about how precisely metaphysical systems should be defined. Metaphysical theses are the core of every type of philosophy, and the creative force and the systematic achievement of every thinker consists in making an authentic and systematic contribution. It would be illusory to attempt a comprehensive survey here. Characterizing some typical positions will provide an impression of the possible variety. The speculative systems of Hegel and Schelling aim at mediating between reason and history, between the absolute and finite, in a consistent form.[11] The ontologies of neothomism and of Nicolai Hartmann set themselves the task of describing the most general determinants of being as such.[12] Kant assigns metaphysics the task of investigating the transcendental presuppositions of any type of knowledge. Collingwood follows this approach but insists on historical variability of the presuppositions.[13] E. E. Harris holds the view that metaphysics has the task of setting up a coherent universal system of concepts in which all scientific knowledge can find a place.[14] Strawson pleads for a descriptive metaphysics that reveals the most general conceptual structures by means of the analysis of the use of language.[15] Finally, Ryle believes that the real task of philosophy consists exclusively in putting forward *reductio ad absurdum* arguments which can be used to test the logical soundness of statements and to point out systematic ambiguities.[16]

After all, we have to keep in mind that none of the philosophers who, in one form or another, reject metaphysical systems can avoid referring to some sort of evidence, a procedure which they object to when it is derived from metaphysical systems. Thus, logical empiricism and the analytical philosophy of language invoke the constitutive role of sense perception and of the use of language respectively. This is to say, they appeal to an insight into theoretical relations which can only be ascertained by means of intellectual evidence and not by mere sensory perception or observation of the use of language. Whether somebody accepts or rejects the theses of Hume's *Enquiry Concerning Human Understanding* or Leibniz's *Monadology* is decided by means of contemplation in one's armchair, in the library, or in philosophical discourse, but not through observation of everyday life, through the study of historical sources or through experiments in the laboratory. In this context, the mere appeal to evidence does not lead to a decision in one sense or another; the question remains open for the time being. Hence, before individual arguments are examined, one can neither grant nor take away the right of philosophical systems to exist.

RESULTS OF THE PHILOSOPHY OF SCIENCE

In view of this situation the following structural comparison between metaphysical systems and scientific theories may be useful. Of course, one cannot expect an exhaustive and final verification from this comparison. Yet, an analysis of the common traits and the differences in the formation of theoretical concepts in both systems of statements can help to achieve a better understanding of metaphysical systems. Such a comparison suggests itself because in the philosophy of science for a long time a detailed (and often highly technical) discussion has been conducted that has led to remarkable results. Hence the question arises whether or to what extent the results found there can be transferred to the study of metaphysical systems.

If one compares the present, highly heterogeneous state of the discussion in the philosophy of science and in analytical philosophy with the far-reaching program that was put forward by the neopositivism of the Vienna Circle (later the label "logical empiricism" came into use), one observes that the original far-reaching claims have been weakened. As an indication of the extent of the original claim we can take M. Schlick's statement in 1930 that: "We are objectively justified in considering that an end has come to the fruitless conflicts of systems. We are already at the present time, in my opinion, in possession of methods which make every such conflict in principle unnecessary;"[17] and he continued: "There is thus no other testing and corroboration of truths except through observation and empirical science."[18]

In order to make this comparison one needs neither to reconstruct the historical development, nor need all the details of the present state of the discussion be taken into consideration. It is sufficient to survey the most important results. For this purpose, five points are of special relevance: protocol sentences, theoretical concepts, the problem of induction, the Duhem-Quine thesis, and paradigm change in the history of science. According to the empiricist view, all synthetic statements, i.e. those which contain information, ought to be reducible to sense perceptions. The stringent development of this program led logical positivism to stipulate the condition that only those statements that can be tested by direct observation are to be considered meaningful and legitimate and hence are to be allowed as part of a scientific theory. The *basic statements* or *protocol sentences* that record the results of scientific experiments are to constitute the final, unquestionable basis of all scientific knowledge. The idea is that, in contrast to the arbitrary, theoretical speculation of metaphysics, this will provide a real empirical point of reference.[19] In his *Tractatus Logico-Philosophicus* the early Wittgenstein formulated this methodological program explicitly and ontologically in terms of logical atomism: "The world is the totality of facts, not of things"; and "If all true elementary propositions are given, the result is a complete description of the world."[20]

In the discussion of this apparently convincing program it became evident that the original claim to rigor could not be maintained. On closer inspection it turns out that apparently simple and unambiguous observation is structured, ambiguous and determined by theory. Our empirical knowledge is not based on isolated elements of experience that are free from theory; it is rather based on theoretically prestructured perceptions which are closely linked with each other.[21] Furthermore, it is not sense experience as such, but language which forms the final accessible element in scientific discussions. In the case of a conflict between different theories it is not the observation as such but rather interpretative statements about observations which oppose each other. This eventually led Wittgenstein to replace his former picture theory of knowledge by his theory of language games. These insights do not supersede the empiricist call for an anchoring of our knowledge in concrete sense experience, but they do severely limit its scope.

The situation is similar with the problem of *theoretical concepts*. In practice, scientific language does require more than simply observation predicates. In order to be able to achieve a systematization, i e. a condensation of the wide empirical data in the interest of mental economy, general, and hence necessarily abstract, concepts are needed. These concepts are necessarily related only indirectly to the concrete observations. Since, in the last analysis, one of the tasks of scientific theories consists in describing and predicting well-defined and empirically proven relations between predictable phenomena, it seems a logical step to think about dispensing with theoretical concepts. But in this case one would be forced to use a very large number of postulates or correspondence rules in order to organize the empirical data. Following this procedure would make it necessary to do without inductive predictions and deductive explanations that use scientific theories. Similarly, we would also be required to dispense with the heuristic function of general hypotheses.[22]

For this reason, one continues to make use of theoretical concepts although they cannot be reduced in a unique and unproblematical way to empirical statements—which are in turn susceptible to the problems mentioned above. To do so it is essential to rely on the basic idea that it is possible in principle by means of operational definitions, interpretative sentences, or correspondence rules, to pin down the empirical content which is assigned to the theoretical concepts used. Thus, it is not the theoretical concepts, or rather the corresponding propositions, themselves, which are directly tested: they merely receive an indirect confirmation by a demonstration of their empirical consequences.[23] Unfortunately, when the attempt is made to elaborate this basic principle of the philosophy of science, acute difficulties are encountered. At this juncture it becomes perfectly clear that the actual practice of science, which is obviously bound up with empirical experience, can only be described by models of the philosophy of science which significantly simplify reality.

The procedure of *generalizing induction*, i.e. the formulation of universal statements on the basis of an inevitably limited number of observed instances, cannot be justified on logical grounds. Nevertheless, no science which wants to go beyond immediate description of past events by making predictions about future events (which can also be exploited for technical purposes) can dispense with such generalizations. Popper's suggestion was to regard scientific theories only as heuristic devices for formulating hypotheses which can be used as long as no negative, falsifying counterexample has been found. But this does not constitute a solution, since without the tacit presupposition of the uniformity of nature every prediction would be equally valid.[24] Furthermore, this would involve a vicious circle because the uniformity of nature can in its turn only be empirically justified on inductive grounds. Certainly the close interconnectedness and the hierarchical relations of dependence between scientific laws increase their plausibility, but still there is no generally agreed theoretical (philosophical) justification for the practical success of the sciences in the use of scientific laws.[25]

It was Quine who by further developing Duhem's research suggested the idea of the inherently holistic interrelation between scientific theories. The *Duhem-Quine thesis* maintains that a coherent theoretical system which is characteristic of the natural sciences cannot be refuted by means of the negative result of a single experiment. In the design and execution of an experiment, in the setting up of the experimental conditions, in the collection and processing of the observational data received as well as in the theoretical interpretation of these various elements, a great number of theories are inevitably involved. The result is that an unexpected experimental deviation cannot be localized unambiguously: there is no *experimentum crucis*. Consequently, the system of theories in question must be accepted or rejected in its totality.[26] The outcome is that the natural sciences which at first seem to be exclusively determined by the natural world turn out to be the result of a certain theoretical (philosophical) interpretation of the structure of the world. This is so because there is no clear-cut method for constructing scientific theories. Neither logical reasoning nor empirical data (the result of experiments) alone provides an authoritative prescription for a certain way of conceptualizing the world. This holds good notwithstanding the fact that the actual course of scientific research in modern times has been successfully directed towards an ever greater and more successful technological manipulation of natural processes.[27]

The discussion initiated by Kuhn about the *change of paradigms* within the history of science points in the same direction.[28] Undoubtedly the processes of nature are today the same as they were three hundred years ago. But the way we conceptualize these processes has changed. Objectively this is possible because our sense experiences are always theoretically "underdetermined" in the sense that they do not by themselves force us to put forward a certain type of theory. Only by means of intellectual spontaneity does a certain interpretation come about through applying specific concepts and through categorizing the elements referred to within a well-defined theoretical context. It was for this reason that in the course of the history of science the very same physical processes were conceptualized and interpreted in so many different ways. In doing this one always, inevitably, refers to certain paradigms, models and ideals of natural order. This insight into the change of paradigmata and into the inevitable element of theoretical choice implied in any type of scientific theory contradicts the naive empiricist notion of a purely accumulative process which results in an ever deeper and more general understanding of nature.

SIMILARITIES AND DIFFERENCES

Metaphysical systems with clearly defined terms and with a systematic structure are particularly suited for a comparison with scientific theories. The importance of the systematic structure of knowledge is underlined by Whitehead's statement: "The true method of philosophical construction is to frame a scheme of ideas, the best one can, and unflinchingly to explore the interpretation of experience in terms of that scheme," the understanding being that this procedure applies, with the appropriate alteration, to any kind of scientific systematization.[29]

A systematically structured metaphysical conception, i.e. one which is not composed of randomly assembled elements, has the same function of systematization and explanation as scientific theories. In both cases intellectual spontaneity is applied in order to formulate a coherent system of statements about a certain area of experience which is defined differently in each case. These systems yield an all-embracing synopsis and structure into which the specific cases in question can be fitted by means of abstract concepts and relations. In neither case is the self-evidence and efficiency of the system in question immediately obvious. Only by means of the consequences deduced from the general statements of the systems in question may the experiences referred to can be dealt with because these consequences provide an interpretation and explanation of the special cases considered in terms of the overall system.

Using the five points dealt with previously, we are now able to discuss in more detail the similarities and differences between metaphysical propositions or theories and scientific ones: Undoubtedly the greatest difference is with respect to the concrete final elements referred to. In the case of the natural sciences these can be taken to be the *protocol sentences* (or alternatively the corresponding observations). Here positivism rejected metaphysics precisely because it had no comparable unambiguous empirical basis that could compete with protocol sentences. Logical positivism has learned that it is necessary to weaken the distinction between empirical facts and theoretical interpretation. This can be seen as reducing the distance between science and metaphysics. As in science a certain dominance of theory formation vis à vis the apparently purely empiricist element has become evident, conceptualization itself turns out to be theoretically prestructured, so that indirectly the burden of proof for metaphysical systems is reduced, though not eliminated.

If we continue the comparison between scientific theories and metaphysical systems, the analogue to scientific observations (protocol sentences) in the case of metaphysics is a rather imprecisely defined conglomerate of everyday experience and scientific knowledge. The way this conglomerate is conceptualized may differ from philosopher to philosopher. In the context of this comparison, it is highly important that, while the natural sciences actively interfere with their object of investigation, metaphysics is essentially passive in its relation to reality. The most illuminating results of modern science are obtained by experimental manipulations which reflect the theoretical framework of the experiment in question. In the sciences the touchstone of the "truth" of every variable and relationship postulated is the outcome of an experiment predicted by means of the theories involved. This is why in general the deductive explanation of a single instance derived from the scientific theory will also yield a corresponding prediction about events in the natural world. In modern times, scientific explanations are not restricted to theoretical interpretation. In this respect they are quite different from the sciences of antiquity and the Middle Ages which were basically confined to a contemplative, passive attitude towards nature, an attitude reinforced by the mutual permeation of science and philosophical ideas about nature. Nowadays, the results of science can always be verified operationally and hence they are available for practical, technological exploitation. The success of modern science manifests itself in technological products which can be interpreted as concrete and palpable proof of the "truth" of scientific theories.

Formally, a similarity between scientific theories and philosophical systems can be observed with respect to the use of *theoretical concepts* which are not open to immediate observation. In both cases the use of universal and abstract concepts which are necessarily "distant" from concrete experience is indispensible. Scientific concepts are designed to investigate specific questions which are defined by the discipline in question. They only claim to refer to a well-defined specific aspect of the world. This specificity applies even in those cases, such as the general theory of relativity, which apply throughout the universe, but which are restricted to specific features of the universe. This is not the case with metaphysics. Its splendor and misery is that it must fulfil its claim to express the most general and the most basic structures of all phenomena in the universe without tying these phenomena to a specific interpretation.

At first glance the situation with respect to *the problem of induction* seems to be similar because in metaphysics as well as in the sciences generalizing conclusions are drawn which cannot be justified on logical grounds. Yet, in spite of all the internal problems of the philosophy of science, in the natural sciences the method of induction is justified pragmatically but not logically through predictions which have been successful.

The *Duhem-Quine thesis* provides a further argument in favor of metaphysical systems. The closed nature and the holistic character of metaphysical systems and the fact that they can be accepted or rejected only in their entirety turns out less strange when it is realized that in principle this feature is common to all scientific theories. Finally, the *change of paradigms* in the course of the history of science can also be adduced in the defence of metaphysical systems. It is easier to accept the apparent incommensurability of metaphysical systems when it turns out that a similar situation obtains even in the allegedly unambiguous and precise sciences. However, notwithstanding the historical change of theoretical conceptions in modern times, the development of science is marked on the whole by certain general tendencies, including the extension of the range of validity of theories, their internal differentiation, and the close interconnections between subareas. Above all else, scientific theories are marked by their ever-increasing capacity for predicting natural phenomena and for technologically manipulating natural processes. In the historical development of metaphysics, no similar uniform trends can be observed. Certainly there is an increase in analytic approaches and methodological problems in modern times, but this is more a change in the way questions are asked than in the way answers are given.

As an outcome of our comparison between metaphysical systems and scientific theories, we can observe a cessation of hostility and perhaps even a mutual reconciliation. Certainly this does not constitute a cogent legitimation of metaphysical systems. They can be best legitimized by showing their real explanatory power, and not by general, abstract considerations.

If one turns one's attention not to the natural sciences but to the humanities, one observes that the criteria of predictability and of technological applicability are no longer relevant. This narrows the gap between metaphysical systems and theories applicable within a specific discipline. As philosophy itself is part of the humanities, it is not surprising that the connection between metaphysical systems and the humanities is closer than that between metaphysics and the natural sciences.

The similarity discussed here could be supplemented by pointing out that metaphysical systems share with scientific theories the heuristic function of stimulating further investigation. Yet, in order to give a complete picture, one important difference between metaphysical systems and scientific theories must be mentioned. Scientific theories fit into the larger context of science as a whole, no matter how specialized the fields of enquiry may be. In contrast to this, metaphysical systems are—like works of art—the achievement of a single individual. The closed synthesis they provide results from a unique act of creativity. This is why they cannot reasonably be developed further. In contrast to this, scientific conceptions are integrated into the conceptual fabric of the discipline and they are open to ongoing development by the scientific community.

Philosophical systems and scientific theories have in common the function of giving a structure to that which otherwise would be unstructured, to ordering conceptually that which otherwise would be unordered, and to explaining that which would otherwise remain unexplained. In the natural sciences, predictions that can be empirically tested play a decisive role. In the case of metaphysical systems, as well as in the case of other explanatory systems in the humanities, a convincing explanation can already be regarded as a "verification" of the system in question. Moreover, a weaker, more indirect process of verification is always possible along the lines of a negative dialectic. A holistic and consistent philosophical system not only provides a taxonomy and an interpretative framework, but as we know from the history of philosophy, every such closed system also constitutes an intellectual challenge. The natural reaction to such a challenge is to attempt to criticize, refute, improve, or transcend the system given. If a philosophical system successfully withstands such scrutiny, this may be regarded as a form of *ex negativo* verification.

NOTES

1. "Ich sitze mit einem Philosophen im Garten; er sagt zu wiederholten

Malen 'Ich weiß, daß das ein Baum ist', wobei er auf einen Baum in unserer Nähe zeigt. Ein Dritter kommt daher und hört das, und ich sage ihm: 'Dieser Mensch ist nicht verrückt: Wir philosophieren nur'." Ludwig Wittgenstein, *On Certainty*, ed. G. E .M. Anscombe and G. H. von Wright, trans. Denis Paul and G. E. M. Anscombe (Oxford: Blackwell, 1969), 4.67; "Es ist, als ob das 'Ich weiß' keine metaphysische Betonung vertrüge." *On Certainty*, 4.82.

2. In his Editor's Introduction, A. J. Ayer calls Hume's theses "an excellent statement of the positivist's position." *Logical Positivism* (New York: Free Press, 1959), 10.

3. C. G. Hempel, "Empiricist Criteria of Cognitive Significance—Problems and Changes," in *Aspects of Scientific Explanation* (New York: Free Press, 1965), 101–171.

4. It is in these terms that A. J. Ayer states: "But I take it to be characteristic of the metaphysician, in my somewhat pejorative sense of the term, not only that his statements do not describe anything that is capable, even in principle, of being observed, but also that no dictionary is provided by means of which they can be transformed into statements that are directly or indirectly verifiable." *Language, Truth and Logic* (London: Pelican Books, 1971), 18.

5. I. Kant, *Critique of Pure Reason*, B XVIII.

6. G. Ryle, *The Concept of Mind* (London: Hutchinson, 1949); P. F. Strawson, *Individuals* (London: Methuen, 1959).

7. "Die wahre Gestalt, in welcher die Wahrheit existiert, kann allein das wissenschaftliche System derselben sein," G. W. F. Hegel, *Phänomenologie des Geistes*, ed. by J. Hoffmeister, (Hamburg: Meiner, 1959), 12.

8. J. Passmore, *Philosophical Reasoning* (London: Gerald Duckworth, 1961), 84f.

9. "Die richtige Methode der Philosophie wäre eigentlich die: Nichts zu sagen, als was sich sagen läßt, also Sätze der Naturwissenschaft." L. Wittgenstein, *Tractatus Logico-Philosophicus* 6.53; " Wovon man nicht sprechen kann, darüber muß man schweigen." *Tractatus* 7. ["The correct method in philosophy would be the following: to say nothing except what can be said, i.e. propositions of natural science.... What we cannot speak about we must pass over in silence." Trans. D. F. Pears.]

10. M. Heidegger, *Die Technik und die Kehre* (Pfullingen: Günther Neske, 1962).

11. Cf. note 7 and F. W. J. Schelling, *System des transzendentalen Idealismus*, ed. R. E. Schulz, (Hamburg: Meiner, 1957).

12. I. M. Bochenski, *Europäische Philosophie der Gegenwart* (Bern: Francke Verlag, 1951), chap. 24 [*Contemporary European Philosophy*, trans. Donald Nicholl and Karl Aschenbrenner, (Berkeley and Los Angeles: Univ. of California Press, 1966), chap. 24]; N. Hartmann, *Zur Grundlegung der Ontologie* (Berlin: de Gruyter, 1935).

13. In 1781, Kant noted in a letter to Marcus Herz that his *Critique of Pure Reason* contains the "metaphysics of metaphysics," *Briefe*, ed. J. Zehbe, (Göttingen: Vandenhoeck, 1970), 89; R. G. Collingwood, *An Essay on Metaphysics* (Oxford: Oxford University Press, 1940), 49f.

14. E. E. Harris, "Method and Explanation in Metaphysics", *The Problem of Scientific Realism*, ed. E. A. MacKinnon, (New York: Appleton-Century-Crofts, 1972), 171. In a similar way, but not restricted to scientific knowledge: A. N. Whitehead, *Process and Reality*, xiv, Preface.

15. Strawson, *Individuals*, Introduction.

16. G. Ryle, "Philosophical Arguments", in *Logical Positivism*, 330.

17. M. Schlick, "The Turning Point in Philosophy", repr. in: *Logical Positivism*, 74; cf. also: V. Kraft, *Der Wiener Kreis* (Wien: Springer, 1968), and J. Joergensen, *The Development of Logical Empiricism* (Chicago: University of Chicago Press, 1951).

18. Schlick, "Turning Point," 56.

19. This is exposed in the articles of O. Neurath and A. J. Ayer in: *Logical Positivism*, 202–236.

20. "Die Welt ist die Gesamtheit der Tatsachen, nicht der Dinge." *Tractatus* 1.1; and "Die Angabe aller wahren Elementarsätze beschreibt die Welt vollständig." *Tractatus* 4.26.

21. P. Duhem, *The Aim and Structure of Physical Theory* (1904/5), tr. P. P. Wiener, (Princeton: Princeton University Press, 1959); W. v. O. Quine,

From a Logical Point of View (Cambridge, Mass.: Harvard University Press, 1953).

22. C. G. Hempel, "The Theoretician's Dilemma," *Minnesota Studies in the Philosophy of Science*, vol. 2, ed. H. Feigl *et al.*, (Minneapolis: University of Minnesota Press, 1958), 87.

23. E. Nagel, *The Structure of Science* (London: Harcourt, Brace & World, 1961), chap. 5.

24. K. R. Popper, *The Logic of Scientific Discovery* (New York: Basic Books, 1959), chap. 4; F. Rapp, "The Methodological Symmetry between Verification and Falsification," *Zeitschrift für allgemeine Wissenschafstheorie* 6 (1975): 139–144.

25. None of the approaches put forward by, e.g., Hume, Kant, Carnap, or Hintikka for the solution of the problem of induction has met with unanimous approval.

26. "Can Theories be Refuted?" *Essays in the Duhem-Quine-Thesis*, ed. S. G. Harding, (Dordrecht: Reidel, 1976).

27. F. Rapp, "Observational Data and Scientific Progress," *Studies in the History and Philosophy of Science* 11 (1980): 153–162.

28. T. S. Kuhn, *The Structure of Scientific Revolutions*, 2nd ed., (Chicago: University of Chicago Press, 1970); *The Structure of Scientific Theories*, ed. F. Suppe, (Urbana: University of Illinois Press, 1974).

29. Whitehead, *Process and Reality*, Preface. I. Leclerc has pointed out that though Whitehead started philosophizing in terms of the philosophical problems of modern science and often returns to these issues in his later work, his metaphysics must not be mistaken as a mere extension of the philosophy of science issues. The "considerable change" of Whitehead's "entire approach to these problems" is indicative of the differences that exist between a metatheory of the sciences and genuine metaphysics. I. Leclerc, *Whitehead's Metaphysics* (London: George Allen and Unwin, 1958), 5; cf. also 31–35 and 224f.

14

The Philosophical Content of Quantum Chemistry

Paul A. Bogaard

> In exact sciences, every theory has a philosophical, mathematical and empirical content. All these three aspects are equally important; if we neglect one of them, we sooner or later get into difficulties. The experience of half a century with quantum mechanics and the enormous literature on its interpretation has shown that good mathematics makes yet not good physics, it is a necessary but not yet sufficient condition. The rejection of metaphysics by the logical positivists... led to a philosophical plight. Positivism and operationalism...have neither solved the great philosophical problems...nor are they a tenable basis for modern science...our best texts still stick to operationalism.... Nevertheless, everybody (including the theoreticians) believes in some kind of realism. It is the duty of the theoreticians to make such a choice of metaphysical regulative principles that the reasonable requirements of realism are fulfilled.[1]

There is nothing unusual, in our day, in being reminded that too restrictive a focus upon the empirical and mathematical content of our scientific theories, has proven short sighted. Nor is it that unusual to find an argument for "some kind of realism." It is unusual to find a theoretical chemist, however, willing to debate the philosophical content of his theories, and (as Hans Primas does in this 1979 lecture on the "Foundations of Theoretical Chemistry") to insist upon the "conceptual recasting of quantum mechanics." This paper will neither provide nor review a conceptual recasting of all quantum mechanics, but it will take up Primas's remarks about a theory's "philosophical content," in order to discuss the "metaphysical principles" which have played out their role in the "conceptual recasting" of chemical theories.

The debates within chemistry, at a theoretical level, from the nineteenth and into the twentieth century illustrate the stake these scientists placed in the conceptual foundations of their theories. The positivist attitude to which Primas alludes silenced much of this debate in its wholesale rejection of metaphysics. Within the last two decades, however, there is again a growing debate amongst chemists about the conceptual underpinnings appropriate to a theoretical understanding of chemical bonding, and of chemical reactions generally.[2] Moreover, Primas himself illustrates a new determination to recognize that this level of debate cannot afford to divorce empirical and mathematical content from its philosophical content—particularly where a significant recasting in conceptualization is required.

By *philosophical content* Primas seems to mean the conceptual underpinnings of a scientific theory, in terms of which its mathematical representation can be interpreted, and which can be actively debated and "recast." These conceptual debates, their being recast, and the assumptions that are made explicit in the process, are of particular philosophic interest; it is to this aspect of scientific theory rather than its mathematical or empirical content that philosophers of science can aspire to make some contribution to the debate.

Primas's concern with the metaphysical principles required for quantum chemistry requires us to attend to a shift from the assumptions typical a century ago, when "chemical bonding" first found a theoretical articulation, to the assumptions being touted in recent years. The argument of this paper will be not only that these changing assumptions are reflected substantively in the theories accepted and in interpreting the mathematical representations being used, but that they have an influence on the overall assessment of chemistry's success and upon its relations to physics and biology. The change in metaphysical assumptions, which is implicated in the conceptual recasting Primas has in mind, is also reflected in the judgement of philosophers and historians as to the stature of chemistry.

In 1925, at the very time chemists were casting about for a new conception of chemical bonding, W. H. Bragg gave voice to their frustration in a set of public lectures.

> If we ask ourselves what binds atoms together into the various combinations and structures...we have got our materials—the bricks, slates, beams and so on; we have our various kinds of atoms. If we look round for mortar and nails we find we have none. Nature does not allow the use of any new material as a cement. The atoms cling together of themselves. The chemist tells us that they must be presented to one another under proper conditions, some of which are very odd; but the combination does take place, and there is something in the atoms themselves which maintain it when the conditions are satisfied. The whole of chemistry is concerned with the nature of these conditions and their results.[3]

New means of conceptualizing chemical bonding are being called for here, and its resolution lies at the heart of chemical theory. The "whole of chemistry" was concerned with articulating a new set of underlying assumptions, and I would argue this was brought about in a way not shared by either physics or the life sciences. It was rooted in the difference between presuming that the basic components within the domain of chemistry's interest are truly "basic"—in some ultimate sense of "atomic," simple, not to be further analyzed—and the current assumption that the complex substances of interest to chemists are invariably comprised of constituents which are themselves complex. This change in assumption was required by the discovery, now more than eighty years old, that atoms are not "a-tomic."

What is unique to chemistry is the extent of the change required in its philosophical content, a degree of conceptual recasting this discovery forced upon neither physics nor biology. The tendency within physics, confronted with the evidence that the atoms, themselves, do not provide an "ultimate component," was to turn its attention to the interior of the atom to seek there for the one (or many) components which will serve as theoretically ultimate. In biology the assumption had always been that the objects of their study were complex, and few biological assumptions were affected by admitting the complexity of whatever constituents it conceives as basic.

This may be an oversimplification, especially because the conceptual change required could be attributed to the theoretical assumptions pertinent to any "molecular" study whether carried on by a chemical physicist, molecular biologist, or quantum chemist. Nevertheless, in between (a) presuming that we can always continue the search through ever more interior levels for an unanalyzable component, and (b) always having assumed that one's subject matter was complex, there is the striking case of those theoretical problems confronting chemists. These problems had been pursued on the explicit assumption that the components were themselves ultimately basic, but came to be understood on the grounds that compounds, and atomic components alike are inescapably complex. We will pay special attention to this transition in assumptions—those pertinent to theories of chemical bonding and chemical reactions generally—partly because these theories can only be interpreted in the light of what Primas calls their philosophical content, and partly because these same concepts and their presuppositions have a major impact on how dependent these theories are thought to be upon the more basic theories of atomic physics.

Consider how this historical transition is usually reconstructed by philosophers of science. In the mid-nineteenth century both Mill and Whewell had agreed (despite their differences) that the properties of chemical compounds were *not* to be explained on the grounds of their atomic constituents as conceived in terms of the mechanical relations typical in their day.[4] In the mid-1920s it was still the position of C. D. Broad that one could not expect to derive the behavior of chemical compounds from that of their constituents.[5] By the end of the 1920s, however, Paul Dirac declared, as he is so often quoted:

> ...the general theory of quantum mechanics is now almost complete...the underlying laws necessary for the mathematical theory of a large part of physics and all of chemistry are thus completely known.[6]

Dirac's judgement has been cast into philosophic jargon, best known perhaps in Ernst Nagel's contention that the laws of chemistry are thereby fully "reducible"[7] (at least in principle) to the quantum theory of atomic physics.

If we are to take Primas and the current concerns of other theoretical chemists seriously, however, Dirac's appraisal must have been at least premature, and thoroughly misleading. In fact there needs to be a reappraisal on both sides of this historical transition. Prior to the establishment of quantum chemistry in the late 1920s, a theoretical explanation of chemical bonding might well have represented a "reduction" in Nagel's sense, had it succeeded. Its underlying assumptions would have supported Nagel's conclusion, despite Mill, Whewell, and Broad, but it did not succeed. Subsequently, the successes in applying the quantum mechanical formalisms to chemical compounds have not constituted a "reduction" (certainly not in Nagel's sense of a "deductive derivation") precisely because the new assumptions required do not support a reductionist interpretation. Nagel like Dirac was construing this success under nineteenth-century assumptions, and the intervention of positivism only served to blind them to the degree they were relying upon outmoded metaphysical principles.

The notion of reduction has worn many faces, unfortunately, and has grown into a more complex set of issues than can be resolved here. The proper interpretation of quantum mechanics generally has grown into an even more complex set of issues which haunts us to this day, but there is much we can learn from the case of theoretical chemistry about the interdependencies of scientific theories and how these dependencies change over time. Despite the quandaries within quantum mechanics itself, there is something we can learn about the limitations of physics as a "chemical reducing agent"![8]

The crux of these issues are the difficulties in the interpretation of quantum theory as applied to chemistry which have frustrated theoretical chemists. As useful as the mathematical formalisms have been, they have not provided an unambiguous resolution of what Bragg was seeking. The conceptual recasting has not been complete. In the words of K. Roby:

We are faced with a situation that is best described as the 'conceptual dilemma of quantum chemistry': agreement with experiment demands more rigorous theory, yet in more rigorous theory the conceptual structure of chemistry is not readily apparent.[9]

This dilemma is the situation Roby claims quantum chemistry still faced fifty years after it had been declared as "reduced" to the theory of atomic physics. If, as Roby suggests, the conceptual structure of chemistry is not apparent, it may be that a deeper appreciation of this problem requires that we attend to the philosophical content of quantum chemistry.

DO WE EXPLAIN BONDING BY LOSING IT?

What is Roby's dilemma? What are these two "horns" he has set for us, that agreement with experiment demands more rigorous theory, but that the conceptual structure of chemistry somehow gets lost in the more rigorous application of this theory?

The theory to which he refers is the quantum theory, or specifically, the formalism of the Schrödinger equation as it is constructed to represent atoms bound in molecules—particularly systems of nuclei and electrons. What Roby means by a more "rigorous" version of this theory we have yet to see. More importantly, we will want to sort out what he may mean by chemistry's conceptual structure as opposed to this theory. Does Roby mean to imply that chemistry has a conceptual structure of its own, independently of the theory which Dirac implies was provided by atomic physics?

What Dirac claimed, back in the 1920s, was that mathematical theory sufficient to chemistry's needs had now been provided. So, perhaps it's a fair distinction with which to begin, to say that atomic physics provided a mathematical formalism, which has been wedded somehow to chemistry's own concepts. Physics has provided a mathematical representation of those systems of atoms that are of interest to chemists, but the *interpretation* of this representation (over and above the quandaries troubling quantum mechanics itself) may be a problem of how to utilize chemistry's own conceptual structure.

Already in 1927 the Schrödinger equation was utilized by Heitler and London to show why two hydrogen atoms could be expected to bonded together into a stable molecule. From that point on we have had the continuing development of quantum chemistry—the basis, presumably, for the optimistic declarations of Dirac and Nagel. But in the mid-70s, almost fifty years later, Roby's reassessment is that "it seems as though the simple bond has got lost."[10] Can it be that chemists have lost sight of the very concept quantum physics is supposed to have explained for them?

The suggestion provided by Roby is that such chemical concepts get lost in the face of more rigorous theory—by which he presumably means the mathematical content of quantum theory, namely, the application of the Schrödinger equation. Linus Pauling, in his classic treatise from 1939, *The Nature of the Chemical Bond*, summarizes the role of this mathematical formalism in this way:

> The fundamental principle of quantum mechanics in which we are interested states that *the energy value W_0 calculated by the equations of quantum mechanics with use of the correct wave function Ψ_0 for the normal state of the system is less than that calculated with any other wave function Ψ that might be proposed*; in consequence, *the actual structure of the normal state of a system is that one, of all conceivable structures, that gives the system the maximum stability*.[11]

Apparently, what the Schrödinger equation is used to calculate, is the total energy of the system for which it has been constructed. This result is of interest to chemists because this energy value can be compared with that calculated for a wide range of possible systems. Insofar as the "wave function" representative of each of these possible systems can be interpreted in terms of structure—literally in terms of spatial arrangement or distribution—a comparison can be made of the total energy associated with each such structure and used to identify that one structure for which the total energy of that system is the least. This will be, as Pauling promises, the structure which has the maximum stability.

Before proceeding we should note that there are already several assumptions in use here, including the classic physical principles of the conservation of energy and that of least action. Prior to Pauling, and prior to quantum theory itself, these assumptions had already been applied to the theoretical questions facing chemists. Physical chemists, in the last years of the nineteenth century, had found they could measure experimentally what they took to be the strength of chemical bonds from acid/base equilibria, temperature transfers, even from osmotic pressure, interpreting these as a measure of the "free energy" already along associated with heats of reaction. Van't Hoff, in particular, recognized that this amounted to setting aside the expectation of identifying the "affinity" responsible for bonding in terms of a specific "force," and conceiving of bonding, instead, in terms of the stability identified with a "diminution" of total energy.[12]

The formalisms of quantum theory provide in a more precise way for the stability of a bonded molecule in terms of total energy—that is to say, that system is most stable whose structure is associated with the least possible energy. Unlike the methods (some of which had already been devised) for measuring these amounts in the laboratory, quantum theory provides the Schrödinger equation in terms of which these amounts can be theoretically calculated. The promise Pauling offered is that, through an appropriate interpretation of these formalisms, the lowest calculated energy can be identified with a specific structure of the appropriate components, thereby providing an explanation for stable bonding which prequantum chemistry never quite managed.

Nineteenth-century chemists had seen, experimentally, the need for conceiving of compounds in terms of their structure, and had measured the strength of affinity but could not provide a theory as to how these factors were mutually related so as to bring about stability. It was typically called bonding, but there was no satisfactory explanation for how this came about, and certainly no theoretical means of calculating its effect. These means are first provided by quantum mechanics, and the attempt to put it into practice we call quantum chemistry. We have noted that some physical chemists had already suspected a reconceptualizing of bonding into an energy minimum might be required, but only the Schrödinger equation has provided the mathematical formalism for calculating this effect.

Why, then, does Roby question the more rigorous use of this formalism, in the attempt to match experimental measurements, and why does he caution us about the conceptual structure of chemistry in this context? A partial answer can be quickly provided: the mathematical fact is that as soon as the Schrödinger equation is applied to a system with more than one electron, its analytic solution is no longer possible. This equation has nevertheless provided the mathematical basis for over fifty years of quantum chemistry due to the finesse with which solutions to the Schrödinger equation can be approximated. Roby's concern is with the more rigorous improvements attempted on these approximations. To assess the cost quantum chemists must pay for this, we need to examine how this is done.

To make these calculations more tractable, complicating factors which (hopefully) are of minor consequence are dropped out. Even if one sets up the Schrödinger equation so as to ignore the portion of the potential energy due to mutual electron repulsion, as one example, the number of variables to be included can be very large. So additional factors entering into the total energy are left out as well, the most typical being that which is called the Born-Oppenheimer approximation, which drops out that portion of the kinetic energy due to the movement of the nuclei. The supposition is that the speed with which the electrons adjust to movements of the nuclei is so fast, comparatively, one should be able to determine the distribution of the electrons independently of the spatial arrangement of the nuclei. One begins, therefore, with the Hamiltonian portion of the equation designed to include only the kinetic energy of the electrons, plus some of the potential terms representing Coulombic repulsion and attraction between them.

Quantum chemists have interpreted the results of such approximations with considerable practical success in terms of "charge density" over three dimensions. That is, the total energy they calculate is the total electronic energy, and this can be done on the basis of a wave function interpreted as representative of electron distribution.[13] Chemists had surmised, well before Schrödinger devised his equation, that electrons were the atomic constituent implicated in chemical bonding. It seemed very likely to many theoreticians that it was the electrostatic attractions and repulsions which were responsible for atoms bonding. What stood in the way of this straight forward explanation was that too many compounds were known on chemical grounds to be comprised of the same or similar atoms. These are the ones that typically produce "covalent" bonds and which G. N. Lewis had argued were brought about by their "sharing" pairs of electrons. A great deal of evidence pointed to this, and by 1920 the idea was widely accepted by chemists and physicists alike, even though no one could say precisely what this "sharing" amounted to (other than it went directly against the usual assumptions about electrons repelling each other).

The dramatic impact of Heitler and London producing the first quantum mechanical calculation for a stable molecule, in 1927, was not only that it was first (if you count the H_2^+ "molecule" with one electron, they weren't quite first) but that they provided a means for calculating a two-electron molecule of two hydrogen atoms—the paradigm of a covalent bond. The success of their approximation could be interpreted as suggesting that, despite electron repulsion, the interaction between these two "charge clouds" somehow produces a lower total energy than the energy of the two atoms calculated separately and added together. This matched expectations based on the Pauli exclusion principle, which simply declared that when electron spin is taken into account, up to two electrons are "permitted" in each state, or orbital, of the system. Such pairing of electrons, when represented mathematically by superposition, seems to lower the total energy more significantly than the Coulombic (electrostatic) attraction of both electrons for the two nuclei, or their mutual screening and transient polarization. All of these factors apparently contribute to stability, but the first is what makes the pairing of electrons so peculiarly effective,[14] that is, it is a quantum effect.

On the other hand, much of the difficulty in calculating this effect results from the fact that the amounts by which the total electronic energy is reduced, are only a small fraction of the total. (It amounts to about 14 percent of the electronic energy in H_2, but less than 3 percent in a molecule no more complex than CH_4. This is rather like determining the weight of a ship's captain by subtracting the weight the ship alone from the weight of the ship with him aboard![15]) The approximations have to be very precise, and what might seem a minor variation in that approximation may have a large impact on the level of energies of interest to chemistry.

As a practical matter of how to proceed, the wave function for a molecular system, in terms of which its energy is calculated, is usually constructed out of known atomic wave functions, since the molecular function cannot be determined analytically. If one begins with wave functions for single electrons in a single atom and linearly combines all the permutations of these for the product of as many as will be needed in the total molecular wave function, and if (to ensure that this trial function is a good one) one linearly combines all the variations that can created by varying their coefficients, then, according to the variation principle, the more of this that is done—up to infinitely many—the better will be the energy value calculated. The more candidates you linearly combine, the lower the energy value; and therefore, the more accurate will be the result.[16]

In practice, however, which "basis" is used (i.e., which orbitals are mathematically "superposed") is chosen so as to ensure that these expansions converge—to make the math tractable—and also so as to make the results interpretable in chemical terms. As E. Steiner explains in his text:

> The restricted Hartree-Fock model, with its concept of a set of molecular (symmetry) orbitals each of which can be occupied by two electrons, forms the basis for much of the chemist's understanding and interpretation of the structure and properties of molecules. We saw however that the two simplifying and valuable properties of the orbitals, namely the double-occupancy and symmetry properties, in general represent constraints on the orbital approximation, and it follows that a lower, and therefore more accurate, energy can be obtained by a relaxation of these constraints.[17]

To relax the two "constraints" to which Steiner refers, would be to lose sight of the symmetry of the molecular orbitals so constructed, and of the distribution of two electrons per orbital. Here, finally, we begin to glimpse examples of those chemical concepts about which Roby was concerned. The schema of chemical concepts is such that without these two constraints it becomes very difficult to interpret the results in terms of electron distribution. Relaxing these constraints has the effect of improving flexibility in the total electronic wave function, which lowers the energy and enhances the calculation of stability, but it also has the effect of worsening our ability to interpret their spatial distribution; or worse still, it implies a fully delocalized distribution.

From this result one can appreciate why Roby describes it as a dilemma: we want theoretical calculations of total energy to be as accurate as possible to match experimental measurements (let alone improve upon them), but when we do press for a more rigorous calculation in this sense, it has the effect of throwing out of focus the very features (like structural distribution) which make chemical sense. What is threatened is that very correlation of structure and maximum stability which Pauling identified as the reward for chemistry in their relying upon the quantum formalism. If so, why was this threat not already apparent to Pauling? Why did we wait through almost fifty years of quantum chemistry before Roby warned of this dilemma?

Roby, for one thing, was not the first to note this difficulty. We might better ask why it began receiving more attention only within the last twenty years. Part of the answer may well be, that until 1960, the Schrödinger equation had been used to perform *ab initio* calculations on only the simplest of molecules. Thereafter, especially with the advent of the computer, a more thoroughly "computational" quantum chemistry developed, which has finally engendered this kind of concern.[18]

Prior to this, quantum chemistry was determined to draw as much that was of chemical interest out of these quantum formalisms as possible. The techniques of approximation, therefore, were designed to meet the interest of chemists. No one approach produced all that the chemist might hope for, but the Valence Bond approach and the Molecular Orbital approach arose as two of the most successful. These two, and all their many variations, have remained in active use because they provide so many alternate means of deploying the mathematical formalisms.[19] The strength of the quantum formalism comes from this extreme flexibility, but philosophers and scientists alike need to be forewarned in assessing the role of such scientific theories and in interpreting them realistically. In the case of quantum chemistry it is not the theory—at least not the mathematical representation in itself—which guides the scientist. As C. Coulson insists in describing the application of the Valence Bond approach:

> But we shall see that these operations are not merely mathematical; each one represents the introduction of some aspect of chemical intuition and experience. It is not unfair to say that in this, as in practically the whole of theoretical chemistry, the form in which the mathematics is cast is suggested, almost inevitably, by experimental results. This is not surprising when we recognize how impossible is any exact solution of the wave equation for a molecule. Our approximations to an exact solution ought to reflect the ideas, intuitions, and conclusions of the experimental chemist.[20]

Alternate mathematical techniques provide alternate means of infusing the formalism with chemical significance, and this cuts both ways. The techniques which distribute electrons over molecular orbitals, and those techniques which combine atomic orbitals as in the Valence Bond approach, provide alternate conceptions of molecular structure and thereby alternate visions of the same reality. In the first case one is led to include in the calculation the effect of "configuration interaction," while in the latter one can readily compute "hybrid orbitals" as the product of specific circumstances. Is either one of these more than an artifact of the technique chosen? From the techniques of other means of approximation, these specific effects do not appear; similarly for the calculation of "resonance energy" or the energy of electron "exchange," these may be artifacts of the technique.

It is difficult to assess in this bewildering array what the conceptual structure of chemistry is, and more important from our philosophical perspective, it is not at all obvious that any of these conceptual interpretations has been provided by atomic physics. Rather, there is good reason to suppose they are based on chemical intuition and chemical evidence.

It might be supposed that by adhering to the underlying theory some one conceptual basis might become more obvious, but the opposite seems to be the case. Roby has warned that when its mathematical representation is pressed to its most rigorous, the theory sweeps away this array of alternate schemes, and leaves us with none; or at most, we are left with the stability of lowest possible energy, but no way of discerning that which would be of chemical interest among totally delocalized electrons.

THE RISE AND FALL OF CONTRASTING INTERPRETATIONS

What is at stake in the loss of this prototypical chemical concept, the chemical bond, is highlighted by the contrast between the interpretation which *might* have been appropriate in the nineteenth century and that which has come to seem more appropriate only in the twentieth century.

It was widely known throughout the nineteenth century that chemical elements would combine in definite proportions—elements were distinguished by John Dalton as chemical atoms of distinct weight—and that these compounds would remain stable. However, the source of their stability was at best a matter of speculation. In the middle of the century, evidence from organic as well as inorganic chemistry converged to emphasize that compounds not only retained a stable composition but that they showed evidence of a stable structure as well. Compounds, it was learned, could be stereochemically as well as stoichiometrically differentiated. The tendencies of any one elemental atom to combine with others could be quantified, thereby, in small whole numbers. In fact, these tendencies to a specific valence (as it came to be called) were taken as an indication of when a particular element's ability to combine was saturated, such that it would combine with *only* so many others.

Why molecules would exhibit only certain valences, and with such consistent compositional and structural results, was not known. In this context the symbolization and terminology of bonding arose, and it was most typically conceived in terms of Dalton's atoms. There were speculations as to the thermal, or magnetic, or electrical origins of this stability, but none of these speculations could account for the spatial distribution and valence saturation of chemical bonding any better than the simple mechanical contrivance that the atoms are held together by hooks and eyes!

Quantum theory has, without question, provided a much more successful means of calculating the effect of these chemical phenomena, and at first glance may even have provided a more satisfactory explanation than any nineteenth- or early twentieth-century theory managed to do. At first glance, it seems to be the same set of concepts—bonding in terms of the stability of valence saturation with structural results—with which the quantum chemist deals. Nineteenth-century speculations were almost invariably in terms of some force which would hold the atoms together, despite their natural tendency to fly apart. Some link, or rivet, or glue was the metaphor needed to conceive of atoms (whose exclusive mode of activity was locomotion) being bound together. To be bonded was not, in this conception, for the constituents to "do" anything, but rather for them to be held. As Bragg lamented, however, nature had by the 1920s revealed no such cement.

The quantum chemists have had to learn to conceive of bonding in a very different way. To a certain extent, chemists and even historians and philosophers of science have known this all along. I would argue they have not fully appreciated the implications of this conceptual recasting of chemical bonding until the last twenty years or so, and even then the philosophical implications are only now emerging.

This conceptual change requires one to begin by assuming that the stability of the compound is not to be conceived as components being forced to stay together, but as their being left alone to enact their own tendency (as a system) to remain in a condition of lowest possible energy. As was admitted at the outset, this reconceptualization is not in itself unique to quantum chemistry. However, what is unique is the idea that the constituents (and in this case their own subconstituents, the electrons) can bring this condition about through their mutually influencing each other, and in ways the nineteenth century could not imagine. It does *not* follow that the restrictions on what results from such mutual interaction (as characterized by the Pauli exclusion principle, for example) can themselves be derived from the quantum formalisms. On the contrary, this is one of the assumptions one must make in order to allow the formalism to work for us. The overall effect, on the other hand, does seem to account for a wide range of chemical phenomena.

I would reconstruct the conceptual recasting which is evident in theoretical chemistry in this way: despite the inability of chemists throughout the nineteenth century to explain chemical bonding, quantum chemists have had available to them a certain set of expectations. With new mathematical means at their disposal, quantum chemists can not only expect stability to be accounted for in terms of the total energy of any molecular system they so choose to calculate, but they also expect that this total will be raised (implying loss of stability) as soon as the number of atoms one tries to combine differs from their known valence, or as soon as the structural results are other than those expected to obtain. These expectations were not derived from some more fundamental physical theory, but from out of chemistry's own long experience.[21] Moreover, it was from out of this experience that it was possible that such calculations could answer chemists' questions, precisely because they were infused with chemical insights.

These expectations were not carried over into quantum chemistry without some conceptual recasting. This is particularly evident in chemical bonding theory, where what arose in the mid-nineteenth century was a theory with a well-developed "interpretation" of what was meant by bonding, firmly rooted in the experimental evidence but in search of a workable "representation." A workable mathematical formalism is just what this early chemical theory failed to provide. When the development of quantum mechanics in the 1920s finally provided a formalism that seemed capable of "saving the phenomena," however, it did so at the cost of the classical conception of what was meant by bonding, and provided little by way of replacement. It arose as a mathematical "representation" in search of an "interpretation."

Chemical experience suggested that what was at stake was the stability of complex structures specified by valence, and these proved to be an invaluable guide for whichever mathematical technique was used to achieve an approximation. In any one case the theory had to be told which effects to account for, whether the wave function should be made up by a mixture of atomic states, or by a pure molecular state (itself made up by the superposition of atomic states). Under these chemical constraints, as Steiner calls them, the quantum theory was rather successfully adapted to the chemical domain. The subsequent success of quantum chemistry, seen in this light, can hardly be modeled in terms of a "derivational deduction." This becomes more dramatically evident when the theoretical representation is pressed into more rigorous service, until the accuracy of energy calculations is improved at the cost of sweeping all chemical intuitions aside, including Pauling's promise that the classic concepts of structure and stability would be correlated.

To my knowledge, the most forceful statement of how thoroughly we are caught up in the web of conceptual recasting has been developed in a series of articles by the English theoretical chemist, R.G. Woolley. For most of the considerations raised so far, one might assume that there remains a distinction between the structural results for the electrons themselves (e.g., is there a hybrid orbital located just where we find a polarizing effect?) and for the

The Philosophical Content of Quantum Chemistry 265

nuclei of the molecule (e.g., do the two hydrogen nuclei stabilize at an angle of 104° from the oxygen nucleus with which they are bonded?). Woolley warns that this remains a significant conceptual ambiguity. He argues that it is the very notion of structure which is lost in a rigorous treatment of quantum chemistry.

> The quantum theory of molecular structure and the role of the Born-Oppenheimer approximation has been discussed in some detail in the recent literature; this paper is a continuation of this discussion in a chemical context, and argues that it will be essential in the future to try to understand an important class of experiments in physical chemistry without reference to the notion of molecular structure. This radical idea is a consequence of an analysis of the idea of molecular structure from "first principles" which shows that if one starts from a description of a molecule as an isolated, dynamical system consisting of the number of electrons and nuclei implied by the stoichiometric formula that interact via electromagnetic forces, one cannot even calculate the most important parameters in chemistry, namely, those that describe the molecular structure. This fact does not mean that "the quantum theory is wrong," nor does it deprive the idea of molecular structure of its general usefulness, for the key word in the above *ab initio* description is "isolated"; it does mean that it is wrong to regard molecular structure as an intrinsic property of a molecule.
>
> The quantum mechanical analysis of the idea of molecular structure that I sketch here is partly an attempt to make clear the fact that quantum theories of the physical and chemical properties of bulk matter could not have been developed to their present-day form without borrowing the notion of molecular structure from classical chemistry. One cannot therefore claim that the hitherto mysterious structural concept underlying chemical explanation is derivable from physical theory and therefore "explained" by quantum mechanics.[22]

Woolley's specific contention is that structure itself cannot be a mere product, at the chemical level, of the interactions of the physical components presumed in the quantum theory. Rather, when left to themselves to evolve into the most stable system (in isolation) they in fact may evolve into no recognizable structure at all. In such a case, not only are electrons delocalized around a semirigid nuclear framework, but the nuclei themselves are fully delocalized. Woolley's suspicion is that this is the inescapable implication of quantum theory, so long as we pursue our most typical techniques for applying the formalism to a system in isolation.

Aware of this concern, what Primas urges us to realize is that there is no real isolation.[23] It is our segmenting the world into isolated portions which is the artifact. A molecule in theoretical isolation may have no structure at all but because a molecule will always be found in some environment, we must look to these environmental influences for the source of those constraints which lead to distinguishable spatial distribution. These influences may be very slight in their energetic effect, but as we have seen, compared to the total energy of a chemical system, the portion that is responsible for its stability may already be a very small percentage of the system's total. Slight influences, therefore, may well be all that is required for structural results—less even for nuclei, perhaps, than for electrons.

The conception Roby, Woolley and Primas require contrasts strongly with that in terms of which chemical phenomena were interpreted a century ago. Instead of atoms as held together they construe atoms as mutually producing a condition of stability. Instead of a force of such strength that it can thwart the natural momentum of the constituents, they expect stability to be brought into effect by energetic changes which are only a small fraction of the momentum of the constituents. The difference in conceptualization is great enough that only in the latter case is stability understood as sensitive to minor variations in its environment. The nineteenth-century conception of bonding would presume that the structural arrangement which resulted was stabilized against all but comparably large external forces; however, under the assumptions evidenced in quantum chemistry, the structure of a chemical molecule is the result of comparatively weak energetic effects, and thus sensitive to even minor perturbations from within its environment. Structure, as Woolley warns, cannot be considered a property of individual molecules, *sui generis*, but only as it arises in an environmental context.

If this be true for "covalently" bonded molecules, it is even more true for "hydrogen bonding" and the bonding circumstances which involve the minor energetic variation in "d-orbital" electrons (which supposedly controls the carrying of oxygen by hemoglobin, for just one example). In all these instances chemical phenomena are represented by theoretical chemists in terms of the basic quantum formalism. They will never be fully interpreted simply in terms of their components, characterized in isolation, without the environmental influences in the context of which both the chemical compounds of these components and the components themselves stabilize into what they are.

THE STATURE OF CHEMICAL THEORY

Thus, reconstructed, the change in fundamental assumptions which has characterized theoretical chemistry is just the opposite of the impression one might get, noting the transition from such prequantum chemistry philosophers such as Mill, Whewell, and Broad to the declarations of Dirac and the derivational reductionism of Nagel. The impression to which they all contribute, is that the developments of quantum theory are responsible for bringing us from the situation in which chemistry was not reduced or even reducible to atomic physics, to a situation in which chemical theory can be and has been reduced to the quantum mechanics as established within atomic physics.

My reconstruction suggests: if chemists and/or physicists had managed to establish a scientific law (one with full mathematical representation), as for example in a world in which electrostatic attraction between truly atomic constituents was sufficient to bring about all forms of bonding, then we would have to conclude with Nagel that chemistry's theory of bonding (and its understanding of reactions generally and everything that would follow in its train, i.e., virtually the whole of chemistry) would via this law have been "reduced" to the theory of atomic physics in which this law was embedded. On the assumption that compounds are nothing more than atomic constituents which some force holds together, we would have not only a clear case of epistemological reduction but an ontological reduction as well. It might remain a convenience, under this hypothetical situation, to consider molecules as a unit, but in reality there would only be atoms—all behavior would really be atomic interaction. In fact, "interaction" would never have a substantive effect, just the pushing and pulling of unchanging atoms from one location to another.

Despite what many scientists in the nineteenth and early twentieth century seem to have hoped for and expected (and many a philosopher, too), theoretical chemistry did *not* unfold in this way. Instead, what has been developed is the Schrödinger equation as the relevant representation, and with quite a different interpretation. What has transpired is not a vision of chemical problems the solution to which is simply isomorphic with a Nagelian deductive derivation. The expectation that whatever transpired would constitute a theoretical reduction—either epistemological or ontological—has in itself been very misleading as the model of philosophic reconstruction. Such a model requires the problems as understood within one theoretical domain to be resolved by newer theories from a more fundamental domain, and where the conceptual landscape remains the same throughout. Only within such a reductionist framework would one assume that the processes and entities at one theoretical level are completely resolvable into those at a lower level. These expectations have cast a shadow over the historical evidence that there has been significant conceptual recasting.

Undoubtedly, chemical theory relies upon basic physical principles, and chemists are dependent upon the work of physicists for much of the mathematical representation they use including various of the techniques for its numerical evaluation. However, these underlying principles have not been sufficient to explain chemical phenomena. The dependency so often proclaimed is no more than the dependence physics itself has upon pure and applied mathematics.

Historically, in fact, the dependency has worked both ways. (This is especially evident in the development of quantum mechanics itself, relying directly upon the periodic table, chemical evidence for molecular stability and composition, and even the sharing of electron pairs.) Historically, chemists have had to rely upon the evidence of their own domain to complete their best depiction of chemical behavior—down to and including their understanding of the bonding of the smallest molecules. There are physical grounds for anticipating that chemical behavior is, in fact, sufficiently separable from its subatomic underpinnings that it must be understood as a product (within broad physical bounds) of its physical, chemical, and biological environment.

We would do better, therefore, to see this conceptual recasting as making necessary a transition from the quite legitimate expectation of chemistry about to be reduced to physics, to a stage of our scientific understanding in which this expectation is shown to be so simplistic and one-sided as to be seriously misleading. The irony is that the strongest claims for "reduction" have been made after this transition and have explicitly claimed as their evidence the reliance of theoretical chemistry upon quantum theory; when their best justification is to be found in the (unfulfilled) expectations which preceded quantum chemistry.

As we find in science so often, and in this particular case of bonding theory, too, older terms and ideas are not simply and quickly thrown away. For a variety of practical reasons of application, ease of communication, and especially teaching, the conception of atoms held together has not been expunged from chemistry. We have also been forewarned that practicing scientists, especially as reflected in their texts, will tend to read their current accomplishments as the culmination of all their predecessors.[24] For these sorts of reason, perhaps, Dirac's claim has often been repeated, that physics provided for quantum chemistry's solution to the problem of chemical bonding.

Once made explicit, the philosophical content of quantum chemistry makes clear that this claim is seriously misleading. The explication of these assumptions, however, is at least as much a philosophical problem as a scientific one, especially insofar as the philosophical task must extend to an assessment of these assumptions as viable metaphysical principles. Only in the context of the positivist denial of metaphysics could the conceptual recasting of chemistry have been so misconstrued as to conclude that it provides a clear case of reduction to physics.

To conclude with one last warning from out of theoretical chemistry:

Chemistry has never been well-treated by fundamental physical theories.... In theoretical chemistry, there is a distinct tendency to throw out typically chemical variables, admitting that they have served a noble purpose in the past but that now they are obsolete. However, the task of theoretical chemistry is the sharpening and explanation of chemical concepts and not the rejection of a whole area of inquiry.

Current quantum chemistry tends to give the impression that the major difficulties in applying quantum mechanics to complex molecular systems are computational. Yet the main stumbling block for the development of genuine theoretical chemistry is not computational but conceptual.... The creation of the physical reality by abstractions is a deep conceptual problem which cannot be discussed separately from more general philosophical problems.[25]

NOTES

1. H. Primas, "Foundations of Theoretical Chemistry," in *Quantum Dynamics of Molecules: The New Experimental Challenge to Theorists*, NATO Advanced Study Series, vol. 57, ed. R. G. Woolley, (New York, 1980), 39–40.

2. In addition to the sources cited in this paper, there are interesting collections of articles, several of which reflect the difficulty in conceptual interpretation: the retrospective articles in the 1970, vol. 24, edition of *Pure and Applied Chemistry*; *Wave Mechanics: the First Fifty Years* (London: Butterworths, 1973); *Quantum Dynamics of Molecules: The New Experimental Challenge to Theorists* (New York: Plenum Press, 1980); and *The Force Concept in Chemistry* (New York: Van Nostrand/ Reinhold, 1981).

3. W. H. Bragg, *The Nature of Things*, in six lectures, (London: G. Bell and Sons, 1925), 25.

4. See J. S. Mill's *A System of Logic* (1837), vol. I, chap. vi, 243ff; and W. Whewell's *Philosophy of the Inductive Sciences* (1847), bk. VI, 376ff.

5. See C. D. Broad's *Mind and its Place in Nature* (London: K. Paul, Trench, Trubnes and Co., 1925), 44ff.

6. *Proc. Royal Soc.* A. 123 (1929): 714.

7. See E. Nagel's *The Structure of Science: Problems in the Logic of*

Scientific Explanation (New York: Harcourt, Brace and World, 1961) and his article in *Mind, Science, and History* (Albany: State University of New York Press, 1970), 117–137.

8. See my "The Limitations of Physics as a Chemical Reducing Agent" in *PSA 1978*, vol. 2, ed. P. D. Asquith and I. Hacking, (East Lansing: Philosophy of Science Association, 1981), 345–356; and S. Brush's comments in his *Statistical Physics and the Atomic Theory of Matter* (Princeton: Princeton University Press, 1983), 231–232.

9. K. R. Roby, "Mathematical Foundations of a quantum Theory of Valence Concepts," in *Wave Mechanics: the First Fifty Years*, 39.

10. Roby is here citing a comment of C. Coulson. Caldirola in *Scientia* 110 (1975): 69–81, cites Dirac himself as saying: "We do not yet have the fundamental laws of quantum mechanics. The laws that we are now using will need to have more important modifications made to them"; and L. Pauling in the discussion recorded during the *International Symposium on the Origins of Life on Earth*, in 1957, is recorded as having lamented that: "...we find it extremely difficult to define a chemical bond!"

11. L. Pauling, *The Nature of the Chemical Bond* (Ithaca: Cornell University Press, 1939) 9.

12. See van't Hoff's "The Relations of Physical Chemistry to Physics and Chemistry," *Journal of Physical Chemistry* 9 (1905): 84.

13. See the warnings in M. Bunge's *Philosophy of Physics* and *Method, Model, and Matter* (both Boston: D. Reidel Publishing, 1973), and the metaphysical assumptions he finds evident in the application of quantum theory.

14. See C. Coulson's *Valence* (Oxford: Oxford University Press, 1961) 116–125; and on the status of the Pauli exclusion principle see 142–145 and especially 147.

15. From Coulson's *Valence*, 10 and 91.

16. See E. Steiner's text, *Molecular Wave Functions* (Cambridge: Cambridge University Press, 1976) chap. 3.

17. *Molecular Wave Functions*, 57.

18. See Steiner's Preface to *Molecular Wave Functions*.

19. Nancy Cartwright describes a number of similar cases in her *How The Laws of Physics Lie* (Oxford: Oxford University Press, 1983).

20. Coulson, *Valence*, 113–4.

21. More dramatic, perhaps, than seeing these nineteenth-century expectations re-emerge in Linus Pauling's classic text of quantum chemistry, is the series of concerns based on these same expectations which were raised by G. N. Lewis in the years *between* the Bohr atom and the Schrödinger equation; see his monograph, *Valence and the Structure of Atoms and Molecules* (The Chemical Catalog Co., 1923).

22. R. G. Woolley, "Must a Molecule Have a Shape?" *Journal of the American Chemical Society*, 100:4 (1978): 1073–1074.

23. See the Primas article cited above, and his "Pattern Recognition in Molecular Quantum Mechanics," *Theoret. Chimica Acta* 39 (1975): 127–148. These themes are more fully developed in his *Chemistry, Quantum Mechanics and Reductionism* (Berlin: Springer-Verlag, 1983).

24. This is the thrust of chap. 11 of Thomas Kuhn's *The Structure of Scientific Revolutions* (Chicago: The University of Chicago Press, 1962).

25. Primas, "Foundations of Theoretical Chemistry," 99–100.

15

The Nature of Chemical Existence

Joseph E. Earley

I

In *The Nature of Physical Existence* (hereafter, NPE), Ivor Leclerc described "the modern concept of nature," and identified as one of its main features the doctrine that the physical existent is "matter, conceived in the Gassendist way as impenetrable, solid atomic bodies." (NPE, 227) After discussing the relationship of this outlook to earlier viewpoints, and how the modern system became dominant with the triumph of Newtonian science, Leclerc argued that it is now necessary to replace "the modern concept of nature." It is his contention that progress in important areas, including science, may be limited by continued use of approaches and categories that no longer have an adequate metaphysical basis. Professor Leclerc then provided a "prolegomena to a new concept of nature," involving a novel specification of physical existence:

> The problem is how precisely are many substances to be conceived as constituting one substance. The theory being here advanced conceives the acting of substances as acting on each other. Now when the acting of the substances on each other is fully reciprocal, I wish to suggest, these actings combine to one single act, with one single form.... It is in virtue of this combined acting, constituting a one acting, that the compound entity acts as a whole, that is, as one, with reference to, and on, other wholes. (NPE, 311)

The key concept in this proposal is "fully reciprocal" acting, further explained as follows:

> If the acting of a particular substance in response to the acting on it of another be more strongly a passive response or reception than itself an acting on, that is, if the feature of acting on in this relationship be recessive by contrast with the aspect of reception, the rela-

tion will not be a unity of a substantial kind, but one in which the recipient substance will be quite changed but will remain substantially quite distinct. (NPE, 312)

In a paper published in 1982,[1] I proposed that certain chemical systems, called dissipative structures, ought to be considered to be unified active entities—that these coherences have as much claim to be "physical existents" as entities of any other class.

In *The Philosophy of Nature* (hereafter, PN) Professor Leclerc provided further discussion of the modern corpuscular concept, including analysis of the important role of chemical thought and practice in the origin, development and spread of this doctrine. He also generously reviewed my suggestion concerning the ontological status of dissipative structures, but he expressed the opinion that the chemical systems I had discussed were better regarded as "societies" rather than as single acting entities. He also provided further specification of his own proposal for a new concept of nature:

> Moreover, as Leibniz and, even more clearly, Kant recognized, physical acting is at once an "acting" and a "reacting," so that when, say, an entity A acts on entity B, B reacts to A both by receiving an effect from A and being affected by A in respect of what it becomes, of its definiteness or character. By this reciprocal transaction there is thus both an exertion of "force" by A's acting, and a "bond" between the two entities by virtue of the two entities acting and reacting. This means that physical acting effects a relation in the full sense of "connecting." This, I venture to suggest, is the philosophical explanation of the physical "bonds" (sometimes spoken of as "forces") which hold a number of entities together to constitute a composite whole.
>
> By reason of the mutual actings and reactings, compound wholes are constituted which have a unity and thereby also a determinate character, which is definitely more than those of a mere aggregate. This means that the actings of the constituents combine to constitute the whole a new physical existent. Since the combined acting of the constituents effects a unity which transcends the constituents per se, the combined acting must have the *whole* entity as its subject—for the combined acting is not reducible to the constituents severally as its subject. Thus, from the combined acting and reacting of the constituents there emerges a new integral entity in the full sense of itself per se capable of acting. By such a compound entity's entering into integration with other such entities, still more complex entities emerge. (PN, 166–167)

Aristotle remarked that those "who dwell in intimate association with nature and its phenomena" may have insights that are philosophically important. (*De Generatione et Corruptione* I, 316a6) Both NPE and PN clearly illustrate that chemical concepts and experimentation have historically been intimately involved with philosophic understanding of nature. This paper will give some examples of what sorts of things are held to exist (and not to exist) by contemporary chemists and reconsider the ontological status of compound entities.

II

We begin with a straightforward case. When zinc metal is added to an aqueous solution of hydrochloric acid, bubbles of an odorless, colorless, flammable gas appear. A variety of evidence leads to the conclusion that this gas is molecular hydrogen, H_2, (now frequently called dihydrogen)—a chemical substance that can be regarded to consist of two hydrogen atoms (each of which, in turn, consists of one proton and one electron). Rather complete discussions of "the covalent chemical bond" that holds the dihydrogen molecule together can be found in textbooks of physical chemistry studied by upper-division undergraduate science students. Mutual interaction of protons and electrons cause the distance between the two protons to be rather closely restricted. Bringing the two positively charged protons closer together than the "equilibrium internuclear distance" engenders forces that tend to push the protons apart, but separating them beyond the equilibrium internuclear distance evokes responses that tend to compress the molecule. Splitting the dihydrogen molecule so as to produce two hydrogen atoms would require a specific, if rather large, amount of energy (the "bond energy" of dihydrogen). The magnitude of that energy can be calculated quite precisely on the basis of well-established principles.

Here we have an example of the clearest kind of chemical existence, let us call it E_1. Interactions between the parts of a sub-microscopic entity give rise to a specific configuration (spatial arrangement of components) of the system such that any deviation from that configuration engenders a response that tends to reduce that deviation (that is, to restore the *status quo ante*). This circumstance is the defining characteristic of chemical structure and of the primary meaning of "existence" for chemists. Chemical systems that have structure, in this sense of having the property of self-restoration after disturbance, are regarded as constituting independently existing entities.

The dihydrogen molecule undergoes continual deformations around the equilibrium configuration. Dihydrogen molecules vibrate incessantly and rotate continually, and, vibrating and rotating, they move rapidly, and frequently collide with each other and with the container. The total energy of motion (kinetic energy) of any sample of the gas is proportional to the (absolute or Kelvin) temperature. At ordinary temperatures, dihydrogen molecules are in rapid, random motion, but they split apart into atoms only exceedingly rarely, because the bond energy of the H-H bond in dihydrogen is larger than the energies molecules generally acquire at normal temperatures.

Diatomic molecules have only one structural parameter (the internuclear distance); the internal potential (nonkinetic) energy of the molecule is specified by that one parameter. Internal potential energy is a minimum at the equilibrium internuclear distance and higher at all other values of that single important parameter. More complicated chemical structures follow the same principle. A molecule of a gaseous organic chemical (such as paradichlorobenzene, the active ingredient of mothballs) has many chemical bonds (like the bond in dihydrogen). At ordinary temperatures, each of these bonds stretches and contracts in an *oscillatory* manner and the angles between the bonds also vary as the molecule vibrates and twists. The large number of parameters involved does not change the situation in any fundamental way; the molecule is said to be *stable*—that is, to exist—because there is a specific arrangement of components that is automatically restored after every variation, no matter how complicated that variation might be.

A crystal—of rock salt (NaCl) or of diamond, for example—requires many parameters to specify its structure. Fortunately for crystallographers (and those who study large molecules) the symmetry of a crystal or of a molecule can introduce great simplifications, so that most of these parameters can be combined to yield a relatively small number of relevant parameters. Even such large aggregations as visible macroscopic crystals have the kind of structure described for dihydrogen—a specific arrangement of components that restores itself after disturbance from outside and also after internal fluctuations (generated by thermal energy) of *every* sort. The pattern of the macroscopic solid of a salt crystal is made up by the juxtaposition of identical microscopic "unit cells" that fit together so as to fill space.[2]

The molecule of methane, CH_4 can appropriately be considered as a carbon nucleus (six protons and about six neutrons, firmly bound together) associated with an "inner core" of two electrons and an eight-electron "valence shell" in which four protons are embedded. (Chemists think of electrons in molecules as diffuse clouds of charge, rather than as discrete negative particles.) A configuration in which the four HCH angles are all the same has lower potential energy than any other configuration; any deviation from that configuration engenders a response that tends to reduce the deformation from tetrahedral geometry. Methane has the geometry it does because of the tendency of electrons to associate in pairs, and from the mutual repulsion of the (negatively charged) electron pairs. At ordinary temperatures methane molecules translate and tumble and also vibrate in several different modes; each of the four bonds continually stretch and contract. The properties of macroscopic samples of methane are due to the microscopic properties of the molecules—methane is a gas because there are no regions of concentration of unbalanced charge (either positive or negative) in the molecule. The microscopic properties of the molecule, in turn, depend on characteristics of the electrons and nuclei that comprise the molecule.

Each reasonably well-formed salt crystal may properly be regarded as a single entity, composed of sodium cations, Na⁺ and chloride anions, Cl⁻ distributed in a specific pattern. The cohesion of the crystal is due to electrostatic (Coulombic) interactions between the ions, and to the fact that the sizes of these ions are such that they pack neatly together in a lattice that has cubic symmetry. When the crystal dissolves in warm water the ions are not changed, they merely become surrounded by dipolar water molecules and disperse through the liquid in such a way that every region of liquid has very nearly the same number of positive cations and negative anions. What molecules and salt crystals have in common is not the nature of the interactions between components (covalent bonds within molecules are rather different from ionic interactions in salt crystals), but the circumstance that those interactions define specific, self-restoring structures—and, therefore, have chemical existence E_1.

III

Entities that have this strong (E_1) sense of existence do not exhaust chemical ontology. There are many classes of entities that are recognized by chemists as having real, if sometimes transient, existence. We can only deal here with a few examples. Consider an experiment that is conceptually simple, although quite complex in practice—collision between two crossed beams, one a stream of molecules and the other a beam of atoms. Dihydrogen molecules can be made to collide with fluorine atoms; alternatively, beams of lithium atoms and hydrogen fluoride molecules can be crossed.[3] Experiments of this kind can be done in high-vacuum apparatus, and one can monitor the direction (relative to the directions of the initial beams) of emergence of the product-molecules—HF molecules and H atoms in the first case and LiF molecules and H atoms in the second. By careful study of whether the reaction products emerge behind or in front of the position at which straightforward calculation indicates they should emerge, physical chemists often infer the existence of "complexes" that have short lifetimes, as low as one millionth of a millionth of a second (10^{-12} second). For a brief time during the reaction the atom and the diatomic molecule constitute an aggregate; this grouping does not last long enough to undergo vibrational motion, but it does persist long enough to rotate as a unit—and that rotation has consequences in respect to how the distribution of product molecules is related to the initial beam directions. The action of the aggregate, as an aggregate, has discernible consequences; therefore, chemists consider that the triatomic "complex" exists. Let us designate this sort of existence (rotational, but not vibrational) as E_2.

The next point of chemical ontology is best approached by considering an important and well-defined class of chemical entity called "the transition state." Entities of this class are remarkable in that (like Santa Claus) *they do not exist* (sorry, Virginia). Suppose a dihydrogen molecule is struck by a rapidly moving hydrogen atom. After the collision there will be an atom and a diatomic molecule (as there was before the collision), but it is possible that the loose atom may have come from the original molecule, and the projectile atom may be part of the final molecule, that is:

(1) H' + H—H → H—H' + H

Consider the situation half-way between the states indicated by the two sides of reaction (1)—the situation in which the new bond is exactly half-formed and the old one exactly half-broken. This specific configuration, uniquely defined for each specific reaction, is designated the "transition state" for the reaction. In favorable cases the configuration of this state can be precisely specified and accurately described. (Santa Claus would be a portly gentleman with a red suit and a white beard.) Bond lengths and the H-H-H angle can be accurately specified for the transition state for reaction (1) but that entity lacks the property that gives real chemical existence. There is one disturbance of the transition-state configuration that does *not* encounter a restoring force. (The variation that leads from the reactants' configuration to the products' configuration is different from all other variations.) The entity cannot "exist" in either of the two senses (E_1 or E_2) discussed above although (as Michael Polanyi first demonstrated over fifty years ago) fruitful chemical conclusions can be obtained by reflecting on its necessary properties (bond lengths, angles, etc.).

Nevertheless John Polanyi (Nobel laureate, son of Michael Polanyi) has predicted[4] the absorption spectrum of the transition state of reaction (1). That is to say, he has given a detailed description of the *color* of something that does *not* exist—that cannot, by definition, exist in either of the two senses (E_1 or E_2) that we have already discussed. The paradox is resolved by noticing that absorption of visible light by a chemical species involves change of the *electronic* energy state of the system—one or more electrons use energy removed from the incident light to become "promoted" to a higher quantum energy state. Electrons are very much lighter that even the lightest atomic nuclei. Electrons move at the speed of light; atomic nuclei move much more slowly. The entire process of light absorption takes about 10^{-30} seconds—essentially *no* atomic motions occur in that short a time. The transaction that is responsible for color can take place thousands of times *during* the collision of two molecules, even during the brief impact of two rapidly moving molecules.

In the particular case of calculating the spectrum of the transition state of reaction (1), Polanyi *fils* imagined a large number of hypothetical experiments in which a hydrogen atom approached a dihydrogen molecule from some particular direction, at some specific speed. All the forces involved in this interaction are well understood; it was possible, in each case, to compute what the positions of each of the three atoms would be as a function of time during the course of each postulated encounter (the trajectory). He also could calculate the probability of an electronic transition for each possible configuration of the three atoms. These two types of calculation were then combined to yield the predicted electronic spectrum—the color—for the three-atom aggregate, although that aggregate does not exist in any strong sense. Entities having this third type of existence—let us designate it as E_3—are capable of exhibiting electronic properties, although they do not persist long enough for vibration or rotation.

Perhaps this point can be clarified by another example. Solutions of diiodine in benzene have a distinctive color, due to absorption of light by a complex, an aggregation of one benzene molecule and one diiodine molecule. This complex *does not exist* in either the E_1 or E_2 senses. When diiodine is dissolved in benzene there will always be, merely by chance, some diiodine molecules that happen to be located directly alongside benzene molecules. When light falls on the system, electronic transitions will occur in which electrons are shuffled back and forth between the members of such chance pairs of adjacent and properly oriented molecules. (Light absorption will be much less likely for all other relative orientations of benzene-diiodine pairs.) Absorption of radiant energy corresponds to a color characteristic of a new entity, even though (on the time-scale of molecular vibration or rotation, 10^{-12} seconds) there is no third chemical entity present, only benzene and diiodine molecules. E_3 is our designation of the type of the existence characteristic of the colored entities in these solutions, aggregations that exist for times of the order of 10^{-30} seconds (long enough for electronic transitions) but not for as long as 10^{-12} seconds (the time needed for vibration or rotation).

IV

Yet another strange sort of entity can be detected in simple gas-phase chemical reactions such as reaction (1). Sometimes, when reaction probability for such reactions is plotted against an experimental variable, a sharp spike of enhanced reaction likelihood appears in the graph at certain values of experimental parameters. These results are interpreted in terms of "resonances"—a type of existence that we will designate E_4. Here, the details of the interactions between the several components of a system trap the components in a complicated pattern of motion, and hold them in intimate contact for more or less extended periods, although no specific chemical bonds are formed.[5] Such trapping requires that the total energy of the system be in certain restricted ranges, neither too high nor too low. (A homely analogy might be a ball shot in a pinball machine that gets trapped between several bumpers for a long time: if the ball were to stop moving it would at once escape the trap, but so long as it has kinetic energy in the appropriate range it may be held indefinitely.) Resonances in chemical systems come into existence when several components, with significant kinetic energy become entangled by the detailed nature of their interactions, in an aggregation that persists, as a coherent unit, long enough for that aggregation, as such, significantly to effect other events. We designate this sort of existence as E_4. "Solitons"[6] in physical systems and "exiplexes" in photochemical reactions also exist in related senses, but we will not discuss them here.

Analogous situations can be observed in condensed-phase chemical systems. One example is the Belousov-Zhabotinski (hereafter, BZ) reaction which involves interaction of bromate ion and a reducing agent (frequently malonic acid), usually in the presence of certain indicators and catalysts.[7] This reaction is remarkable in that it proceeds in an *oscillatory* way, rather than merely changing from reactants to products directly. With the usual indicators present, the reaction solution turns red, then blue, then red, then blue, and so on. The system alternates between those two colors repeatedly, while the chemical energy of the reactants is released, with the production of low-energy products, including carbon dioxide. In the absence of stirring, intricate spatial patterns spontaneously develop; if the reaction is carried out in a continuously stirred tank, with reactants continuously supplied and the overflow removed, oscillations of color will continue indefinitely.[8] An especially important feature of this system is that, within certain rather wide limits, perturbations (whether introduced externally or arising from within the system) are damped out—all conceivable fluctuations engender responses that tend to reduce the fluctuation, rather than amplify it. We designate this sort of coherence as E_5. This sort of aggregation shares an important characteristic with the molecules and crystals that exemplify existence, E_1. In both cases variations away from a reference arrangement are damped out; in the case of E_1, the reference arrangement is a spatial configuration of component entities—in the case of E_5 the reference arrangement is more complex and interesting. The E_5 arrangement does not involve self-identical 'things' here and there at a specific time, but rather interactions of entities that are themselves undergoing continual change and are distributed over rather large regions. A further difference between E_1 and E_5 is that, in the latter case, the reference arrangement is not a single state definable without reference to the passage of time, but rather a sequence of states, each of which recurs after the lapse of a specific interval of time.

There is a close analogy between E_5 and E_4. In both cases components are trapped in intricate more or less long-lasting behavior patterns by details of dynamic interactions that occur between components. In E_4 resonances the components are single entities, such as atoms or molecules. E_5 coherences are intrinsically more complex; vast numbers of several sorts of component entities are involved in the interaction. This complexity does not destroy the analogy, any more than the transition from a one-parameter diatomic molecule to a crystal or macromolecule alters the fundamentals of E_1.

In contradistinction to E_1, E_2 and E_3, both E_4 and E_5 are *far from equilibrium* structures. These coherences require a source of energy (either internal or external) in order to come into being, and for their existence to be prolonged. In the BZ reaction, for instance, the high chemical energy of the reactants is dissipated as the reaction proceeds; this flux of energy keeps the oscillation in being. Such arrangements are called dissipative structures. A flame in a gas jet is such an entity; it will continue to exist just so long as high-energy chemicals (gas and dioxygen) are provided. Flames (and instances of the BZ reaction) are chemical entities, in the sense that we designate E_5. The interactions that give rise to E_4 and E_5 have the property of filling time in a way that is quite comparable to the way in which extended crystal structures fill space.

The type of existence designated E_5 is a better model for entities of wide human interest than either the corpuscular model of the physical existent, or the E_1 class of chemical existence typified by the hydrogen molecule. Human social groupings (The New York Yankees, for example) persist as recognizable entities over extended periods of time—and that persistent group identity has discernible consequences. Each of the human individuals that constitute those social groupings is always in the process of development and change. The continued existence of the group depends on the availability of resources (box office receipts for the Yankees) and also influences the types of development that are necessary or possible for component entities. The existence of such macroscopic coherences must be taken with full seriousness. There is no warrant for expecting that there is, anywhere or anywhen, some type of entity that is not composite in closely related senses. Existences of the class E_5 need to be taken into account—they are *physical existents* if any such exist. In these cases, it is clear that the persistence of a unified center of effective action also depends on coherences of both smaller and larger scales; this is equally true, if less apparent, for other sorts of coherence. (In the institutional analog, invalids make poor Yankees; baseball's place in American culture is also important.) This is not a defect in the concept of E_5; it is a general characteristic of being, and of all beings whatsoever—or so I claim.

V

Everything that chemists deal with is composed of microscopic constituents; to that extent chemists warmly embrace the outlook that Leclerc designates as the "modern concept of nature." There is one important aspect of that worldview, however, that chemists do not, in general, share. Chemists *do not hold* that there is a single fundamental level of description—that there is any *one* scale of time or size (or single group of classes of entities) in terms of which *all* interesting questions can be answered. According to Leclerc, one of the main features of the modern concept is the doctrine that there are, in fact, *ultimate* components into which things can be resolved and that it these "atoms" which do, could, or should ground *all* explanations. Turn-of-the-century chemists identified these minima as the atoms of the elements; in mid-century, physicists sought a restricted set of truly "elementary" particles; in our own time, public-choice economists consider individual human agents to be ultimate: all of these attitudes may be regarded as manifestations of the complex of attitudes that Leclerc terms the "modern concept of nature."

Ian Hacking has pointed out that ontologies that scientists use depend in important ways on the types of problems with which they deal.[9] Chemists frequently need to worry about the spin of nuclei and consider properties of individual atoms and of such subatomic particles as electrons and neutrons, but they are more likely to be engaged with more or less coherent aggregates such as molecules and the other entities that were discussed above, and with higher-level structures that form the primary subject matter of engineers or of biologists. Chemists agree that it may be possible to learn a great deal more about the internal structure of quarks, but would generally maintain that it is not likely that such information will be pertinent to the problems with which they are concerned.

Similar considerations apply *a fortiori* to biologists, who frequently are concerned with chemical matters, but rarely get into the physico-chemical arcana that many chemists relish, although biologists are more likely to deal with questions of ecology, large-scale integrations of food chains and biogeography than are chemists. Maynard Smith's concept of the evolutionarily stable strategy[10] bears close and important analogies to the chemical concept of the dissipative structure. David Hull and others have engaged in vigorous controversy, which they unabashedly term *metaphysical*,[11] concerning the "units of selection," i.e. what sort of entities ought to be considered fundamental in discussions of biological evolution. As in chemistry, there is *no single level* of description that is fundamental.

To the extent that chemists, biologists, and other scientists have abandoned the notion of a fundamental class of units adequate for all descriptions they have moved away from an essential metaphysical feature of the "modern concept of nature."

VI

In PN Professor Leclerc rejected my identification of dissipative structures (E_5 in this paper) as integrated active entities because "those structures are wholes which are not per se agents." (PN, 168) In NPE (311), he states: "The action of one compound 'atom' on another is not, by the scientific evidence, an aggregate acting of the electrons and protons individually on each other, but of each 'atom' as a whole on others." This description does not apply to dissipative structures; if such a description were characteristic of compound individuals functioning as unified physical existents, then rejection of my suggestion would be well-founded. But I know of no scientific evidence to support the contention that the action of 'atoms' on each other differs in any way from the (properly weighted) sum of the aggregate actings of the components. It is difficult to conceive situations in which the two alternative descriptions would be discernibly different from each other, providing only that proper account be taken of the constraints that arise from the structures (internal to the existents) that define the entities in question.

Is the sound of a well-rehearsed chorus different from the arithmetic sum of the sounds made by the individual singers? Are the properties of the methane molecule merely the sum of the properties of the components? The sound of the chorus in performance is certainly different from the tumult that rises from the champagne party after the concert, but only because sounds emitted by the choristers during the performance are carefully coordinated, while the babble of the same people during the party has little or no organization. The sound of the chorus in both cases is the arithmetic sum of the sounds made by the chorus members.

Are the properties of methane merely the sum of the properties of the components? Again the answer is affirmative; providing one considers atomic kernels (nuclei plus inner electrons) and valence electrons as the components of the molecule then the properties of the molecule follow from the properties of the components, and of *the symmetry of the structure in which they are united*. This symmetry also depends on the components.

Crystals have extension because unit cells combine to fill *space*: networks of interaction that define existence E_5 fill *time* in a quite analogous way. In these E_5 cases, sequences of states periodically recur in time, just as specific distributions of atoms periodically recur in the spatial arrangement of a crystal. In PN, Leclerc indicates that it was the question of the nature of extension that brought Leibniz to understand the crucial importance of relations (PN, 39,146) and that the same problem was the occasion of Kant's 1769 realization of the primacy of the perceiver and the activity of perception. (PN, 104) It seems that it will require a judicious *combination* of these two insights to understand the metaphysical significance of the new concept of nature that is emerging from contemporary science.

Is it the internal composition of an entity, alone, that decides whether the thing is a unified source of action or is not such a unified source? Or is it, instead, some characteristic of the percipient that determines whether a thing is one or many? I suggest that the chemical examples crudely sketched in sections I to IV indicate that *both* the internal composition of an entity *and* the interactions of that entity with the external world are important in deciding whether a thing is a unified source of action or whether it is a multiplicity.

Does the benzene-iodine complex exist, or does it not? It depends on how one looks for the supposed entity. If the probe is visible light, the complex evidently exists, because there is a visible color, associated with the complex, that can be detected not only with a spectrometer but even with the unaided eye. Electronic transitions take only 10^{-30} seconds; the two molecules are near enough to each other for a long enough time for the color to be apparent. However, if one uses a slower technique, such as nuclear magnetic resonance or infrared spectroscopies, then all evidence indicates that there is no such thing as a benzene-iodine complex. The aggregation does not persist long enough to be detected by *those* techniques. The measurement technique does not *cause* the existence (however fleeting) of the aggregation: the pre-existing properties of benzene and diiodine and the consequent characteristics of the properly oriented molecular pair formed by these two entities determines what there is for the measuring technique to discern. Existence is not a univocal concept; aggregations that are unified with respect to some measures are composite with respect to other interactions. Any adequate ontology must be able to deal with this general characteristic of existence.[12]

We are now at an intellectual watershed as significant as that of the seventeenth century—the scientific and social changes we are witnessing are equally far-reaching. Ivor Leclerc has delineated major philosophical problems that face contemporary culture, and has made an inspiring beginning toward their solution.

MAJOR WORKS OF IVOR LECLERC CITED

NPE *The Nature of Physical Existence* (New York: Humanities Press, 1972).

PN *The Philosophy of Nature* (Washington: The Catholic University of America Press, 1986).

NOTES

1. J. E. Earley, "Self-Organization and Agency: In Chemistry and in Process Philosophy," *Process Studies* 11 (1981): 242; "Aggregation, Actualities and Attractors," *Mondes en Développement* 54–55 (1986): 225.

2. D. R. Nelson, "Quasicrystals," *Scientific American* 255:2 (August 1986): 42–51; V. Sasisekharan, "A new method for generation of quasi-periodic structures with n-fold axes; Application to five and seven folds," *Pramana-J. Phys.* 26 (1986): L283–L293.

3. Y. T. Lee, "Molecular Beam Studies of Bimolecular Reactions: F + H_2 and Li + HF," *Ber. Bunsenges. Phys. Chem.* 86 (1982): 378–386.

4. H. R. Mayne, R. A. Poirier, and J. C. Polanyi, "Spectroscopy of the transition state (theory). II. Absorbtion by $H_3{*}O$ in $H + H_2$ $H_3{*}O$ $H_2 + H$," *J. Chem. Phys.* 80 (1984): 4025.

5. C. C. Marston and R. E. Wyatt, "Semiclassical theory of resonances in 3D chemical reactions. I. Resonant periodic orbits for $F + H_2$," *J. Chem Phys.* 81 (1984): 1819; G. Hose, H. S. Taylor and Y. Y. Bai, "Fundamentals and mechanisms of quantum localization in multidimensional correlated systems," *J. Chem. Phys.* 80 (1984): 4363; S. Gee and D. R. Truax, "Dynamics of coherent states," *Physical Review A* 29 (1984): 1627.

6. M. Lakshmanan, ed., *Solitons* (New York: Springer-Verlag, 1988); C. Rebbi, "Solitons," *Scientific American* 240:2 (February 1979): 92–116.

7. I. R. Epstein, K. Kustin, P. DeKepper, M. Orban, "Oscillating Chemical Reactions," *Scientific American* 248:3 (March 1983): 112–123; G. Nicolis and I. Prigogine, *Exploring Complexity* (New York: Freeman, 1989).

8. W. Geiseler and H. H. Foellner, "Three steady-state situations in an open chemical reaction system," *Biophysical Chemistry* 6 (1977): 107.

9. Ian Hacking, *Representing and Intervening* (Cambridge: Cambridge University Press, 1983), especially chap. 16, "Experimentation and Scientific Realism."

10. John Maynard Smith, *Evolution and the Theory of Games* (Cambridge: Cambridge University Press, 1982).

11. David Hull, *The Metaphysics of Evolution* (Albany: State University of New York Press, 1989).

12. This and related questions are considered in *Individuality and Cooperative Action,* ed. J. E. Earley (Washington D.C.: Georgetown University Press, 1991).

16

What Is Time?

Ilya Prigogine

It is a great privilege to contribute to this collective volume in honor of Ivor Leclerc. I have been reading with great excitement his books, and specially his monograph on *The Nature of Physical Existence*, where he concludes:

> Once again, as in the seventeenth century, the 'philosophy of nature' must not only be brought into the forefront, but the recognition of its intrinsic relevance to and need by the scientific enterprise must be restored. Then it will be seen that there are not two independent enterprises, science and philosophy, but one, the inquiry into nature, having two complementary and mutually dependent aspects.[1]

When I remember the path that I followed in my work, I feel that I have been quite fortunate. As a result of my personal taste and my early formation, I was interested in evolutionary time as manifest so clearly in archeology and art. This brought me to the study of irreversibility in the physical sciences, and reinforced my conviction that the role of time was not adequately treated in classical physics. Therefore, my philosophical convictions have reinforced my interest in science and vice versa. In my youth, time was considered as a solved problem. What to add, after all, to Newton and Einstein?

Today, the situation has changed drastically. Nonequilibrium systems are in the center of interest of modern science. The constructive role of irreversibility is well recognized.

Still, the problem remains: "What is time?" Here also I believe that some progress has been realized, as we begin to have a glimpse into the nature of time in the physical world around us. Of course, much remains to be done, and I shall limit my discussion here to nonrelativistic aspects, ignoring the fascinating problems which arise in high-energy physics or in cosmology.

Ivor Leclerc emphasizes in his book that since the Renaissance, primality has been given to space over time. The mechanical conceptualization of nature implies, as Leclerc aptly said, that "nature is completely understandable in terms of changeless substances and their locomotion."[2] Moreover, for the whole of traditional physics, this locomotion was expressed in terms of time-reversible, deterministic laws such as Newton's laws, or, in quantum mechanics, Schrödinger's equation.

Here we come to one of the great paradoxes which are confronting physics today: on one side, the enormous importance of irreversibility on the phenomenological level of description; on the other side, the absence of any reference to a direction of time on the fundamental level. As is well known, it was Boltzmann's work which acted as a catalyst to bring forward this splitting in our description of the physical world. After many discussions, Boltzmann retreated to a mere probabilistic interpretation of irreversibility. In this view, irreversibility was only the effect of a more "probable" evolution of the universe, but was devoid of any fundamental meaning. In short, as Einstein wrote, irreversibility would be "only an illusion."

However, the situation has changed drastically since Boltzmann's time. We now know that most elementary particles are unstable. We know also that our universe has a history. Closer to the scale which we shall consider in this short presentation, we have learned that not all dynamical systems are equivalent. The modern theory of dynamics, due mainly to Poincaré and Kolmogorov, has proven that dynamics does not exclude randomness and the existence of a temporal horizon (related to the so-called Lyapounov exponents). In addition, nonequilibrium thermodynamics has shown how irreversibility leads to coherent structures. Therefore, we have to reconsider the situation. This is the aim of the work which my colleagues and I have been pursuing over the last years.

We shall refer here to one class of dynamical systems, the Large Poincaré's systems or LPS (definition follows), because they are the type of system we deal with in everyday physics and chemistry. Still, interesting results also have been obtained for some other classes of dynamical systems. I refer here to our earlier work.[3] However, in this short presentation, I shall concentrate on Poincaré nonintegrable systems.

In 1889, Poincaré asked a basic question: can we eliminate interactions within the framework of the classical dynamical description? As a matter of fact, his original question was not so general, but this is of no concern here.

Should the answer have been affirmative, our universe would then be isomorphic to a noninteracting gas, formed by particles without any interactions or collisions.

Obviously, no organization would then be possible; no life and no human civilization. It is, therefore, fortunate that Poincaré's answer was negative: we cannot in general eliminate interactions. Systems where this is so correspond to what Poincaré called *nonintegrable systems*.

What is Time?

Poincaré went further and indicated the reasons for this nonintegrability. The reason is *resonance*. As is well known, resonances may appear for a variety of systems such as systems presenting coupled oscillations, collisions or quantum jumps. All these systems belong to the class of nonintegrable systems. Resonance means that there exists a relation between the various frequencies ω_i (for a definition of resonance, consult my *From Being to Becoming*[4] or any monograph dealing with dynamics):

$$n_1\omega_1 + n_2\omega_2 ... = 0$$

For a finite system, n_1, n_2...are integers, and resonance means that there exists a rational relation between the frequencies i. However, in the limit of large systems (where we have to replace Fourier series by Fourier integrals), the relation becomes:

$$k_1\omega_1 + k_2\omega_2 ... = 0$$

where the k_1, k_2...are real numbers.

Rational points are dense, but the "measure" is negligible with respect to the measure of irrationals. We see that in a finite system, resonances are rare. This situation is dealt with in the so-called KAM (Kolmogorov-Arnold-Moser) theory.

In the limit of infinite systems (LPS), every point becomes a resonance point, and the theory becomes much more simple. These are the systems we shall discuss: a gas or a liquid in which collisions occur; or quantum systems in which there are quantum jumps, such as matter-radiation interactions.

Let us try to understand what time means for this class of dynamical system. Irreversibility is obviously related to some time ordering. We know for example that a flower which fades is at a "later" stage than a bud. Obviously also, the neolithic revolution antedates the industrial one. In all biological and human systems, there is no problem about time ordering, but in physics, there is one. Consider two positions of an undamped pendulum: each of them may come "before" the other. This is not true for all dynamical systems. Consider for example the so-called Friedrichs model: a two-level atom which can go from the higher level to the lower one, with the emission or the absorption of a photon.

Whatever we may do, after some time the particle will appear in the ground state, with the emission of a photon. Therefore, there is a natural order in time. The transition from the particle to the photon may be associated with the future. The transition from the photon to the excitation of the particle is associated with the past. As is well known, quantum mechanics is described by a wave function, which is evolving in the so-called Hilbert space. In this problem we may associate a direction of time with the evolution of the wave function in the Hilbert space, but this is exceptional. In general, there is no

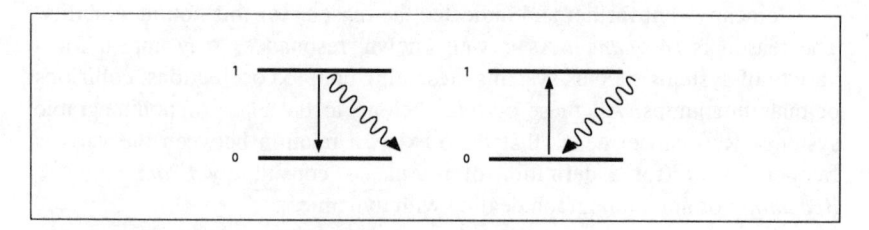

Fig.1 Friedrichs model for the two-level atom
(emission or absorbtion of a photon).

time ordering possible in the Hilbert space; while, as we shall indicate, there is a natural time ordering on the level of statistical ensembles (the so-called Gibbs ensembles, in classical or quantum mechanics).

Ensembles are described by probability functions (or by density matrix in quantum mechanics). This probability function contains all the information we have about the ensemble, such as the velocity distribution, binary or higher order correlations and so on. Let us consider a N-body system in which the particles undergo collisions.

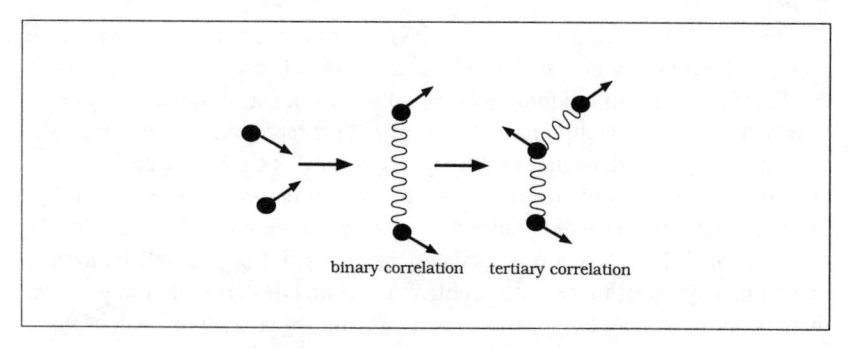

Fig.2 N-body particle systems with Newtonian collisions.
Flow of correlations.

Once two particles collide, they keep the memory of their collision. If you perform a velocity inversion, they come back and collide again. So they are in a special position. It's like two people who talk and then separate, but there is something remaining, some memory of the discussion they had. Now, the two particles are not alone in the universe. There is a third particle coming in; then a fourth. Therefore, the number of particles involved in correlations—the degree of the correlations—is growing larger and larger; there is a *flow of correlations*. It is exactly like the propagation of gossip in a society.

So, there is a close association between the *flow of correlations* and time ordering. Time is flowing in the direction of the increasing degree of correlations. In this view, irreversibility is not related to particles but to the relation among particles. The state of the system incorporates in a sense a memory of its past. This flow of correlations can be studied by computer experiments, be it for classical or quantum systems. It is the flow of correlations which is the mechanism through which thermal equilibrium is established.

Binary correlations are established very quickly, while multiple correlations require more and more time. Even to build up the binary equilibrium correlation function $g(r)$ takes a longer and longer time as r becomes larger.[5] In addition to binary correlations we have three-particle correlations, four-particle correlations, and multi-million-particle correlations that will take a geological time to build up. Therefore, we don't believe that there is any object at equilibrium in the universe. What is in equilibrium is the local environment, the first neighbors, but correlations involving billions of particles are not in equilibrium. In every object the arrow of time starting from the "big bang" is still present and will go on forever. Fortunately, only local equilibrium is required to ensure the usual thermodynamical properties of systems.

Using these ideas, we can readily understand the qualitative difference between two trajectories in a LPS. Suppose we start from A and go to B. In A, we have no correlations. From A to B we have a successive creation of correlations; from B to A we have a progressive destruction of correlations.

A -> B "dispersion" of correlations
B -> A "reconcentration" of correlations

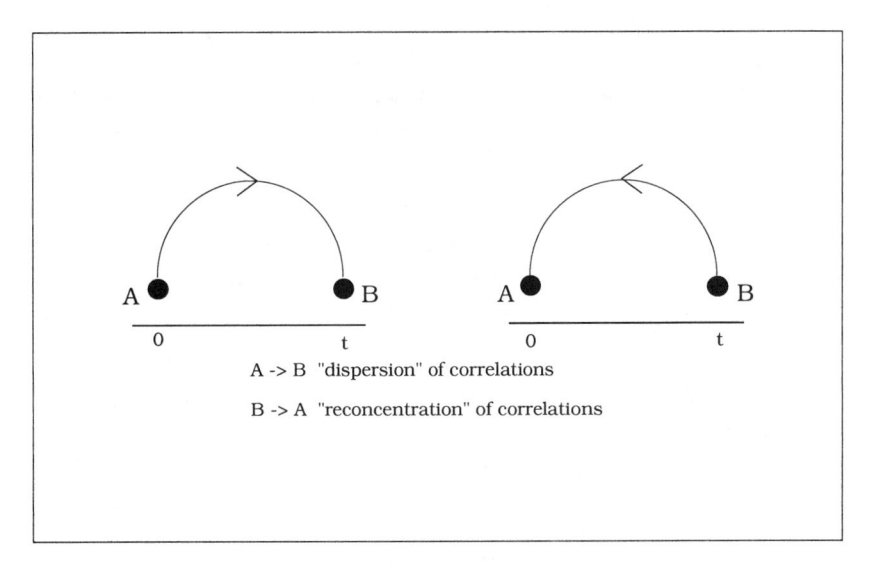

Fig. 3 Possible and forbidden evolutions in a system presenting correlations among its components.

Over the last years, we have used these ideas to build a quantitative theory leading to the *incorporation of time on the microscopic level*.[6] In fact, our theory combines two problems which we have inherited from the nineteenth century. One is the nonintegrability problem of Poincaré, and the other is the "time paradox." The resonances we have described lead to the so-called small denominators problem. Indeed, in all methods of solution, there appear denominators of the form $k_1\omega_1 + k_2\omega_2\ldots$. As these denominators vanish, we have the Poincaré catastrophe, preventing integrability.

What we have shown is that we can solve the problem of nonintegrability for LPS, and eliminate the problem of the Poincaré catastrophe by giving an appropriate prescription for handling these small denominators.

As an example, let us consider the Friedrich model presented above. The Poincaré denominator is then of the form:

$$\frac{1}{\omega_k - \omega_1}$$

where ω_k is the frequency associated to the photon, and ω_1 is the frequency associated to the particle. This denominator may vanish, but we may give a meaning to this expression by adding a small imaginary part.

$$\frac{1}{\omega_k - \omega_1} \rightarrow \frac{1}{\omega_k - \omega_1 \pm i\epsilon}$$

This is standard mathematical procedure. However, for the LPS, we have to go one step further: we have to specify when we have $+i\epsilon$ and when we have $-i\epsilon$. Now, as summarized in the appendix, there is a close association between the sign of i and the direction of time. In short:

$$-i\epsilon \rightarrow Future$$
$$+i\epsilon \rightarrow Past$$

Therefore, in the Friedrichs model, we shall use $-i\epsilon$ for a transition to the ground state with emission of a photon and $+i\epsilon$ for the inverse process. We may then show that the Poincaré divergences disappear. In this way, we come to a generalization of quantum mechanics for LPS which include the direction of time on the microscopic level.[7]

In quantum mechanics, the basic quantity is the state of the system, the wave function, which is a time-symmetrical law. The distinction between past and future introduces a new type of state, with a broken time symmetry, and which evolves according to a law that also has a broken time symmetry, such as an exponential decay towards the future.

However, in general, the introduction of a time ordering can only be made on the level of statistical description, which involves correlations. On the level of statistical description we can introduce our rule for giving a meaning to the Poincaré denominators. All transitions to higher order correlations are treated as oriented towards the future, while transitions to lower order correlations are treated as oriented towards the past. In this way, we can eliminate entirely the Poincaré catastrophe and solve the problem of the small denominators for LPS, but this solution introduces automatically a broken time symmetry. In fact, there are two solutions: one in which the degree of correlation increases with time, and the other in which it decreases asymptotically. Obviously, the world in which we live is the first one.

In summary, in this way we have connected the problem of the arrow of time with the Poincaré problem, and given a meaningful method for the construction of the arrow of time in both classical and quantum mechanics. As the direction of time is introduced on the level of distribution functions, this level becomes the "fundamental" one for description. As a result, quantum mechanics is now formulated as a theory of density matrices, and no more of wave functions (for integrable systems, we naturally recover the usual results).

An important consequence is that we have then to distinguish three levels. The statistical level is precisely the level at which irreversibility appears. Instead of the "classical" distinction between a microscopic, reversible level, corresponding to trajectories in classical mechanics and to wave functions in quantum mechanics, and a macroscopic, irreversible level, we have now a three-level distinction. From bottom to top, we have first, the level of trajectories and wave function, second, the statistical level, into which we can incorporate time ordering and irreversibility, and third, the macroscopic level.

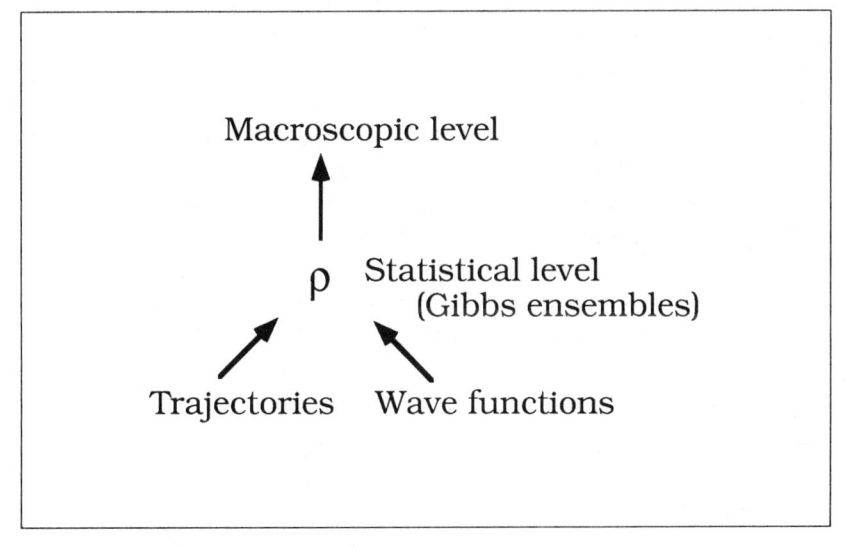

Fig. 4 Three levels of physical description.

We can show that starting from the statistical level we can obtain all the results of macroscopic physics, such as the second law, nonequilibrium structures, dissipative chaos, and so on. By contrast, if we start with trajectories or wave functions, we can show that they are destroyed by the requirement of the introduction of a well-defined time order. Therefore, not only do we have to deal with the quantum mechanical "collapse of the wave function," but also with a corresponding situation of classical mechanics, where the traditional concept of trajectories is destroyed by the randomness related to Poincaré's resonances. For highly unstable systems, the traditional description, classical or quantum, becomes thus a short time approximation.

In quantum mechanics there were two types of processes, corresponding respectively to unitary transformations within the Hilbert space and nonunitary ones, leading from wave functions to density matrices. Obviously, this situation was not satisfactory. Our approach unifies these two aspects. We show that in general the theory has to be formulated on the level of density matrices whenever instability, such as manifest by resonances, is to be taken into account. This instability may come either from the quantum system proper, or from the measurement apparatus, which acts as an intermediate between the microscopic and the macroscopic worlds.

We have now to reconsider the traditional views on the role of time in nature. Leclerc emphasized that in the Newtonian description space was playing the central role, time being only a parameter. In the Einsteinian view also, space is predominant, time being in a sense reduced to space through the velocity of light. This geometrical view of the universe remains quite popular, as testified for example by the recent book by Hawking, *A Brief History of Time*.[8] The formulation presented here emphasizes the autonomy of time as expressing an intrinsic order in the processes going on in the universe. Moreover, the arrow of time expresses a *relation* among the objects—be it among particles or fields. Time is not in the objects, but results from the dynamics.

Of course, these new concepts have to be tested through computer experiments and physical predictions. We have already performed various computer experiments to test these ideas for simple cases. Insofar as known to us at present, all consequences of our approach appear to be confirmed. More details are to be found in subsequent publications.

ACKNOWLEDGMENTS

I want to thank my colleagues of Brussels and Austin, specially T. Petrosky and F. Mayné. This work was done with the help of the Department of Engery, the Welch Foundation and the European Community.

APPENDIX

Let us indicate briefly what we mean by the close association between the direction of time and the complex plane.

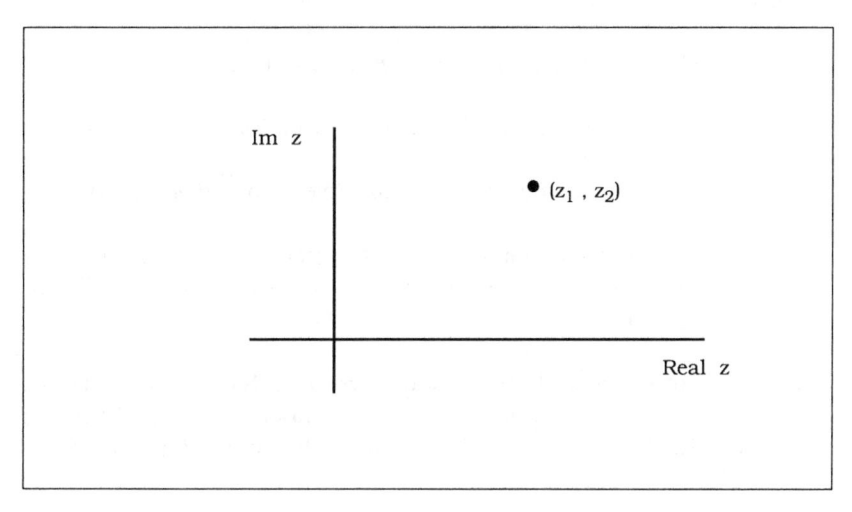

Fig. 5 Complex plane.

Let us consider the function
$$e^{-izt}$$
where z is a complex variable $z = z_1 + iz_2$. Suppose we are interested in large, positive times, then we need to take $z_2 < 0$ to obtain the expression:
$$e^{-iz_1 t} e^{-iz_2 t}$$
which vanishes for $t \to +\infty$. In contrast, this expression diverges for $t \to -\infty$. Therefore, if we are interested in large, negative times, we have to take $z_2 > 0$ in order to obtain
$$e^{-iz_1 t} e^{-iz_2 t}$$
which vanishes for $t \to +\infty$.

The sign of $i\varepsilon$ in Poincaré's denominator is, therefore, related to the direction of time we are considering. This means that, according to the type of process we are describing (increase or decrease of correlations) we have to specify the sign of $i\varepsilon$. These types of rules have been used long since to distinguish incoming waves from outgoing ones (Sommerfeld conditions). The novelty introduced here is that we use them in each step of the perturbation calculation associated to Poincaré's systems.

NOTES

1. I. Leclerc, *The Nature of Physical Existence* (London: George Allen and Unwin, 1972), 351.

2. I. Leclerc, *The Nature of Physical Existence*, 148.

3. B. Misra, I. Prigogine and M. Courbage, *Physica* 98A (1979): 1.

4. I. Prigogine, *From Being to Becoming* (New York: Freeman, 1980).

5. I. Prigogine, E. Kestemont and M. Mareschal, in *From Chemical to Biological Organization*, ed. M. Markus, S. C. Müller and G. Nicolis, (Berlin: Springer, 1988).

6. T. Petrosky and H. Hasegawa, *Physica* A 160 (1989): 351–385, where earlier references can be found. This is closely related to the results obtained by E. C. G. Sudershan, C. B. Chiu and V. Gorini, *Phys. Rev. D* 18, 8: 2914–2929.

7. T. Petrosky, S. Tasaki and I. Prigogine (to appear).

8. Steven W. Hawking, *A Brief History of Time. From the Big Bang to Black Holes* (New York: Bantam Books, 1988).

Section Five
Subjectivity and God

17

God, Necessary and Contingent; World, Contingent and Necessary; and the Fifteen Other Options in Thinking about God: Necessity and Contingency as Applied to God and the World

Charles Hartshorne

HARTSHORNE'S MODEL
Revised by Joseph Pickle

	I	II	III	IV
1.	N.n	C.n	NC.n	O.n
2.	N.c	C.c	NC.c	O.c
3.	N.cn	C.cn	NC.cn	O.cn
4.	N.O	C.O	NC.O	O.O (the most false?)

Interpretations

Columns:
I. God is in all respects necessary (or absolute, etc.)
II. God is in all respects contingent (or relative, etc.)
III. God is (in diverse respects) necessary and contingent
IV. God is impossible (or has no modal status)

Rows:
1. World (what is not God) is in all respects necessary
2. World is in all respects contingent
3. World is (in diverse respects) necessary and contingent
4. World is impossible (or has no modal status)

About this table the following claims seem legitimate: it is as definite a discovery in the metaphysics of religion as I, or for all I can see, anyone now living, or since Whitehead, have made. Its "intellectual beauty," in the poet Shelley's phrase, is striking, thanks to the elegant form in which my dear friend Dr. Pickle of Colorado College showed me how to arrange it. (An inelegant form is in my book on *Creative Synthesis*,[1] and another incomplete one in the article "Pantheism and Panentheism" in the Eliade *Encyclopedia of Religion*.[2])

It is as powerful an instrument for thinking analytically, rationally, about the theistic problem as is now available, especially if it be realized that it can be taken as only one of a series of analogous tables that can be made using other similarly abstract polarities besides that of necessary-contingent, including absolute-relative, independent-dependent, infinite-finite, abstract-concrete, simple-complex, and object-subject.

In each such table the sixteen items are so related that fifteen must be false and the remaining one true, if the zeroes are interpreted broadly. What William L. Reese and I attempted in *Philosophers Speak of God*[3] (and I had done some work on previously) has in these tables reached what looks like a fairly definitive form. Before us, centuries and millennia of theological and antitheological discussions had been unconsciously but grossly oversimplifying the theistic problem. They committed the "fallacy of many questions." Does God exist? Answer, Which God? At least six of the sixteen items, each standing for a doctrine, can reasonably be termed theistic: the first three in columns I and III (some would say, also in column II). The first and third items in row 4 fit what Hegel calls acosmism or mystical monism, as in Hinduism in some form. More pluralistic varieties of Hinduism may fit *N.c,* or classical theism, others perhaps *NC.c,* or *NC.cn*. The Bengali School of Sri Jiva Goswami, two of whose representatives I met in this country and one of whom wrote a dissertation under me in Chicago, easily fit the last mentioned modal combination. In column IV are the explicitly atheistic theoretical possibilities.

The reader will have noticed that in *NC.cn* the spatial order of the modal symbols has been reversed. In mathematical combinatory theory this permutation does not produce a new combination, so that the "16" for the total is not affected. I permute the order to call attention to the conceptual truth that the contrast between *N* and *n* can most reasonably be interpreted as follows. God, as single being, individual, or (analogically) person, exists necessarily, whether all God's qualities are necessary (*N* standing alone) or whether there are also contingent divine qualities, *NC*. Column II is scarcely theistic in the sense of the high religions. Even classical theologians who rejected the ontological argument, as Aquinas did, never did so because they believed in a merely contingent deity. However, the contingency of the world need not mean that instead of this actual world there might have been no world at all. In *cn* it means that there might have been a different world, but there could not have been no world at all. The supreme creative power could not have simply refrained from creating. I am among those who see nothing glorious in an ability to do nothing.

In all uses C (or c) means, *could* have been otherwise, and N (or n) means *could not* have been otherwise; where the two are combined the contrasting applications mean something in God (or the world) could, and something could not, have been otherwise. *World* is defined through the idea of God, for it is only divine creativity or love that makes the world a single reality. If there must be some world, it is because God must have some creatures. God is not *merely contingently* creative but essentially so; yet just *how* or *what* divine Creativity does is contingent.

Reasonably clear examples of many, perhaps all, of the options can be found represented in the history of philosophy in the West and in India. Aristotle was definitely committed to $N.cn$; in the Middle Ages, Christians virtually unanimously affirmed $N.c$ (except for Cusanus who came close to $NC.cn$, and for Scotus Erigena, with whom almost nobody agreed). Al Ghazali, the orthodox Islamic thinker, and Jewish Maimonides were much the same in their metaphysics. Stoics and Spinoza conformed to $N.n$ in their total denial of contingency. Indian extreme monism conforms to $N.O$, more pluralistic Hindus vary, some fitting $N.c$, some (the Bengali School of Sri Jiva Goswami) to $NC.c$ or $NC.cn$. Column IV locates the explicit atheists.

The first three items in column II contain what has usually been understood as belief in a "finite God." $C.n$ may fit J. S. Mill, and $C.c$ Wm. James. $Nc.cn$ patterns Plato's mature theism, if with several scholars we collapse Plato's two Gods into one, with two aspects. In early modern times two Italians, F. Socinus and Postello, came close to this pattern. Much later Fechner and Pfleiderer in Germany, Jules Lequier in France, Varisco in Italy, and W. P. Montague in the United States came closer still; finally Whitehead came very close indeed. My revisions of Whitehead, I hope, only make the fit more consistent.

The conviction I have had throughout my career that metaphysical inquiry has historically not been done in accordance with elementary logical rules, but that it can be done in accordance with them, is confirmed in this case. Other elementary fallacies besides that of many questions, including fallacies of division and composition, or of confusing contraries with contradictories (e.g. all or none, forgetting some) appear in many famous writers. However, to define metaphysics by such misuses of words, as Wittgenstein seems to do, I regard as a viciously "persuasive" definition.

The question of how polar contraries are to be applied in theism is not the only one concerning which controversies have raged. There are also issues about seemingly more concrete ideas, including mind, soul, experience, knowledge, love, feeling, purpose. These can apply to deity only through analogical generalization from human or other animal examples.

Apart from exceptionally mystical persons we do not definitely and consciously perceive God, and hence must either identify God with some abstraction, the Absolute, say—and this in my opinion has little to do with religion—or else find some way of distinguishing *in principle* between mind or purpose as in human or other animals, and as in God. What then defines God as dealt with in the high religions? The old term was perfection, (or *ens realissimum*), but this terminology as traditionally used (Plato, Kant) was ambiguous or begged an important issue similar to that between *NC* and just *N*. To remove the ambiguity I distinguish A, or absolute perfection, from *R* or relative perfection.

The distinction is quite definite. In some dimensions of value there can, it is reasonable to suppose, be an unsurpassable maximum. Thus, divine knowledge (or better, love) can be all-inclusive of what there is; divine goodness can take all sentient beings ideally well into account, but what has historically been a mere assumption, (sometimes supported by weak or fallacious arguments) was that value in every relevant sense admits of an absolute maximum. Against this I argue as follows. Aesthetic value, which is basically what happiness is, in no clear way admits of such a maximum. It would have to mean entirely harmonious and absolutely intense experience. I have yet to learn what Plato could have meant by "absolute beauty," and I challenge anyone to say what we can mean by it. I find it a leap into the dark, or a mere absurdity. A "contented oyster" may experience harmony, but what about the intensity of its enjoyments? We are told that God enjoys perfect bliss, and does not suffer pain or sorrow, yet that God knows and loves those who do suffer and sorrow. What would suffering be to a total nonsufferer?

With some ancient heretics, and with Berdyaev and Whitehead, I see the idea of an all-knowing, all-loving but simply nonsuffering deity as incoherent. Whitehead's "the fellow-sufferer who understands," goes right to the point. Only God could have this relation to *all*, and *fully* understand all. At our best we do *infinitely less* than this.

Plato had one advantage over Whitehead, as only a few in the history of this subject have seen, and as Aristotle not only did not see but tried to make a virtue of not seeing (followed in this by Whitehead, alas); Plato saw that possible analogies between what we know about our fellow creatures and ourselves fall into two large classes. A member of one, the usual class, takes some relation between a single person (or animal) and another person, animal, creature, or set of creatures, as like, and yet vastly inferior to, the relation of God to the creatures. Thus, God is friend, judge, ruler, or parent (surely not father, I beg you, in preference to mother), or admirable role model. Plato, with awesome profundity, wisdom, and cogent logic, saw the advantages of a quite different basis for the theistic analogy, that of a mind or psyche to its own body. In modern science and metaphysics this analogy works far better than it could in Plato's day. The Greeks knew next to nothing of the microstructure of nature—atoms and their subatomic particles, molecules, cells, and single-celled animals and plants. The Greeks had psychological and sociological insights, but of what a "body" consists their ignorance was simply vast.

Our ignorance is also vast, but theirs was vaster by many orders of magnitude. One's body is a huge population of self-active creatures over which each of us in a fashion (when awake) rules, and in whose weal and woe we sensitively participate and which we love with a partly innate love. We are each a quasi-deity in what T. L. Peacock somewhat miscalled our "animal republic." Plato in the *Phaedrus*, *Timeaus*, and *Laws*, Book Ten, showed a wisdom that was more than twenty centuries ahead of its time and can only now be adequately appreciated. Aristotle, Philo, Plotinus, and a thousand others who were misled by these, missed the Platonic point. A few theologians, Montague, McIntosh, and Pfleiderer, in this century, and some Hindus a long time ago, have used the mind-body analogy, but none so well as Whitehead virtually does while thinking he must reject it. This is a psychological paradox.

I began my graduate studies much more definitely concerned with Plato than with any other author before Spinoza, and I have taken Paul Shorey, Burnet, and Cornford seriously as commentators. By still other scholars, several of them friends, I have been supported in my sense that Aristotle only in some ways improved upon Plato, while in other ways failed to understand his great teacher. By his enormous influence he helped hundreds of philosophers and theologians to miss some of Plato's best insights.

From the table one can see at a glance that among the sixteen possibilities for theorizing, only one of which could be true, there is also only one that can survive the application of Leibniz's rule: in metaphysics only denials have been mistaken, metaphysical affirmations alone can be true. The argument for the rule is clear: the most general conceptions (those dealt with in metaphysics) cannot lack instantiation. The famous assertion, "there might have been nothing," is not a genuine affirmation but the contradiction, or sheer nonsense, of "the being of total non-being." To say, "nothing exists," or "there is nothing," is clearly self-refuting, and I believe the less direct formulations can be shown to be so. Bergson, in *Creative Evolution*,[4] convinced me if I needed convincing of the following: 'nothing', or 'non-being', has genuine meaning only if it is given a limited sense, such as *my non-being*, or as *nothing to the purpose in hand*. To my knowledge, not one of the great Greeks tried to completely generalize "nothing." Buddhism seems sometimes to do this, as does Heidegger; I have only this to say: whatever of importance can be conveyed by talking or writing in this manner can be as well or better said otherwise.

God, Necessary and Contingent; World, Contingent and Necessary 301

Another rule that helps to narrow down the selection from the options is the principle of contrast. The function of concepts is to distinguish. If nothing is contingent, then 'necessary' performs no job; if nothing is necessary, then 'contingent' loses its sense. Similarly with 'absolute' and 'relative'. I recall some writer who wrote, "nothing is absolute," yet also directly, or very plainly, indirectly, wrote that causal determination of events is absolute. I challenge his choice of instantiation for 'absolute', but commend his implied giving up of *'everything* is relative'. *N.n* and *C.c* violate this principle, and so do the philosophies of Spinoza and the Stoics and, in the opposite way, Wm. James, J. S. Mill, and various others who want even God to be a merely contingent reality. Theism has an advantage over atheism at this point, for it admits a contrast between the "all possible others surpassing" (or "by no others surpassable") being and the "by others surpassable" beings.

Here is another rule. If Q is a contingent proposition and P entails Q, then P is also contingent. Hence, if "God knows that you and I contingently exist" is true then, since this requires that you and I exist (infallible knowledge could not err), the proposition that God has this knowledge is itself contingent. Hence, there is something contingent in God, and *N.C* and *N.cn* are both self-contradictory unless it is false that God knows contingent things or truths. This is precisely why Aristotle denied divine knowledge of contingent aspects of the world, for he did deny contingent aspects of God. His God is the "unmoved mover." Spinoza's (wholly necessary) God was said to know all things, hence Spinoza denied the contingency of these things. Before medieval theology Aristotle, after it Spinoza, employing the same logical principle in opposite ways, showed the illogicality of that theology. In still other ways Carneades showed it also.

Why were classical theism (*N.c*), Aristotelian theism (*N.cn*), or Spinoza's classical pantheism (*N.n*) as popular as they were at various times and places? This, too, the table helps to explain. *N.n* and *N.c* are simple, and human weakness tends to like extreme simplicity. *N.c* has the further advantage of conforming to the rule of contrast. *N.cn* is more complex; and (at a price) it can avoid trouble with the necessary knowledge of contingency problem. Also, it caters to the human tendency to react to danger, risk, and fear by seeking an escape into a realm in which there are no changes, hence no changes for the worse. That this might logically mean no concrete good, as well as no concrete evil, is set aside. The multiplication table, or the number series, is timeless enough. To the ancients the heavenly bodies, species of animals, and (if they admitted them) atoms, seemed in essential respects changeless.

That *C.c* appealed to some is explained by the ease with which we can say, "take anything that exists, we can think of it as not existing." With ordinary things this makes good sense; our own coming to be, for example, is clearly an extremely chancy thing, a throw of the dice of generation. Also, if our parents had freedom, they might have behaved differently and not had just us as offspring. However, that I might never have existed does not mean that instead of me there might have been nothing. It means that every portion of space-time might have been occupied in such a manner that I could not have been there also. I have not invented this meaning; it is quite classical. That there might not have been human beings has, in no way that I have ever seen, been shown to entail that there might have been no beings. The possible emptiness of specific classes has nothing to do with the possible emptiness of all, including the most general or abstract classes. The most general ideas (including that of deity), in my judgement, cannot intelligibly lack instantiation.

How, you may be thinking, can 'God' stand for an extremely general idea, considering that God is envisaged as a single being or individual? Here is one more way in which dual transcendence has been missed. God is not *an* individual but *the* unique individual who alone has strictly *universal* functions, prehending all, hence influenced by all; equally, dual transcendence adds, prehended (at least felt) *by* all; and therefore *influencing* all. Of no mere nondivine creature can this be said. I will never influence Plato by getting him to prehend me, and I prehend and am influenced by him only in an indirect, complex, and incomplete manner.

Because of the unique generality of its subject matter, metaphysics cannot use the scientific method of observational falsification, as Popper was the first to see clearly. Science cannot legitimately deny God, and it need not affirm God. It does need to affirm something metaphysical, and here, too, I agree with Popper. At least it should, and scientists largely do, affirm a basic realism. The being of humanity is not Being Itself.

A metaphysics that denies God cannot, I think, amount to much. Here I agree with A. Comte. No wonder Hume (who half denied God) turned to history, and Bertrand Russell to dear knows what. Theism alone, as Peirce said, following Kant, "enables us to unify our general ideas." Nietzsche's substitute for God, the eternal recurrence, with causal determinism, has some of the worst faults of some theisms.

As the great religions, also Plato, Aristotle, and the Stoics define God, column II is atheistic. Some Anglo-American monolithic empiricists, J. S. Mill, Wm. James, E. S. Brightman, have tried to be theists without supra-empirical considerations; but they neither meet the crucial Popperian criterion of empirical (conceivable observational) falsifiability, nor do they achieve impressive positive results for very many of us. I admired Carnap, who was certainly no theist, for his refusal to call himself an atheist. On the religious question he was a positivist. 'God' has not been given, he thought *could not* be given, a "cognitive meaning," unless one that would fit only primal superstitious forms of religion which science is adequate to discredit. This is my view, so far as most traditional explications of empirical or nonmetaphysical theism are concerned. Brightman was really a metaphysical partisan of dual transcendence—the finite-infinite [or infinite-finite] God.

That God is *exclusively* necessary (column I) is open to objections so clear and cogent that I am reminded of Chesterton's phrase, missing the truth "as if by magic." (1) Freedom, by its natural intuitive meaning, connotes contingency, that what was decided might have been decided otherwise. If God's "let there be light" was a free act, there was something contingent in God. The classical theists (*N.c*) said God could have refrained from creating. Ergo. (2) *N* (or *A*) by itself means that God can receive nothing from any contingent (or free) decision of the creatures. God, it was thought, is the great giver, but the divine capacity to receive from others is zero. Think what parents receive from children, and what we all receive from observing nature and one another. Is God to receive *nothing* from the creatures? Then how can we "serve God" in a genuine sense, however analogical? (3) Why were these absurdities foisted upon believers? The answer is clear: since God's intrinsic value is held to be absolutely maximal, incapable of increase, there can be nothing to add. Not the Bible, but Plato gave this argument (in his middle period). He knew better in the end, but his followers mostly did not, alas. The argument assumes, and collapses entirely without, the *logical possibility* of an absolute maximum of value, and this not in some dimensions only, or according to some criteria only, of the relevant dimensions or criteria of value, but all of them.

I see no sound reasons for this assumption. Quite the contrary. Optimal *intrinsic* value is best conceived as aesthetic, as harmonious and intense experiencing. A contented oyster would have harmony, but what about intensity? Experience exhibits intensity as varying with variety and quantity of experienced data. A high-pitched sound cannot have the massiveness, the volume, of a low-pitched sound. Can any mere white light have the beauty of a panorama of colors? If beauty is some form of unity in variety, what could maximal variety be? It could not be *all possible* variety, for there are "incompossibles." Leibniz knew this but utterly failed to see the theistic consequence. Kant rightly rejected the attempted proof that there can be no contradiction in the idea of deity as maximal intrinsic value. The proof was indeed fallacious for the reason Kant gave. Alas for human fallibility, this did not prevent Kant from continuing to retain the classical theistic view of the idea of God; it only confirmed for him his doctrine that, while we can rationally believe in God, we should view this as faith not knowledge. Strictly speaking, all our knowledge is faith (as Peirce in his youth declared); only God simply knows; however, some faiths are far better and more truly knowledge than others. If deconstructionists deny this, so much the worse for them and the rest of us if they are taken more seriously than they deserve. Their work, at least as much as any, needs to be deconstructed.

The Leibniz rule clearly favors column III and row 3. In all four cases of the latter, c can be taken to attribute contingency to every nondivine active singular in a radical sense in which *NC* does not need to attribute contingency to God. Thus, c may mean that you or I, for instance, might not have existed at all, whereas the divine existence obtains no matter what. Not mere divine existence but divine actuality is contingent. Indeed actuality, as I use this word, is contingent in all applications. Divine actuality is how, or in what concrete states, the divine essence is instantiated. The class of such states cannot be empty, whereas the class of your or my states might have been (and once was) empty, and so with every nondivine individual. Deity will in every possible case be actualized somehow, but I might have been actualized nohow. For this distinction between existence and actuality I have found no clear precedent; it has been called by David Tracy my "breakthrough." It was, I think, suggested to me by Whitehead's choice for his concept of unit actuality (again my term), "actual entity." 'Actual' contrasts with 'possible', not with 'existent'. We do not naturally say, "events exist"; rather, they actually happen or occur. Nor is it natural to say, "experiences exist." Individuals or species exist, provided events or experiences actualize what makes them individuals or species.

'Existence', naturally employed, is less concrete than actuality, so, too, is necessity compared to contingency. That is why it is only existence that can (in God, or in "some world or other") be necessary, whereas actuality cannot be so—provided we avoid using 'actual' for being somehow actualized, concretized, or instantiated. So long as the dichotomy, essence-existence, is taken as exhaustive, so long will neoclassical philosophy be poorly understood. Triadic divisions are radically more illuminating than merely dichotomous ones. Peirce and no one else taught me this, but he never quite decided how to apply it to his belief in God. This was my opportunity.

Few of the principles appealed to in this essay are my invention; I am, it seems, the first to put them together. Eclecticism is closer to the sound method in philosophy than some seem to suppose. The philosophers I admire most tried to act on this presumption. As for Victor Cousin, the French "eclectic" philosopher, when I finally looked him up I found him a thinker of admirable good sense and good will.

Among the bizarre features of much theistic discussion is the fact that, although 'God' stands for the supremely important and good reality, yet words like 'necessary' and 'contingent', or 'absolute' and 'relative', or 'infinite' and 'finite', have no unambiguous *value* connotations. "Absolutely false" is as natural as "absolutely true." A great *mis*fortune, a great *good* fortune, a wicked deed, a noble or kind deed, they can all be contingent. A divine

God, Necessary and Contingent; World, Contingent and Necessary 305

act is, by definition of 'divine', good, but unless it is unfree it is contingent, and God could have done otherwise. 'Otherwise' does not have to mean less good, for it is a baseless assumption that to a definite concrete situation there is one best possible kind of concrete response. It is good to speak kindly to a neighbor, but there is no one best possible way to do this. What practical decisions require is not the hopeless search for the "best possible" response to each situation but only a response about *as good* as any other possible one. Concreteness is always partly new and undeducible from abstractions, such as principles, rules or laws, plus concrete details of the past.

Whitehead, for the first time in history, said the precise truth here: each new concrete actuality (or experient occasion) is a process in which "the many become one and are increased by one." An experience is a unity, but its causal conditions are previous such unities, those in one's own personal series and also those in other series. Psychologists are not even trying (still less, if possible, are physicists) to find a formula for determining exactly how the new unity is derived from the previous multiplicity. No wonder they talk about behavior rather than experience! Yet all intrinsic values, the roots of motivations, are in experiences. Nor do 'infinite' and 'finite' ordinarily function as unambiguously evaluative. If the creative process had no absolute beginning, as Aristotle and Whitehead assume, then there may have been an infinity of small or large satisfactions, and also of dissatisfactions.

A unique advantage of the most nearly symmetrical and also completely *positive* doctrine, *NC.cn*, is its implication that between Creator (neoclassical theism can use this word, provided it be understood that every creature is—Lequier, Fechner, Whitehead—partly self-creative) and creature there is genuine analogy (likeness in principle as well as difference in principle). This analogy, N to n and C to c, makes communication between God and other beings possible, and we human persons can know not merely what God is not but, in abstract outline, what God is. Precisely this is what religion demands. Another advantage is that with it we avoid the absurdity of the three theistic items in row 2, *N.c*, *C.c*, and *NC.c*, which posit zero necessity in God's having some world or other rather than no world at all. Of all forms of worshipping a zero this seems the least sensible. In God is indeed zero possibility of divine wickedness, and this infallible goodness is indeed worshipful, but not freedom to produce nothing, no creatures at all. Definitely, explicitly, deliberately Whitehead—probably also Peirce, Bergson, with all the old Greeks—avoided this absurdity. God's freedom is not to have no world at all. If some world is not better than no world, what can we possibly do to "serve" or express love for God? What sense does the idea of divine love then have? A God for which the world has no intrinsic value intelligible in divine terms and a world for which God has no intrinsic value intelligible in human terms—how can that view be religious? Only by chicanery (I have to agree with Russell here) did

Leibniz, the classical theist, avoid admitting the necessity of the world as it is. His "sufficient reason" entails this necessity, or do not ask me what it means! Crusius definitely anticipated me here, back in Kant's time. I learned about this from Kant and then from reading Crusius.

The explicitly atheistic column IV shows the following oddities. In the first option (thirteenth out of sixteen) the world is wholly necessary, there is no contingency anywhere (vs. the principle of contrast) and no ground for the alleged necessity in an intelligible cosmic power. In option two (fourteenth) there is no necessity anywhere, nothing to limit collapse toward mere chaos or nonentity. Item three (fifteenth) means a not merely contingent world and therefore, some sort of cosmic order, but no cosmic orderer adequately powerful enough (which means intrinsically good enough) for the job. According to atheistic option four (or sixteenth) modal logic lacks application. Quine, followed by Richard Martin, rejected this logic, but his position here has won no general agreement, and it deprives philosophy of a logical backbone. Aristotle, Peirce, Whitehead, Kripke, Popper are my experts here.

If neither 'necessary' nor 'contingent' is an unequivocal word of praise or dispraise, and the same is true for 'absolute' and 'relative', or 'infinite' and 'finite', are not 'independent' and 'dependent', or 'indifferent to' and 'responsive to' others, in the same value-neutral class—like *very*, as in 'very good' and 'very bad'? Why was Aristotle so sure that a being whose consciousness is the mere "thinking of thinking," wholly indifferent to, unmoved by, joy or sorrow in anyone else, is the most admirable or divine reality, the role model for the stars and ourselves? Was Plotinus, with his worship of pure unity, any better? Fairly obviously unity is not by itself the supreme good, nor is complexity in principle bad. In spite of the poet Shelley the "white radiance of eternity" is not better than the many colors that life, like stained glass, produces. Is there not a subtle idolatry in worshipping such one-sided, extreme abstractions? Why our predecessors fell into this stance is capable of various explanations, but the details I leave for other occasions.

Tradition was not wrong in using both value and value-neutral concepts to distinguish God from all else. Without the latter we are unable, in using value terms for God, to avoid childish, even grossly destructive forms of anthropomorphism. Countless beings are in some way dependent, but only God can be dependent as God is dependent; countless beings are in some way independent, but only God can be independent as God is independent. Similarly with the other polarities mentioned. Also with fixity or permanence, and change or novelty. Creatures change by increase or decrease, and their change has a beginning and an end. Divine change is exclusively increase, and without beginning or ending. Divine dependence is in *ideally sensitive* responses of love to *all* creatures, ours is infinitely less than this.

Consider power, meaning ability to influence others. Some persons have had great power—Alexander, Napoleon, Hitler—for evil as well as some power for good, with Hitler having probably the least for good and the most for evil. (Or did Stalin surpass him in this?) Tradition was, however, partly right about power. Being and power (Plato uses the second to define the first) are *primarily* good. Every organism, until near death, is a largely harmonious functioning of bodily parts. "Unbearable pain" cannot be and is not borne. I am sure that I have never borne it, in spite of ulcers and some breaking of bones. We live essentially because we want to, though our cells by their primitive little pulses of feeling have enough momentum to complicate the matter somewhat; still, with simply no satisfaction, we scarcely live.

What, I ask, gives a human stream of consciousness its power over its cells in the central nervous system and hence over muscles? Answer, in brief: a human experience pools the life and feeling in the cells; they are sensitive to us because we are sensitive to them. Whitehead spells this out. There is "feeling *of* feeling" both ways, and always on both sides there is some "satisfaction." Why is this not the fulfilment of Plato's aborted scheme, a cosmos in which the whole, as in a human body, is sensitive to its parts, and in which all the parts are, or are moved by, self-moving and, hence, besouled and at least sentient agents? Why could Plato not carry out this project? Because Plato, like all the ancients (apart from rather wild guesses), knew *nothing* of the microworld, the indeed self-moving constituents of all so-called matter. He saw two limitations on cosmic teleology, (1) the freedom of many (all) psyches, and (2) the existence of portions of nature from which self-motion or soul appeared wholly absent. Only the first limitation is real. We can know what no ancient Greek could about "matter."

Still another argument for the truth of *Nc.cn* is the following. The only *completely* symmetrical (and therefore, not beautiful and probably not true in this realm of timeless necessity) of the sixteen mathematical options is *O.O*, which is the same as *OO.OO*. Against this, besides the primacy (which I learned first from Lancelot Whyte) of asymmetry or directional order, are the other rules, that of positivity (Leibniz), or of contrast (Wittgenstein), or of polarity (M. Cohen). Nearly all tradition favors the application of modality to existents as well as to propositions. How could what an unconditionally necessary proposition (conditional necessity is not represented by the table) affirm what exits only contingently? I conclude that *O.O*, the most negative option, is also the *most completely false* of the options. From this I infer that the most true option can only be the opposite, the most positive, and this is *NC.cn* The permutation in *cn*, and the asymmetry it introduces, is not genuinely negative (in spite of the prefix *a*), for symmetry is itself a negation, the collapse of directional order. Denying symmetry is a not-not, an affirmation. Plato's denial of strict equality (a symmetrical relation) in nature was a stupendous affirmation of the rich diversity of reality.

Those who know Peirce's idea of a diagram in the strict mathematical sense will see that the table is such an instrument. It structurally corresponds (partially and in a controlled way) with the structure of the concepts represented, according to rules of interpretation. Such a diagram does what no mere rhetoric could, with reasonable efficiency, to lay bare the conceptual relationships of the ideas in question. Scientists and logicians know this. It is time all philosophers should know it. How well did Sartre know it? Or the deconstructionists?

The table of theisms, atheisms, and acosmisms, plus the literally "positivistic" doctrine of Leibniz that all metaphysical truth is positive (hence that the extreme negative formula, total non-being, is a mere misuse of words); plus the principle of contrast or of polarity (M. Cohen), that the most general or abstract contraries must be applied together so neither pole can lack instances; plus finally the conceptual primacy of nonsymmetry over symmetry (equal to simply means neither greater nor less than)—all this together seems to come close to justifying neoclassical theism, or the principle of dual transcendence, NC, and the correlative principle of dual immanence, cn. If more is wanted I can only refer to my not otherwise available six theistic arguments in *Creative Synthesis and Philosophic Method*. (I now prefer not to call them proofs because, although their structure involves no formal fallacy, so far as I can see, their formulation requires more than logical constants and may be unacceptable to some philosophers. Like the Hartshorne-Pickle table, each argument is stated as an exhaustive set of (3 or 4) mutually exclusive options other than the neoclassical theism common to them all.)

From either procedure it is clear that although rigorous formal logic by itself does not suffice (and even in mathematics intuition is required) to determine a "metaphysique" (a neologism for a system of noncontingent existential truths), logic does have an invaluable role to play in arriving at such a system. It enables us to exhaust the options. Without this we have at best only poetry, or amateur and very likely inferior or antiquated science (especially psychology), or ingenious language games, or raw, uncritical common sense.

Another essential element in metaphysics is in the use of historical arguments, treating the history of philosophy as a laboratory of intellectual experiments in theories, and arguments for or against theories, and in judgments about theories and arguments. If earlier philosophers had no valuable capacities to judge these things, what is the likelihood that we have? Their lack of later achieved observations and instruments of observation is neither irrelevant nor necessarily decisive. Although what philosophy in its central metaphysical concerns most needs are not contingent and special facts, but rather completely universal abstract principles, such is the fallibility of human rationality that the impressive successes of science are only too likely to lead to extreme formulations, or overstatements, of genuinely empirical and contingent truths so as to exclude some metaphysical truth. For example, the stately and largely predictable movements of the heavenly bodies, or of bodies falling to the earth (Galileo), for two thousand years and more tended to conceal from educated intelligences the *pervasive* presence of what Plato called the self-movement of soul, what others call freedom or creativity, and what Leibniz (and many since Leibniz) agree with Plato is in some form and degree psychical, wherever—and that is everywhere, on some level of magnitude—there is *active singularity, genuine agency.*

The historical method of argument is prominent in Peirce, Whitehead, Popper; much less so in Carnap, Quine, and many contemporaries. Rorty uses it, but in my judgment, more cleverly than carefully. Deconstructionists seem to me to fail to come to grips with the great thinkers of the past. Yes, there was much ambiguity, but there were also penetrating glimpses of definite truths.

Still another thing separates me from many: the importance of Darwinian biology. No matter how rational or spiritual we rational animals may be, animals we certainly are. Human mentality is not cosmic mentality and may not be the best planetary mentality there is in the huge numbers of galaxies. Finally, either the cosmos as a whole is besouled or it is not. How this dilemma is resolved is not a detail or a trifle for philosophy. Even for psychology as allegedly an observational science it deserves consideration, and there are anthropology and comparative religion. Biology itself is gambling on a questionable guess if it does not take seriously the possibility that comparative psychology has only for convenience and practicality its lower boundaries with the higher animals, or even with unicellular plants and animals. Animals seem to *want* to live, escape danger, and mate. Also what is called culture (learning from elders) is generalizable beyond any easily established lower limit. An English tit discovers how to get the milk from lidded milk bottles, and soon most of the tits are doing this. Evolution does not need divine guidance in the rigid manner of the old teleologies (which contradicted freedom and also made providence responsible for monstrosities); however, the basic *orderliness* of nature is not explained by science. Rather, it is assumed and by observation particularized. If more or less narrowly limited freedom is everywhere, as metaphysicians now tend to assume (and physicists do not much quarrel with this), why may not the laws constituting this order be indeed divinely established, that is, by cosmic freedom and cosmic psychicality?

In the lifetime of Darwin, evolution was cordially accepted by some English and American theists. Soon after Darwin's death my maternal grandfather and my father both Episcopal clergymen whose piety was manifest, did this. It is also reasonably arguable that Darwin's nontheism was not grounded in his positive theories, but in his already almost antiquated faith in determinism which was not required for those discoveries.

I close with some points of agreement with tradition. Although mere eternity or unchangeability is not better than mere temporality or changeability, yet whereas in temporality there is both good and evil, in mere eternity there is only good. The strictly necessary, which is the same as the strictly eternal (Aristotle), can have no unfortunate or undesirable aspects. The argument is that terms of disapproval make sense with temporal, contingent circumstances that *might have been* avoided or not have occurred, but they are absurd if applied to the eternal or necessary. The eternal can, however, be good and beautiful in its abstract way. I see here another reason for theism. If life lacks overall meaning without God, and I can think no otherwise, then nontheism implies an *eternal and necessary defect* in reality. Most regrettable—but such regret must be *absolutely futile*. Life itself has to be basically affirmative and optimistic. I hold with Albert Schweitzer (and against Sartre) that it is irrational to toy with suppositions that render living as such nonsensical.

Our extremely intelligent daughter, Dr. Emily H. (Mrs. Nicolas) Goodman—brought up, like her parents and grandparents, to believe in human freedom—says her religion is belief in an *"eternal rightness* in reality." This is what I tried to explain in the previous paragraph. In mere eternity nothing can be bad or wrong but something must be good or right. This necessary good is the defining essence of deity, an extreme abstraction, but a precious and beautiful one (*NC*.) It is, after all, not wholly surprising if its rightness and beauty has been persistently identified with the fullness of the divine life, perpetually resynthesizing itself in response to an ever-increasing treasury of past creatures, through cosmic epoch after epoch. If we acquire some skimpy outline awareness of the vastness of this treasury as in this epoch, we do well. The rest we can leave to God. Our business is in this world and its reasonably inferable past and reasonably projectable future.

We rational, or at worst (as someone has said) rationalizing, animals may boast, with Milton, that our thoughts "wander through eternity" or, with George Meredith, that our science has made us aware of "unalterable law." Such boasts add not an iota to our actual knowledge. Fragments that we are, what we can know is also fragmentary—except for the uttermost abstractions that enable us to make some sense in principle of our place in that besouled cosmos apart from which (*per impossibile*) we and the creatures which we know would indeed be as "nothing." This partial and abstract knowledge is our precious gift from the interplay of Creator-creaturely freedom that, more or less as Darwin plus Mendel, Sewall Wright, and other biologists have conceived it, in billions of years has produced our species. The process was worthwhile all along, for as Aristotle rightly said, all the forms of life are in themselves beautiful and, as a mystic has said, are cherished by God. We are, it seems, the greatest single asset of life on this planet and its greatest single danger. (Freedom cannot be wholly safe.) It is for us to mitigate the dangers, while enriching the good. Practice, or *praxis*, is indeed the bottom line.

NOTES

1. Charles Hartshorne, *Creative Synthesis and Philosophic Method* (London: SCM Press, 1970).

2. Mircea Eliade, Editor in Chief, *Encyclopedia of Religion* (New York: Macmillan, 1986).

3. Charles Hartshorne and William Reese, *Philosophers Speak of God* (Chicago: University of Chicago Press, 1953).

4. Henri Bergson, *Creative Evolution*, trans. Arthur Mitchell, (New York: H. Holt and Company, 1911, 1931, 1937).

18
Persons and God

Hywel D. Lewis

I

We live in a strange world. Most of us readily adapt ourselves to this and learn to live in the world as we find it. Few pause to wonder at the way things are, not even when led to think about the astonishing consistencies in the constant variations involved in our perceptions of the world around us. We accept things in terms of what we have learnt to expect, including the complexities and minutiae of expert accounts of how things come to be, whether close at hand in the experience of each one or in distant heavenly bodies and in other constellations vastly remote in space or time. The consistencies, *mutatis mutandi*, guarantee the accounts that are given and make possible all our persistent manipulations of things in the world around us, including the provision and maintenance of what we have learnt, will sustain and nourish us in our present existence. It seems perverse to raise any question about this or to speculate about our hopeless plight if the world and the response of its ingredients were different. If, as sometimes happens, they seem different, we take it that there is some explanation of such perplexing phenomena, whether we find it or not, which will bring it within the framework of the world in which we find ourselves and live out our lives. We would not exist without the basic consistency of things. How could we survive at all if things began to behave in any old way?

Even the most sceptical must admit this and marvel with us at the way things are and their making possible the lives we have. Some young creatures adapt themselves with astonishing rapidity and sureness from the time they are born. A young pony, for instance, licked by its mother and thrust the appropriate ways, struggles to its feet and very soon is able to run along with its mother without dashing itself against possible obstacles. Most young creatures learn to get their own nourishment from a parent in one of several ways in which they may participate themselves.

Some persons remove the strangeness of this by invoking the now familiar term 'instinct'. Young creatures have an instinct which guides them. Others insist that the use of this term simply provides a general name for many things which are not thereby explained at all. Others contend that there is much more than many realize in the notion of instincts as explanatory factors,[1] but I do not think they succeed in removing the general essential mystery of the way we find things to be and our good fortune on account of it.

I must insist, with perhaps some repetition not easily avoidable, that what I have been stressing does not just apply or manifest itself in circumstances or events to which we would normally be apt to apply the word 'wonderful', such as scenery or exceptionally fortunate coincidences like a very powerful swimmer being at hand when some being is in difficulties in the water, or, closer to our concern today, when stranded whales have the unplanned nearness of persons able to handle them and get them effectively out to sea again and on their course, or, better still in the light of recent events, find some gap in a wall of ice which blocks their way. We can think endlessly of such wonders, escapes, achievements, and so forth, but it is not in this sense that I refer now to the wonder we find in the world around us. The enumeration and multiplication of wonderful events, such as we might normally have in mind in the use of a word like 'wonderful', has little proper relevance to my present concern. Such events happen within the general consistency of all things as we find them in the world around us. Strange things are not altogether out of line. There is always some explanation in principle, however hard to find.

This does not mean that there may not be some events or occasions which fall altogether outside the framework within which things are normally understood in relation to one another. I have myself maintained, and shall do so again, that moral freedom of choice is of this sort. But it involves a very exceptional, I should say unique, situation arising from the peculiar nature of moral responsibility and obligation. Since, as I maintain, our natures or characters do not determine the course we take here, there is no explanation required or possible beyond the making of the choice itself. This is a unique situation which would not itself be possible without the normal determination of events around us, other than the moral choices of others, and of our own nature as they have developed, subject again to measures of indeterminism due to occasional moral choices. The assumption within which we normally function, including accepting the guidance of people whom we have reason to believe to be better informed and with sounder insight than ourselves, in my view, is that all other than free moral choice, fits somewhere into the general framework out of which everything comes and has its place assigned. The inevitable sequences of events generally cannot be accounted for itself in the same way as particular courses of events or occasions related within the framework.

We come to accept the inevitability of the framework because we find that things so happen and come to accept that this is how things are, with variations prescribed by the course of events itself, throughout the entire finite system which is all we ourselves directly encounter. There is no argument, a priori or otherwise, which we may invoke to establish the general necessity of all things as they are. I would not even say that we have an intuition to this effect. We realize that without a framework of consistent sequences such as I have noted, all would be meaningless and pointless and could not exist at all in any recognizable shape. How or why it is in fact so, we cannot say in terms of any finite consideration or inspection of the world as it is. We find that fortunately things fall together in this way, more fully apprehended by some gifted people than others. We assume from the long range of unbroken sequences in all we observe that things have to be so, but we cannot properly establish within the finite framework in which we operate normally, that this is inevitable or will continue. We have to accept the world and live in it as we find it.

The nagging question remains however as to why, subject to some tantalizing problems still unresolved, the finite universe seems to be throughout the consistent framework which our minds may tackle and deprive of its secrets within itself.

Two lines of reply may suggest themselves here, and they have both been commended to us from time to time.

The first is that, in all accounts of ourselves and our environment, however complete we make them, we are pushed back from one finite relationship to others until we have at last to postulate an origin of things in which they simply sprang into being out of just nothing but having the forms and sequences which we discover in due course and extend in principle to everything.

There is strictly no reason why this should not be. But I find it hard to believe that anyone seriously believes it—first, just nothing, and then a real world in which fascinating things happen. The vital word here is 'real', not the attractive and exciting features of the world, but simply that there is a world. The real question here is whether we can suppose that anything comes into being out of nothing. Thinkers of long ago have maintained with vigorous confidence that "out of nothing, nothing comes." It is hard not to agree. Why should things, coming into being out of nothing, do so at just the time they did, or in the shape they did. It is hard to find a reason why things could not come to be out of nothing. It just seems impossible. It is out of all reason, a mere blind happening.

If we reject, as I am inclined to do out of hand, the notion that there was just nothing and, then, the world, or any world or universe, as we find it, we are apt to turn to our second alternative and say that the finite universe has always been. There never was a wholly original, unheralded beginning.

However far back you go you will find something. The universe never began, it has always been. This may sound very plausible at first, and it seems to leave us with no awkward problems. We can all, we are apt to think, conceive of the world having always been. But this is in fact a very extraordinary use of 'always'. This word is usually invoked where there are very long stretches of time involved. "There is always snow on the top of Everest," "It is always cold in the Arctic or at the North Pole," "It is always warm at the Equator." But there was a time when the top of Everest was not cold, indeed when there was no Everest at all. At one stage, a long time ago, it was very warm in far northern regions and the entire earth was steaming and burning away, as it does still even in the far north deep below the surface, as volcanoes in far northern regions and springs of steaming water illustrate well. In a limited finite way we can use the word 'always' with ease and without misleading anyone.

It is very different if we think of 'always' in an absolute sense. Does the term mean anything when used in that way? However far back we stretch our thoughts, there must be a terminus somewhere. As the medievals, to invoke them again, wondered, how could we ever reach now if there was not time from which we began, or the course of events which led to the things that are now—how could they become as they are now if they never started.

I am not referring here to the beginning of this particular planet earth, or our particular constellation centered on the sun. Scientists may tell us with confidence about such beginnings and speculate very plausibly about others of which they are less certain. We may find it strange to think of the universe without this world. But that is not impossible, and we know that some factors existing at the time brought it about. It is quite different to think of the external universe as a whole not having any beginning but stretching back and back to nowhere.

What then do we say? Is there any conclusion to be drawn? Yes, I think we should say that the entire finite universe is dependent upon or sustained by an ultimate and radically different reality of which we thus speak as a transcendent reality. As such we can have no notion what it is like in itself, but we have to regard it as the source or ground of all that is. We cannot know the transcendent in itself, not just because we are not yet clever enough, as might be said of some persisting puzzlement in the finite world with which we are familiar, but because our thinking does not enter into any realm other than finite existence. We have no notion what it would be like to have intelligent awareness ranging beyond things in their limitations and interrelatedness as they present themselves. It is tempting, as many indeed have found it, to reject this kind of truck with an ultimate mystery altogether, and in an agnostic and empiricist age this is the line that most will take. They are not presumptuous enough to offer their own empiricist account of the bafflements noted earlier about beginning and range in time and space. They prefer rather to leave such matters alone or to treat them as pseudo problems which only the immature or uninitiated will waste time upon today. We shall make no progress, they assert; and in a way they are right for no plausible solution can ever present itself within the parameter of the way philosophical and the like exercise are pursued by us.

Yet the stark facts remain. The world around us and ourselves are certainly real enough, and they have their antecedents. Unraveling these further and further may continue with profit and worthwhile insights, but the question remains, uneliminated by any agnostic shrugging of shoulders or an air of superiority to such concerns, the question remains of whether there is any unavoidable stopping place, which it would indeed be hard to maintain, or the supposition that the world as we find it, the finite world, has been forever. I strongly maintain that being involved in this dilemma is not a state of mind to be cured by greater skill or familiarity with special techniques. The questions I have asked are not technical ones. They are matters of stark, simple puzzlement, genuine and unavoidable within the ways our thought normally proceeds. Those who raise them are not trifling with mysteries of their own contriving.

Indeed, some very notable thinkers down the ages have concerned themselves extensively with just the issue I have been raising, from Plato and his friends in ancient Greece to St. Augustine and his associates to Aquinas and on to Descartes and Spinoza and their contemporaries among empiricists and rationalists of their time to Kant and Hegel and post-Hegelian idealists right to our own time in the work of exceptionally fine writers of today, among whom I would give pride of place to the much underestimated C. A. Campbell.[2] It would, in my view, be a very advantageous thing for influential thinkers of today to set themselves carefully to consider what Plato may have meant by saying that The Good was "beyond being and knowledge." He certainly did not mean that it was an illusory unreality or a figment of the brain of carelessly speculative thinkers. For all these philosophers some ultimate beyond the proper grasp of our thought was the most supreme reality there is.

Quite possibly these much admired thinkers of the past were deluded in supposing they were dealing with a genuine problem of some supreme transcendent reality, as many things which held people's thought in the past, and some factors of which they had no doubt are quite exploded in the light of all we know today. People in the past have taken such matters as the alleged flatness of their earth with great seriousness and taken with great concern many possibilities which we must ascribe today to ignorant naivete. Could the question of the supposed grounding of all finite existences in an ultimate transcendent be the same, a genuine issue in the past but today a delusion to be easily dispelled?

It seems evident to me that this cannot be the case. Further information about finite facts and better understanding about their interrelationships has little relevance to the issue of the ultimate status of finite reality as a whole and the initiation and maintenance of it.

We stay then with the notion of some supreme reality related to the world we know in some way of which we have no understanding and itself a total mystery. This has been stressed in many contexts of thought or religious scriptures. In the Bible the *locus classicus* is the story of Moses at the burning bush. Moses wanted to have better information about God, to be told something more specific, in order to convince his fellow countrymen and Pharaoh and his fellow Egyptians that he really was on a mission from God to request the restoration of the freedom of his people. But nothing was given him beyond the assurance of God's existence.

In the same way, in many other places, the Bible, while giving varied accounts, some sharply out of character with the rest, persists in regarding the nature and functioning of God as in itself beyond our understanding. Our minds do not reach directly beyond finite existence, however intimate in other ways the relationship may be. A further intimation of the same caution is the restriction even on the use of the name itself, not mainly out of fear of presumptuous pride, but because the extension could mean nothing and was apt to deprive God of his essentially transcendent mystery. In seeking or seeming to reduce this mystery we are in serious danger of making God other than he is and no longer a proper object of worship.

The oneness of God is stressed in the same way. Any multiplicity of being would set us in a condition where the relation of one factor to another would require explanation in similar ways to finite existences, and raise the same problems over again. But thinking along these ways, the attitudes and procedures of some religions have been apt to culminate, in some faiths, in a notion of an all-inclusive oneness into which limited finite existences are absorbed. Everything becomes a feature of the ultimate one. The one whole of being becomes everything. The consequence of this is just to annul finite reality and, as in some forms of Buddhism at least, to dispense altogether with finite realities like ourselves—in fact there is only the One and our own fulfilment and destiny is to appreciate that. I will not write more here about what seem to me the calamitous consequences of holding such a view, notably in the way of indifference to avoidable evil and a passive acceptance of whatever fate seems to befall us.

It must suffice for the present to insist that the genuine reality of finite things around us, whether mind-dependent or fully objective as we normally assume, must not be imperiled. Metaphysics gives us no entitlement to question or thrust aside the genuine reality of finite existences, including especially ourselves. It is ourselves that, in the present sense, we know best. To think of ourselves as even distinctive modes or appearances of the one Whole, as much Hinduism and Western post-Hegelian idealism were apt to do (chiming in closely in this respect with one another), appears to me a very grave distortion. We must start our religious thinking with acceptance of what we clearly find to be the case, most of all about ourselves. We are not figments or shadows of some other being. We find ourselves at any particular time as real as anything can be. Whatever may be said about the multifarious factors that have brought us to ourselves as we are now, and however mistaken we may be about them or their like, we find ourselves to be the conscious creatures that we are now; and our immediate physical reality, the apprehended state of our bodies now, sitting as I am at this table now, we find this beyond any possible dispute, whatever further analysis may say of it, and the relegation of it to a mode of some quite different existent we find utterly unacceptable, not primarily because of the affront to our pride, but as out of accord with the brute fact[3] of our present awareness of ourselves now. I shall return to this major issue in a moment. All I wish to stress now is that our apprehension (very sound and significant as it certainly is) of the essential oneness of ultimate transcendent being gives no warrant whatsoever to the absorption of finite things, as we experience them, in ourselves or outside ourselves, into some radically different whole of being in which our identity as distinct finite creatures is lost. Nothing gives us a right to pretend like this with undisputable facts of experience, or call these latter into question.

Some of the most impressive and influential of modern Hindu thinkers have stressed this themselves, most notably Sri Aurobindo, and I may perhaps refer here to what I have said earlier about him,[4] with eloquent quotations from his work, such as his vigorous condemnation of the "will to annul life itself in an immobile reality or an original nonexistence."[5] As the distinctness and finality of personal identity is so important and central for us in further ways, it may be well to pause a little here and say more about this vital matter before we proceed.

II

It is remarkable how completely philosophers of today have rejected any form of Cartesian dualism. The name is perhaps not very fortunate in an age where "isms" are apt to be frowned upon, but it is not mainly a matter of the name. The notion of mental existence being radically different from bodily things and procedures is rejected outright from the start by most philosophers, and especially the more highly regarded and influential ones; it is rejected as one which recent thought has made entirely implausible. This appears to me to be largely a slavish following of fashion, and it seems to be altogether at odds with what all of us take for granted every moment of our lives.

Take my own experience now. I see the room around me, the walls, the furniture, the table at which I write, and the paper in front of me. If I raise my head I see trees in the garden and the familiar field beyond them. I may be mistaken about some of these things, but I cannot be mistaken about the nature of the sort of experience I am myself having and I find this, though related to the world around me and conditioned by it and especially by my own bodily state, altogether different in nature from any extended physical existence. It makes sense to ask how wide the table is, but there is no point in asking how wide or how long my seeing it is. The seeing is not itself extended, nor are my thoughts about what I see.

There is, admittedly, a bodily factor in my experiences, most patently perceptual ones. My eyes have to be open and directed the right way, and the retina of my eyes have to be stimulated in a way that is itself "relayed," as we put it, to my brain. All sorts of physical defects or failures may affect, or hinder altogether, the experience of seeing the room and proceeding with my writing, but these, and the like conditions, are not part of the experience of seeing. That ensues upon the affectation of the brain and is not itself extended or in any other way physical or physiological. It has, for instance, no shape or color. It is just an experience through which I pass, and I am aware of this simply by having this experience of which I can give no account beyond the content of it, seeing a table and writing paper, etc. I do not observe this experience as I observe things happening around me, and nobody else observes it or knows directly what it is like.

The outside observer may note the state of my body, and having no reason to question whether I am well and normal, he can readily conclude that I am seeing things around me as I have noted. He may even put this in the terms that he was watching and thereby seeing me all the time I was seeing the table, etc., but he was not strictly seeing my seeing. All he could see was my body and its posture and objects in front of me. If I deny that he was seeing me having the experience of seeing the table, etc., he will need very powerful evidence, such as that I had a sudden illness (a stroke perhaps) or some mysterious blindness. But a stricter account would be that he saw me looking. He did not see the seeing, that is just not the sort of thing which can be seen. I do not see it myself, nor does any other.

No one need deny, and few would attempt to do so, that we are constantly subject, in all our experience, or our mental existence and reactions, to physical or bodily conditions. I could do none of the things I have been doing during the past ten minutes if my body failed. At any moment I am bodily conditioned. That may not be so evident in some sorts of experience as in others, like seeing or hearing. I may be deep in some train of thought or some highly abstract exercise, and no one could easily tell what this is like without my telling him myself—and I may in fact be just pretending. I am the only one who directly knows what is happening to me, or what I do, in nonphysical ways at any time. The body conditions much of this, but that does not make it a bodily occurrence itself. This is the mistake of which many seem to be guilty at present. They take the constant dependence on the body to be tantamount to making the essential nonbodily functioning, which is my experience, itself bodily in some strange way.

My seeing, hearing, thinking, and all else that proceeds as my genuine mental life is a nonbodily process. I am essentially a nonbodily existent, and not only do I function mentally in ways radically different from bodily changes and extending well beyond anything that could be known from bodily circumstances, like my meditation in accordance with the nature of thought itself, but I am able, within familiar limits, to bring about some change (or cause something to happen) in my own body. There may be no objection in principle to mental efficacy at a distance, and telepathy, as the direct influence of one mind on another, is treated very seriously in parapsychology. But normally at least we function in the world through our own bodies.

Some of the things one can accomplish in this way are very limited. I could not, even to save my life, or that of another, leap more than a few feet, two or three at most by now, over an obstacle barring my way. Even a trained athlete could not manage more than three or four times that. With a burning forest behind one and closing in no one could leap fifty feet to safety across a chasm. But in other ways we can bring things about at vast distances. A friend could telephone me from Australia or South America and say that he was an assessor for an appointment for which a former pupil of mine was a candidate, and that he would like my opinion of the candidate. I may give a very favorable report and that could have a substantial influence on the ultimate decision. Suitably qualified and trained people could affect things in outer space in this way or, some day, in a distant planet in some other constellation. But this could only be done by bringing about some change in one's own body first, such as causing intelligible speech coming from my mouth or signs on paper.

This dependence on one's own body must not be taken to mean that we are just bodily creatures. The nature of thinking itself is usually decisive. Communication of this is usually, as are other exchanges of opinion, through bodily media but that itself involves the exercise of considerable, and sometimes difficult and ingenious, mental achievements.

That this functioning of continuous mental operations in ways that could not be learnt from the physical media of our bodies in themselves, in other words our genuine and distinctive mental existence, that this should be so largely questioned or fused in people's understanding of it, with bodily states themselves, appears to be a quite extraordinary feature of the attitudes of several people highly intelligent themselves and engaged primarily in distinctively intellectual activities. They belie all that they normally do.

A good example of this has been noted by me elsewhere;[6] it is in the work of the influential American philosopher John Searle. In his Reith Lectures at Oxford he said in one place that, "the characteristic experience that gives us the conviction of human freedom, and it is an experience from which we are unable to strip away the conviction of freedom, is the experience of engaging in voluntary, intentional human actions."[7] He adds that, "The experience of freedom, that is to say the experience of the sense of alternative possibilities, is built into the very structure of conscious, voluntary, intentional human behavior."[8] In amplification of this he also said:

> The cases of top-down causation only work because the mental events are grounded in the neurophysiology to start with,...like the rest of nature, its features are determined at the basic microlevels of physics.... Such a 'bottom-up' picture of the world allows for top-down causation (our minds, for example, can affect our bodies). But the top-down causation only works because the top level is already caused by and realised in the bottom level."[9]

I can make little of this, and I have been bold enough elsewhere[10] to describe it as eventually prevarication. There is a firm admission that our minds can affect our bodies, but this, it seems, is only possible because the working of our minds is already determined and realized in the bottom level. There seems to be no real scope for the mind to make a difference to what happens simply because of what it is in itself. The issue here is not that of ultimate absolute freedom. We do have that, but only, in my view, when we believe that we have a moral obligation to do something opposed to our desires as a whole—a "conflict of duty and interest," as it is often put. In such cases nothing decides what we do and what happens besides our own free choice. Searle does not draw this distinction and seems to think, as do many others today, that his own account of the influence of our minds covers all that comes to us as important freedom. But at this level, the one he takes seriously, his view presents serious difficulty, for we are bound to ask how can the alleged efficacy of our minds, and thereby their freedom in any sense be acknowledged when the course of our thoughts and wishes and all our experience and mental processes, is itself settled initially at the bottom level of physiology.

Behind many stances like those of Professor Searle lies the assumption that everything, in the last analysis, must be open to scientific explanation. But respect for science does not require us to bring everything under its sway. One is not bound to be out of touch with the thought of today if one questions whether an empiricist or scientific account can be given of consciousness. What matters most for us individually is the course of our own consciousness, our thoughts, feelings, wishes, and intentions, etc., but none of this is observable. While there are bound to be physiological and other physical conditions of these mental processes, they are not themselves states of our bodies, and they are, together with the like states of minds of other persons, what we essentially are as human beings. Each one knows his own experience in having it and communicates with others in a mediated way through observation of their bodies, sounds, sight etc., and the significance he has come to ascribe to physical states and performances as the reasonable explanation of them. The communication is mediated but is not itself the physiological mediation, and it is the source or essence of all we value, or regard with admiration, affection, love, etc., or their opposites.

The unique factor in all this is one's own individual consciousness, and it should always be a source of wonder to us that this distinctive awareness of each one enters into the rich and valuable communication of persons in society. We do not know any other mind expressly as one knows one's own. This could cause a sense of isolation in one's own existence but we acquire from birth the habit of the to and fro of communication. It is nonetheless a remarkable feature of our existence and is important not only as a fact of our being, with which we should be deeply impressed if we think reflectively about it, but a clue to much else in the total human situation which we do not directly experience but gives our existence its significance. In itself this is not a religious attainment, and what I have just been stressing could be accepted or agreed to by thinkers of no religious conviction. It is a matter of straight philosophical thinking, but it provides the key to much in our religious awareness as well, and without the distinctiveness of mental awareness in itself, there is little likelihood that religious thinking could get started at all. Of this we shall have to take further note shortly.

It might be thought that telepathy, if well established, and the like paranormal events, provide an exception here. But I do not think there is the slightest reason for regarding such occurrences, where established, as involving any immediate awareness of another mind such as we have of one's own. This possibility seems to me just unacceptable, and we may say this without any discredit to paranormal assumptions and study in themselves.

III

Many of those who would agree closely with what has been said in the earlier part of this paper would, nonetheless, be apt to draw very unsound conclusions from it. I have maintained that our inability to account for finite realities, and their interrelations, beyond their place in the consistent system of finite relations we in fact find to be the case, requires an ultimate ground or source of all there is, as we find it, which is essentially transcendent and thereby beyond the power of our understanding to know what it is like in itself or how it operates. From this it is assumed that we have no need to pay much regard to reason and to consistency with our ordinary insights in the world we in fact inhabit, and within which we function, when we attempt to say things more specific about God in whatever further or mediated way seems possible. Hence, a spate of random indulgences in sheer unreason; we are talking about a suprarational transcendent and can therefore, it is supposed, say what we like or cling to whatever ill-founded traditional or customary notions appeal to us or seem, by their customary usage as a rule, to have some credibility.

I have commented, sometimes in very severe criticism, on such procedures in earlier writings such as my *Morals and the New Theology* and *Morals and Revelation*. An intriguing example on which I commented in the earlier volume is that of Reinhold Niebuhr when he declared that there is no big sin or little sin because all we do is equally and essentially evil. We are fallen creatures and can therefore do nothing that is not essentially evil. There can be a more or less in the harm we do, some of our deeds being beneficial and in that regard commendable, but at the heart of things, in our inner purposing, all is equally evil. How such a friendly and agreeable person as Niebuhr could say this always puzzled me. It shows, I think, how far a thoroughly misleading commitment could take us. On Niebuhr's view the actions of Mother Teresa in getting abandoned and dying people off their bit of a street to the comfort and attention and companionship of her own hospice, or the decision of Father Damien to stay to minister to and help those hopelessly ill in a leper colony where he could be virtually certain, as happened, of succumbing to the vile infliction himself—all this is as vicious in itself as the cruelties and terror inflicted by the minions of Hitler or Goering on helpless prisoners thrown to their mercy, if that is the word, in appalling concentration camps. We may admit that Mother Teresa has latterly reaped some personal advantage in the way at least of known and public esteem, but few could anticipate this and the supposition that she went to work with anything approaching such a personal gain in mind is to fly in the face of what ordinary reasonable thinkers would believe. However we may wish to stretch the limits or our consideration, we are living here in a world of ridiculous fantasy altogether at odds with our normal reactions.

I shall not pursue this further, having said enough about it already.[11] But it is important to make it as clear as possible, from the start, that we have a peculiarly difficult and vital issue on our hands, in any thought about religion today, namely how can we with our essentially finite understanding, find the validation and appropriate selectiveness of the bolder and more precise things we say about God and his relations to ourselves and our world. Until we face up to this question and find some truly convincing answer to it, the drift away from religion, most of all among enlightened and intellectual people, will continue, perhaps intensifying to the virtual elimination of religion except where it persists as a part of ancient history or a sentimental adherence to earlier stages of their lives among the elderly in the ranks of the faithful.

Eloquent articulation of articles of faith will not arrest this. The decline is already far advanced, and there is no lasting escape in the frequency of the reaffirmation of the faith in this or that respect, however endearing to those who have seen different days. The vital issues must be faced, and platitudinous affirmations of ancient dogmas will not achieve this. The vindication must be there, too. That is vital if we are to retain respect and credibility. If the central question is ignored or covered up in obscurity, nothing else will serve or survive.

Nor is there any easement of this dilemma by more expert or intensified rational activity. The issue is not the inadequacy or incompleteness of reasoning procedures as such but that we are dealing initially with a transcendent and thus suprarational existent. This can only be met by finding the appropriate justification for what can be ascribed to God, or treated as what he says or his procedures, beyond the requirement that he should *be* as a reality beyond the domain of our understanding.

Some have spoken of the God of the heart distinct from a God of the mind, but there can be no God of the heart which is not initially a God of the mind in the senses indicated earlier. A mere God of the heart is no God but the object of idolatrous worship to be altogether avoided. The issue remains of how we can speak of a transcendent God in relation to ourselves and the world around us. This is a peculiarly difficult question, and there can be no more vital question for our time than this.

IV

I add now some further observations on the questions I have just noted and which I regard as the crucial question today as in the past, for religious people and for all who are concerned about religion whatever their own commitment may be. It is the question how we may vindicate, or render reasonably plausible, anything we specifically ascribe to God, or claim as his distinct affirmation, beyond the initial assurance that a transcendent being who is the source and ground of our own existence, or who bestowed on us in some way our existence, cannot himself be thought to fall at any point below the sensitivity and insight, in ethical matters especially, which we have acquired ourselves and observe at our best. This is not a new, or even an exclusively Jewish or Christian conviction. Plato was very insistent that we must never speak of God as anything but the author of good and never of evil.[12] He was thinking primarily of the influence on the young of what they are taught about God. He was not thinking mainly of worship but of education, stressing especially how impressionable the young are in all such respects and apt to imitate what is presented to them as the highest and finest. Nonetheless, it is not implausible to think that the author of beings with our power of appreciation and sense of worth should himself never fail in any such respect. It is not difficult to agree with Plato that God must be always the author of good and never of evil.

Can we then get no further than the general affirmation of the inherent goodness of God as God? Many suppose that we are restricted here to two choices. First, we may take it that wherever there is an ascription to God in religious practice or scriptures, this must always be given full credit as a communication from God and carry that authority—it is 'the Word' of God. Alternatively, we may say that there never is an authenticated communication of that kind, never an unambiguous 'Word of God'—all that purports to be so is a fabrication, not always perhaps recognized by the agent himself to be so, designed to give the insights or convictions of the prophet or the like agent a special importance or appeal, to present more vividly what might otherwise seem more mundane and require support beyond its inherent impressiveness.

But we are not restricted in these ways. There is much in religious practice and ordinances and in distinctive religious scriptures, which seems to reflect, or be a response to, an explicit direction or intimation from God himself, but which we would not dream nowadays of seriously ascribing to God in that way—it is often entirely out of character for God as we have come to think of him in an enlightened context. In the book of Joshua, for example, there are many references to battles which the Israelites had to fight to secure for themselves the Promised Land in which they hoped to settle as their special domain, and we read there also of the part which God played in their attainment of this end. In the celebrated chapter, he is described as himself hurtling a shower of stones,[13] like hail, after the retreating enemy to cut short their escape and chance to reassemble again as a formidable force. On another occasion the day is ending before the pursuit and slaughter is complete and God miraculously lengthens the day and holds back the setting of the sun[14] to provide time before the enveloping dark made it difficult or insecure to continue with the pursuit to its eliminating end.[15]

How far this was ever meant as genuine history is hard to tell. Some scholars go out of their way to remind us that the Bible is not, and was never intended to be, a historical book. It seems that many have got into the way of taking it so and without discrimination of giving a historical significance to all that we read about God there. It seems that there is much, besides the disturbing passages of which I have made special mention, which we must reject outright as intimations to us of the mind of God.

We seem, therefore, bound to conclude that there is no strict a priori rule, in scriptures or religious practice, by which we can specifically say about God that certain things which are expressly said to be his own utterances, give us a precise insight into what we must say about him beyond anything that directly follows from his being God. If there is divine utterance or revelation, we have to discover what is the proper ground for saying that.

Some parts of the Bible seem to be better qualified than others to serve this purpose. The splendid chapter 58 of Isaiah would be one. The first verse gives us God's instructions to the prophet to "spare not" and to "cry aloud." Then there follows the body of what he is to cry. He is to warn the people of the perils of a false affectation of religion.

> Is not this the fast I have chosen?, to loose the bans of wickedness, to undo the heavy burdens, and to let the oppressed go free and that ye break every yoke? Is it not to deal thy bread to the hungry, and that thou bring the poor that are cast out to thy house? when thou seest the naked that thou cover him; and that thou hide not thyself from thine own flesh?... Then shalt thou call; and the Lord shall answer; thou shalt cry, and he shall say, Here I am.... And they that shall be of thee shall build the old waste places, thou shalt raise up the foundations of many generations; and thou shalt be called, The repairer of the breach, The restorer of paths to dwell in.

It is God who speaks in these words and the rest of the chapter, which I have not quoted, it is his message to the prophet telling him what he is to say, and we have no difficulty here in respect of the appropriateness of the ascription of all that is said in these remarkable words to God. The difficulty which some may still feel, however, is to find what it is in such an exhortation, beyond a custom and familiar habit, which induces us to say, "This cannot be the words of man but must come from God and is a superb example of God's intervention in our world." Could it not all be the perception and insight of a highly gifted and deeply concerned person? Why must we say of this and the like passages that they take us beyond inspired moral insight and must be regarded as expressly the intervention of God in the lives of people?

I do not think we can say this if the passages are taken in themselves. Our clue must be found in the way we communicate with one another and come to know other persons. I have already insisted, as a central theme in connection with many related matters, that the knowledge we have of other persons, and of their attitudes and purposes, never has the immediacy and initially unquestionable certainty that we have of our own experiences and of ourselves as the persons having them. This does not mean that we may not give misleading accounts of ourselves, deliberately or without any intention to mislead. We may use words that turn out to be misleading, and we may in retrospect or later reflections about ourselves, often affected by the views we like to have of ourselves, have a very false impression of ourselves and convey this to others, sometimes with highest intentions of presenting what is strictly true. We may not always be the best interpreters of our own states and purposes. Nevertheless, it does seem inherently impossible to have any experience without knowing at the time what it is and that we ourselves are having it. It is our experience at the time, whether we reflect on the fact or not.

This does not preclude our having the most intimate and lively relations with one another or, as we are apt to put it, sharing one another's experiences. However close the latter may be and however important a feature of our lives together and as members of society, the mediated character of even our very close and continuous relationships is an abiding factor. We never have the experiences of others, in any respect, as we have our own. However I may grieve over the misfortune of a friend or relative, or "share" his pain or dismay, so that I may be disposed to say with more credibility than that of the legendary schoolmaster, that it hurts me more, yet I never have the grief or pain as it is for my friend. I may learn of it and in that way share the grief or hurt, but I do not have myself the pain which my friend or close relative has. That is something which he "lives through" in the terms made familiar some time ago by a celebrated philosopher.[16]

Admittedly, our lives would be very different and lacking in most that enriches them now if we did not share our lives in the sense already admitted. A completely solitary existence from the start, by whatever means we survived, is almost impossible to envisage. But with all the allowances we have to make in this respect, the fact remains, with all the complexities it may bring in the way of service or of malignant purpose, that no one strictly has any experience other than his own. In this respect we are essentially solitary beings and there is much importance in some ways in bringing this out. Some very notable modern writers have so brought this out, sometimes very movingly.[17] It is not always perverse to assign importance to solitude, and in some situations it may be important to instruct and educate people about this and about the pitfalls of living too extensively in a private world of our own or, as it may also be put, in a silent inner world. Solitude is a feature of existence with which we must learn to cope without excessive indulgence.

There is much further that may be said on this theme, as perceptive thinkers have learnt to appreciate better today, but I do not wish to pursue the theme further on its own account here. The point at the moment is that we must not expect essential features of our finite existence to be left out of account when we turn our minds to religious matters. The most persistent offender here, in present day thinking especially, is the kind of monism to which I have already referred, namely the view that all we take to be limited finite existence is some mode, or in some other way an ingredient, in the being of God. The problem which is the central concern of this paper and which I have ventured to describe as the major issue for our time, is easily settled, for if we are modes of the being of God, then all our experience is *ipso facto* the experience of God. All experience is God's experience, and there is no question how it is communicated to us. In having any thought we have the thought of God.

This is very like "the short way" in regard to the problem of evil. How does a good God, a being essentially of love and care, allow so much terrible evil in the world, whether it be the so-called natural or nonmoral evil, like acute suffering or the moral evil of properly vicious conduct. An almighty God could eliminate it all. In reply to this it is sometimes said that all is the work of one universal mind, which directs itself altogether to good, and where there seems to be grave evil, this is just the way some things appear when seen out of their full context in the comprehensive will and experience of God. The problem of evil vanishes because where God is all in all there can be no evil. This view is found in both Eastern and Western thought, especially in the West in work like that of famous idealists. It is hard to see how this is possible when so many of the philosophical idealists were themselves persons of great ethical integrity and concern. Bradley might invoke as well his doctrine of the suprarational character of ultimate being, but while this is not without its place here, it is hard to see how one who was so concerned to stress the genuine moral responsibility of a person for actions which are truly *his own* in Bradley's own phrase in the famous chapter one of *Ethical Studies*, how such a person could regard all reality, including our own conduct, as an appearance of the one all-inclusive reality of God.

I do not think therefore that we can look for a genuine easement of the problem of divine communication and its warrant in the repudiation of our own distinctness and patent existence as genuinely finite beings. We have still to ask what is the basis and justification of our ascription of certain affirmations to God and our confidence in his constant communication to us and what we even boldly describe as his presence? Where does the word of man stop and the word of God begin?

This is where we must heed very carefully the warning not to seek the answer in close analysis and consideration of impressive seeming individual cases. We must rather take our cue from our essentially mediated knowledge of one another. For, in relation to God also, there are occasions when the firm and profound awareness of the inevitable being of God is closely associated with evaluations and requirements of basic importance in our lives here and now. This blend of religious awareness with other insights may form distinctive patterns similar to those by which we recognize and understand one another, and we come to appreciate in due course, and with deepening certainty, what are the things which, though fully capable of being understood in finite terms, are underlined as the communications of God's greatest concern about our own attitudes and conduct. In religious awareness we have, thus, no need to suppose that we are lifted to some entirely new realm or become familiar with some exceptional matters which are normally beyond our ken. The novelty and impressiveness comes, not in the content of what we learn in itself, novel and remarkable though that may be at its own level of finite understanding, but in the intrusion of God into human experience to specify his especial concern about what we are and do. It is not an inspired grasp of matters beyond normal apprehension altogether that the prophet gains but a deepening sense of the place and relevance of some insights and perceptions in the wholeness of our total and sustained relationship with God.

This is itself made evident in some of the most impressive parts of the Bible and other scriptures. The chapter I have quoted a little earlier from Isaiah is a good example, and it leads the way to the moving pronouncements of Jesus in the beatitudes where we learn that, "Blessed are the pure in heart for they shall see God." It is not some peculiar visionary insights that are promised here but just the sort of refinement which the pure in heart attain and represent in their own commitment and awareness of the God, that is as much beyond their understanding as ours, being involved in a fully encompassing way in all that the integrity and selflessness that a pure heart implies. Piety and deep devotion and humble association together, without pretentious exhibition and with prayerful regard to the developing understanding of God in the scriptures, is the way to the reward promised to the "pure in heart." It is not a facile simplicity but a frame of mind which may be as evident in high attainment as in the simplest obedience. It is the last thing that should be mimicked. It is a way of life for all.

V

I must stress here again the point that has been made earlier, and which is implicit in much that I have said throughout, namely that identity in the case of conscious beings is radically different from identity as we think of it and find it in various entities in the external world, this cup, this table, this room, this house, this village, etc. The latter depend largely on location and various attributes discovered and ascribed to particular entities. The first sort of identity is found in one's own ascription of experiences and attributes, purposing oneself as the distinct ultimate being one finds oneself to be, and which cannot be identified further by locations or any further description. I find myself to be the being that I am and ascribe anything further that may be said of me to this one nonobservable being that I am and which you learn about in a more mediated way by which you also ascribe such experiences or reactions to me. The failure to observe this radical distinction between the two sorts of identity has been a source of much confusion in philosophy over the years and at no time more than today when the centrality of the notion of identity for many major issues in philosophy has been well and extensively recognized and the meaning of the term itself made the subject of frequent contributions to major journals, often by distinguished writers.

It has been unfortunate that, along with the recognition of the importance and decisiveness of the notion of identity in recent years has gone the general inclination of philosophical thought towards some kind of empiricism and the assumption that all genuine reality must be of one kind. This accounts for the persistence of attempts to bring mental existences within some framework of special relationships such as those to which we ascribe external events when we identify them or place them in our mode of understanding.

The views which I have outlined are sharply at variance with central themes of some nonChristian religions, especially some vital forms of Buddhism deriving from early Buddhist writings which are extensively taken to bring us as near the teaching and thought of Buddha himself as we are ever likely to get. The continuity which is involved in such doctrines of rebirth or of life eternal is not that of some subject or like reality which itself remains the same through varied states or modes of experience. It depends, rather, on interrelationships which establish one kind of continuity. In presenting this, very clearly and effectively, in his book *Rationality and Mind in Early Buddhism*[18] Professor Frank Hoffman uses the observation of Wittgenstein that, "the strength of a cord does not always depend on there being a single strand which runs from end to end, but sometimes depends on the inter-relationship between over-lapping and criss-crossing fibres,"[19] none of which runs the entire length of the cord. This is an intriguing view of personal continuity, and many are attracted to it. But it does not do any justice to the distinctiveness of our individual awareness of a particular experience or doing being one's own which is sometimes said to be *sui generis*.[20] This is the continuation of what Professor Roderick Chisholm has called "being me," and it is this that persons concerned about personal continuity have in mind, however difficult it may prove to give an adequate or independent account of the awareness in question, familiar and evident to all at the time though it may be.

It is the patterning of the sense of the being of God, beyond our understanding though this may be, in the consciousness of individual centers or subjects of consciousness, that becomes distinctive in a way like our unquestioned general understanding of one another, and this becomes in due course the core of our knowledge of God in more specific ways as his own intrusion or involvement in our lives which does not require us to have freakish or mysterious insight or vision of something quite outside the normal range of the life of most of us. It is in this vein also that we should talk about "the Person of Christ" and the special role we ascribe to him in our own relationship to God. He is also distinctive in a way that can be understood, not only by mystics or others who have experiences radically different from the rest of us, but by all who are prepared to make the effort and observe the demanding conditions set out for it. This is the point where the philosopher must hand over to the theologian, and I shall not say more about it now.

NOTES

1. D. W. Hamlyn, for example. See *In Defense of Free Will* (London: Allen & Unwin, 1967).

2. C. A. Campbell's main books are *In Defence of Free Will* (London: Allen & Unwin, 1967), and *Selfhood and Godhood* (London: Allen & Unwin; New York: Macmillan, 1957). His first book, *Scepticism and Construction* (London: Allen & Unwin) was also a remarkable one.

3. Of "brute facts" in knowledge and perception much may be found in the work of H. A. Prichard and his mentor Cook Wilson. See the posthumously published collection of Cook Wilson's papers, *Statement and Inference*, vol. 2, (Oxford: The Clarendon Press, 1926), for his famous article "Rational Grounds of Belief in God."

4. In my *World Religions*, jointly with R. L. Slater, (London: Watts, 1966, and Penguin), chap. IX.

5. Sri Aurobindo, *The Life Divine* (New York: The S. A. Library, 1949), 374.

6. In my article "Immortality," in *The Review Expositor* (Fall 1985): 549–562.

7. John Searle, *Minds, Brains and Science* (Cambridge: Harvard University Press, 1984), 95.

8. Searle, 98.

9. Searle, 93–94.

10. In my article "Immortality," (see fn. 6), 7.

11. See my *Morals and the New Theology* (London: V. Gollancz; New York: Harper, 1947), chap. V, on the notion of 'Universal Sin'.

12. See *Republic* Book 2, 379–383.

13. Josuah, chap. 10, verse 11.

14. Josuah, chap. 10, verse 13.

15. It was common practice in early societies to eliminate their enemies in this way after a success in battle. This is reflected in a line of his *Ymadawiad Arthur* [*Morte d'Arthur*] by Professor T. Gwynn Jones who has Bedwyr (Sir Bedever in English literature), not knowing how severely Arthur is wounded, saying, a little distraught, how hard it is that Arthur himself is not leading the chase: "Neud, tost nad erlynnit ti."

16. Samuel Alexander, *Space, Time, and Deity* (London: Macmillan, 1920), 11.

17. See, for example, an extraordinary book in style and substance by Patrick Leigh Fermor, *Time to Keep Silence* (London: F. Murray, 1982).

18. Frank Hoffman, *Rationality and Mind in Early Buddhism* (Delhi: Mortilal Banarsidass, 1984), chapter 4 especially.

19. Hoffman, 51. The reference is to *Philosophical Investigations*.

20. For example by Professor H. P. Rickman in his excellent article "Exorcising the Ghost of the Machine," *Philosophy* (Oct. 1988). Professor Rickman presents the case for dualism with extraordinary care and a caution not to overstep the mark and say more than is warranted and necessary. I very warmly commend his article to all who are interested in this issue, whatever side they take.

Contributors

Paul A. Bogaard participated in Ivor Leclerc's graduate seminars at Emory University during the late 1960s. Many of the topics in Leclerc's *The Nature of Physical Existence* and *The Philosophy of Nature* were presented for discussion in these seminars. His own papers have appeared in *Isis*, *Studies in the History and Philosophy of Science*, and publications of the Philosophy of Science Association. In addition to co-editing this volume, he has edited and authored the Introductory essay for *Profiles of Science and Society in the Maritimes before 1914* (1990). He has served as Department Head, Associate Dean of Faculty, and is currently Professor of Philosophy at Mount Allison University in Sackville, New Brunswick.

W. Norris Clarke, S.J., is Professor of Philosophy at Fordham University. He holds advanced degrees from Fordham, the Catholic University of Leuvin, and an honorary degree from Villanova. He has authored many papers, and his books include *New Themes in Christian Philosophy* (1968), *The Idea of God* (1969), *God, Knowable and Unknowable* (1973), and *The Philosophical Approach to God* (1980). He has been President of the Metaphysical Society of America, and the Americal Catholic Philosophical Association.

Jude P. Dougherty is Professor and Dean in the School of Philosophy, the Catholic University of America. He has published many papers and authored *Recent American Naturalism* (1960), co-authored *Approaches to Morality* (1966), and edited *The Good Life and its Pursuit* (1985), amongst others. He has been the general Editor for *The Review of Metaphysics* since 1971 and *Studies in Philosophy and the History of Philosophy* since 1978. He has been President of the American Catholic Philosophical Association, the Society for Philosophy of Religion, and the Metaphysical Society of America.

Joseph E. Earley is Professor of Chemistry at Georgetown University, Washington, DC. He has authored many papers on chemical kinetics and inorganic chemistry, and several on process philosophy. He was editor of *Individuality and Cooperative Action* (1991). He was chairman of the Georgetown University chemistry department (1984-1990).

Lewis S. Ford attended Nathaniel Lawrence's Yale graduate seminar which Ivor Leclerc also visited in 1957-58. *Whitehead's Metaphysics* had not been published, but it was made available in typescript. He has published numerous articles in such journals as *The Journal of Religion, The Modern Schoolman, International Philosophical Quarterly, The Review of Metaphysics.* He is the founding editor of *Process Studies,* now in its twentieth volume. He edited *Two Process Philosophers* and (with George L. Kline) *Explorations in Whitehead's Philosophy.* He has written *The Lure of God: A Biblical Background for Process Theism* (1978) and *The Emergence of Whitehead's Metaphysics* (1984), using the method of compositional analysis on the text of *Process and Reality.* He has taught at Raymond College (the University of the Pacific), Pennsylvania State University, and is currently Professor of Philosophy at Old Dominion University, Norfolk, Virginia.

Errol E. Harris is John Evans Professor of Moral and Intellectual Philosophy (Emeritus) of Northwestern University and has held teaching appointments at several institutions in South Africa, Britain, and America. He was Roy Roberts Distinguished Professor of Philosophy in the University of Kansas (1962-1966), Cowling Professor at Carlton College (1977), and Distinguished Professor of Christian Philosophy at Villanova University (1982). He delivered the Terry Lectures at Yale University in 1957, the Werner Lectures at Clark University, the Machette Lectures at Tulane University, and the Gilbert Ryle Lectures at Trent University. He has published a large number of books and articles, the best known of which are *Nature, Mind and Modern Science* (1954), *Hypothesis and Perception* (1970), *Salvation from Despair* (1973), *Formal Transcendental and Dialectical Thinking* (1987), *An Interpretation of the Logic of Hegel* (1983), *The Reality of Time* (1988), and *Cosmos and Anthropos, A Philosophical Interpretation of the Anthropic Cosmological Principle* (1991).

Charles Hartshorne is Emeritus Ashbel Smith Professor of Philosophy at the University of Texas in Austin. Educated at Haverford and Harvard, with post-doctoral studies in Europe, he has taught at five universities in the United States, including the University of Chicago (27 years) and the University of Texas (25 years), and five abroad in Germany, Australia, Japan (twice), India, and Belgium. At Emory University in Atlanta (7 years), he taught, besides philosophy, an adult education course on songbirds, on which he has written a book (to be reissued in 1992). He has written all, or substantial parts, of more than 20 philosophical books and more than 400 essays in periodicals, *Festschriften,* or symposia on philosophical or theological topics, and 16 on ornithological ones. With Paul Weiss he edited six of the eight volumes of *The Collected (Philosophical) Papers of Charles S. Peirce* (1931-35).

George L. Kline is Milton C. Nahm Professor Emeritus of Philosophy at Bryn Mawr College, Pennsylvannia. He edited and contributed the introduction to *Alfred North Whitehead: Essays on his Philosophy* (1963, and

1989), with Lewis S. Ford he co-edited and contributed a chapter ("Form, Concrescence, and Concretum") to *Explorations in Whitehead's Philosophy* (1983). His "Concept and Concrescence: An Essay in Hegelian-Whiteheadian Ontology" appeared in *Hegel and Whitehead: Contemporary Perspectives on Systematic Philosophy*, ed. George R. Lucas, Jr., (1986).

Hywel D. Lewis, after studies at the University College of North Wales, Bangor, and Oxford, returned to a lectureship in Bangor. While there he published six books in Welsh, plus *Morals and the New Theology* (1947) and *Morals and Revelation* (1951). In 1955 he was appointed to the Chair of History and Philosophy of Religion, King's College, University of London. Among his many later works are *Our Experience of God* (1959) and *The Elusive Self* (Vol. I, 1969, and Vol. II, 1982). He was the founding Editor of *Religious Studies*, President of the The Mind Association, the Aristotelian Society, The Society for the Study of Theology, and the International Society of Metaphysics. At the time of his death, he held honorary degrees from St. Andrews and Emory, and had given the Gifford Lectures (St. Andrews), the Wilde Lectures (Oxford), and at least ten other named lectures in Britain, Canada, India and the United States.

Hugo A. Meynell took his B.A. and Ph.D. degrees at Cambridge University, and lectured for eighteen years in the Philosophy and the Theology and Religious Studies Departments in the University of Leeds. He is the author of ten published books, including *Freud, Marx and Morals* (1981), *The Intelligible Universe* (1982), *An Introduction to the Philosophy of Bernard Lonergan* (1986), *The Nature of Aesthetic Value* (1986), and *The Art of Handel's Operas* (1986). Since 1981 he has been teaching in the Religious Studies Department at the University of Calgary.

Edward Pols has advanced degrees from Harvard, and has taught at Harvard, Princeton, and Bowdoin College. He was most recently Kennan Professor of Humanities at Bowdoin. His many publications include *The Recognition of Reason* (1963), *Whitehead's Metaphysics: A Critical Examination of Process and Reality* (1967), *Meditation on a Prisoner: Towards Understanding Action and Mind* (1975), and *The Acts of our Being: A Reflection on Agency and Responsibility* (1982). He has been President of the Metaphysical Society of America.

Ilya Prigogine is Director of the International Institute of Physics and Chemistry at Brussels, Ashbel Smith Professor, and Director of the Ilya Prigogine Center for Studies in Statistical Mechanics, Thermodynamics and Complex Systems at the University of Texas at Austin. He holds the Nobel Prize for Chemistry, 1977, many other prizes, medals, and more than 20 honorary degrees. In 1989 he was created a Vicomte by His Majesty the King of

Belgium. Of the 16 monographs he has authored, and co-authored, at least half appear in several translations. His *La Nouvelle Alliance, Les Metemorphoses de la Science* with I. Stengers (1979) has appeared in at least sixteen languages, *From Being to Becoming: Time and Complexity in the Physical Sciences* (1980) in eight, and most recently with G. Nicholis, *Exploring Complexity* (1989) in six languages.

Friedrich Rapp is Professor of Philosophy at the University of Dortmund. He studied Physics and Mathematics at the Polytechnic Institute Darmstadt (Germany) (M.A.) and Philosophy at the University of Fribourg/Switzerland (Ph.D.). In 1976 he was named Professor of Philosophy at the Polytechnic University of Berlin and since 1985 has been at the University of Dortmund. His publications include: *Analytical Philosophy of Technology* (German, 1978, Spanish, 1981, Chinese, 1986), *Fortschritt: Entwicklung und Sinngehalt einer philosophischen Idee* (1992), co-editor with H.-W. Schütt of *Contributions to a Philosophy of Technology* (1974), *Naturverständnis und Naturbeherrschung* (1981), *Philosophy and Technology* (1983, with P. Durbin), *Whitehead's Metaphysics of Creativity* (English, 1990, with R. Wiehl).

Albert Shalom was, at the time of his death, Professor Emeritus of McMaster University. His first degrees were obtained at the University of Cape Town, South Africa. On leaving South Africa, he was a research fellow at the Centre National de la Recherche Scientifique (CNRS), in Paris, visiting professor in the U.S., and then professor at McMaster University in Canada. He was a corresponding member of l'Institut de France (section: Académie des sciences morales et politiques). He was the author of *R. G. Collingwood: philosophe et historien* (1967) and of *The Body/Mind Conceptual Framework and the Problem of Personal Identity* (1985; 2nd printing in 1989 included a Preface by Ivor Leclerc). He was also the author of some twenty articles—mainly on time, the person and conceptualization—the more recent of which are in *The Review of Metaphysics*, in the Polish journal *Dialectics & Humanism*, in a recent volume of J. T. Fraser's series *The Study of Time*, and in the 1991 issue of *La Revue de Métaphysique et de Morale*. He was a member of the International Society of America, of the International Society for the Study of Time, and of the Canadian Philosophical Association.

Donald W. Sherburne, Professor of Philosophy and Chair of the Department at Vanderbilt University, holds advanced degrees from Oxford and Yale Universities. Author of *A Whiteheadian Aesthetic* (1961) and *A Key to Whitehead's PROCESS AND REALITY* (1966), he was co-editor (with David Ray Griffin) of the Corrected Edition of Whitehead's *Process and Reality* (1978). He served as Editor of the interdisciplinary journal, *Sound-*

ings, from 1980 to 1985 and as President of the Southern Society for Philosophy and Psychology.

Gordon Treash studied under Ivor Leclerc at Emory University and has been a member of the Department of Philosophy at Mount Allison University in Sackville, New Brunswick, Canada since 1966. His publications include: a translation from German into English and introduction to Kant's *The One Possible Argument for a Demonstration of the Existence of God* (1979), a set of excerpts of work by Adolph Friedrich Hoffmann and Christian August Crusius, which along with a closely related and hitherto untranslated essay of Kant's will appear under the title of *Logic and Metaphysics: Hoffmann, Crusius, Kant*. He was responsible for extensive editorial work on the translation of Kant's late essay, *What Progress Has Metaphysics Made in Germany Since the Days of Leibniz and Wolff* (1983). He also translated the majority of essays in the study, *Whitehead's Metaphysics of Creativity* (1990), into English. A participant in the Fifth, Six and Seventh International Kant Congresses, his papers appear in the *Proceedings* of those meetings.

Jan Van der Veken is Professor of Philosophy at the Institute of Philosophy, Catholic University of Leuven (Belgium). He wrote a doctoral dissertation on *The Absolute in the Philosophy of Marice Merleau-Ponty*. He has published extensively on process thought in Dutch, and is the chairman of the European Society for Process Thought. At Leuven, he is the Director of the Center for Metaphysics and Philosophy of God. He also has published in the area of phenomenology and religious language.

Reiner Wiehl is Professor of Philosophy at the University of Heidelberg. His philosophic interests include: philosophical psychology, hermeneutics and ontology. Amongst his publications are a translation, introduction and commentary on Plato's *Sophist* (1967), an introduction to Whitehead's philosophy in the German translation of *Adventures of Ideas* (1971), *Die Vernunft in der menschlichen Unvernunft. Das Problem der Rationalität in Spinozas Affektenlehre* [Reason in Human Irrationality. The Problem of Spinoza's Doctrine of Affects]) (1983), and papers on philosophical psychology and action theory.

A Bibliography of the Published Work of Ivor Leclerc

BOOKS

Whitehead's Metaphysics. London: Allen & Unwin; New York: Macmillan Co., 1958. 2nd edition, New York: Humanities Press, 1965. Paperback edition: Indiana University Press, 1965. 2nd Paperback edition: Lanham, MD.: University of America Press, 1986.

The Nature of Physical Existence. London: Allen & Unwin, in the Muirhead Library of Philosophy; New York: Humanities Press, 1972. Paperback edition: Lanham, MD.: University of American Press, 1986.

The Philosophy of Nature. Washington, D.C.: Catholic University of America Press, 1986.

Whitehead's Philosophy—Between Rationalism and Empiricism. Institute of Philosophy, Katholieke Universiteit Leuven, 1984.

Editor:

The Relevance of Whitehead. Philosophical Essays Commemorating the Centenary of the Birth of Alfred North Whitehead. London: Allen & Unwin; in the Muirhead Library of Philosophy; New York: Humanities Press, 1961.

The Philosophy of Leibniz and the Modern World. Nashville: Vanderbilt University Press, 1973.

Co-translator (with Eva Schaper):

An Introduction to General Metaphysics. Translation, *Einleitung in die Allgemeine Metaphysik*, by Gottfried Martin. London: Allen & Unwin; New York: Humanities Press, 1961.

ARTICLES IN BOOKS

"Form and Actuality." In *The Relevance of Whitehead*, ed. Ivor Leclerc, 169–189. London: Allen & Unwin; New York: Humanities Press, 1961.

"Whitehead and the Problem of Extension." In *Alfred North Whitehead: Essays in his Philosophy*, ed. G.L. Kline, 117–123. New York: Prentice-Hall, 1963.

"Whitehead and the Theory of Form." In *Process and Divinity*, ed. W.L. Reese and E. Freeman, 127–137. Lasalle: Open Court Publishing Co., 1964.

"Leibniz and the Analysis of Matter and Motion." In *The Philosophy of Leibniz and the Modern World*, ed. Ivor Leclerc, 114–132. Nashville: Vanderbilt University Press, 1973.

"The Meaning of 'Space' in Kant." In *Kant's Theory of Knowledge*, ed. Lewis White Beck, 87–94. Dordrecht/Holland: D. Reidel Publishing Company, 1974.

"Some Main Philosophical Problems involved in Contemporary Scientific Thought." In *Mind in Nature*, ed. John B. Cobb and D. R. Griffin, 101–108. Washington, D.C.: University Press of America.

"Concepts in Space." In *Probability, Time and Space in the Eighteenth Century*, ed. Paula R. Backscheider, 53–67. New York: Fordham University Press, 1983.

"Über die Notwendigkeit, zur Philosophie der Natur zurückzukehren." In *Whitehead: Einführung in seine Kosmologie*, ed. Ernst Wolf-Gazo, 105–123. Freiburg/Munich: Verlag Karl Alber, 1980.

"Being and Becoming in Whitehead's Philosophy." In *Explorations in Whitehead's Philosophy*, ed. Lewis S. Ford and George L. Kline, 53–67. New York: Fordham University Press, 1983.

"Process and Order in Nature." In *Whitehead and the Idea of Process*, First International Whitehead Symposium, 1981, ed. Harald Holz and Ernst Wolf-Gazo, 119–136. Munich: Karl Alber Verlag, 1984.

"The Metaphysics of the Good." In *The Good Life and Its Pursuits*, ed. Jude P. Dougherty, 51–71. Washington, D.C.: Paragon House Publishers, 1984.

"Time and Physical Existence." In *Nature, Time and History*, ed. B. P. Schurer and Guy Debrock, 1–11. Nijmegen: Faculty of Science of the Catholic University of Nijmegen, 1985.

"God and the Issue of Being." In *Religious Studies*, Vol. 20, Special Issue for H. D. Lewis, 63–79. Cambridge: University Press, 1984.

"The Metaphysical Quest and the History of Philosophy." In *Philosophers on Their Own Work*, ed. André Mercier and Maja Svilar, 171–183. New York: Peter Lang, Bern/Frankfurt am Main, 1985.

"Foreword" to the *The Body/Mind Conceptual Framework and The Problem of Personal Identity*. By Albert Shalom, IX–XII. Atlantic Highlands, N.J.: Humanities Press International, Inc., 1985.

"Whitehead and the Problem of Knowledge of Nature." In *Hegel and Whitehead*, ed. George F. Lucas, 167–185. Albany: State University of New York Press, 1986.

"Whitehead and the Dichotomy of Rationalism and Empiricism." In *Whiteheads Metaphysik der Kreativität*, Second International Whitehead Symposium, ed. Friedrich Rapp and Reiner Wiehl, 13–31. Munich: Karl Alber Verlag, 1987. *Whitehead's Metaphysics of Creativity*, Albany: State University of New York Press, 1990.

"The Relation between Natural Science and Metaphysics." In *The World View of Contemporary Physics*, ed. Richard F. Kitchener, 25–33. Albany: State University of New York Press, 1988.

"Individual and Society in Metaphysical Perspective." In *Person and Society*, ed. George F. McLean and Hugo Meynell, 39–48. Lanham, Md.: University Press of America, 1988.

"God and the Problem of Being." In *Person and God*, ed. George F. McLean and Hugo Meynell, 3–13. Lanham, Md.: University Press of America, 1988.

"Metaphysics as a Discipline." In *The Nature of Metaphysical Knowledge*, ed. George F. McLean and Hugo Meynell, 3–20. Lanham, Md.: University Press of America, 1988.

"The Issue of the Nature of Metaphysics." In *Religion, Reason and the Self*, ed. T.A. Roberts and Stewart S. Sutherland. Cardiff: University of Wales Press, 1989.

ARTICLES IN JOURNALS

"Internal Relatedness in Whitehead." *The Review of Metaphysics* 6 (1952): 297–299.

"Whitehead's Transformation of the Concept of Substance." *The Philosophical Quarterly* 3 (1953): 225–243. Spanish translation by Professor Jorge Perez Ballaster, *Convivium* 1 (1956): 181–208.

"Whitehead's Philosophy." *The Review of Metaphysics* 11 (1957): 68–93.

"The Nature of Metaphysics." *The Review of Metaphysics* 11 (1958): 426–440.

"The Analysis of 'Act'." *Proceedings of XII International Congress of Philosophy* 6 (1958): 235–241.

"Being and Becoming in Whitehead's Philosophy." *Kant-Studien* 51 (1959–60): 427–437.

"The Metaphysics of Aesthetic Experience." *Proceedings of IV International Congress on Aesthetics*, Athens (1960): 670–73.

"The Structure of Form." *Revue Internationale de Philosophie* (Whitehead Centenary Issue) 56–57 (1961): 185–203.

"Whitehead and the Problem of Extension." *The Journal of Philosophy* (Whitehead Centenary Issue) 18 (1961): 559–565.

"Individuals." *Philosophy* 38 (1963): 20–30.

"The University and the Unity of Knowledge." *The Emory University Quarterly* 20 (1964): 32–40.

"Kant's Antinomie der Teilung und die Metaphysik von Whitehead." *Kant-Studien* 56 (1966): 25–41.

"Kant's Second Antinomy, Leibniz and Whitehead." *The Review of Metaphysics* 20 no. 1 (1966): 25–41.

"Atomism, Substance, and the Concept of Body in Seventeenth Century Thought." *Filosofia* (Edizioni di Filosofia della Scienza) 18 (1967): 1–6.

"Die Frage nach der Metaphysik. Zu G. Martin *Allgemeine Metaphysik*." *Kant-Studien* 58 (1967): 247–262.

"The Problem of Metaphysics." *International Philosophical Quarterly* 8 (1968): 276–290.

"A New Theory of the Physical Existent as a Compound Actuality." *Akten des XIV. Internationalen Kongresses für Philosophie* (1968): 305–313.

"The Problem of the Physical Existent." *International Philosophical Quarterly* 9 (1969): 40–62.

"Das Problem des Physikalisch Existenten." *Kant-Studien* 60 (1969): 61–83.

"Whitehead and the Problem of God." *The Southern Journal of Philosophy* (Special Issue on Whitehead), ed. Lewis S. Ford, 7 (1969): 447–455.

"Whitehead on Physical Existence: a Rejoinder." *International Philosophical Quarterly* 10 (1970): 126–128.

"A Rejoinder to Justus Buchler on Whitehead." *Process Studies* 1 (1971): 55–59.

"The Meaning of 'Space' in Kant." *Proceedings of the Third International Kant Congress*, ed. Lewis White Beck (1972): 393–400.

"The Necessity Today of the Philosophy of Nature." *Process Studies* 3: 158–168.

"Über die Notwendigkeit, zur Philosophie der Natur zurückzukehren." *Studia Leibniziana* Band 6 Heft 1 (1974): 93–106.

"The Philosophy of Nature in the Seventeenth and Eighteenth Centuries." *International Philosophical Quarterly* 16 (1976): 135–149.

"The Ontology of Descartes." *The Review of Metaphysics* 34 (1980): 135–149.

"Motion, Action, and Physical Being." *International Philosophical Quarterly* 21 (1981): 17–27.

"Metaphysics and the Theory of Society." (translated into Bulgarian) *Philosophska Missl* 11 (1981): 81–88.

"Metaphysics of Social Relations." (translated into Polish) *Dialectics and Humanism* (Polish Journal) (1981).

"Metaphysics and the Theory of Society." *Dialectics and Humanism* (1981).

"The Problem of God in Whitehead's System." *Process Studies* 14 (1985): 301–315.

Index of Names

Acton, H. B., 90–91, 96
Adickes, E., 35–40
Al Ghazali, 298
Alexander, S., 296, 332
Altizer, T. J. J., ix
Aristotle, ix, 1, 18, 27–28, 50, 60, 70, 94, 122, 134, 165, 172, 175, 185, 203, 209, 221, 227, 239–240, 274, 298–302, 305, 306, 310–311. *See also* categories; conceptualization; form; justice; matter; metaphysics; physics; principle
Arnauld, A., 66
Augustine of Hippo, St., 203–204, 316
Aurobindo, S., 318, 331
Austin, J. L., 239
Avicenna, ix
Averroes, ix
Ayer, A. J., 210, 215, 223, 249

Bacon, F., 70
Bai, Y. Y., 284
Barth, K., 93
Baumgarten, A. G., 49
Beck, L. W., 56, 57
Berdyaev, N., 299
Bergson, H., 105, 108, 155, 158, 300, 305, 311
Berkeley, G., 186. *See also* idealism
Bochenski, I. M., 250
Boehme, J., 76, 92
Boethius, 60
Bogaard, P. A., x, 5
Bolman, F., 90–91, 92, 93
Boltzmann, L., 286
Bonaventure, St., 170
Bradley, F. H., 40, 112, 328. *See also* idealism

Bragg, W. H., 253, 255, 263, 269
Bréhier, E., 93
Brightman, E. S., 302–303
Broad, C. D., 255, 267, 269
Brown, R. F., 92
Brucker, J. J., 52
Brush, S., 270
Buber, M., 178
Bunge, M., 270
Burnet, J., 300

Caldirola, 270
Campbell, C. A., 308, 331
Caputo, J. D., 149
Carnap, R., 239, 251, 257, 302, 309
Carneades, 301
Cartwright, N., 271
Cassirer, E., 36
Chardin, T. de, 115
Chesterton, G. K., 303
Chisholm, R., 96, 217, 223, 330
Chiu, C. B., 294
Chomsky, N., 195
Christian, W. A., 153, 161
Clarke, W. N., x, 4, 99, 106, 180
Cloots, A., xi, 3
Cohen, M., 307–308
Collingwood, R. G., 241, 250
Comte, A., 302
Copernicus, N., 59–60. *See also* copernican revolution
Copleston, F., 74, 80, 86, 90, 91, 92, 93, 94, 96
Cornford, F. M., 300
Coulson, C., 261, 270, 271
Courbage, M., 294
Cousin, V., 304
Crusius, C. A., 306

345

Cusanus, N., 298

Dalton, J., 262
De Raeymaeker, L., 179, 180
Darwin, G., 309–310
DeKepper, P., 284
Delbrück, M., 187
Democritus, 10
Descartes, R., ix–x, 16, 45, 61–62, 150–151, 164, 167, 171, 185, 193, 200, 203–209, 211–214, 217, 221, 222, 316. *See also* cogito; dualism; extension; skepticism; subjectivism; substance
de Sitter, W., 66
Devlin, P., 208, 235
de Volder, B., 51
Dewey, J., 151
Dirac, P., 240, 242, 253, 255, 270
Dougherty, J., x, 4
Duhem, P., 244, 250. *See also* Duhem-Quine thesis
Durkheim, E., 228, 236
Dworkin, R., 224, 235

Earley, J. E., x, 5, 283
Eddington, A., 59, 64, 66
Einstein, A., 59, 65–66, 285–286. *See also* physics
Eliade, M., 297
Emmet, D., 109–110, 153, 161
Epicurus, 10
Epstein, I. R., 284
Esposito, J. L., 91
Eslick, L. J., 102, 108

Faraday, M., 61
Fechner, G. T., 298, 305
Feinberg, J., 236
Felt, J., 180
Fermor, P. L., 332
Fichte, J. G., 73–75, 77, 80–82, 89–90, 186, 206, 210, 213–14, 222

Foellner, H. H., 284
Ford, L., x–xi, 3, 111–114, 117–118, 119
Foucault, M., 220
Frank, M., 94, 324
French, P. A., 225–226, 232, 235
Freud, S., 116, 186, 220

Galileo, G., 60, 309
Garland, W. J., 141
Gassendi, P., 62. *See also* atoms
Gee, S., 284
Geiseler, W., 284
Gierke, O., v. 232, 236
Gilson, E., 221
Goethe, J. W., 28
Goodman, E. H., 310
Gorini, V., 294
Goswami, S. J., 297–298
Grene, M., 111, 115–117, 120
Gwynn Jones, T., 332

Hacking, I., 282, 284
Hall, E., 153, 161
Hamlyn, D. W., 331
Hampe, M., 38
Harris, E. E., ix, 3, 241, 250
Hartmann, N., 241, 250
Hartshorne, C., x, 5, 108, 308, 311
Hasegawa, H., 294
Hawking, S., 292, 294
Hegel, G. W. F., ix, 3, 18–19, 37, 73, 78, 84, 88–90, 93, 106, 150–151, 154–155, 170, 172, 186, 239–241, 249, 297, 316. *See also* idealism; language; spirit
Heidegger, M., 3, 86, 92, 98–99, 106, 114, 174, 222, 241, 250, 300
Heisenberg, W., 59, 62
Heitler, H., 256, 259
Held, V., 236
Hempel, C., 239, 249, 250
Hessen-Rheinfels, E. von, 66
Hintikka, J., 251
Hobbes, T., 61–62

Index of Names

Hocking, W. E., 119
Hoffman, F., 330, 332
Honderich, T., 225, 235
Hose, G., 284
Huber, P. W., 225, 235
Hull, D., 281, 284
Hume, D., 43, 79, 86, 89, 95, 100, 107, 113, 138, 173–174, 210–215, 222, 227, 238–39, 242, 249, 251, 302. *See also* justice; principle; skepticism; substance
Husserl, E., 217

Jackson, H., 192
James, W., 298, 301–302
Jaspers, K., 228–229, 236
Joergensen, J., 250
Jung, C., 87, 96

Kant, I., ix–x, 9–16, 18–22, 26, 29–41, 42–55, 57–58, 73, 80, 81, 86, 89, 117, 186, 210–214, 222, 239–241, 249, 250, 251, 273, 282, 299, 302–303, 306, 316. *See also* copernican revolution; critical philosophy; monad; pan-subjectivism; theory
Keane, K., 180
Kemp Smith, N., 47
Kepler, J., 60
Kestemont, E., 294
Kierkegaard, S., 78, 80
Kline, G., x, 3, 111–114, 117–119
Knutzen, M., 50
Kolmogorov, H., 286–287
Kraft, V., 250
Kretzmann, N., 180
Kripke, S., 306
Kuhn, T., 245, 251, 271
Kustin, K., 284

Laplace, P. S., 60, 62 58, 59
Leclerc, I., ix–x, 2, 5, 73, 108, 119, 122–124, 127, 135, 137, 144, 146, 162, 175, 251, 272–273, 281–283, 285–286, 292, 294
Lee, Y. T., 284
Leibniz, G. W., ix–x, 3, 18, 40, 49–52, 54, 57–60, 63, 65, 67–71, 124, 140, 210–211, 213, 222, 239–240, 242, 273, 282, 300, 303–304, 306–309. *See also* metaphysics; monad
Lequier, J., 298, 305
Lewis, C. S., 96
Lewis, G. N., 259, 271
Lewis, H. D., vii, x, 5, 231, 236
Locke, J., 43, 45, 62, 126, 155, 158, 168, 172, 174, 179, 181, 210, 212. *See also* substance
London, F., 256, 259
Lonergan, B., 80, 84, 94, 95, 96, 167
Lovejoy, A., 180
Lucretius, 101
Lucas, G., 57–58

Mach, E., 66
MacIntyre, A., 224–225, 227, 235
Malebranche, N., 186
Maimonides, 298
Marcel, G., 178
Mareschal, M., 294
Margoshes, A., 89, 91
Maritain, J., 181
Marston, C. C., 284
Martin, L., 121
Martin, R., 306
Marx, K., 80, 220
Maxwell, C., 61
May, L., 225–226, 235
Mayne, H. R., 284
McIntosh, D. C., 300
McTaggart, J. M. E., 95
Mendel, G., 310. *See also* genetics
Meredith, G., 310
Merleau-Ponty, M., 158
Meynell, H. A., ix, x, 3, 72, 94, 95
Mill, J. S., 254–255, 267, 269, 298, 301–302
Milton, J., 310

Misra, B., 294
Montague, W. P., 298, 300
Montaigne, M. de,221
Moore, G. E., 80, 95
Murphy, A. E., 109

Nagel, E., 251, 255–256, 267, 269. *See also* reduction
Nelson, D. R., 284
Neurath, O., 215, 222, 250
Newton, I., 47, 49, 59–60, 64, 285. *See also* atoms; materialism; physics; science; theory
Nicolas, M. J., 180
Nicolis, G., 284
Niebuhr, R., 323
Nietzsche, F., 93, 108, 302
Nobo, J., 123, 153, 158, 162, 163

O'Connell, M. J., 181

Parmenides,113, 197
Passmore, J., 249
Paul, St., 77
Pauling, L., 257–258, 261, 270, 271
Peacock, T. L., 300
Pegis, A., 180
Peirce, C. S., ix–x, 73, 302–305, 308–309
Petrosky, T., 294
Pfleiderer, O., 298, 300
Philo,300
Pickle, J., 296–297, 308
Pieper, J., 177, 181
Planck, M., 59, 61
Plato, ix, 17–18, 48, 52, 80, 94,98, 105, 110, 113, 133–134, 142, 172, 185–186, 202, 204–205, 207–209, 221, 299–300, 302–303, 307, 309, 316, 324. *See also* creativity; form; good; idea; realism; receptacle; world
Plotinus,170, 300, 306
Poincaré, H., 274, 275, 277–280, 282.

See also nonintegrable system
Poirier, R. A., 284
Polanyi, J., 277–278
Polanyi, M., 117, 277, 284
Pols, E., xi, 4
Popper, K., 81, 95, 244, 251, 302, 306, 309
Poser, H., 38
Postello, G., 298
Prichard, H. A., 331
Prigogine, I., x, 5, 284, 294
Primas, H., 252, 254, 266, 269, 271
Pullum, G. K., 120

Quine, W. v. O., 216, 223, 244, 250, 306, 309. *See also* Duhem-Quine thesis

Rapp, F., x, 4, 251
Ratzinger, J., 178, 181
Reese, W. L., 297, 311
Rickman, H. P., 332
Roby, K., 255–256, 258–262, 266, 270
Rorty, R., 309
Russell, B., 89, 160, 173, 222, 302, 305
Ryle, G., 239, 241, 249, 250

Sartre, J. P., 3, 111–118, 120, 310
Sasisekharan, V., 284
Schelling, F. W. J., ix, 3, 37, 73–96, 241, 250
Schlick, M., 210, 215, 223, 242, 250
Schmitz, K., 180
Schopenhauer, A., 93
Schrödinger, E., 66, 259. *See also* Schrödinger equation
Schweitzer, A., 310
Sciama, D. W., 66
Scotus Erigena, J., 298
Searle, J., 321, 331
Sellars, P., 216
Shalom, A., vii, x, 4
Shankhara,91
Sharma, C., 91

Index of Names

Shearson, W., 181
Shelley, P. B., 297, 306
Sherburne, D. W., xi, 3, 144, 153, 158, 162
Shorey, P., 300
Slater, R. L., 331
Smith, J. M., 284
Smith, M., 281
Smith, N. K., 47
Socinus, F., 298
Spinoza, B., ix, 3, 10, 74, 90, 100, 103–104, 106, 239–240, 298, 300–301, 316. *See also* substance
Stegmüller, W., 239
Steiner, E., 260, 264, 270, 271
Stern, D., 195
Stokes, W., 102–103, 108, 109
Strawson, P., 222, 239, 241, 250
Sudershan, E. C. G., 294

Tasaki, S., 294
Taylor, H. S., 284
Thomas Aquinas, St., ix, 81, 95, 96, 165–172, 176–179, 181, 229, 236, 297, 316. *See also* neothomism; thomism
Thurlaw, Baron, 218
Tierney, B., 232, 236
Tillich, P., 94
Tracy, D., 304
Treash, G., ix, x, 3
Truax, D. R., 284

Van der Vecken, J., xi, 3, 109

van 't Hoff, J. H., 257, 270
Varisco, B., 298
Veatch, H., 180
Villon, F., 111

Waldstein, M., 181
Weizsäcker, V., v. 38, 41
Weyl, H., 66
Whewell, W., 254–255, 267, 269
White, A., 86, 89–90, 91, 92–93, 94, 96
Whitehead, A. N., ix–x, 2–5, 16–29, 31–35, 37–41, 42–44, 52, 56, 58, 63, 65, 68–69, 71, 98–107, 108, 109, 111–119, 122–147, 148, 150, 152–162, 164, 167, 171–172, 189, 239–240, 245, 250, 297–300, 304–306, 309. *See also* categories; copernican revolution; language; metaphysics; self
Whyte, L., 307
Wiehl, R., ix, 3, 7, 38
William of Ockham, 173. *See also* nominalism
Wilmot, L. F., 105, 110
Wilson, C., 331
Wisdom, J., 222, 288
Wittgenstein, L., 215–216, 220, 238–239, 241, 243, 249, 298, 307, 330
Wojtyla, K., 234
Wolff, C., 49
Woolley, R. G., 264–266, 271
Worf, B. L., 120
Wright, S., 310
Wyatt, R. E., 284

Index of Subjects

Absolute, the, 74-76, 87-91, 95-96, 99, 299
   and human subject, 74
   as God, 77-78, 82, 86
   contrasted with finite, 76-77, 88
Abstraction, 23, 41
Action, reciprocal, 272-273, 283
Activity,
   as foundation, 207, 209, 211, 214-220
   ego as, 75
   substantial, 99-106
Actual,
   as ambiguous, 152-153, 157-163
   as past, 124, 152, 157, 159
   world, 140
Actual entity, 29, 65, 68-69 99-102, 105, 111-113, 118, 122-133, 135, 137, 139-141, 143-145, 153, 157-162, 304
   as past, 3, 135, 152, 157
   as reasons, 125-127, 140-141
   as substance, 167, 172
   subject as, 160
Actuality, 123-136, 145, 146, 152, 304-305
   as reason, 136, 143
   as togetherness, 172
   contrasted with existence, 304
   contrasted with potentiality, 132, 141, 143
   ontological principle vested in, 135
Ambiguity, systematic,
   passive contrasted with active, 151-153
   process contrasted with product, 151-158
   See also Language.
Analytic philosophy, 241-242

Antecedent, contrasted with consequent, 77-79
Art, 76, 83-84
Atheism, 298, 301-302, 306, 308
Atoms, 63-64, 67-68, 256, 281
   atomic physics, 254, 256, 262, 267
   atomism, 10, 253-254, 262, 266
   Dalton's, 263
   Gassendi's, 272
   Newton's, 172
   organic, 16
   reduction to, 281

Being, 114, 117-118, 143-145, 164-179
   as being, 202, 205
   contrasted with becoming, 111-113, 123, 128, 158, 205
   contrasted with beings, 98-99, 104
   ground of, 199
   in itself, 114-115, 117, 171, 174-179
   organized, 11-13, 20
Belousov-Zhabotinski reaction, 279-280
Bifurcation of nature, 16-17
Biology, 62, 254, 281, 287. *See also* Evolution; Genetics.
Body, 12, 16, 27, 30, 40, 300. *See also* Dualism.
Bonding. *See* Chemistry.
Born-Oppenheimer approximation, 258-265
Buddhism, 300, 317, 330

Capital punishment, 226
Category, 44-45
   Aristotelian, 45
   categorical scheme, 28

Category *(continued)*
  contrasted with ideas, 52
  of life, 23–24
  of reversion, 134, 139, 145, 147
  of the Ultimate, 100–101, 107–108
  Whitehead's categorical system, 40
Causality, 15, 20, 24–25
  as ultimate, 38
  causal history, 25–30
  causalism, 10–11
  causal processes, 27–28
  causal relations, 22
  final causation, 61, 70–71
  mechanical contrasted with teleological, 15, 20, 24, 30
  See also Teleology.
Causa sui, 100–101, 104–105
Change of place, 26–28
Chemistry,
  chemical bonding, 5, 253–269, 272–276
  experimental, 261
  modes of chemical existence:
    chemical entity, 5
    chemical molecule, 274–276, 279, 282
    chemical resonance, 278, 280
    dissipative structures, 279–282
    short-lived complex, 276–277
    transition state, 277–278
  theoretical, 266–67, 269
  See also Quantum theory, quantum chemistry.
Cogito, 1, 116, 205–207, 209
  as proposition, 217
Cognition, 31–35
Concept, 184–185
  and temporality, 194, 196–198
  Aristotelian conceptualism, 134
  conceptual foundation of science, 252–269
  conceptual framework, 185, 189
  foundation of, 195
  theoretical, 242–244
Concrescence, 22–24, 113, 123–134, 136–143, 147, 153, 155, 157, 159
  and creativity, 101, 108
Concrete, the, 32, 41
Consciousness, 114–117
Constitution, as ambiguous, 154, 157–160
Contingent, contrasted with necessary, 299–311
Copernican revolution, 60–61
  Kant's Copernican turn, 21–22, 26, 31
  Whitehead's Copernican turn, 21–23, 26, 31, 34–35
Cognition, 45–46
Court decisions,
  Hymowitz v. Lilly, 228
  Roe v. Wade, 226
Creative process, 305, 309
Creativity, 3, 65, 69, 98–110, 118, 126–127, 141, 143–144
  as Aristotelian matter, 103
  as metaphysical explanation, 101–103
  as Platonic *hypodochè,* 103–104
  as transition and concrescence, 101
  subject as, 102
Critical philosophy, Kant's, 74
  critique of reason, 19–20, 24
  critique of teleological judgment, 9–16, 24

Decision, 123–125, 129, 133, 136, 146–148, 162
  as ambiguous, 150–158
Deduction, objective, 46
Determinism, 79, 85, 96
  causal determinism, 302
Dissipative structures, 292. *See also* Chemistry.
Dualism, Cartesian, 187–190, 193, 318–322
  mind/body, 61–63, 185–187, 194, 318–322
  See also Body.
Duhem-Quine thesis, 242, 245, 247

Index of Subjects

Ego, as activity, 75
Emergence, 185–188, 190–192, 195–197, 273
Empiricism, 63, 173, 212–214, 238, 240, 243–245
    as reductionism, 330
    logical empiricism, 241–242
Entropy, 62
Eternal objects, 125, 128, 130–134, 138, 140, 143–145, 152–153
    as pure potentiality, 134
Event, 45, 47, 313–314
Evil, 317, 324–325
    problem of, 99–100, 324–325, 328
Evolution, 61–63, 69–70, 81, 115, 184–185, 187–188, 192–193, 281, 309
    of universe, 286–287
Existence, contrasted with actuality, 304
Experience,
    empirical, 243–245
    objects of, 30–31
    scientific, 29
Experiment, 242, 244–246, 256–258, 260–261, 265, 276, 292
Explanation, 79, 245–246, 248
    as necessitarianism, 84, 86–87
    See also Teleology, teleological explanation.
Extension, Cartesian, 186
    as result of activity, 50–51

Fatalism, 10, 29
Feeling, 137
    of feeling, 34, 307
    physical, 131
    propositional, 129
    pure feeling, 19, 34
    rationality of, 19
Final causation, 61, 70–71
Form,
    Aristotelian, 186
    contrasted with matter, 12, 14–15, 18
    of organisation, 28–29
    of the Good, 208–209, 316

Platonic, 147
    substantial, 165
Foundation, 14–15, 75, 85, 101, 118
    as metaphor, 200, 202–220
    foundationalism, 215–218
    ideas as, 185
    metaphysical, 14–15
    of science of nature, 201, 204–206, 208–209, 212–217
    of spatial-temporal universe, 198
    philosophical, 16–18, 185
    See also Metaphysics.
Freedom, 85, 100, 303, 309–311
    divine contrasted with human, 77, 79, 86, 88, 96
    human, 321
    infinite, 74
    moral and legal, 230, 313
Free will, 85

Genetics, Mendelian, 59
Geometry, Euclidean, 50
Giffords draft, 125, 127, 129, 131, 134, 138, 139, 142, 146–147
God, 1, 5, 55, 60, 62, 69, 77–78, 82, 85–87, 89, 93, 95–96, 104–107, 110, 124–128, 131–135, 138–139, 143–144, 147, 165–166, 169–171, 179, 186, 196, 199, 296–331
    as actual entity, 99–100, 107
    as master of time, 192
    as perfect being, 205–207, 209–210
    as transcendent, 317–318, 322–331
    as triune, 169–170, 178–179
    consequent and primordial nature of, 87–89, 93, 109, 137, 148
    contrasted with creativity, 98
    contrasted with real entities, 104, 107
Good, Platonic, 208–209, 316
Guilt, collective, 4, 224, 226–235

Hinduism, 297, 318
Horizons, 115
Hylozoism, 9–10, 15

Idealism, 3, 9–11, 17, 63, 81, 84, 88, 95, 318, 328
  Berkeley's, 44–46, 58, 186
  Bradley's, 58
  German, 73–74, 81–82, 99
  nineteenth-century, 206, 213–214, 218
  subjective, 81–82, 85
  transcendental, 10, 20, 44, 46, 75–76
Ideas, 52
  Platonic, 185, 196
  representative, 207
  transcendental, 46–52
Immediate given, the, 21–24, 27, 29–35
Immortality, 118
Induction, problem of, 242, 244, 247, 251
Ingression, 152–153, 161–162
Intelligibility, 196–197
Intentionality, as subjectivity, 21
Interaction, 4–5, 300, 307
  as correlation, 288–291
  as resonance, 287, 292
  chemical, 253–269, 274–280
  physical, 286–287
Internalization, 22–24, 28
  contrasted with externality, 12, 26, 28
  of time, 192, 198–199
Irreversibility, 5
  in nature, 285–286, 289, 291

Judgment, 13–15, 25, 30
  determining, 14–15, 24–25, 30
  particular and universal in, 14
  reflective, 11, 14–15, 24–25, 30, 37
  teleological, 9–16, 36
Justice, 225, 227

Knowledge, 30–35
  a priori contrasted with a posteriori, 15, 19, 24, 26
  empirical, 14–15, 19
  natural, 20, 30
  scientific, 18

Language,
  analytical philosophy of, 241–242
  disambiguation of, 150–160
  moral, 85–86
  See also Ambiguity, systematic.
Law, 224, 225, 230
Lawfulness, 12–15, 18, 30, 35
Life, 12, 15, 23–24

Materialism, 17, 47, 54, 63
  as mechanism, 61–63, 72
  as metaphysics, 203
  as reduction, 75, 80, 83, 85, 89
  Newtonian, 54
Mathematics,
  as certain knowledge, 205
  as synthetic, 214–215
Matter, 9–10, 13–15, 36, 38, 40, 75
  and form, 12, 14–15, 18
  Aristotelian, 103–104
  living, 9, 16
  See also Body; Material.
Metaphysics, 17–22, 73, 80, 88–89, 98, 110, 238–240, 245
  Aristotelian, 122
  as contrasted with physics, 18–20, 28
  as first philosophy, 201–206, 208–210, 214, 218, 221
  as foundation, ix–xi, 1–5, 245
  Leibnizian, 18–20
  of natural science, 3, 245, 252–269, 272–283
  of nature, 175–176
  of religion, 296–311
  of Spirit, 19
  Whitehead's contemporary, 22, 24–35
  See also Foundation.
Mind. *See* Dualism.
Monad, 50–52, 55, 64–69, 171, 211
  Kantian, 49–52
  Leibnizian, 64–69
Monism, 328
Motion, 10, 12–15, 25–30, 40, 50
Myth, 87–88, 94
  mythology, 78–79, 195

Index of Subjects

Nature, 42–55
   as dynamic, 9, 49–55
   as model, 42–46
   as visible spirit, 75
   bifurcation of, 16–17
   modern concept of, 272, 281–282
   organic, 9
   philosophy of, 15, 75–76, 80, 84
Necessity and contingency, 5, 170, 299–311
Neoplatonism, 218
Neothomism, 99, 241
Nominalism, 173
Non-equilibrium systems, 285–286, 289, 292

Object,
   as extended, 47
   as related, 47–48, 51
   contrasted with subject, 22–23
   of experience, 54
   of possible experience, 30–31
   of possible knowledge, 14, 31–35
Objectification, 128
Objective, 82–83
   data, 21, 23, 32
   deduction contrasted with subjective derivation, 46
   immortality, 118
One, the, 217–218
Ontological argument, 297
Ontological principle, 3, 20–21, 100, 107, 109, 122–148
Ontology,
   of groups, 234
   of substance and thing, 21, 27, 29–30
   used by science, 281
Organism, 13, 16, 29, 69
   forms of organization, 28–29
   organic living being, 12
   organic nature, 9
   organized being, 11–13, 20
   philosophy of, 13, 16, 42, 55
Ousia, 112

Panpsychism, 9–11, 15–17, 20–26, 28–29, 32–33
   Cartesianism as, 20
Pansubjectivism, 17–20
   Kantianism as, 20
Pantheism, 29, 77, 301
Paradigm change, 243, 245, 247
Part, contrasted with whole, 12, 29
Past, 111, 113, 117–118, 123–128, 131–141, 144
   as concrete, 113–114
Perception, 20–30
Person,
   as related, 170–178
   as social, 165, 173–174, 176–179
   known as other, 326–330
   of the trinity, 170, 178
   personal identity, 318, 329–330
   personhood, 226, 234,
   collective, 234
   corporate, 232
Phenomenalism, 20–21, 39
Philosophy,
   analytical, 241–242
   negative and positive, 78–80
   of identity, 82
   of nature, 15, 75–76, 84
   of organism, 13, 16–17, 42, 55, 117, 128, 138
   of science, 242–245
   process, 98
   transcendental, 10, 14, 21, 30, 35–36, 39
Physical existence, 192, 272–273, 280, 282–283
   dissipative structures as, 273, 280
   See also Chemistry, modes of chemical existence.
Physics, 254, 287
   Aristotelian, 26–27
   as contrasted with metaphysics, 18
   atomic, 254, 256, 262, 267
   classical, 18
   Einsteinian, 63, 292
   electrodynamics, 18, 40

electromagnetic fields, 61–62, 64
empirical contrasted with philosophic, 75
   mathematical, 17–18
   modern, 59, 63, 65–71, 285–286
   Newtonian, 28, 63, 172, 286, 292
   nonequilibrium thermodynamics, 286–292
   relativistic, 61–62, 64
Positivism, 214, 302
   logical, 239, 243, 246, 252–253, 268
   unity of science as, 214–216
Power, 306–307
Prehension, 65, 127, 131, 153, 162
   as feeling, 131, 139, 147,
   negative, 147
Principle,
   Aristotelian, 122, 125, 135, 140–144
   cognitive, 30
   Hume's, 132, 138–139, 141
   metaphysical regulative, 252
   of contradiction, 210, 213
   of identity, 76–77
   of reflective judgement, 11
   of relativity, 141
   of subjectivity, 17, 20, 39
   of sufficient reason, 127, 140–41, 210–211, 221
   of verification, 239–249
   ontological, 3, 20–21, 100, 107, 109, 122–148
   sensationalist, 48
   subjectivist, 125, 128, 137–141, 148–149
   teleological, 9–16, 20
Process,
   and existence, 119
   and product ambiguity, 151, 154–155, 158
   causal, 26–29, 32–34
   cognitive, 32–35
   metaphysics, 111
   philosophy, 98
Proposition, 130
   as foundation, 207, 209, 211,
214–220
   as product of language, 220
Protocol statements, 215, 242–243, 246
Purposiveness, 9–11, 15, 25, 29–30, 37, 39

Quality, primary and secondary, 192–193
Quantum theory, 61–62, 67, 255–258, 263, 265
   quantum chemistry, 252–271
   quantum mechanics, 252, 286–288, 290–292
   See also Chemistry; Physics.

Real, the,
   directly and indirectly known, 202
Realism, 189–190, 302
   empirical, 20, 31
   of purpose, 9–11
   Platonic, 134
   radical, 4, 200, 202, 207, 219–220
Reality,
   as intelligible, 73
   as process, 112, 119
   felt need for, 200–204, 218–220
   physical, 22
   transcendent, 5, 315–318, 322–324
Reason, 31, 33–35, 136, 143
Receptacle, Platonic, 103
Reduction, 5, 12–13, 34–35
   Nagel's, 255, 267
   nondeducible, 305
   of scientific theory, 255–256, 267–268
   to constituents, 273
   scientism as, 80
Relation, 148
   as intrinsic dimension of being, 164–166, 170, 177
   modes of, 19
   scheme of, 64–67,
Relativity, theory of, 61–62, 64
Responsibility, 4,

Index of Subjects

collective, 225, 227, 233–235
  entailed by guilt, 230
  of aggregate, 233
Right, 230, 235

Schrödinger equation, 256–258, 261, 267, 271, 286–287
Science, 79–80, 83
  as mathematical physics, 17
  as necessitarian, 86
  metaphysical foundations of, 14–17
  Newtonian, 61, 63, 272
  paradigm of, 17–18, 28
Scientism, 80
Self 17, 32, 37
Self restoring systems, 274–276
Sentience, 187–188, 190, 194–195
Simple location, 22
Skepticism, 19, 21, 39
  Cartesian, 204–207
  Humean, 19, 40
Societies, 39–40, 273, 280, 305, 307
Soul, 177–178
  contrasted with body, 22–23
Space-time, 27, 61, 63–67, 71
Spirit, Hegel's metaphysics of, 19
Structures,
  dissipative, 292
  isolated contrasted with related, 265–266
Subject, 1–4, 42, 45, 78–83, 90, 117, 124, 184–186
  as actual entity, 160
  as conceptualizing, 196
  as ontological, 43
  as primary instance of being, 172
  contrasted with object, 45, 74–83, 89, 196
  creativity as, 102
Subjective aim, 136–139, 143
Subjectivist principle, 125, 128, 137–141, 148–149
Subjectivity, x–xi, 2–5, 113, 184, 191–195, 198
  Cartesian, 118

metaphysics of, 9–41
transcendental, 34–35, 197–198
Substance, 50, 55, 122, 164–181
  and thing ontology, 21–27, 29–30
  as related, 4, 174–175, 177, 179
  Cartesian conception of, 164, 167, 171–172, 174
  Humean conception of, 164, 173–174
  Lockean conception of, 164, 168, 172, 174
  Spinozistic conception of, 100, 104, 107
  substantial activity, 99–106
Synthetic a priori, 213, 222
System,
  Poincaré nonintegrable, 286–287, 290
  resonances in, 287, 290, 292

Teleology, 11, 15, 20, 24, 30, 70–72
  and God, 105
  contrasted with mechanical, 9–15, 20, 24, 30
  cosmic, 307, 309
  teleological explanation, 61–62, 65, 70–71
  teleological judgment, 9–16, 36
Temporality, 114, 310
  and being, 184, 196–198
  as constitutive, 188–192
  temporal identity, 191–199
  See also Time.
Theism, 10–11, 29, 298, 301–305, 308
Theory,
  scientific, 242, 246–248, 252–256, 258, 260–264, 267
  theoretical concepts, 242–244, 247
Thomism, transcendental, 3, 73, 80–82, 86–87
Thought, contrasted with knowledge, 45–46
Time, 4–5, 285–293
  See also Temporality.
Togetherness, 125, 135, 138, 142, 149, 172

Understanding, 80–81
  contrasted with sensibility, 24, 30
  human, 30–31
  the creator's, 10
Unity, 12–15, 18
Unity of science, 214–216
Universal, contrasted with particular, 14
Universe, 79–80, 84, 88, 102, 286–288
Unmoved mover, 301, 306

Verification principle, 239–249
Vienna circle, 214–216, 242

Whole, 12, 29, 67–69, 71
World,
  as mechanical, 60–63
  as theoretical construct, 42–43, 44, 46
  contrasted with subject, 39
  Platonic conception of, 52